Lonely planet

NEW ENGLAND'S
BEST TRIPS

31 AMAZING ROAD TRIPS

D1153905

Benedict Walker

Isabel Albiston, Amy C Balfour, Robert Balkovich,
Gregor Clark, Adam Karlin, Brian Kluepfel,
Regis St Louis, Mara Vorhees

SYMBOLS IN THIS BOOK

 Top Tips

 History & Culture

 Essential Photo

 Link Your Trips

 Family

 Walking Tour

 Tips from Locals

 Food & Drink

 Eating

 Trip Detour

 Outdoors

 Sleeping

☑ Telephone Number	@ Internet Access	🍴 English-Language Menu
⊘ Opening Hours	🛜 Wi-Fi Access	👪 Family-Friendly
P Parking	🥗 Vegetarian Selection	🐾 Pet-Friendly
⊖ Nonsmoking	🏊 Swimming Pool	
❄ Air-Conditioning		

MAP LEGEND

Routes
```
      Trip Route
      Trip Detour
      Linked Trip
      Walk Route
      Tollway
      Freeway
      Primary
      Secondary
      Tertiary
      Lane
      Unsealed Road
      Plaza/Mall
      Steps
)= = Tunnel
      Pedestrian
      Overpass
- - - Walk Track/Path
```

Boundaries
```
- - - International
- - - - State/Province
      Cliff
```

Hydrography
```
      River/Creek
      Intermittent River
      Swamp/Mangrove
      Canal
      Water
      Dry/Salt/
      Intermittent Lake
      Glacier
```

Route Markers
```
97  US National Hwy
5   US Interstate Hwy
44  State Hwy
```

Trips
1	Trip Numbers
9	Trip Stop
🏃	Walking tour
↱	Trip Detour

Population
```
✪  Capital (National)
◎  Capital
   (State/Province)
●  City/Large Town
•  Town/Village
```

Areas
```
   Beach
   Cemetery
   (Christian)
   Cemetery (Other)
   Park
   Forest
   Reservation
   Urban Area
   Sportsground
```

Transport
```
✈  Airport
Ⓑ  BART station
Ⓣ  Boston T station
🚟  Cable Car/
   Funicular
Ⓜ  Metro/Muni station
Ⓟ  Parking
Ⓢ  Subway station
Ⓡ  Train/Railway
Ⓣ  Tram
Ⓤ  Underground station
```

Note: Not all symbols displayed above appear on the maps in this book

PLAN YOUR TRIP

ON THE ROAD

CONTENTS

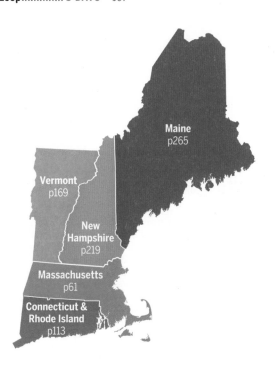

Maine
p265

Vermont
p169

New Hampshire
p219

Massachusetts
p61

Connecticut & Rhode Island
p113

Contents cont.

ROAD TRIP ESSENTIALS

COVID-19

We have re-checked every business in this book before publication to ensure that it is still open after the COVID-19 outbreak. However, the economic and social impacts of COVID-19 will continue to be felt long after the outbreak has been contained, and many businesses, services and events referenced in this guide may experience ongoing restrictions. Some businesses may be temporarily closed, have changed their opening hours and services, or require bookings; some will unfortunately have closed their doors permanently. We suggest you check with venues before visiting for the latest information.

WELCOME TO

NEW ENGLAND

New England is one of America's best road-tripping regions; steeped in history and culture, chock-full of culinary and architectural delights and crisscrossed by scenic byways from the ancient Appalachians to the shores of the mighty Atlantic.

The trips in this book embrace the thrill of the open road, taking in both well-known travel hot spots and off-the-beaten-track treasures. Come cruise the fabled coastlines of Maine and Cape Cod, the White Mountains' spectacular granite summits and the fiery fall foliage of the Berkshires and Green Mountains. From historic sites like Plimoth Plantation and Nantucket to big cities and contemporary art museums, these trips traverse pumpkin patches and cranberry bogs, red barns and white-steepled churches, covered bridges and lighthouses.

Along the way, sample cuisine from the best clam shacks, lobster joints and farm-to-table eateries, and stay at cozy B&Bs, vintage hotels and classic roadside motels. And if you've only got time for one trip, make it one of our seven Classic Trips, which take you to the very best of New England. Turn the page for more.

Mt Washington Mt Washington Auto Road
MIHAI_ANDRITOIU/SHUTTERSTOCK ©

NEW ENGLAND HIGHLIGHTS

Classic Trip 2
Fall Foliage Tour
The ultimate fall foliage trip, featuring dappled trails and awesome views.   5–7 DAYS

Classic Trip 25
Maritime Maine
Lighthouses, lobster shacks, maritime museums and early sunrises.   5 DAYS

Classic Trip 26
Acadia National Park
Swoop up Cadillac Mountain, then roll past cliffs on Mount Desert Island.   3 DAYS

St Leonard

Clair

Dickey

CANADA
USA

Allagash Wilderness Waterway

St Lawrence River

Québec City

QUEBEC

Lac St-François

Sherbrooke

NEW BRUNSWICK

Perth-Andover

Ashland

Presque Isle

Bridgewater

Knoles Corner

Woodstock

Fredericton

St Stephen

Passamaquoddy Bay

Lubec

Baxter State Park

Mt Katahdin (5267ft)

Millinocket

Rockwood

Moosehead Lake

Kennebec River

Appalachian Trail

Howland

Milo

Bangor

Belfast

Camden

Rockland

Penobscot Bay

Bar Harbor

Acadia National Park

West Grand Lake

MAINE

Jackman

Bingham

Oquossoc

Rumford

Mooselookmeguntic Lake

Pittsfield

Waterville

Augusta

Brunswick

Sebago Lake

Berlin

Littleton

Lincoln

White Mountain National Forest

Mt Washington (6288ft)

North Conway

VERMONT

Morrisville

Stowe

Montpelier

Long Trail

St Albans

Burlington

Lake Champlain

Middlebury

Saranac Lake

Lake Placid

Adirondack Park

NEW YORK

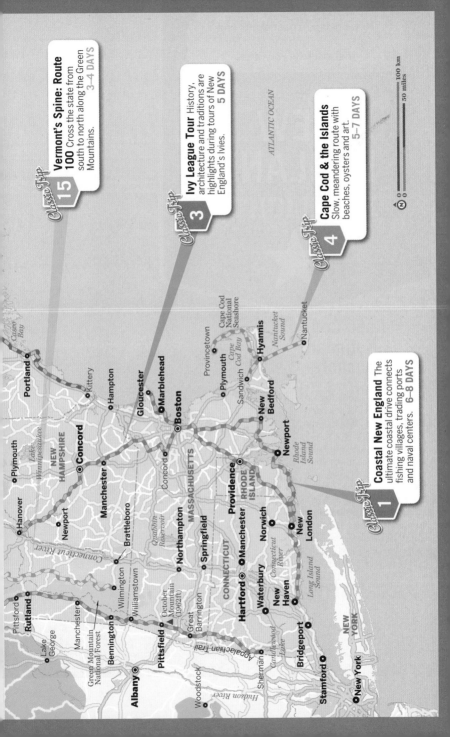

Classic Trip 15

Vermont's Spine: Route 100 Cross the state from south to north along the Green Mountains. **3–4 DAYS**

Classic Trip 3

Ivy League Tour History, architecture and traditions are highlights during tours of New England's Ivies. **5 DAYS**

Classic Trip 4

Cape Cod & the Islands Slow, meandering route with beaches, oysters and art. **5–7 DAYS**

Classic Trip 1

Coastal New England The ultimate coastal drive connects fishing villages, trading ports and naval centers. **6–8 DAYS**

ATLANTIC OCEAN

100 km
50 miles

Casco Bay

Portland

Kittery

Hampton

Plymouth

Lake Winnipesaukee

NEW HAMPSHIRE

Concord

Hanover

Newport

Manchester

Brattleboro

Concord

Gloucester

Marblehead

Boston

Provincetown

Cape Cod National Seashore

Plymouth

Cape Cod Bay

Sandwich

Hyannis

Nantucket Sound

Nantucket

New Bedford

MASSACHUSETTS

Northampton

Springfield

Quabbin Reservoir

Connecticut River

Providence

RHODE ISLAND

Newport

Rhode Island Sound

Pittsford

Rutland

Manchester

Green Mountain National Forest

Bennington

Williamstown

Wilmington

October Mountain (1062ft)

Pittsfield

Great Barrington

Appalachian Trail

CONNECTICUT

Hartford

Waterbury

New Haven

Manchester

Norwich

New London

Connecticut River

Long Island Sound

Lake George

Manchester

Albany

Woodstock

Sherman

Candlewood Lake

Bridgeport

NEW YORK

Stamford

New York

Hudson River

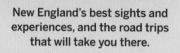

New England's best sights and experiences, and the road trips that will take you there.

NEW ENGLAND
HIGHLIGHTS

Cape Cod National Seashore

The outer edge of Cape Cod is a collage of sand dunes, salt marshes and seaside forest, home to prolific bird and marine life. Since the 1960s, this wild world has been preserved under the auspices of the Cape Cod National Seashore. Drive along the shoreline on **Trip 4: Cape Cod & the Islands**, stopping to climb historic lighthouses, swim at wind-whipped beaches and stroll along scenic boardwalks.

Trips 4 5

Cape Cod National Seashore Salt marshes on the coast

Fall Foliage White Mountains

Fall Foliage

New England is radiant in autumn, when mountainsides burst into a mosaic of red, gold, orange and crimson leaves, juxtaposed against verdant meadows and granite crags. On **Trip 2: Fall Foliage Tour** or **Trip 15: Vermont's Spine: Route 100**, drive through vivid streamers of seasonal foliage – stopping to chug fresh-pressed cider – before the earth goes to sleep under a thick blanket of snow.

Trips 2 7 8 14 15 16 17 19 20

Acadia National Park

The Precipice. The Beehive. Thunder Hole. Is this a James Bond movie or Acadia National Park? The dilemma on **Trip 26: Acadia National Park**: stop to explore or keep on driving? Park Loop Rd, with its gentle curves and crafted viewpoints, was designed with drivers in mind. It tugs you forward. But the adventures pull you sideways. So drive it twice – first without stopping, then again to explore.

Trip 26

Appalachian Trail

The AT traverses 14 states and more than 2100 miles. Five of those states and 730 of those miles are in New England. **Trip 7: Berkshire Back Roads** offers access to the lush slopes of western Massachusetts; **Trip 20: White Mountains Loop** hits New Hampshire's majestic granite peaks; and **Trip 28: Great North Woods** traverses the Great North Woods of Maine.

Trips 2 3 7 8 14 15 19 20 27 28 31

Lighthouses Portland Head Light

BEST BEACHES

Hammonasset Beach A long pine-backed beach set amid salt marshes and meadows.
Trip 12

Ellacoya State Park Family fun on the shores of New Hampshire's favorite lake. **Trip** 22

Sand Beach Ponder the Milky Way over the Atlantic at an evening ranger talk. **Trip** 26

Weston's Beach Kayak, canoe or tube your way to this sandy bend along Maine's Saco River.
Trip 29

Lighthouses

More than 60 lighthouses pepper Maine's coast, with dozens more in Massachusetts, Rhode Island and Connecticut. Their historic importance is evident on **Trip 25: Maritime Maine**, which curves past fishing villages, ports and maritime museums. But their vital connection to local lives doesn't truly grab you until you visit on a fog-thick morning, with foghorns wailing and waves smashing against the rocks.

Trips 1 4 10 25 26

13

Newport Mansions Rosecliff, Newport

Newport Mansions

Newport's natural beauty has long attracted wealthy holidaymakers. As early as the 18th century Manhattan's 'society' families flocked here for relaxing escapes, purchasing generous parcels of land and erecting sumptuous summer mansions. On **Trip 9: Rhode Island: East Bay**, take our walking tour down ritzy Bellevue Ave and admire Italianate palazzos, French châteaux and English manors, cloned from steeple to cellar.

Trips 1 9

BEST HIKES

Housatonic River Walk Follow the foliage-clad banks of this idyllic river. **Trip** 7

Mt Greylock Climb Massachusetts' tallest mountain for glorious views of five states. **Trip** 8

Camel's Hump Enjoy sweeping vistas from an iconic Vermont peak. **Trip** 17

Mt Monadnock Tread in Thoreau's footsteps up America's most-climbed mountain. **Trip** 23

Precipice Trail Scale cliff-side ladders in Maine's Acadia National Park. **Trip** 26

15

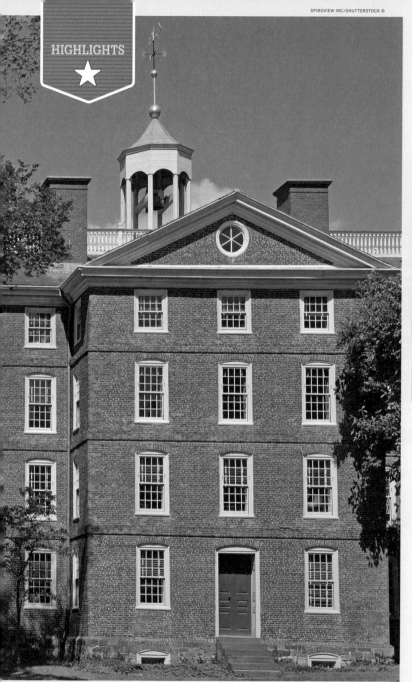

Ivy League Universities University Hall, Brown University

LAURA STONE/SHUTTERSTOCK ©

Colonial History Nathan Hale Homestead, Coventry

White Mountains

Hikers love the White Mountains, a region of soaring peaks and lush valleys that covers one quarter of New Hampshire. More than 700,000 acres are protected in the White Mountain National Forest. As you'll see on **Trip 20: White Mountains Loop**, this wilderness is made accessible by the Appalachian Mountain Club, which manages the hut-to-hut hiking network.

Trips 2 20 24

Ivy League Universities

New England is home to four of the eight Ivy League universities. Steeped in tradition, these institutions are known for academic excellence and rich histories. Study up on **Trip 3: Ivy League Tour**, starting on the bucolic green of Dartmouth College, with subsequent stops at the more urban campuses of Harvard, Brown and Yale.

Trip 3

Colonial History

New England's rural hinterland presents a rich tableau of the country's Colonial past. On **Trip 11: Quiet Corner** or **Trip 14: Litchfield Hills Loop**, trace the footsteps of Revolutionary heroes, human rights activists, religious thinkers and reformists, and discover the region's deep historical roots.

Trips 1 5 11 14

17

Vermont Farms

From apple and blueberry picking to artisanal-cheese sampling and pumpkin festivals, Vermont farms welcome visitors and encourage you to learn how they produce the fare that lands on your plate. Experience the state's agricultural bounty to the max on **Trip 16: Cider Season Sampler**, when the harvest hits full swing and leaves erupt in red, yellow and copper.

Trips 16 17 18 21

Maritime New England

The southeastern corner of Connecticut is unlike any other in New England. The heritage of its seafaring days lives on in the country's largest maritime museum, Mystic Seaport, and the US naval base in Groton, visited on **Trip 1: Coastal New England**. Come for seafaring tales, as well as cruises in tall ships, wooden-boat regattas and restaurants serving seafood.

Trips 1 4 6 9 10 25 26

(left) **Maritime New England** Tall ship at Salem Maritime National Historic Site; (below) **Ben & Jerry's Ice-Cream Factory** Ice-cream tasting and tours

Ben & Jerry's Ice-Cream Factory

After winding your way through the scenic curves and rural villages on **Trip 15: Vermont's Spine: Route 100**, there's only one thing left to do – eat ice cream at Chunky Monkey HQ, aka the Ben & Jerry's Factory. Take a tour and learn how two schoolmates turned a $5 ice-cream-making correspondence course into Vermont's most delicious export.

Trip 15

BEST DRIVING ROADS

Mohawk Trail This scenic byway follows a former Native American footpath. **Trip** 8

CT 169 Explore Connecticut's farms and 200-year-old villages. **Trip** 11

VT 100 Meander through the scenic heart of Vermont's Green Mountains. **Trip** 15

US 2, Champlain Islands Island-hop across Lake Champlain. **Trip** 18

Kancamagus Hwy Cruise past majestic vistas of granite peaks. **Trip** 20

19

Ipswich Fried clams

Seafood

When in New England, it's obligatory to eat as much fresh-steamed, butter-drenched lobster as possible. But there's more to life than the celebrity crustacean: delights from the deep include crabs, clams (quahogs), oysters, scallops and flaky fried fish.

4 **Cape Cod & the Islands** Feast on seafood galore at some of the region's best restaurants.

6 **Around Cape Ann** Pull up a picnic table for fried clams and steamed lobsters at a waterfront clam shack.

10 **Rhode Island: Coastal Culture** Celebrate summer with clam cakes on a sunny bayside terrace.

25 **Maritime Maine** Lobster rolls, haddock and chowder – look for the shacks and no-frills eateries along the coast.

Outdoor Activities

Rolling hills and rocky peaks; rushing rivers and glass-like lakes; windswept beaches and sandy dunes: these are what entice thousands of avid outdoor adventurers to New England every year.

2 **Fall Foliage Tour** Go zip-lining in Bretton Woods or cruise Lake Champlain on a 43ft schooner.

20 **White Mountains Loop** Embrace the views on a hut-to-hut hike amid New England's highest peaks.

26 **Acadia National Park** Hike, bike, kayak and stargaze on Mount Desert Island, a multisport mecca.

28 **Great North Woods** Canoe and fish on magnificent Moosehead Lake, or climb Mt Katahdin, Maine's highest peak.

Beer & Wine

Despite the region's Puritan roots, modern-day New England is jam-packed with microbreweries and wineries where you can wet your whistle. Just don't drink and drive!

12 **Connecticut Wine Trail** Tour Connecticut's Atlantic-facing vineyards for award-winning cabernet franc.

16 **Cider Season Sampler** Try organic brews, crisp hard ciders, and an unconventional wine made with Vermont maple syrup.

18 **Lake Champlain Byway** Pull yourself away from the lake to visit Vermont's most creative microbrewery.

27 **Old Canada Road** The Liberal Cup and the Kennebec River Brewery are mug-lifting members of the Maine Beer Trail.

Newport White Horse Tavern

Art & Architecture

New England's art and architecture span the centuries, from historic homes to contemporary museums and galleries.

1 Coastal New England
Take in Boston's historic downtown, Newport's astonishing clifftop mansions, and the grounds of Yale University in New Haven.

3 Ivy League Tour
Discover Orozco murals, a magnificent Shaker dwelling and the brick and stone beauty of America's oldest college campuses.

17 Northeast Kingdom to Camel's Hump Visit villages lost in time, tour a historic round church and explore a barn full of larger-than-life puppets.

30 Mainely Art With galleries and art walks galore, you can take home the local scenery in Belfast, Camden and Rockport.

History

From Plymouth Rock to Revolutionary War sites to Mark Twain's Victorian mansion, New England's multilayered history is palpable at every turn.

5 Pilgrim Trail Chart the arrival and settlement of the New World's earliest incomers from Europe.

9 Rhode Island: East Bay Tour Pilgrims' houses and ancient burial grounds, drink at the oldest tavern and visit America's first synagogue.

19 Southern Vermont Loop Learn about Bennington's role in the American Revolution, the Lincoln family home and Norman Rockwell's place in Vermont.

25 Maritime Maine
Maine's coastal heritage, from shipbuilding and seafaring to fishing, is traced at museums along the coast.

Wildlife

The northern states are home to moose, bears, deer and other land mammals; dolphins, whales and seals frolic in the coastal waters; and the region's forests, lakes and marshes are full of migrating and resident birdlife.

4 Cape Cod & the Islands Onshore sanctuaries shelter abundant birdlife, while Stellwagen Bank attracts magnificent marine mammals.

13 Lower River Valley
Spot bald and golden eagles migrating down from Canada for the winter.

22 Lake Winnipesaukee
Bobcats, mountain lions and loons inhabit the quieter nooks of Lake Winn.

24 Woodland Heritage Trail With a 95% success rate, the odds are good you'll see a moose on the Gorham Moose Tour.

CURRENCY
US dollar ($)

LANGUAGE
English

VISAS
Check if you're eligible for the US Visa Waiver Program and apply online before departure at: https://esta.cbp.dhs.gov/.

FUEL
Gas stations are everywhere and open late. Expect to pay $2.25 to $2.55 per US gallon. Non-US credit cards won't work at many pumps: prepay inside – you'll be refunded what you don't use.

RENTAL CARS
Daily rates for compact autos hover around $30 to $50; weekly rates start around $200. Rate shopping on sites like kayak.com can save you plenty.

Budget (www.budget.com)

Enterprise (www.enterprise.com)

Hertz (www.hertz.com)

Rent-A-Wreck (www.rentawreck.com)

IMPORTANT NUMBERS
AAA (☏800-222-4357)

Emergency (☏911)

Road Conditions (☏511)

Climate

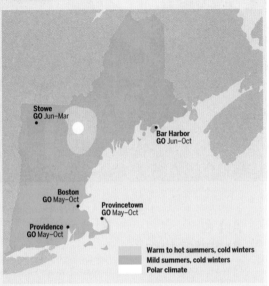

Stowe
GO Jun–Mar

Bar Harbor
GO Jun–Oct

Boston
GO May–Oct

Provincetown
GO May–Oct

Providence •
GO May–Oct

Warm to hot summers, cold winters
Mild summers, cold winters
Polar climate

When to Go

High Season (May–Oct)
» Accommodation prices increase by 50% to 100%; book in advance.

» May promises temperate spring weather and blooming fruit trees. July and August are hot and humid (somewhat less so in mountain areas).

» September and October bring harvest season and cooler weather, with peak foliage in October.

Shoulder (Mar–Apr)
» Weather remains wintry throughout March; April sees some sunshine and spring buds.

» There's less demand for accommodations; negotiate lower prices (also applies to beach areas in May and early June).

Low Season (Nov–Feb)
» With snow comes ski season (usually from December onward), meaning higher prices in mountain resorts.

» Prices for accommodations are significantly lower elsewhere.

» Some sights in seasonal destinations close.

Your Daily Budget

Budget: Less than $150

» Camping, dorm bed or budget hotel: $30–100

» Bus tickets: $10–20

» Street food: mains $8–12

» NPS walking tours and free-admission days at museums: free

Midrange: $150–300

» Double room in a midrange hotel: $100–250

» Car rental for a portion of the trip: from $30 per day

» Admission to museums and parks: $10–20

Top End: More than $300

» Double room in a high-end hotel: from $250

» Eating at the region's finest restaurants: mains from $25

» Tickets to concerts, events and tours: $30–100

Eating

The following price ranges refer to a standard main course at dinner. Unless otherwise stated, a service charge and taxes are not included.

$ less than $15

$$ $15–25

$$$ more than $25

Sleeping

The following price ranges refer to a double room with bathroom in high season. Unless otherwise indicated, breakfast is not included. Rates do not include taxes, which cost 5.7% to 15% depending on the state.

$ less than $150

$$ $150–250

$$$ more than $250

Arriving in New England

Logan International Airport4 (Boston, MA) The T (subway, $2.75) and the free silver line bus connect Logan airport to the city center from 5:30am to 2:30am; a taxi costs $25 to $35 and takes about 20 minutes.

Bradley International Airport (Hartford, CT) The Bradley Flyer bus runs to the city center ($1.75, 30 to 40 minutes) roughly hourly from 4:45am to midnight; a taxi costs $45 and takes about 20 minutes.

Cell Phones

Most modern smartphones work on US networks, but roaming charges for calls, SMS and data (especially background data) can ruin your perfect road trip when you get home to the bill. If your phone is unlocked, you'll save money and headaches buying a pre-paid SIM card in the USA.

Internet Access

Connect to free wi-fi at tourist information centers, shopping malls, most chain restaurants and almost all hotels. Bring plug adapters for your non-US model device chargers (and check they auto-sense voltage).

Money

ATMs are readily available. Major credit cards are accepted almost everywhere.

Tipping

Many service providers depend on tips for their livelihoods, so tip generously for good service.

Baggage carriers $1 per bag

Housekeeping $2 to $5 per day, $5 to $10 per week

Servers and bartenders 15% to 20%

Taxi drivers 15%

Tour guides $5 to $10 for a one-hour tour

Useful Websites

Appalachian Mountain Club (www.outdoors.org) Fantastic resource for hiking, biking, camping, climbing and paddling in New England's great outdoors.

New England Network (www.newengland.com) New England travel resources from *Yankee Magazine*.

Lonely Planet (www.lonelyplanet.com/usa/new-england) Destination information, hotel reviews and more.

Opening Hours

Shorter hours and seasonal closures generally apply in colder months.

Banks and offices 9am to 5pm Monday to Friday; occasional Saturday trading

Bars and pubs 5pm to midnight, some until 2am on weekends

Restaurants breakfast 6am to 10am, lunch 11:30am to 2:30pm, dinner 5pm to 10pm daily

Shops 9am to 7pm Monday to Saturday; some open Sundays

For more, see Road Trip Essentials (p330).

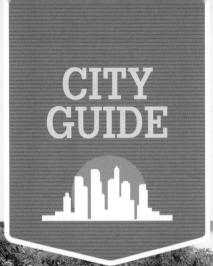

CITY GUIDE

BOSTON

Narrow streets and stately architecture recall a history of revolution and transformation. Today, Boston is still forward-thinking and barrier-breaking. Follow the Freedom Trail to learn about the past; stroll along the Rose Kennedy Greenway to appreciate the present; and visit the galleries, clubs and student haunts to envision the future.

Boston Quincy Market

Getting Around

Boston is best explored with a combination of your own two feet, the city's excellent bike-share program, Blue Bikes (www.bluebikes.com) and the nation's oldest subway, the MBTA (www.mbta.com) – known locally as the 'T.'

Parking

Free spaces are scarce and meter readers ruthless. Relatively affordable parking lots are located under the Boston Common and in the Seaport District.

Where to Eat

Boston's most famous eating area is the North End, packed with *salumeria* (delis), *pasticceria* (pastry shops) and *ristoranti*. The Seaport District is the place to go for seafood, while the giant Quincy Market food court offers something for everyone.

Where to Stay

Almost all neighborhoods offer easy access to great sights, dining and entertainment, though rooms here can be expensive. Beacon Hill and Back Bay are particularly charming. Although the West End is somewhat drab, its hotels offer good value for their convenience to downtown.

Useful Websites

Boston.com (www.boston.com) The online presence of the *Boston Globe*.

Boston Magazine (www.bostonmagazine.com) Local lifestyle, culture and cuisine.

Universal Hub (www.universalhub.com) Bostonians talking to each other.

Lonely Planet (www.lonelyplanet.com/usa/boston) Info, reviews, tips and more.

Trips Through Boston:

TOP EXPERIENCES

➡ Frolic on the Common
Picnic on the 50-acre lawn of America's oldest public park, or take a pedal-boat ride at the adjacent Public Garden. (www.boston.gov/parks/boston-common)

➡ Follow the Redbrick Road
Sample Boston's Revolutionary sights along the well-marked Freedom Trail from Boston Common to Bunker Hill. (www.thefreedomtrail.org)

➡ Root for the Red Sox
Join the 'Fenway faithful' at America's oldest major league baseball stadium. (www.redsox.com)

➡ Appreciate some Art
Boston's Museum of Fine Arts is famed for its eclectic galleries, notably the one devoted to American painter John Singer Sargent. (www.mfa.org)

➡ Go to Harvard
Absorb four centuries of academic prestige on a campus tour of America's oldest college, which has graduated eight American presidents and dozens of Nobel laureates. (www.harvard.edu)

➡ Stroll around Beacon Hill
Wander the lantern-lit cobblestone streets and flower-bedecked town houses of Boston's loveliest enclave.

➡ Explore the North End
Munch on cannoli in the bakeries of Boston's Little Italy or prowl among 17th-century tombstones in the Old North Church cemetery.

➡ Dine in the Seaport District
Snag a waterside table, gorge on fresh lobster and down a microbrew or two in this hip restaurant district with views galore. (www.bostonseaport.xyz)

TUPUNGATO/SHUTTERSTOCK ©

NEW ENGLAND
BY REGION

New England is a road-tripper's dream, whether you're lobster-shack-hopping along Maine's Atlantic shoreline or climbing through a canopy of multicolored autumn maples on a Vermont back road. Here's your guide to what each state has to offer.

Vermont (p169)

Framed by blazing fall leaves, blankets of snow or the exuberant greens of spring and summer, Vermont's blend of bucolic farmland, mountains and small villages is road trip heaven. The delightful lakeside city of Burlington is just the icing on the cake.

Sip cider and follow fiery foliage on Trip 16

Connecticut & Rhode Island (p113)

Rhode Island is famed for the opulent mansions of Newport's Bellevue Avenue and Providence's hip, heritage downtown, while Connecticut boasts New Haven's Ivy League Yale. Dig a little deeper in each state for historic villages, maritime museums, verdant farmlands and seemingly endless shores.

Ogle the Newport Mansions on Trip 9

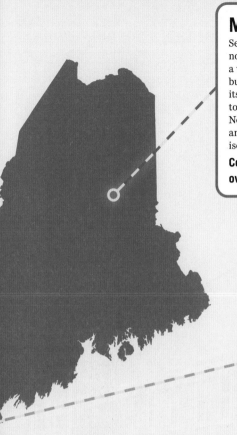

Maine (p265)

Sequestered in the nation's northeastern corner, Maine is a world unto itself, from the bustling summer scene along its supremely scenic coastline to journeys deep into the Great North Woods for fishing, boating and a sense of delightful, wild, isolation.

Count lighthouses and linger over lobster on Trip 25

New Hampshire (p219)

Wherever you go in New Hampshire, nature is always close by. Zigzag through the White Mountains' breathtaking granite notches, frolic on the shores of Lake Winnepesaukee, or take a cultural break in the artsy villages around Mt Monadnock and the history-packed seaside streets of Portsmouth.

Embrace lakeside living on Trip 22

Massachusetts (p61)

Massachusetts is New England's most populous and culturally diverse state. Here museums, galleries and historic sites vie for attention with an amazing variety of landscapes, from Cape Cod's windswept dunes to the Berkshires' pastoral mountain scenery.

Hunt for antique treasures and take long walks on the beach on Trip 4

NEW ENGLAND
Classic Trips

1

LUKAS PROSZOWSKI/SHUTTERSTOCK ©

26

What Is a Classic Trip?

All the trips in this book show you the best of New England, but we've chosen seven as our all-time favorites. These are our Classic Trips – the ones that lead you to New England's iconic sights, top activities and unique experiences. Turn the page to see our multistate Classic Trips and look out for more Classic Trips throughout the book.

Above: Acadia National Park, Maine
Left: Marblehead, Massachusetts

Classic Trip

Coastal New England

This drive follows the southern New England coast. A week of whale-watching, maritime museums and sailboats will leave you feeling pleasantly waterlogged.

1

TRIP HIGHLIGHTS

15 miles

Peabody Essex Museum, Salem
A collection of treasures from around the world

35 miles

Boston Harbor Islands
An island escape, minutes from downtown Boston

115 miles

Newport
Music, mansions and maritime culture

FINISH
New Haven

Mystic Seaport Museum
An amazing 17 acres of maritime history

152 miles

Gloucester
START
Marblehead

New Bedford

Groton

6–8 DAYS
240 MILES / 386KM

GREAT FOR...

BEST TIME TO GO
Sites are open and weather is fine from May to September.

ESSENTIAL PHOTO
Pose for a snap alongside *Man at the Wheel*.

BEST TWO DAYS
The first 35 miles (stops one to four) showcase coastal New England, past and present.

1 Coastal New England

From a pirate's perspective, there was no better base in Colonial America than Newport, given the easy access to trade routes and friendly local merchants. Until 1723, that is, when the new governor ceremoniously hanged 26 sea bandits at Gravelly Point. This classic trip highlights the region's intrinsic connection to the sea, from upstart pirates to upper-crust merchants, from Gloucester fisherfolk to New Bedford whalers, from clipper ships to submarines.

VERMONT

Greenfield○
Deerfield○   Millers Falls
Cummington○
Williamsburg○   (91)   Amher
Leeds○
Northampton○
Belchertow
(90)   ○ **Holyoke**
○ **Chicopee**
Westfield○
Springfie
Southwick○
○Granby
○Canton   **Manchest○**
Hartford ◎   ○
Glastonbu
(84)
Marlborough○
Meriden○   ○Middletown
Wallingford○

FINISH
9
New   (95)   Guilford   Clint○
p166 **Haven**   Long Island Sound

① Gloucester

Founded in 1623 by English fisherfolk, Gloucester is among New England's oldest towns. This port on Cape Ann has made its living from fishing for almost 400 years, and has inspired works like Rudyard Kipling's *Captains Courageous* and Sebastian Junger's *The Perfect Storm*. Visit the **Maritime Gloucester museum** (☏978-281-0470; www.maritimegloucester. org; 23 Harbor Loop; adult/child $10/7; ⊙10am-5pm late May-early Oct, closed Tue-Thu

mid-Oct–May; ⊕) to see the working waterfront in action. There is plenty of hands-on educational fun, including an outdoor aquarium and the excellent Stellwagen Bank National Marine Sanctuary (www.stellwagen.noaa. gov). **Capt Bill & Sons Whale Watch** (☏978-283-6995; www.captbillandsons. com; 24 Harbor Loop; adult/child $48/32; ⊕) boats also depart from here.

Don't leave before you pay your respects at the **Gloucester Fishermen's Memorial**, where Leonard Craske's famous

statue *Man at the Wheel* stands.

✕ ⊨ p39, p89

The Drive » Head out of town on Western Ave (MA 127), cruising past *Man at the Wheel* and Stage Fort Park. This road follows the coastline south through swanky seaside towns like Manchester-by-the-Sea and Beverly Farms, with glimpses of the bay. After about 14 miles, cross Essex

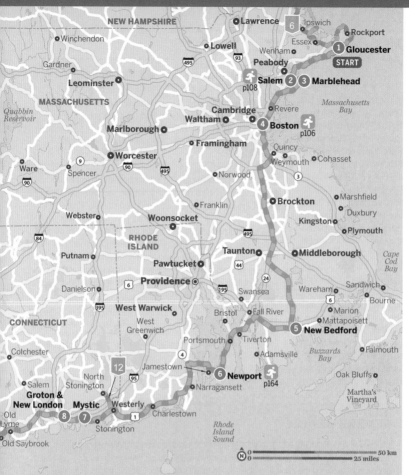

Bridge and continue south into Salem. For a quicker trip, take MA 128 S to MA 114.

TRIP HIGHLIGHT

② Salem

Salem's glory dates from the 18th century, when it was a center for clipper-ship trade with the Far East, thanks to the enterprising efforts

⑤ LINK YOUR TRIP

6 Around Cape Ann

Head north from Gloucester for more quaint coastal culture.

12 Connecticut Wine Trail

Continue south along the coast for a tasty tour through New England's wine country.

of merchant Elias Hasket Derby. His namesake Derby Wharf is now the center of the **Salem Maritime National Historic Site** (www.nps.gov/sama; 160 Derby St; 9am-5pm May-Oct, 10am-4pm Wed-Sun Nov-Apr), which includes the 1871 lighthouse, the tall ship *Friendship* and the state custom house.

Many Salem vessels followed Derby's ship *Grand Turk* around the Cape of Good Hope, and soon the owners founded the East India Marine Society to provide warehousing services for their ships' logs and charts. The new company's charter required the establishment of 'a museum in which to house the natural and artificial curiosities' brought back by members' ships. The collection was the basis for what is now the world-class **Peabody Essex Museum** (978-745-9500; www.pem.org; 161 Essex St; adult/child $20/free; 10am-5pm Tue-Sun;), which contains an amazing collection of Asian art, among other treasures.

A stroll around town reveals some impressive architecture – grand houses that were once sea captains' homes.

✕ 🛏 p39, p81

The Drive ≫ Take Lafayette St (MA 114) south out of Salem center, driving past the campus of Salem State College. After crossing an inlet, the road bends east and becomes Pleasant St as it enters Marblehead center.

----

❸ Marblehead

First settled in 1629, Marblehead is a maritime village with winding streets, brightly painted Colonial houses, and sailing yachts bobbing at moorings in the harbor. This is the Boston area's premier yachting port and one of New England's most prestigious addresses. Clustered around the harbor, Marblehead center is dotted with historic houses, art galleries and waterside parks.

The Drive ≫ Drive south on MA 129, exiting Marblehead and continuing through the seaside town of Swampscott. At the traffic circle, take the first exit onto MA 1A, which continues south through Lynn and Revere. Take the VFW Pkwy (MA 1A) to

---

REVERE BEACH

Cruising through Revere, MA 1A parallels the wide, sandy stretch of Revere Beach, which proudly proclaims itself America's first public beach, established in 1896. Scenic but soulless, the condo-fronted beach belies the history of this place, which was a raucous boardwalk and amusement park for most of the 20th century. Famous for roller coasters, dance halls and the Wonderland dog track, Revere Beach attracted hundreds of thousands of sunbathers and fun-seekers during summer months.

The area deteriorated in the 1970s due to crime and pollution. In 1978 a historic blizzard wiped out many of the remaining buildings and businesses, and the 'Coney Island of New England' was relegated to the annals of history.

Revere Beach benefited from a clean-up effort in the 1980s; nowadays, the beach itself is lovely to look at and a safe place to swim. Unfortunately, dominated by high-end condominium complexes, the area retains nothing of its former charm. Only one vestige of 'old' Revere Beach remains: the world-famous **Kelly's Roast Beef** (781-284-9129; www.kellysroastbeef.com; 410 Revere Beach Blvd; sandwiches $9-15, mains $13-25; 10am-1am Sun-Thu, to 2:30am Fri & Sat), which has been around since 1951 and still serves up the best roast-beef sandwiches and clam chowder in town. There's no indoor seating, so pull up some sand and enjoy the view. Beware of the seagulls: they're crazy for roast beef.

the Revere Beach Pkwy (MA 16) to the Northeast Expwy (US 1), which goes over Tobin Bridge and into Boston.

TRIP HIGHLIGHT

4 Boston

Boston's seaside location has influenced every aspect of its history, but it's only in recent years that the waterfront has become an attractive and accessible destination for visitors. Now you can stroll along the **Rose Kennedy Greenway** (☎617-292-0020; www.rosekennedygreenway.org; 👫), with the sea on one side and the city on the other. The focal point of the waterfront is the excellent **New England Aquarium** (☎617-973-5200; www.neaq.org; Central Wharf; adult/child $27/19; ⏰9am-5pm Mon-Fri, to 6pm Sat & Sun, 1hr later Jul & Aug; P 👫), home to seals, penguins, turtles and oodles of fish.

From Long Wharf, you can catch a ferry out to the **Boston Harbor Islands** (www.bostonharborislands.org; ⏰9am-dusk mid-Apr–mid-Oct; ⛴from Long Wharf) for berry picking, beachcombing and sunbathing. Harbor cruises and trolley tours also depart from these docks. If you prefer to keep your feet on dry land, take a walk to explore Boston's flower-filled parks and shop-lined streets.

✗ 🛏 p39, p81

The Drive ≫ Drive south out of Boston on I-93. You'll

PARKING IN BOSTON

PARKING IN BOSTON

Parking in downtown Boston is prohibitively expensive. For more affordable rates, cross the Fort Point Channel and park in the Seaport District. There are some (relatively) reasonable deals to be found in the parking lots on Northern Ave (near the Institute of Contemporary Art); alternatively, head for the Necco Street Garage (further south, off A St), which charges only $5 per day on weekends and $10 for overnight parking on weekdays.

recognize the urban 'hood of Dorchester by pretty Savin Hill Cove and the landmark Rainbow Swash painted on the gas tank. At exit 4, take MA 24 S toward Brockton, then MA 140 S toward New Bedford. Take I-195 E for 2 miles, exiting onto MA 18 for New Bedford.

5 New Bedford

During its heyday as a whaling port (1765–1860), New Bedford commanded some 400 whaling ships – a vast fleet that brought in hundreds of thousands of barrels of whale oil for lighting lamps. Novelist Herman Melville worked on one of these ships for four years, and thus set his celebrated novel *Moby Dick* in New Bedford.

The excellent, hands-on **New Bedford Whaling Museum** (www.whalingmuseum.org; 18 Johnny Cake Hill; adult/child $17/7; ⏰9am-5pm Apr-Dec, to 4pm Tue-Sat & 11am-4pm Sun Jan-Mar) commemorates this history. A 66ft skeleton of a blue whale welcomes you at the entrance. Inside, you can tramp the decks

of the *Lagoda,* a fully rigged, half-size replica of an actual whaling bark.

The Drive ≫ Take I-195 W for about 10 miles. In Fall River, head south on MA 24, which becomes RI 24 as you cross into Rhode Island. Cross the bridge, with views of Mt Hope Bay to the north and Sakonnet River to the south, then merge onto RI 114, heading south into Newport.

TRIP HIGHLIGHT

6 Newport

Blessed with a deep-water harbor, Newport has been a shipbuilding base since 1646. Bowen's and Bannister's Wharf, once working wharves, now typify Newport's transformation from a working city-by-the-sea to a resort town. Take a narrated cruise with **Classic Cruises of Newport** (☎401-847-0298; www.cruisenewport.com; 24 Bannister's Wharf; adult/child from $25/20; ⏰May-Oct) on *Rum Runner II,* a Prohibition-era bootlegging vessel, or *Madeleine,* a 72ft schooner.

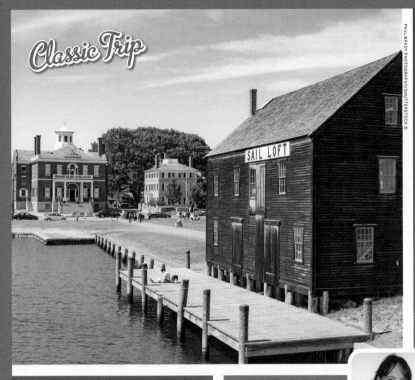

Classic Trip

PAUL BRADY PHOTOGRAPHY/SHUTTERSTOCK ©

CO LEONG/SHUTTERSTOCK ©

WHY THIS IS A CLASSIC TRIP
ISABEL ALBISTON, WRITER

Pretty seaside towns and worthwhile museums are two highlights of this trip, but another is the drive itself. It's hard to beat the exhilaration of driving with the window down, hair whipping in the wind, with the Atlantic at your side and the open road ahead, grabbing glimpses of grand mansions that allow you to slip, for a moment, into a different life.

Above: Salem Maritime National Historic Site
Left: Breakers, Newport
Right: Mystic Seaport Museum

PAUL LATHAM/SHUTTERSTOCK ©

Although its pirate days are over, Newport's harbor remains one of the most active yachting centers in the country, while its waterfront boasts a standout lineup of other attractions. Make sure to tour at least one of the city's magnificent mansions, such as the **Breakers** (☏401-847-1000; www.newportmansions.org; 44 Ochre Point Ave; adult/child $24/8; ⊙9am-5pm Apr–mid-Oct, hours vary mid-Oct–Mar; P) or **Rosecliff** (☏401-847-1000; www.newportmansions.org; 548 Bellevue Ave; adult/child $17.50/8; ⊙9am-4pm Apr–mid-Oct, hours vary mid-Oct–Mar; P), then stop in for a visit at **Fort Adams** (☏401-841-0707; www.fortadams.org; 90 Fort Adams Dr; tours adult/child $12/6; ⊙10am-4pm late May–Oct, shorter hours Nov & Dec), one of the largest seacoast fortifications in the USA. In summer it's the venue for the **Newport Jazz Festival** (www.newportjazz.org; tickets adult/child from $65/15; ⊙Aug) and the **Newport Folk Festival** (www.newportfolk.org; check website for pricing; ⊙late Jul).

✕ ⍿ p39, p123

The Drive » Head west out of Newport on RI 138, swooping over Newport Bridge onto Conanicut Island and then over Jamestown Bridge to pick up US 1 for the drive into Mystic. The views of the bay from both bridges are a highlight.

TRIP HIGHLIGHT

7 Mystic

Many of Mystic's clipper ships launched from George Greenman & Co Shipyard, now the site of the **Mystic Seaport Museum** (☎860-572-0711; www.mysticseaport.org; 75 Greenmanville Ave; adult/child $29/19; ⏰9am-5pm Apr-Oct, 10am-4pm Thu-Sun Nov-Mar; P ♿). Today the museum covers 17 acres and includes more than 60 historic buildings, four tall ships and almost 500 smaller vessels. Interpreters staffing all the buildings are glad to discuss their crafts and trades. Most illuminating are the demonstrations on such topics as ship rescue, oystering and whaleboat launching. The museum's exhibits also include a replica of the 77ft slave ship *Amistad*.

If the call of the sea beckons, set sail on the **Argia** (☎860-536-0416; www.argiamystic.com; 12 Steamboat Wharf; adult/child $52/42; ⏰May-Oct), a replica of a 19th-century schooner, which cruises down the Mystic River to Fishers' Island Sound.

The Drive » The 7-mile drive from Mystic to Groton along US 1 S is through built-up suburbs and light industrial areas. To hop across the Thames River to New London, head north along North St to pick up I-95 S.

---

8 Groton & New London

Groton is home to the US Naval Submarine Base, the first and the largest in the country. It is off-limits to the public, but you can visit the **Historic Ship Nautilus & Submarine Force Museum** (☎800-343-0079; www.ussnautilus.org; 1 Crystal Lake Rd, Groton; ⏰9am-5pm Wed-Mon May-Oct, to 4pm Nov-Apr; P), which is home to *Nautilus,* the world's first nuclear-powered submarine and the first sub to transit the North Pole.

Across the river, New London has a similarly illustrious seafaring history, although these days it's built a reputation for itself as a budding creative center. Each summer it hosts **Sailfest** (www. sailfest.org; ⏰Jul), a three-day festival with free entertainment, topped off by the second-largest fireworks display in the Northeast. There's also a **Summer Concert Series**, organized by **Hygienic Art** (☎860-443-8001; www. hygienic.org; 79 Bank St; ⏰2-7pm Tue-Fri, noon-7pm Sat, noon-4pm Sun).

The Drive » It's a 52-mile drive from Groton or New London to New Haven along I-95 S. The initial stages of the drive plow through the suburbs, but after that the interstate runs through old coastal towns such as Old Lyme, Old Saybrook and Guilford.

---

9 New Haven

Although most famous for its Ivy League university of Yale, New Haven also played an important role in the burgeoning antislavery movement when, in 1839, the trial of mutineering Mendi tribesmen was held in New Haven's District Court.

Following their illegal capture by Spanish slave traders, the tribesmen, led by Joseph Cinqué, seized the schooner *Amistad* and sailed to New Haven seeking refuge. Pending the successful outcome of the trial, the men were held in a jailhouse on the green, where a 14ft-high bronze memorial now stands. It was the first civil-rights case held in the country.

For a unique take on the New Haven shoreline, take the 3-mile round trip on the **Shore Line Trolley** (☎203-467-6927; www. shorelinetrolley.org; 17 River St, East Haven; adult/child $10/7; ⏰10:30am-4:30pm daily Jul & Aug, Sat & Sun May, Jun, Sep & Oct; ♿), the oldest operating suburban trolley in the country, which takes you from East Haven to Short Beach in Branford. A wealth of art and architecture is packed into the streets of downtown New Haven.

✕ ⎘ p39, p59, 147

Eating & Sleeping

Gloucester ❶

✕ Virgilio's Italian Bakery   Deli $

(www.facebook.com/Virgilios-Bakery-333
299483409677; 29 Main St; sandwiches $6-8;
⏱8:30am-5pm Mon-Sat) Primarily a takeout
joint, Virgilio's has excellent sandwiches and
other Italian treats. Try the famous St Joseph
sandwich – like an Italian sub on a fresh-
baked roll. Pick one up and head down to the
waterfront for a picnic.

Salem ❷

⛖ Hotel Salem   Design Hotel $$$

(☎978-451-4950; www.thehotelsalem.com; 209
Essex St; micro/d from $199/238; ❄🛜) Rooms
at this swish new design hotel are thoughtfully
designed with plush beds, bold artwork and
contemporary decor. New 'micro rooms' cater
to more budget-minded travelers. Common
spaces include a delightful mid-century-Modern
lounge area and a rooftop bar.

Boston ❹

✕ Saltie Girl   Seafood $$$

(☎617-267-0691; www.saltiegirl.com; 281
Dartmouth St; small plates $12-18, mains $18-40;
⏱11:30am-10pm; ⓉCopley) A delightfully
intimate place to feast on tantalizing dishes that
blow away preconceived notions about seafood.
From traditional Gloucester lobster roll to tinned
fish on toast to irresistible torched salmon belly,
this place is full of lovely surprises.

✕ Paramount   Cafeteria $$

(☎617-720-1152; www.paramountboston.
com; 44 Charles St; mains $17-24; ⏱7am-
10pm Mon-Fri, from 8am Sat & Sun; 🖉🚼;
ⓉCharles/MGH) This old-fashioned cafeteria
is a neighborhood favorite. A-plus diner fare
includes pancakes, home fries, burgers,
sandwiches, and big, hearty salads. Banana and
caramel French toast is an obvious go-to for the
brunch crowd. Don't sit down until you get your
food! The wait may seem endless, but patrons
swear it is worth it.

Gryphon House   B&B $$

(☎617-375-9003; www.innboston.com; 9 Bay
State Rd; r $268-335; Ⓟ❄🛜; ⓉKenmore) This
beautiful five-story brownstone is a paragon of
artistry and luxury overlooking the picturesque
Charles River. Eight spacious suites have
different styles, including Victorian, Gothic and
arts and crafts, but all have 19th-century period
details as well as perks such as entertainment
centers, wet bars and gas fireplaces.

Newport ❻

✕ Anthony's Seafood   Seafood $$

(☎401-846-9620; www.anthonysseafood.net;
963 Aquidneck Ave; mains $12-32; ⏱11am-
8pm Mon-Sat, from noon Sun) This wholesale,
takeout and dine-in seafood joint in Middletown
is always hopping, testament to the quality and
freshness of the seafood. It's a great place to
try a quahog (also known as 'stuffies' or stuffed
clams). Portions are enormous!

⛖ The Chanler at
Cliff Walk   Boutique Hotel $$$

(☎401-847-1300; www.thechanler.com;
117 Memorial Blvd; d/ste from $325/525;
Ⓟ♿❄🛜) Don't pull up in less than a BMW
at this beautiful boutique hotel. Affording a
remarkable cliff-top position near the beginning
of Newport's legendary Cliff Walk (p165), the
Chanler is a gorgeous 19th-century mansion
boasting sumptuous rooms. Several luxury villa
suites are hidden in its immaculate gardens.
Service is appropriately first-class. Truly a
destination hotel worth every penny.

New Haven ❾

⛖ New Haven Hotel   Boutique Hotel $$

(☎800-644-6835; www.newhavenhotel.
com; 229 George St; d from $169) This robust
downtown hotel is both stylish and affordable.
The hotel occupies a handsome mid-last-
century brick building with bright, modern
common areas, while guest rooms are airy with
large windows, clean lines, dark woods and sink-
into-me bedding. Reasonable rates mean it's
understandably popular. Book in advance.

Classic Trip

Fall Foliage Tour

Touring New England in search of autumn's changing colors has become so popular that it has sprouted its own subculture of 'leaf-peepers.' Immerse yourself in the fall harvest spirit.

2

TRIP HIGHLIGHTS

212 miles — 7 — St Johnsbury

Lake Champlain
Cruise the lake on a 43ft schooner for the best views

8

North Conway
FINISH

327 miles

Bretton Woods
Zipline 1000ft through a golden leaf canopy

● Manchester

47 miles

Berkshires
Pack a picnic in the Berkshires' gourmet shops

4

10 miles

2

Sherman ●
START

Kent
Autumn foliage framing the Housatonic River

5–7 DAYS
375 MILES / 603KM

GREAT FOR...

BEST TIME TO GO
Mid-September to late October for the harvest and autumn leaves.

ESSENTIAL PHOTO
Kent Falls set against a backdrop of autumnal colors.

BEST FOR OUTDOORS
Ziplining through the tree canopy in Bretton Woods.

Kent Falls State Park Kent Falls

Classic Trip

2 Fall Foliage Tour

The brilliance of fall in New England is legendary. Scarlet and sugar maples, ash, birch, beech, dogwood, tulip tree, oak and sassafras all contribute to the carnival of autumn color. But this trip is about much more than just flora and fauna: the harvest spirit makes for family outings to seasonal fairs, leisurely walks along dappled trails and tables groaning beneath delicious seasonal produce.

1 Candlewood Lake

With a surface area of 8.4 sq miles, Candlewood is the largest lake in Connecticut. On the western shore, the **Squantz Pond State Park** (📞203-312-5023; www.ct.gov; 178 Shortwoods Rd, New Fairfield; weekdays/weekends May-Sep $15/22; 🕐8am-sunset; P🐾) is popular with leaf-peepers, who come to amble the pretty shoreline. In Brookfield and Sherman, quiet vineyards with acres of grapevines line the hillsides. Visitors can tour **White Silo Farm** (📞860-

355-0271; www.whitesilowinery. com; 32 CT 37, Sherman; tastings $8; 🕐11am-6pm Fri-Sun Jun-Dec; P🐾), where the focus is on specialty wines made from farm-grown fruit. On the lake's further shore, **Lover's Leap State Park** (📞860-424-3200; Still River Dr, New Milford; 🕐8am-sunset) allows a short walk over a classic iron bridge to a divine view of the Housatonic River.

Consider taking a late-afternoon hot-air balloon ride with **GONE Ballooning** (📞203-262-6625; flygone@aol.com; 88 Sylvan Crest Dr, Southbury;

adult/under 13yr $250/125; 🚶) in nearby Southbury.

🍴 p49

The Drive >> From Danbury, at the southern tip of the lake, you have a choice of heading 28 miles north via US 7, taking in Brookfield and New Milford (or trailing the scenic eastern shoreline along Candlewood Lake Rd S); or heading 26 miles north along CT 37 and CT 39 via New Fairfield, Squantz Pond and Sherman, before reconnecting with US 7 to Kent.

TRIP HIGHLIGHT

② Kent

Kent has previously been voted *the* spot in all of New England for fall foliage viewing. Situated prettily in the Litchfield Hills on the banks of the Housatonic River, it is surrounded by dense woodlands. For a sweeping view, hike up Cobble Mountain in

🔗 LINK YOUR TRIP

8 Mohawk Trail
Pick up the Mohawk Trail at Williamstown for more spectacular mountain vistas and rural New England charm.

15 Vermont's Spine: Route 100
Branch off US 7 at Manchester and take Vermont's dazzlingly scenic VT 100 north along the eastern slopes of the Green Mountains.

Macedonia Brook State Park (☎860-927-3238; www.ct.gov; 159 Macedonia Brook Rd; ⊙mid-Apr–Sep; **P** 🐾), a wooded oasis 2 miles north of town. The steep climb to the rocky ridge affords panoramic views of the foliage against a backdrop of the Taconic and Catskill mountains.

The 250ft waterfall at **Kent Falls State Park** (462 Kent Cornwall Rd/CT 7; Mon-Fri free, Sat & Sun $15; ⊙8am-sunset) is spectacular, and not too challenging a climb, with plenty of viewing platforms along the way.

The 2175-mile Georgia-to-Maine Appalachian National Scenic Trail (www.appalachiantrail.com) also runs through Kent and up to Salisbury on the Massachusetts border. Unlike much of the trail, the Kent section offers a mostly flat 5-mile river walk alongside the Housatonic, the longest river walk along the entire length of the trail. The trailhead is accessed on River Rd, off CT 341.

✕ 🛏 p163

The Drive › The 15-mile drive from Kent to Housatonic Meadows State Park along US 7 is one of the most scenic drives in Connecticut. The single-lane road weaves between thick stands of forest, past Kent Falls State Park with its waterfall (visible from the road), and through West Cornwall's picturesque covered bridge, which spans the Housatonic.

- - - - - - - - - - - - - - - - - - - -

③ Housatonic Meadows State Park

During the spring thaw, the churning waters of the Housatonic challenge kayakers and canoeists. By summer the scenic waterway transforms into a lazy, flat river, perfect for fly-fishing. In **Housatonic Meadows State Park** (☎860-927-3238; www.ct.gov; 90 CT 7 North, Sharon; ⊙8am-sunset), campers vie for a spot on the banks of the river while hikers take to the hills on the Appalachian Trail. **Housatonic River Outfitters** (☎860-672-1010; www.dryflies.com; 24 Kent Rd South/CT 7, Cornwall Bridge; ⊙8am-5pm Sun-Thu, to 6pm Fri & Sat) runs guided fishing trips with gourmet picnics.

Popular with artists and photographers, one of the most photographed fall scenes is the **Cornwall Bridge** (West Cornwall), an antique covered bridge that stretches across the broad river, framed by vibrantly colored foliage.

On Labor Day weekend, in the nearby town of Goshen, you can visit the **Goshen Fair** (www.goshenfair.org; ⊙early Sep) – one of Connecticut's best old-fashioned fairs, with ox-pulling and wood-cutting contests.

🛏 p49

The Drive › Continue north along US 7 toward the Massachusetts border and Great Barrington, 27 miles away. After a few miles you leave the forested slopes of the park behind and enter expansive rolling countryside dotted with large, red-and-white barns. Look out for hand-painted signs advertising farm produce and consider stopping overnight in Falls Village, which has an excellent B&B.

- - - - - - - - - - - - - - - - - - - -

`TRIP HIGHLIGHT`

④ Berkshires

Blanketing the western-most part of Massachusetts, the mountains of the Berkshires turn

LOCAL KNOWLEDGE:
KENT FALLS

Kent is a great place to base yourself in the fall, with lots of accessible spots for viewing the leaves and good amenities in the pretty town center. The best hiking trail in season is the section that connects with the Appalachian Trail at Caleb's Peak, with fantastic views. If you're less able to hike, the easiest way to get a beautiful vista is to head 5 miles south out of town on US 7 to Kent Falls State Park, which is unmissable on your right. The falls are right before you and there are lots of easy trails into the forest.

crimson and gold as early as mid-September. The effective capital of the Berkshires is **Great Barrington**, a formerly industrial town whose streets are now lined with art galleries and upscale restaurants. It's the perfect place to pack your picnic or rest your legs before or after a hike in nearby **Beartown State Forest** (☎413-528-0904; www.mass.gov/dcr; 69 Blue Hill Rd, Monterey; parking $15). Crisscrossing some 12,000 acres, hiking trails yield spectacular views of wooded hillsides and pretty Benedict Pond.

Further north, **October Mountain State Forest** (☎413-243-1778; www.mass.gov/dcr; 317 Woodland Rd; ☺sunrise-sunset) is the state's largest tract of green space (16,127 acres), also interwoven with hiking trails. The name – attributed to Herman Melville – gives a good indication of when this park is at its loveliest, with its multicolored tapestry of hemlocks, birches and oaks.

✗ p49

The Drive ›› Drive north on US 7, the spine of the Berkshires, cruising 11 miles through Great Barrington and Stockbridge. In Lee, the highway merges with scenic US 20, from where you can access October Mountain. Continue 16 miles north through Lenox and Pittsfield to Lanesborough. Turn right on N Main St and follow the signs to the Mt Greylock State Reservation entrance.

⑤ Mt Greylock State Reservation

At 3491ft, Massachusetts' highest peak is perhaps not very high, but a climb up the 92ft **War Veterans Memorial Tower** rewards you with a panorama stretching up to 100 verdant miles, across the Taconic, Housatonic and Catskill ranges, and over five states. If the weather seems drab, driving to the summit may well lift you above the gray blanket, and the view with a layer of cloud floating between trees and sky is magical.

Mt Greylock State Reservation (☎413-499-4262; www.mass.gov/locations/mount-greylock-state-reservation; 30 Rockwell Rd, Lanesborough; ☺9am-4:30pm Jun-early Oct, shorter hours rest of year) has some 45 miles of hiking trails, including a portion of the Appalachian Trail. Frequent trail pull-offs on the road up – including some that lead to waterfalls – make it easy to get at least a little hike in before reaching the top of Mt Greylock.

🛏 p49

The Drive ›› Return to US 7 and continue north through the quintessential college town of Williamstown. Cross the Vermont border and continue north through the historic village of Bennington. Just north of Bennington, turn left on VT 7A and continue north to Manchester (51 miles total).

⑥ Manchester

Stylish Manchester is known for its magnificent New England architecture. For fall foliage views, head south of the center and take the **Mt Equinox Skyline Drive** (☎802-362-1114; www.equinoxmountain.com; VT 7A, btwn Manchester & Arlington; car/motorcyle & driver $20/12, each additional passenger $5, under 10yr free; ☺9am-4pm late May-Oct) to the summit of 3848ft Mt Equinox, the highest mountain accessible by car in the Taconic Range. Wind up the 5.2 miles – with gasp-inducing scenery at every turn – seemingly to the top of the world, where the 360-degree panorama unfolds, offering views of the Adirondacks, the lush Battenkill Valley and Montreal's Mt Royal.

Classic Trip

WHY THIS IS A CLASSIC TRIP
BRIAN KLUEPFEL, WRITER

Imagine you are a painter. Or a hiker. Or a writer (oh, that's me). As the hills of New England turn from the color of old broccoli to an autumnal range of browns, yellows, oranges and reds, you can't help but be inspired: to paint, hike, write or just gawk at this wonder as it frames waterfalls, christens the hummocks and hills, and is brilliantly reflected in awaiting lakes.

Above: Cornwall Bridge, West Cornwall
Left: Mount Washington Cog Railway, Bretton Woods
Right: Berkshires

DENE MILES/SHUTTERSTOCK ©

If early snow makes Mt Equinox inaccessible, visit 412-acre **Hildene** (☎general info 800-578-1788, tour reservations 802-367-7968; www.hildene.org; 1005 Hildene Rd/VT 7A; adult/child $23/6, guided tour $7.50 extra; ⏰9:30am-4:30pm), a Georgian Revival mansion that was once home to the Lincoln family. It's filled with presidential memorabilia and sits at the edge of the Green Mountains, with access to 8 miles of walking trails.

✕ ⌸ p49, p213

The Drive ≫ Take VT 7 north, following the western slopes of the Green Mountains through Rutland and Middlebury to reach Burlington (100 miles) on the shores of Lake Champlain.

- - - - - - - - - - - - - -

TRIP HIGHLIGHT

❼ Lake Champlain

With a surface area of 490 sq miles straddling New York, Vermont and Quebec, Lake Champlain is the largest freshwater lake in the US after the Great Lakes. On its eastern side, **Burlington** is a gorgeous base for enjoying the lake. Explore it on foot, then scoot down to the wooden promenade, take a swing on the four-person rocking benches and consider a bike ride along the 7.5-mile lakeside bike path.

For the best offshore foliage views, we love the *Friend Ship* sailboat at **Whistling Man Schooner Company** (☎802-825-7245; www.whistlingman.com; 1 College St; cruises day adult/

child $50/35, sunset/moonlight adults only $55/35; late May-early Oct), a 43ft sloop that accommodates just 17 passengers. Next door, **Echo Leahy Center for Lake Champlain** (802-864-1848; www.echovermont. org; 1 College St; adult/child $14.50/11.50; 10am-5pm;) explores the history and ecosystem of the lake, including a famous snapshot of Lake Champlain's mythical sea creature.

✖ p49, p205

The Drive » Take I-89 S to Montpelier, savoring gorgeous views of Vermont's iconic Mt Mansfield and Camel's Hump, then continue northeast on US 2 to St Johnsbury, where you can pick up I-93 S across the New Hampshire line to Littleton. Take the eastbound US 302 exit and continue toward Crawford Notch State Park and Bretton Woods. The drive is 115 miles.

TRIP HIGHLIGHT

8 Bretton Woods

Unbuckle your seat belts and step away from the car. You're not just peeping at leaves today – you're swooping past them on ziplines that drop 1000ft at 30mph. The four-season **Bretton Woods Canopy Tour** (603-278-4947; www.bretton woods.com; 99 Ski Area Rd; per person $99-110; tours twice daily year-round, additional times during peak periods) includes a hike through the woods, a stroll over sky bridges and a swoosh down 10 cables to tree platforms.

If this leaves you craving even higher views, cross US 302 and drive 6 miles on Base Rd to the coal-burning, steam-powered **Mount**

Washington Cog Railway (603-278-5404; www. thecog.com; 3168 Base Station Rd; adult $72-78, 4-12yr $41; daily Jun-Oct, Sat & Sun late Apr, May & Nov;) at the western base of Mt Washington, the highest peak in New England. This historic railway has been hauling sightseers to the mountain's 6288ft summit since 1869.

🛏 p229

The Drive » Cross through Crawford Notch and continue 20 miles southeast on US 302, a gorgeous route through the White Mountains that parallels the Saco River and the Conway Scenic Railroad. At the junction of NH 16 and US 302, continue 5 miles on US 302 into North Conway.

----

9 North Conway

Many restaurants, pubs and inns in North Conway come with expansive views of the nearby mountains, making it an ideal place to wrap up a fall foliage road trip. Consider an excursion on the antique steam Valley Train with the **Conway Scenic Railroad** (603-356-5251; www.conwayscenic. com; 38 Norcross Circle; Notch Train coach/1st class/dome car $59/73/85; Notch Train mid-Jun–Oct;); it's a short but sweet round-trip ride through Mt Washington Valley from North Conway to Conway, 11 miles south, with the Moat Mountains and the Saco River as a scenic backdrop.

✖ 🛏 p49, p229

DETOUR:
KANCAMAGUS SCENIC BYWAY

Start: 9 North Conway

Just south of North Conway, the 34.5-mile Kancamagus Scenic Byway, otherwise known as NH 112, passes through the White Mountains from Conway to Lincoln, NH. You'll drive alongside the Saco River and enjoy sweeping views of the Presidential Range from Kancamagus Pass. Inviting trailheads and pull-offs line the road. From Lincoln at the highway's western end, a short drive north on I-93 leads to **Franconia Notch State Park** (603-745-8391; www.nhstateparks.org; I-93, exit 34A; 8:30am-5pm mid-May–Jun & Sep-early Oct, to 5:30pm Jul & Aug, to 4:30pm mid-late Oct), where the foliage in September and October is simply spectacular.

Eating & Sleeping

Candlewood Lake ❶

✕ American Pie   Bakery $$

(☎860-350-0662; www.americanpiecompany.
com; 29 Sherman Rd/CT 37, Sherman; mains
$10-22; ⊗7am-8pm Tue-Thu, to 9pm Fri & Sat,
to 3pm Mon) A local favorite serving up 20
varieties of housemade pie, including pumpkin
and blueberry crumb, alongside burgers, steaks
and salads, offering the sort of homespun
goodness you'd expect next to the Sherman
Post Office. The pecan pie weighs more than
a watermelon. Located dangerously close to
where Routes 39 and 37 intersect.

Housatonic Meadows
State Park ❸

🛏 Falls Village Inn   Inn $$$

(☎860-824-0033; www.thefallsvillageinn.com;
33 Railroad St, Falls Village; d/ste $259/309;
P 🤖) The heart and soul of one of the smallest
villages in Connecticut, this inn originally served
the Housatonic Railroad. Now the five rooms are
styled by interior decorator Bunny Williams (the
'Green' has a claw-foot tub), and the Tap Room
is a hang-out for Lime Rock's racers.

Berkshires (Great Barrington) ❹

✕ Baba Louie's   Pizza $

(☎413-528-8100; www.babalouiespizza.com;
286 Main St; small pizzas $10-14; ⊗11:30am-
3pm & 5-9:30pm) Baba's is known for its organic
sourdough crust. There's a pizza for every taste,
running the gamut from the fan-favorite Dolce
Vita with figs, gorgonzola and prosciutto to the
dairy-free Vegetazione with artichoke hearts,
broccoli, tofu and soy mozzarella.

Mt Greylock State Reservation ❺

🛏 Bascom Lodge   Lodge $

(☎413-743-1591; www.bascomlodge.
net; 1 Summit Rd; dm/d/tr/q without bath
$40/125/170/190; ⊗Sat & Sun May–mid-Jun,
daily mid-Jun–Oct; P) High atop Mt Greylock,
this lodge was built as a federal work project

in the 1930s. In the lobby, inviting leather
sofas are arranged around a stone fireplace: a
sociable place for a drink come nightfall. Rooms
have shared bathrooms, comfortable beds and
wonderful views.

Manchester ❻

🛏 Ash Street Inn   B&B $$

(☎603-668-9908; www.ashstreetinn.com;
118 Ash St; r $199-219; P ❄ 🤖) Dating from
1885, this Victorian home has been thoughtfully
renovated into a comfortable B&B. Rooms all
come with top-of-the-line sheets and towels,
plush robes, high-speed internet and good
lighting for business travelers who need to get a
little work done. It's just a one-minute walk from
Manchester's Currier Museum of Art.

Lake Champlain (Burlington) ❼

✕ City Market   Market $

(☎802-861-9700; www.citymarket.coop; 82
S Winooski Ave; cold & hot buffet per lb $7.99;
⊗7am-11pm; 🍴) If there's a food coop heaven,
it must look something like this. Burlington's
gourmet natural-foods grocery (recently
expanded to a second location in the city's
South End) is chock-full of local produce and
products, with hundreds of Vermont-based
producers represented. Especially noteworthy
are the huge takeout deli and hot bar, and the
massive microbrew-focused beer section.

North Conway ❾

🛏 Cabernet Inn   Inn $$

(☎603-356-4704; www.cabernetinn.com; 3552
White Mountain Hwy/NH 16; r $129-239; 🤖) This
1842 Victorian cottage is north of North Conway
center, near Intervale. Each of the 11 guest
rooms has antiques and queen beds, while
pricier rooms also have fireplaces and/or hot
tubs. Common spaces include two living rooms
with fireplaces and a shady deck, while the large
gourmet kitchen is the source of a decadent
country breakfast (included in rates).

Classic Trip

Ivy League Tour

This trip celebrates history and education as it rolls between New England's Ivies, where campus tours sneak behind the gates for an up-close look at the USA's greatest universities.

3

TRIP HIGHLIGHTS

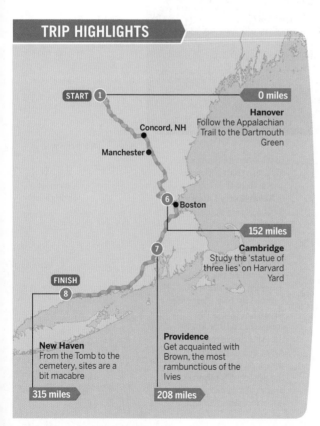

START ① — **0 miles**

Hanover
Follow the Appalachian Trail to the Dartmouth Green

Concord, NH

Manchester

⑥ ● Boston

152 miles

⑦

Cambridge
Study the 'statue of three lies' on Harvard Yard

FINISH
⑧

New Haven
From the Tomb to the cemetery, sites are a bit macabre

315 miles

Providence
Get acquainted with Brown, the most rambunctious of the Ivies

208 miles

5 DAYS
315 MILES / 507KM

GREAT FOR...

BEST TIME TO GO
Catch student-filled campuses from September to November.

 ESSENTIAL PHOTO

Stand beside the statue of John Harvard, the man who didn't found Harvard.

 BEST FOR HISTORY

Learn about the USA's oldest university during a Harvard tour.

Cambridge John Harvard statue, Harvard University

51

Classic Trip

3 Ivy League Tour

What's most surprising about a tour of the Ivy League? The distinct personalities of the different campuses, which are symbiotically fused with their surrounding landscapes. Compare fresh-faced Dartmouth, with its breezy embrace of New Hampshire's outdoors, to enclaved Yale, its Gothic buildings fortressed against the urban wilds of New Haven. But the schools all share one trait — vibrant, diverse and engaged students who dispel any notions that they're out-of-touch elites.

TRIP HIGHLIGHT

❶ Hanover, New Hampshire

When the first big snowfall hits **Dartmouth College** (☎603-646-1110; www.dartmouth.edu), an email blasts across campus, calling everyone to the central **Green** for a midnight snowball fight. The Green is also the site of elaborate ice sculptures during Dartmouth's **Winter Carnival** (www.dartmouth.edu; ☺Feb), a weeklong celebration that's been held annually for more than 100 years.

North of the Green is **Baker-Berry Library** (☎603-646-2704; http://dartmouth.edu; 25 N Main St; ☺8am-2am Mon-Fri, 10am-2am Sat & Sun), which holds an impressive mural called the *Epic of American Civilization*. Painted by José Clemente Orozco, it traces the course of civilization in the Americas from the Aztec era to modern times. At 4pm, stop by the adjacent **Sanborn Library** (☺8am-midnight daily, teatime 4pm Mon-Fri), where

tea is served during the academic year for 10¢. This tradition honors a 19th-century English professor who invited students for chats and afternoon tea. For a free student-led **walking tour** (☑603-646-2875; http://dartmouth.edu; 10 N Main St, 6016 McNutt Hall) of the campus, stop by the admissions office on the 2nd floor of McNutt Hall on the west side of the Green. Call or check online to confirm departure times.

The collection at Dartmouth's revamped **Hood Museum of Art** (☑603-646-2808; http://hoodmuseum.dartmouth.edu; 6 E Wheelock St; ◷10am-5pm Tue & Thu-Sat, to 9pm Wed, noon-5pm Sun) includes nearly 70,000 items. The collection is particularly strong in American pieces, including Native American art. One highlight is a set of Assyrian reliefs dating from the 9th century BCE.

LINK YOUR TRIP

12 Connecticut River Byway

From Hanover, drive south on NE 10 for riverside history.

21 Connecticut Wine Trail

From New Haven, jump from grades to grapes by heading southwest along US 1.

Classic Trip

From the museum, turn left onto E Wheelock St and walk toward the Hanover Inn. You'll soon cross the Appalachian Trail, which runs through downtown (from here, it's 431 miles to Mt Katahdin in Maine, the start/finish point for the trail).

The Drive ≫ From Hanover, follow NH 120 E to I-89 S. Take exit 117 to NH 4 E, following it to NH 4A. Turn right and follow NH 4A 3.5 miles to the museum.

❷ Enfield Shaker Museum

The Enfield Shaker site sits in stark contrast to today's college campuses. In fact, the two couldn't be more different – except for the required communal housing with a bunch of nonrelatives. But a trip here is illuminating. Set in a valley overlooking Mascoma Lake, the Enfield Shaker site dates from the late 18th century. At its peak, some 300 members lived in Enfield. Farmers and craftspeople, they built impressive wood and brick buildings and took in converts, orphans and children of the poor – essential for the Shaker future since sex was not allowed in the pacifist, rule-abiding community.

By the early 1900s the community had gone into decline and the last family left in 1917.

The **museum** (📞603-632-4346; www.shakermuseum.org; 447 NH 4A, Enfield; adult/6-10yr/11-17yr $12/3/8; ⏲10am-5pm Mon-Sat, noon-5pm Sun; 🅿) centers on the Great Stone Dwelling, the largest Shaker dwelling house ever built. You can also explore the gardens and grounds. The guide might even let you ring the rooftop bell. Spend the night on the 3rd and 4th floor of the building; **accommodations** s/d/tr $110/135/160; 🅿🛜) feature traditional Shaker furniture, but not phones or TVs, although there is wi-fi.

The Drive ≫ Return to I-89 S. After 54 miles, take I-93 N 3 miles to exit 15E for I-393 E. From there, take exit 1 and follow the signs.

❸ Concord, New Hampshire

New Hampshire's capital is a trim and tidy city with a wide Main St dominated by the striking **State House** (📞603-271-2154; www.gencourt.state.nh.us; 107 N Main St; ⏲8am-4pm Mon-Fri), a granite-hewed 19th-century edifice topped with a glittering dome.

Nearby, the New Hampshire schoolteacher Christa McAuliffe, chosen to be America's first teacher-astronaut, is

honored at the **McAuliffe-Shepard Discovery Center** (📞603-271-7827; www.starhop.com; 2 Institute Dr; adult/3-12yr $12/11; ⏲10:30am-4pm daily mid-Jun–early Sep, Fri-Sun rest of year; 🅿). She died in the _Challenger_ explosion on January 28, 1986. The museum also honors New Hampshire native Alan B Shepard, a member of NASA's elite _Mercury_ corps, who became America's first astronaut in 1961. Some exhibits feel a bit tired, but you can view a life-size replica of a NASA rocket and the _Mercury_ capsule that transported Shepard to space. For hands-on adventure, you can try to land a _Discovery_ space shuttle from inside a mock cockpit and learn about space travel to Mars and the power of the sun. There's also a planetarium.

✖ p59

The Drive ≫ Return to I-93 S, passing through Manchester before entering Massachusetts. Follow I-495 S toward Lowell.

❹ Lowell

In the early 19th century, textile mills in Lowell churned out cloth by the mile, driven by the abundant waterpower of Pawtucket Falls. Today, the historic buildings in the city center – connected by the trolley and canal boats – comprise the Lowell National Historic

Park, which gives a fascinating peek at the workings of a 19th-century industrial town. Stop first at the **Market Mills Visitors Center** (📞978-970-5000; www.nps.gov/lowe; 246 Market St; ⏱9am-5pm May-Nov) to pick up a map and check out the general exhibits. Five blocks northeast along the river, the **Boott Cotton Mills Museum** (📞978-970-5000; www.nps.gov/lowe; 115 John St; adult/child $6/3; ⏱9:30am-5pm May-Nov; 🎫) has exhibits that chronicle the rise and fall of the industrial revolution in Lowell, including technological changes, labor movements and immigration. The highlight is a working weave room, with 88 power looms. A special exhibit on **Mill Girls & Immigrants** (40 French St; ⏱1:30-5pm May-Nov, from 11am Jun-Sep) examines the lives of working people, while seasonal exhibits are sometimes on display in other historic buildings around town.

The Drive ›› Take the Lowell Connector to US 3 heading south. In Billerica, exit to Concord Rd. Continue south on Concord Rd (MA 62) through Bedford. This road becomes Monument St and terminates at Monument Sq in Concord center. Walden Pond is about 3 miles south of Monument Sq, along Walden St (MA 126) south of MA 2.

⑤ Concord, Massachusetts

Tall, white church steeples rise above ancient oaks in Colonial Concord, giving the town a stateliness that belies the American Revolution drama that occurred centuries ago. It is easy to see how so many writers found their inspiration here in the 1800s.

Ralph Waldo Emerson was the paterfamilias of literary Concord and the founder of the transcendentalist movement (and, incidentally, a graduate of Harvard College). His home of nearly 50 years, the **Ralph Waldo Emerson Memorial House** (📞978-369-2236; www.facebook.com/emersonhouseconcord; 28 Cambridge Turnpike; adult/child $10/7; ⏱10am-4:30pm Thu-Sat, from 1pm Sun mid-Apr–Oct), often hosted his renowned circle of friends.

One of them was Henry David Thoreau (another Harvard grad), who put transcendentalist beliefs into practice when he spent two years in a rustic cabin on the shores of **Walden Pond** (📞978-369-3254; www.mass.gov/dcr; 915 Walden St; parking $15; ⏱dawn-dusk). The glacial pond is now a state park, surrounded by acres of forest. A footpath circles the pond, leading to the site of Thoreau's cabin on the northeast side.

The Drive ›› Take MA 2 east to its terminus in Cambridge. Go left on the Alewife Brook Pkwy (MA 16), then right on Massachusetts Ave and into Harvard Sq. Parking spaces are in short supply, but you can usually find one on the streets around the Cambridge Common.

TRIP HIGHLIGHT

⑥ Cambridge

Founded in 1636 to educate men for the ministry, Harvard is America's oldest **college** (📞617-495-1000; www.harvard.edu; Massachusetts Ave; tours free). The geographic heart of the university – where redbrick buildings and leaf-covered paths exude academia – is **Harvard Yard**. For maximum visual impact, enter the yard through the wrought-iron Johnston Gate, which is flanked by the two oldest buildings on campus, **Harvard Hall** and **Massachusetts Hall**.

The focal point of the yard is the **John Harvard statue**, by Daniel Chester French. Inscribed 'John Harvard, Founder of Harvard College, 1638,' it is commonly known as the 'statue of three lies': John Harvard was *not* the college's founder but its first benefactor; Harvard was actually founded in 1636; and the man depicted isn't even Mr Harvard himself! This symbol hardly lives up to the university's motto, *Veritas* (truth).

Classic Trip

WHY THIS IS A CLASSIC TRIP
AMY BALFOUR,
WRITER

America's most esteemed universities become less imposing as you explore their sprawling grounds. During the school year, the energy on the various campuses is downright invigorating, and you'll feel like a student yourself as you delve into each school's history and soak up the culture. The many quirky traditions prove that these smartypants students are just as weird as the rest of us.

Above: Harvard Square, Harvard, Cambridge
Left: Harkness Tower, Yale, New Haven
Right: Baker-Berry Library, Dartmouth, Hanover

DAN LEWIS/SHUTTERSTOCK ©

Most Harvard hopefuls rub the statue's shiny foot for good luck; little do they know that campus pranksters regularly use the foot like dogs use a fire hydrant.

The revamped **Smith Campus Center** (📞617-495-6916; www.commonspaces.harvard.edu/smith-campus-center/about; 30 Dunster St; ⏰7am-midnight Sun-Fri, to 1am Sat) across from the yard is also worth a look. Hosting lectures, movies and several cafes, it's sure to be a campus hub. It's also home to 12,000 plants!

Overflowing with coffeehouses and pubs, bookstores and record stores, street musicians and sidewalk artists, panhandlers and professors, nearby **Harvard Square** exudes energy, creativity and nonconformity – and it's all packed into a handful of streets between the university and the river. Spend an afternoon browsing bookstores, riffling through records and trying on vintage clothing, then camp out in a local cafe.

✕ 🛏 p59

The Drive » Hop on Memorial Dr and drive east along the Charles River. At Western Ave, cross the river and follow the signs to I-90 E (toll road). Cruise through the tunnel (product of the notorious Big Dig) and merge with I-93 S. Follow I-93 S to I-95 S. Take I-95 S to Providence.

Classic Trip

TRIP HIGHLIGHT

⑦ Providence

College Hill rises east of the Providence River, and atop it sits **Brown University** (📞401-863-1000; www.brown.edu; 1 Prospect St), the rambunctious younger child of an uptight New England household. Big brothers Harvard and Yale carefully manicure their public image, while the little black sheep of the family prides itself on staunch liberalism. Founded in 1764, Brown was the first American college to accept students regardless of religious affiliation, and the first to appoint an African American woman, Ruth Simmons, as president in 2001. Of its small 700-strong faculty, five Brown professors, and two alumni have been honored as Nobel laureates.

The campus, consisting of 235 buildings, is divided into the Main Green and Lincoln Field. Enter through the wrought-iron **Van Wickle Gates** on College St. The oldest building on the campus is **University Hall**, a 1770 brick edifice that was used as a barracks during the Revolutionary War. Free tours of the campus begin from the **Brown University Admissions Office** (📞401-863-2378; www.brown.edu/about/visit; 45 Prospect St).

✕ 🛏 p59, p123, p131

The Drive ≫ Take Memorial Blvd out of Providence and merge with I-95 S. The generally pleasant tree-lined interstate will take you around the periphery of Groton, Old Lyme, Guilford and Madison, where you may want to stop for a coffee or snack. Exit at junction 47 for downtown New Haven.

TRIP HIGHLIGHT

⑧ New Haven

Gorgeous, Gothic Yale University is America's third-oldest college. Head to the **Yale University Visitor Center** (📞203-432-2300; http://visitorcenter.yale.edu; 149 Elm St; ⏱9am-4:30pm Mon-Fri, 11am-4pm Sat & Sun) to pick up a free map or take a free one-hour tour.

The tour does a good job of fusing historical and academic facts and passes by several standout monuments, including Yale's tallest building, **Harkness Tower**. Guides refrain, however, from mentioning the tombs scattered around the campus. No, these aren't filled with corpses: they're secret hang-outs for senior students. The most notorious **Tomb** (64 High St) is the HQ for the Skull & Bones Club, founded in 1832. Its list of members reads like a who's who of high-powered politicos and financiers over the last two centuries.

New Haven's spacious **green** has been the spiritual center of the city since its Puritan fathers designed it in 1638 as the prospective site for Christ's second coming. Since then it has held the municipal burial grounds – graves were later moved to Grove St Cemetery – several statehouses and an array of churches, three of which still stand. A short walk along the green also passes numerous spots (p166) for appreciating art and architecture.

✕ 🛏 p39, p59, p147

Eating & Sleeping

Concord (New Hampshire) ❸

✕ Granite   Modern American $$

(✆603-227-9005; www.graniterestaurant.com; 96 Pleasant St; mains lunch $11-18, dinner $15-25; ⏰7-10am, 11:30am-2:30pm & 5-9pm Mon-Thu, to 10pm Fri & Sat, 7am-2:30pm & 5-8pm Sun) In a grand turreted Victorian building, Granite serves fine New American cuisine all day long, from breakfasts of cinnamon French toast with New Hampshire maple syrup, to crab cake BLTs with Old Bay aioli at lunchtime, to espresso-rubbed pork tenderloin for dinner.

Cambridge ❻

✕ Mr Bartley's Burger Cottage   Burgers $

(✆617-354-6559; www.mrbartley.com; 1246 Massachusetts Ave; burgers $14-21; ⏰11am-9pm Tue-Sat; Ⓣ Harvard) Packed with small tables and hungry college students, this burger joint has been a Harvard Square institution for more than 50 years. Bartley's offers two dozen different burgers, including topical newcomers with names like Trump Tower and Tom Brady Triumphant; sweet-potato fries, onion rings, thick frappés and raspberry-lime rickeys complete the classic American meal. Be aware that this place is old school: credit cards not accepted; no bathroom on-site.

⊨ Kendall Hotel   Boutique Hotel $$

(✆617-566-1300; www.kendallhotel.com; 350 Main St; r $248-317; Ⓟ❄️📶; Ⓣ Kendall/MIT) Once the Engine 7 Firehouse, this city landmark is now a cool and classy all-American hotel. Its 65 guest rooms exhibit a firefighter riff, alongside the requisite creature comforts. The hotel excels with its service, style, and appetizing breakfast spread. The on-site Black Sheep restaurant is worth visiting for lunch or dinner too.

Providence ❼

✕ birch   Modern American $$$

(✆401-272-3105; www.birchrestaurant.com; 200 Washington St; mains $20-30; ⏰5-10pm Thu-Mon) With a background at Noma in Copenhagen, chef Benjamin Sukle and his wife, Heidi, now have their own place: the understated but fabulously good birch. Its intimate size and style (seating surrounds a U-shaped bar) means attention to detail is exacting in both the decor and the food, which focuses on under-utilized, hyper-seasonal produce.

⊨ The Dean Hotel   Boutique Hotel $

(✆401-455-3326; http://thedeanhotel.com; 122 Fountain St; d from $109) The Dean epitomizes all that is design in Providence. It features a beer hall, a karaoke bar, a cocktail den and a beer hall downstairs; upstairs has eight quirky, design-themed rooms that provide a stylish urban oasis from the fun and frivolity downstairs. If you're a cool kid and you know it, you belong here.

New Haven ❽

✕ Modern Apizza   Pizza $$

(✆203-776-5306; www.modernapizza.com; 874 State St; pizzas $10-20; ⏰11am-11pm Tue-Sat, 3-10pm Sun) This local favorite, although usually heaving with diners, has smaller queues than its better-known counterparts. Servers have perfected the efficient turnaround of patrons, but in a 'keep everybody happy,' as opposed to a 'feed them and get them out the door,' kind of way. The pizzas are massive. Despite the name, Modern has been tossing dough since 1934. If gluten is not your friend, don't fret! There's no surcharge for a gluten-free pie base here.

⊨ Study at Yale   Hotel $$$

(✆203-503-3900; www.thestudyatyale.com; 1157 Chapel St; r $250-389; Ⓟ📶) The Study at Yale manages to evoke a mid-century modern sense of sophistication (call it 'Mad Men chic') without being over the top or intimidating. Ultra-contemporary touches include in-room iPod docking stations and cardio machines with built-in TV. Room and lobby furniture was all replaced fairly recently. There's also an in-house restaurant and cafe, to which you can stumble for morning snacks.

Massachusetts

CITY STREETS AND COW-DOTTED PASTURES, WINDSWEPT BEACHES AND FOREST-COVERED MOUNTAINS: Massachusetts offers an incredible diversity of landscapes. The state is small, but its scenery will satisfy your craving for eye candy (surely the foremost requirement for a rewarding road trip). When you're ready for a pit stop, the Commonwealth has you covered, with a tantalizing spread of local specialties, such as fruit and vegetables straight from the farm and succulent seafood right out of the ocean. So fuel up, because you have a lot to do. Massachusetts trips show off four centuries of dramatic history, rich displays of artistry and creativity, and thrilling opportunities for outdoor adventure. Buckle up and enjoy the ride.

Nantucket Main Street

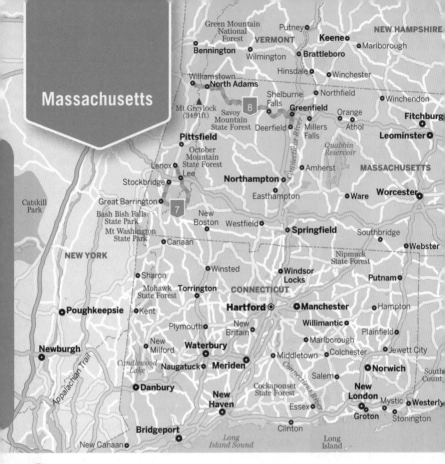

Cape Cod & the Islands 5–7 days
This slow, meandering route includes the Cape's best beaches, oysters and art. (p65)

Pilgrim Trail 4–5 days
This trip for history buffs explores the New World's earliest settlements. (p75)

Around Cape Ann 2–3 days
A cruise along the North Shore features clam shacks and coastal scenery. (p83)

Berkshire Back Roads 2–3 days
Drive through the Berkshires, enjoying inspired arts performances in splendid mountain settings. (p91)

Mohawk Trail 2–3 days
This storied scenic highway is a conduit for history, art and adventure. (p99)

DON'T MISS

Stellwagen Bank

This National Marine Sanctuary is a rich feeding ground for humpback whales. See them on Trip 4

Gould's Sugar House

Fluffy pancakes and homemade ice cream show off delicious maple syrup, made at this family farm. Taste the goodness on Trip 8

Rocky Neck Art Colony

Artists have converted Gloucester's colorful fishing shacks into galleries and studio space, open for your visit on Trip 6

Nauset Light

The iconic red-and-white beacon has been shining the light since 1877. Climb to the top on Trip 4

Commercial Street

'Eclectic' doesn't begin to describe Provincetown's main drag, with art galleries, pet parades and gay cabaret. See the show on Trips 4 5

Stellwagen Bank National Marine Sanctuary Breaching humpback whale

Classic Trip

Cape Cod & the Islands

4

A drive down the cape offers a beach for every mood. Besides sun, surf and sand, there are lighthouses to climb, oysters to eat, art and antiques to buy, and trails to hike.

TRIP HIGHLIGHTS

128 miles

Provincetown
A breeding ground for artistic, intellectual and alternative culture

FINISH 8

Wellfleet

6

105 miles

START
Sandwich **Yarmouth Port** **5**

Cape Cod National Seashore
Hiking, biking, swimming and sunbathing amid miles of pristine dunes and beaches

Hyannis

96 miles

Brewster Tidal Flats
A spectacular seascape for a sunset

3

Nantucket
Cobblestone streets lined with blooming trees and 19th-century mansions

46 miles

5–7 DAYS
128 MILES / 206KM

GREAT FOR...

BEST TIME TO GO

Enjoy fine weather but avoid the crowds in May, June or September.

ESSENTIAL PHOTO

Brewster's otherworldly tidal flats are particularly photogenic at sunset.

BEST FOR FOOD & DRINK

Slurp oysters and devour classic pastries in Wellfleet.

Cape Cod Brewster Tidal Flats

65

Classic Trip

4 Cape Cod & the Islands

As the sun sets and the sky darkens, you slide your car into place alongside dozens of others facing the massive screen. Roll down the window, feel the salty breeze and recline your seat. After an exhilarating day at the beach, it's time to sit back and enjoy a double feature at the drive-in. Sound like something out of a 1950s fantasy? It's summer on Cape Cod.

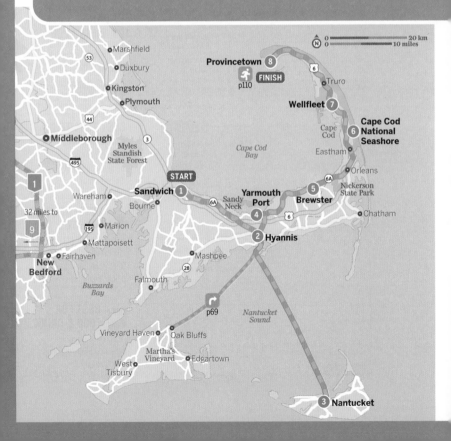

❶ Sandwich

Cape Cod's oldest town (founded in 1637) makes a perfect first impression as you cross over the canal from the mainland. In the village center, white-steepled churches, period homes and a working grist mill surround a picturesque swan pond.

Fun for kids and adults alike, the nearby 100-acre **Heritage Museums & Gardens** (☎508-888-3300; www.heritagemuseumsand gardens.org; 67 Grove St; adult/child $18/7; ⏰10am-5pm mid-Apr–mid-Oct;) sports a vintage-automobile collection, an authentic 1908 carousel and unusual folk-art collections. Too tame? Within the complex, an adventure park houses

zip lines, rope bridges and aerial trails.

Before leaving town, take a stroll across the **Sandwich Boardwalk** (parking is $15 in summer), which extends 1350 scenic feet across an expansive marsh to **Town Neck Beach**. From MA 6A, head north onto Jarves St, go left at Factory St and right onto Boardwalk Rd.

The Drive ❯❯ Heading east on MA 6A, also known as Old King's Hwy, wind your way past cranberry bogs, wetlands and Shaker-shingle cottages. In Barnstable, take a right on MA 132 and head to the more commercial southern side of the cape. For a faster but less scenic version of this trip, take the Mid-Cape Hwy (US 6) instead of 6A.

❷ Hyannis

Most people traveling through Hyannis are here to catch a ferry to Nantucket or Martha's Vineyard (just like you). Fortunately, the village port has a few sights to keep you entertained while you wait for your boat – or even longer.

Take a walk through the **HyArts District** (☎508-862-4678; www. hyartsdistrict.com; 250 South St; ⏰11am-6pm Fri-Sun May–mid-Jun, to 8pm daily mid-Jun–Aug, to 6pm Sep-early Oct), which includes the **Guyer Barn** community art space and neighboring studios, the colorful artist shanties near the ferry

docks, and the art-strewn **Walkway to the Sea**.

Politics aficionados will know that Hyannis has been the summer home of the Kennedy clan for generations. Back in the day, JFK spent his summers here – times that are beautifully documented with photographs and video at the **John F Kennedy Hyannis Museum** (☎508-790-3077; www.jfkhyannismuseum.org; 397 Main St; adult/child $12/6; ⏰9am-5pm Mon-Sat, from noon Sun Jun-Oct, shorter hours rest of year). There's also a JFK Memorial at the family-friendly **Veterans Beach** (Ocean St;), about a half-mile south of the Hy-Line Cruise dock.

🛏 p73

The Drive ❯❯ Leave your car in Hyannis and take a one-hour catamaran trip or a cheaper two-hour ferry trip to Nantucket. Don't miss the picturesque Brant Point Lighthouse as the ferry pulls into Nantucket harbor.

TRIP HIGHLIGHT

❸ Nantucket

Nantucket is New England at its most rose-covered, cobblestoned, picture-postcard perfect. The island's main population center, Nantucket Town was once home port to the world's largest whaling fleet. Now a National Historic Landmark, the town boasts leafy streets lined with

LINK YOUR TRIP

1 Coastal New England

From Hyannis, take I-195 to New Bedford to intersect with this trip through maritime New England.

9 Rhode Island: East Bay

A longer trip on I-195 will zip you to Providence to take in the pleasures of picturesque Rhode Island.

gracious period homes and public buildings. For the finest stroll, walk up cobbled **Main Street**, just past the Pacific National Bank (c 1818), where the grandest whaling-era mansions are lined up in a row.

While strolling the streets, pay a visit to the excellent **Nantucket Whaling Museum** (☎508-228-1894; www.nha.org; 13 Broad St; museum & sites/all access $20/25; ☉9am-5pm late May–mid-Oct, shorter hours rest of year, closed Jan), which occupies a former spermaceti (whale oil) candle factory. The evocative exhibits relive Nantucket's 19th-century heyday as the whaling center of the world.

Close to town, there's a pair of family-friendly beaches to cool off at. For wilder, less-frequented strands, you'll need to cycle or hop on a bus to **Surfside** or **Nobadeer**

Beach, 3 to 4 miles south of town.

 p73

The Drive >> Ferry back to Hyannis Port to pick up your car. From South St, turn north on Lewis Bay Rd/Camp St, and then turn right on Yarmouth Rd. Continue north for 3 miles, then turn right on MA 6A and continue into Yarmouth Port.

- - - - - - - - - - - - - - - - - -

4 Yarmouth Port

Nearly 50 historic sea captains' homes are lined up along MA 6A in Yarmouth Port, in a stretch known as **Captains' Mile**. Most of them are private homes; however, the Historical Society of Old Yarmouth maintains the 1840 **Captain Bangs Hallett House** (☎508-362-3021; www.hsoy.org; 11 Strawberry Lane, Yarmouth Port; tour adult/child $5/free; ☉1-4pm Fri-Sun mid-Jun–mid-Oct). For more historic sites in Yarmouth Port, pick up the free self-guided *Captains' Mile* walking-tour booklet or download a PDF online (www.yarmouthcapecod.com/captains-mile-walking-tour).

CAPE COD POTATO CHIP FACTORY

On your way into Hyannis, stop at the **Cape Cod Potato Chip Factory** (☎888-881-2447; www.capecodchips.com; 100 Breed's Hill Rd; ☉9am-5pm Mon-Fri) for a free self-guided tour and a free sample. From MA 132 (just west of the airport), take Independence Dr a half-mile north to the factory.

Alternatively, stroll or walk 1 mile up Center St to **Grey's Beach**, also known as Bass Hole. A terrific quarter-mile-long boardwalk extends over a tidal marsh and creek, offering a unique vantage point for viewing all sorts of sea life.

The Drive >> Continue east on MA 6A through the classy village of Dennis and on to Brewster. This section of road (between Barnstable and Brewster) is lined with old homes that have been converted into antique shops. Take the time to stop and browse, and come home with treasures ranging from nautical kitsch to art-deco cool.

- - - - - - - - - - - - - - - - - -

TRIP HIGHLIGHT

5 Brewster

Brewster's best-known landmark is the **Brewster Store** (☎508-896-3744; www.brewsterstore.com; 1935 Main St/MA 6A; ☉6am-10pm Jun-Sep, 7am-5pm Mon-Fri, 6am-4pm Sat, to 2pm Sun Oct-May), an old-fashioned country store that has been in operation since 1866. Penny candy is still sold alongside the local newspaper. Upstairs, you'll discover a stash of museum-quality memorabilia as old as the building.

When the tide goes out on Cape Cod Bay, the bayside beach becomes a giant sandbar, offering opportunities to commune with crabs, clams and gulls, and to take in brilliant sunsets. Best

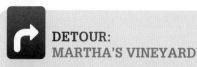

DETOUR:
MARTHA'S VINEYARD

Start: ② Hyannis or ③ Nantucket

Your island destination is Oak Bluffs, the Vineyard's mecca for summer fun. Originally a retreat for a revivalist church group, it's now a retreat for beach-bound, ice-cream-eating party people.

In the mid-19th century, the members of the Methodist Camp Meeting Association (CMA) enjoyed a day at the beach as much as a good gospel service. They first camped out in tents, then built some 300 wooden cottages, each adorned with whimsical filigree trim. From bustling Circuit Ave, slip down the alley to discover the **Campgrounds**, a world of gingerbread houses adorned with Candyland colors. For a peek inside one, visit the **Cottage Museum** (☎508-693-5042; www.mvcma. org; 1 Trinity Park; adult/child $3/0.50; ☺10am-4pm Mon-Sat, from 1pm Sun Jun–mid-Oct), which contains exhibits on CMA history. The brightly painted cottages surround emerald-green **Trinity Park** and its open-air **Tabernacle** (1879), where the lucky descendants of the campers still gather for community singalongs and concerts.

Further north on Circuit Ave, you can take a nostalgic ride on the **Flying Horses Carousel** (☎508-693-9481; www.mvpreservation.org; Oak Bluffs Ave; per ride/10 rides $3/25; ☺11am-4:30pm Sat & Sun May–mid-Jun, 10am-10pm daily mid-Jun–Aug, 11am-4:30pm daily Sep–early Oct; ⛹), a National Historic Landmark that has been captivating kids of all ages since 1876. It's the country's oldest continuously operating merry-go-round, where the antique horses have manes of real horse hair.

Beginning just south of the Steamship Authority's ferry terminal, a narrow strip of sandy **beach** runs unbroken for several miles. There is also a scenic **bike trail** (with plenty of places to rent) connecting Oak Bluffs with other parts of the Vineyard. From Hyannis, **Hy-Line Cruises** (adult/child round trip $59/39, one hour) operates a high-speed passenger ferry to Oak Bluffs several times daily from May to October. It also has a ferry link between Nantucket and Oak Bluffs.

---

access to the tidal flats is via the **Point of Rocks** or **Ellis Landing Beaches** (parking is $20 in summer). Pick up a parking sticker and check the tide charts at the town hall.

 p73

The Drive » Head east on MA 6A out of Brewster, then hop on US 6, lined with roadside motels and clam shacks. It's a quick trip through Orleans and Eastham to your next destination.

TRIP HIGHLIGHT

⑥ Cape Cod National Seashore

Extending some 40 miles around the curve of the Outer Cape, the Cape Cod National Seashore is a treasure trove of unspoiled beaches, dunes, salt marshes, nature trails and forests. Start your explorations at the **Salt Pond Visitor Center** (☎508-255-3421;

www.nps.gov/caco; 50 Nauset Rd, cnr US 6; ☺9am-4:30pm), which offers a wonderful view of the namesake salt pond. Numerous walking and cycling trails begin right at the visitor center; this is also the place to purchase a parking permit if you intend to spend time at any of the National Seashore beaches.

After this brief introduction, take Nauset Rd and Doane Rd to the

Classic Trip

WHY THIS IS A CLASSIC TRIP
ISABEL ALBISTON, WRITER

Coastlines like Cape Cod are worth taking time over, stopping on a whim when a beach is just too beautiful to drive past. Jump out of the car to hike a trail or splash in the sea when the sun comes out. Snap photos that could never capture the screeching seagulls, crashing waves, and gasps of salty air inhaled between mouthfuls of seafood.

Above: Commercial Street, Provincetown
Left: Nantucket Whaling Museum
Right: Nauset Light, Cape Cod National Seashore

picturesque **Coast Guard Beach** (Ocean View Dr) for swimming and bodysurfing. Afterward, drive along the aptly named Ocean View Dr to **Nauset Light** (☎508-240-2612; www.nausetlight.org; ⊙tours 1-4pm Sun May-Oct, plus 4:30-7pm Tue & Wed Jun-Aug), which has been shining on the cape since 1877 (and gracing the packets of Cape Cod potato chips for over 30 years).

The Drive » Take Nauset Rd back to the Mid-Cape Hwy and continue north to Main St in Wellfleet. For a scenic detour, turn right off the highway onto Le Count Hollow Rd, then left on Ocean View Dr. From here, Long Pond Rd will cross the highway and deposit you on Main St in Wellfleet center.

- - - - - - - - - - - - - - - - - -

❼ Wellfleet

Wellfleet is one of Cape Cod's unsung gems, offering some unspoiled beaches, a charming historic center and plenty of opportunities to slurp glorious oysters.

By day, browse the galleries that are sprinkled around town. (The Wellfleet Art Galleries Association map has descriptive listings.) Or spy on the birdlife at Mass Audubon's 1100-acre **Wellfleet Bay Wildlife Sanctuary** (☎508-349-2615; www.mass audubon.org; 291 US 6, South Wellfleet; adult/child $5/3; ⊙trails 8am-dusk, nature center 8:30am-4:30pm late May-early Oct;), where

Classic Trip

LGBTIQ+ PROVINCETOWN

While other cities have their gay districts, in Provincetown the entire town is the gay district.

A-House (Atlantic House; 508-487-3169; www.ahouse. com; 4 Masonic Pl; Little Bar noon-1am, Macho Bar & club 10pm-1am) P-town's gay scene got its start here and it's still the leading bar in town.

Boatslip Beach Club (508-487-1669; www. boatslipresort.com; 161 Commercial St; tea dances daily from 4pm Jun-early Sep, Fri-Sun mid-Sep-May) Hosts wildly popular tea dances each afternoon.

Crown & Anchor (508-487-1430; www.onlyatthecrown. com; 247 Commercial St; hours vary) A popular complex that attracts lesbians and gay men. Hosts lots of shows and events.

trails cross tidal creeks, salt marshes and sandy beaches.

At night, park your car at the 1950s-era **Wellfleet Drive-In** (508-349-7176; www.wellfleetcinemas.com; 51 US 6, South Wellfleet; tickets adult/child $12/9; late May-mid-Sep;), where everything except the feature flick is true to the era. Grab a bite to eat at the old-fashioned snack bar, hook the mono speaker over the car window and settle in for a double feature.

For a more raucous night, head to **Cahoon Hallow Beach**, where the cape's coolest summertime hang-out is housed in the former lifeguard station, now known as the **Beachcomber** (508-349-6055; www.thebeachcomber.com; 1120 Cahoon Hollow Rd; 11:30am-1am late May-early Sep).

 p73

The Drive » US 6 continues north through Truro, passing Truro Vineyards and Pilgrim Heights. On the right, the picturesque East Harbor is backed by pristine parabolic dunes; on the left, wind-blown beach shacks front Provincetown Harbor.

Alternatively, take the slower-going Shore Rd (MA 6A), which branches off in North Truro and eventually becomes Commercial St in Provincetown.

TRIP HIGHLIGHT

8 Provincetown

Provincetown is far out. We're not just talking geographically (though it does occupy the outermost point on Cape Cod); we're also talking about the flamboyant street scenes, brilliant art galleries and unbridled nightlife. Once an outpost for fringe writers and artists, Provincetown has morphed into the hottest gay and lesbian destination in the Northeast. Even if you're only in town for a day,

you'll want to spend part of it admiring the art and watching the local life as you stroll along Commercial Street.

Provincetown is also the perfect launching point for whale watching, since it's the closest port to **Stellwagen Bank National Marine Sanctuary**, the summer feeding ground for humpback whales. **Dolphin Fleet Whale Watch** (800-826-9300, 508-240-3636; www.whalewatch.com; 307 Commercial St; adult/child $52/31; mid-Apr-Oct;) offers up to 10 tours daily, each lasting three to four hours.

p73, p81

Eating & Sleeping

Hyannis ②

🛏 Anchor-In   Hotel $$$

(📞508-775-0357; www.anchorin.com; 1 South
St; r $206-316; ❄ @ 🛜 🏊) This family-run
boutique hotel puts the chains to shame. The
harbor-front location offers a fine sense of place,
and the heated outdoor pool is a perfect perch
from which to watch fishing boats unload their
catch. The rooms are bright and smart, with
water-view balconies. If you're planning a day trip
to Nantucket, the ferry is just a stroll away.

Nantucket ③

🍴 Company of
the Cauldron   Modern American $$$

(📞508-228-4016; www.companyofthecauldron.
com; 5 India St; 4-course dinners $60-89;
🕧6:30-10pm Mon-Sat mid-May–Jan) A splendid
choice for a romantic dinner, this intimate
restaurant has attentive service and top-rated
food. It offers only reserved seating times and
four-course prix-fixe dinners, with the likes of
rosemary-skewered shrimp followed by beef
tournedos. As the chef concentrates his magic
on just one menu each evening, it's done to
perfection. Book early for Lobster Monday.

Brewster ⑤

🍴 Brewster Fish House   Seafood $$$

(📞508-896-7867; www.brewsterfishhouse.com;
2208 Main St/MA 6A; mains $28-38; 🕧11:30am-
3pm & 5-9:30pm) It's not an eye-catcher from
the outside, but it's heaven inside for seafood
lovers. Start with the chunky lobster bisque.
From there it's safe to cast your net in any
direction; dishes are fresh and creative. There's
just a dozen tables, and no reservations, so try
lunch (mains $17 to $19) or an early dinner to
avoid long waits.

🛏 Old Sea Pines Inn   B&B $$

(📞508-896-6114; www.oldseapinesinn.com;
2553 Main St/MA 6A; r $130-170, ste $210-425;
@ 🛜) Staying here is a bit like staying at
Grandma's house: antique fittings, sleigh beds

and sepia photographs on the bureau. This
former girls' boarding school dating from 1840
has 24 rooms: some small; others commodious,
with fireplace; some suited to families. Mosey
out to the rocking chairs on the porch and soak
up the yesteryear atmosphere.

Wellfleet ⑦

🍴 PB Boulangerie & Bistro   Bakery $

(📞508-349-1600; www.pbboulangeriebistro.
com; 15 Lecount Hollow Rd, South Wellfleet;
pastries $3-5; 🕧bakery 7am-6pm Wed-Sun,
bistro 5-9:30pm Wed-Sat, 10:30am-2pm Sun)
A Michelin-starred French baker setting up
shop in tiny Wellfleet? You might think he'd
gone crazy, if not for the line out the door.
You can't miss PB: it's painted pink and set
back from US 6. Scan the cabinets full of fruit
tarts, chocolate-almond croissants and filled
baguettes and you'll think you've died and gone
to Paris.

Provincetown ⑧

🍴 Canteen   Modern American $

(📞508-487-3800; www.thecanteenptown.com;
225 Commercial St; mains $10-16; 🕧11am-9pm
Sun-Thu, to 10pm Fri & Sat; 🍴 👶) Cool and
casual, but unmistakably gourmet – this is
your optimal P-town lunch stop. Choose from
classics like lobster rolls and barbecued pulled-
pork sandwiches, or innovations like cod *banh
mi* and shrimp sliders. We strongly recommend
you add crispy brussels sprouts and a cold
beer to your order and then take a seat at the
communal picnic table on the sand.

🛏 AWOL   Boutique Hotel $$$

(📞508-413-9820; www.awolhotel.com; 59
Province Lands Rd; r $397-639; 🕧May-Oct;
🅿 ❄ 🛜 🏊) Overlooking the salt marsh and
away from the bustle of Provincetown's main
drag is AWOL, a new boutique hotel with a
tropical 1960s vibe. Wood and wicker furniture
is featured both in the rooms and on the large
front lawn, which is set up with lounge chairs
and fire pits, perfect for sipping a tiki cocktail
under the moonlight.

Pilgrim Trail

Follow in the footsteps of the country's earliest European settlers, visiting the sites that commemorate their struggles and celebrate their successes in making their home in the New World.

5

TRIP HIGHLIGHTS

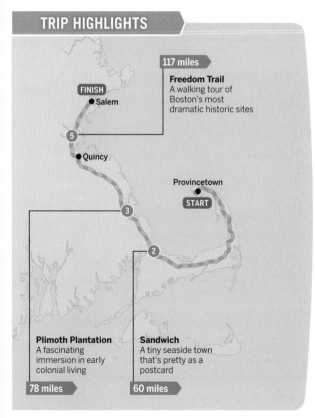

117 miles

Freedom Trail
A walking tour of Boston's most dramatic historic sites

FINISH
● Salem

5

● Quincy

Provincetown ●

START

3

2

Plimoth Plantation
A fascinating immersion in early colonial living

78 miles

Sandwich
A tiny seaside town that's pretty as a postcard

60 miles

4–5 DAYS
147 MILES / 237KM

GREAT FOR...

BEST TIME TO GO

Most sites are open from April to November.

 ESSENTIAL PHOTO

The Dexter Grist Mill in Sandwich is photogenic.

 BEST FOR FAMILIES

Plymouth is packed with interesting and educational fun.

Sandwich Dexter Grist Mill

Pilgrim Trail

Your car is a time machine, transporting you back 400 years. The region's living museums allow you to experience firsthand what life was like for the colonists as they settled in the New World. Explore the sites and structures – churches and trading posts, homesteads and grist mills – that are still standing from those early days.

1 Provincetown

Most people don't know that months before the 'official' landing on Plymouth Rock, the Pilgrims arrived at the tip of Cape Cod. Despite the protected harbor and good fishing, they were unable to find a reliable source of freshwater, so they headed off to Plymouth. But not before signing the Mayflower Compact, which is considered the first governing document of the Plymouth Colony. The **Pilgrim Monument** (☎508-487-1310; www.

55 miles to
25

○ Rockport
○ Gloucester

FINISH

Peabody ○ 6 Salem p108
○ Marblehead

Lexington ○

107

Cambridge
Waltham ○ ○ ● 5 Boston p106

90

Quincy 4 ● ○ Weymouth
93 ○ Cohasset

Massachusetts Bay

○ Norwood

Stroughton ○ 3 Rockland ○ Marshfield

○ Franklin ● Brockton

Easton
495 24 ○ Bridgewater
1 ○ Kingston
3 Plymouth

START
Provincetown 1
p110

Truro ○ Cape Cod
National
Wellfleet ○ Seashore

Taunton ○ Middleborough 3
24 Myles Standish
State Forest
○ Pawtucket 495

○ Providence
138 24 Freetown
Fall River Wareham ○
Warren ○ State Forest Bourne ○
Fall River ○ 195 ○ Marion p77

Cape Cod Bay

○ Eastham
Brewster ○ ○ Orleans

2 Sandwich

6 6 ○ Chatham

○ Hyannis

○ Portsmouth New
Bedford *Buzzards
Bay* ○ Falmouth ○ Mashpee *Nantucket
Sound*

N 0 ▬▬▬ 20 km
0 ▬▬▬ 10 miles

pilgrim-monument.org; 1 High Pole Hill Rd; adult/child $12/4; ⊘9am-5pm Apr, May & Sep-Jan, to 7pm Jun-Aug) commemorates the signing of the compact, as do a few exhibits at the on-site **Provincetown Museum**. Climb 252ft (116 steps) to the top of the tall tower for magnificent views of Provincetown Harbor and the National Seashore.

In addition to its historic interest, Provincetown is a cauldron of contemporary creativity, which you can see for yourself on a walk (p110) along artsy Commercial St.

✕ ⇦ p73, p81

The Drive » Head out of Provincetown on US 6, passing picturesque East Harbor and windblown beach shacks. You'll also pass Pilgrim Heights, where the settlers found fresh water, and First Encounter Beach, site of the first violent clash with the native population. From Orleans, continue west on US 6 or take slower, more scenic MA 6A, which shows off the cape's historic villages.

LINK YOUR TRIP

1 Coastal New England

See more of maritime Massachusetts and Connecticut.

25 Maritime Maine

For a round of lighthouse photos and lobster feasts, take I-95 to Kittery.

DETOUR: BOURNE

Start: ② Sandwich

Bourne is not as picturesque as nearby Sandwich, but it is historically significant, thanks to its strategic location at the northeastern corner of Buzzards Bay, halfway between the Manomet and Scusset Rivers. Here, in 1627, the Pilgrims founded the Aptucxet Trading Post, which allowed easy access to the Dutch settlements to the south. The trading center would eventually lead to the construction of the Cape Cod Canal, which was built so traders could avoid the cape's hazardous eastern shore.

Nowadays, the **Aptucxet Trading Post Museum** (☎508-759-8167; www.bournehistoricalsociety.org; 6 Aptucxet Rd; adult/child $6/4; ⊘10am-4pm Tue-Sat, noon-3pm Sun late May–mid-Oct) is an eclectic little museum, built on what is believed to be the oldest remains of a Pilgrim building ever found. Although the simple, unpainted clapboard structure standing today is a replica built on the original foundation, it's still possible to imagine Pilgrims, Wampanoag and Dutch coming here to barter goods, seeds, tools and food. To reach the Aptucxet Trading Post, take MA 6A out of Sandwich and continue on Sandwich Rd for 7 miles along the Cape Cod Canal. Once in Bourne, turn right on Perry Rd and take the first left on Aptucxet Rd.

TRIP HIGHLIGHT

② Sandwich

With the waterwheel at the old mill, the white clapboard houses, and the swans on the pond, the center of Sandwich is as pretty as a Cape Cod town can be. The restored 17th-century **Dexter Grist Mill** (☎508-888-4361; Water St; adult/child $4/3; ⊘11am-4:30pm Mon-Sat, 1-4pm Sun Jun-Oct) on the edge of Shawme Pond has centuries-old gears that still grind cornmeal. Nearby, **Hoxie House** (☎508-888-4361; 18 Water St; adult/child $4/3; ⊘11am-5pm Mon-Sat, from 1pm Sun mid-Jun–mid-Oct) is the oldest house on Cape Cod. The 1640 salt box–style structure has been faithfully restored, complete with antiques and brick hearth, giving a good sense of early-settler home life.

The Drive » Hop on US 6 heading west over the Sagamore Bridge. Stay on MA 3 or branch off to MA 3A, which hugs the coast for the 14 miles north to Plymouth.

MASSACHUSETTS **5** PILGRIM TRAIL

3 Plymouth

Plymouth is 'America's Home Town,' where the Pilgrims first settled in the winter of 1620. An innocuous, weathered ball of granite – the famous **Plymouth Rock** (Water St) – marks the spot where they (might have) stepped ashore in this foreign land, while **Mayflower II** (www.plimoth.org/what-see-do/mayflower-ii; State Pier, Water St; 👪) is a replica of the small ship in which they made the fateful voyage. Many museums and historic sites in the surrounding streets recall the Pilgrims' struggles, sacrifices and triumphs.

The best is **Plimoth Plantation** (📞508-746-1622; www.plimoth.org; 137 Warren Ave; adult/child $28/16; ⏰9am-5pm Apr-Nov; 👪), a historically accurate re-creation of the Pilgrims' settlement. Everything in the 1627 English Village – costumes, implements, vocabulary, artistry, recipes and crops – has been painstakingly researched and remade. Costumed interpreters, acting in character, explain the details of daily life and answer your questions as you watch them work and play. The on-site **Wampanoag Homesite** replicates the life of a Native American community in the same area during that time. Unlike the English Village, the homesite is staffed by indigenous people speaking from a modern perspective.

🍴 p81

The Drive » Take MA 3 north for about 25 miles. In Quincy, take the Burgin Pkwy 2 miles north into the center.

Plymouth Plimoth Plantation

4 Quincy

Quincy was first settled in 1625 by a handful of raucous colonists who could not stand the strict and stoic ways in Plymouth. History has it that this group went so far as to drink beer, dance around a maypole and engage in other festive Old English customs, which enraged the Pilgrims down the road. Nathaniel Hawthorne immortalized this history in his fictional account *The Maypole of Merrimount*. Eventually, Myles Standish arrived from Plymouth to restore order to the wayward colony.

What earns this town the nickname 'The City of Presidents' is that it is the birthplace of John Adams and John Quincy Adams. The collection of houses where the Adams family lived now composes the **Adams National Historic Park** (www.nps.gov/adam; 1250 Hancock St; adult/child $15/ free; ☺9am-5pm mid-Apr–mid-Nov). Besides the homes, you can also see where the presidents and their wives are interred in the crypt of the **United First Parish Church** (www. ufpc.org; 1306 Hancock St;

suggested donation adult/ child $5/free; ☺11am-4pm Mon-Sat, from noon Sun mid-Apr–mid-Nov).

The Drive » Take Newport Ave north out of town and merge onto I-93 heading north. Continue on the Central Artery straight through (and under) Boston, experiencing firsthand the benefits of the infamous Big Dig. Take exit 26 onto Storrow Dr for downtown Boston.

TRIP HIGHLIGHT

5 Boston

Ten years after the Pilgrims settled in Plymouth, they were followed by a group of Puritans – also fleeing the repressive Church of England – who founded the Massachusetts Bay Colony about 40 miles up the coast. The Puritans' first seat of government was on the north shore of the Charles River, where excavations have uncovered the foundations of Governor John Winthrop's home, known as the **Great House** (City Sq; ⊙dawn-dusk). Winthrop is buried alongside other early settlers in the **King's Chapel Burying Ground** (☎617-523-1749; www.kings-chapel.org; 58 Tremont St; suggested donation $3, tours adult/child $7/3; ⊙church 10am-4:30pm Mon-Sat, 1:30-5pm Sun, hourly tours 10am-3pm).

Not too many physical structures remain from these earliest days of Boston's settlement. The city's oldest dwelling (1680) is **Paul Revere House** (☎617-523-2338; www.paulreverehouse.org; 19 North Sq; adult/child $4.50/1; ⊙9:30am-5:15pm mid-Apr–Oct, to 4:15pm Nov–mid-Apr, closed Mon Jan-Mar, where the celebrated patriot lived. The oldest church (1723) is **Old North Church** (Christ Church; ☎617-858-8231;

www.oldnorth.com; 193 Salem St; adult/child $8/4, plus $2 for tour; ⊙10am-4pm Nov-March, 9am-6pm April-Oct), where two lanterns were hung on the eve of the American Revolution. To see these and other sites from Boston's revolutionary history, follow the **Freedom Trail** (☎617-357-8300; www.thefreedomtrail. org), which connects the most prominent historic landmarks. For a contemporary perspective, stroll around the city's green spaces and shopping places.

✗ 🛏 p39, p81

The Drive » As you exit Boston to the north, take US 93 to US 95/MA 128. At the fork, stay on MA 128. Take exit 25A to MA 114, and follow the signs to Salem center. Alternatively, for a scenic seaside route, take MA 1A all the way up the coast through Swampscott and Marblehead.

----

6 Salem

Founded by English fisherfolk in 1626, Salem was part of the Massachusetts Bay Colony. **Salem Pioneer Village** (www.facebook.com/Pioneer-Village-Salem-1630-121882794516520; Forest River Park; $6; ⊙tours 12:30pm, 1:30pm & 2:30pm

Sat & Sun Jun-Oct) is an outdoor, interactive museum that gives visitors an idea of what daily life was like for settlers.

Salem is most famous – or infamous – as the site of the witch trials in 1692, when 19 people were hanged as a result of witch-hunt hysteria. Don't miss the **Witch Trials Memorial** (Charter St), a simple but dramatic monument that honors the innocent victims. To understand more about how this hysteria snowballed, visit the **Witch House** (Jonathan Corwin House; ☎978-744-8815; www.thewitchhouse.org; 310 Essex St; adult/child $8.25/4.25, guided tour $2; ⊙10am-5pm mid-Mar–mid-Nov, noon-4pm Thu-Sun mid-Nov–mid-Mar). This was the home of Jonathan Corwin, a local magistrate who investigated witchcraft claims.

The town has dozens of other related sites, as well as a month-long Halloween extravaganza in October. But there's a lot more to Salem than bed knobs and broomsticks. Take a walk (p108) and discover the town's many historical charms.

✗ 🛏 p39, p81

Eating & Sleeping

Provincetown ❶

✖ Mews
Restaurant & Cafe   Modern American $$$

(📞508-487-1500; www.mews.com; 429 Commercial St; mains $19-44; ⏱5-10pm, also 10am-2pm Sun mid-May–Sep) A fantastic water view, the hottest martini bar in town and scrumptious food add up to Provincetown's finest dining scene. There are two sections: opt to dine gourmet on lobster risotto and filet mignon downstairs, where you're right on the sand, or go casual with a juicy Angus burger from the bistro menu upstairs. Reservations recommended.

🛏 Carpe Diem   Boutique Hotel $$$

(📞508-487-4242; www.carpediemguesthouse. com; 12-14 Johnson St; r $349-599; P ❄ 🛜) Sophisticated yet relaxed, this boutique inn blends a soothing mix of smiling Buddhas, orchid sprays and artistic decor. Each guest room is inspired by a different LGBTIQ+ literary genius; the room themed on poet Raj Rao, for example, has sumptuous embroidered fabrics draped over the modern furniture. The on-site spa includes a Finnish sauna, a hot tub and massage therapy.

Plymouth ❸

✖ Blue Blinds Bakery   Bakery $

(www.blueblindsbakery.com; 7 North St; mains $5-9; ⏱6am-9pm Sun-Thu, 7am-3pm Fri; 🖉 👪) Blue Blinds is a cozy house – it feels like a home, really – with plants in the windows, a fire in the fireplace and folks sipping coffee on the shady front porch. The baked goods are out of this world, including fresh-baked organic breads, muffins and pastries. Breakfast is served all day, but the sandwiches and homemade soups are also divine.

Boston ❺

✖ Island Creek Oyster Bar   Seafood $$$

(📞617-532-5300; www.islandcreekoysterbar. com; 500 Commonwealth Ave; oysters $3, mains lunch $13-21, dinner $24-36; ⏱4-11pm Mon-Fri, 11:30am-11:30pm Sat, 10:30am-11pm Sun; 🚇Kenmore) Island Creek claims to unite farmer, chef and diner in one space – and what a space it is. It serves up the region's finest oysters, along with other local seafood, in an ethereal new-age setting. The specialty – lobster-roe noodles topped with braised short ribs and grilled lobster – lives up to the hype.

🛏 Liberty Hotel   Hotel $$$

(📞866-961-3778, 617-224-4000; www. libertyhotel.com; 215 Charles St; r from $375; P 🍽 ❄ 🛜; 🚇Charles/MGH) It is with intended irony that the notorious Charles St Jail has been converted into the classy Liberty Hotel. Today, the 90ft ceiling soars above a spectacular lobby. All 298 guest rooms come with luxurious linens and high-tech amenities, while the 18 in the original jail wing boast floor-to-ceiling windows with amazing views of the Charles River and Beacon Hill.

Salem ❻

✖ Red's Sandwich Shop   Diner $

(www.redssandwichshop.com; 15 Central St; mains $6-10; ⏱5am-3pm Mon-Sat, 6am-1pm Sun) This Salem institution has been serving eggs and sandwiches to faithful customers for over 50 years. The food is hearty and basic, but the real attraction is Red's old-school decor, which comes complete with counter service and friendly faces. It's housed in the old London Coffee House building (around since 1698).

Around Cape Ann

6

There's more to Cape Ann than widows' walks and sailing lore. This drive offers salt marshes and windswept beaches, oases of art and antiques, and more clam shacks than you can shake a shucker at.

TRIP HIGHLIGHTS

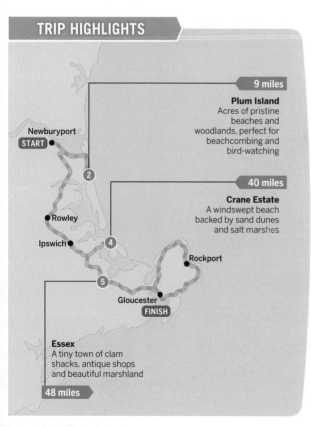

9 miles

Plum Island
Acres of pristine beaches and woodlands, perfect for beachcombing and bird-watching

Newburyport
START

2

40 miles

Crane Estate
A windswept beach backed by sand dunes and salt marshes

Rowley

Ipswich

4

Rockport

5

Gloucester
FINISH

Essex
A tiny town of clam shacks, antique shops and beautiful marshland

48 miles

2–3 DAYS
54 MILES / 87KM

GREAT FOR...

BEST TIME TO GO

The water is warmest from July to September.

ESSENTIAL PHOTO

The red fishing shack at Rockport Harbor is called Motif No 1 for its artistic appeal.

BEST FOR OUTDOORS

Parker River Wildlife Refuge offers excellent hiking, swimming, kayaking and canoeing.

Around Cape Ann

Somebody – a New Englander, no doubt – once said that 'the humble clam...reaches its quintessence when coated and fried.' The big-bellied bivalve – lightly battered and deeply fried – supposedly originated in Essex, Massachusetts, so Cape Ann is an ideal place to sample the specialty. This North Shore route takes you from clam shack to clam shack, with breaks for beachcombing, bird-watching, gallery hopping and plenty of picture taking.

❶ Newburyport

Situated at the mouth of the Merrimack River, the town of Newburyport prospered as a shipping port and silversmith center during the late 18th century. Not too much has changed in the last 200 years, as Newburyport's brick buildings and graceful churches still show off the Federal style that was popular back then.

Today the center of town is a model of historic preservation and gentrification. Admire

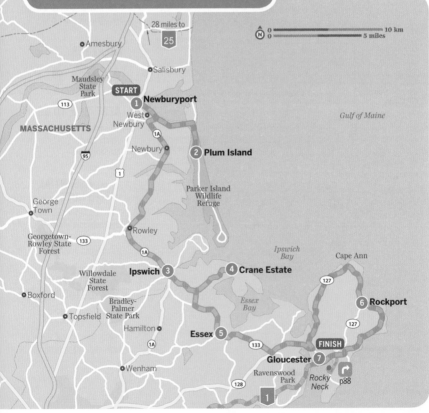

the public art as you take a stroll along the **Matthews Memorial Boardwalk**, which runs along the Merrimack and ends at the granite **Custom House Maritime Museum** (www.custom housemaritimemuseum.org; 25 Water St; adult/child $7/5; ⊙10am-4pm Tue-Sat, from noon Sun May-Dec, 10am-4pm Sat & Sun Jan-Apr). From here, you can browse in the boutiques along State St or admire the art galleries on Water St.

The Drive ❯❯ Go east on Water St, which follows the coastline out of town. It becomes the Plum Island Turnpike before passing the eponymous airport and the Parker River Visitor Center. Cross the river onto Plum Island and turn right on Sunset Dr to reach the wildlife refuge.

LINK YOUR TRIP

1 Coastal New England

Continue south from Gloucester and follow the coastline all the way through Connecticut.

25 Maritime Maine

From Newburyport, drive 26 miles north on I-95 to Kittery to experience the coastal culture of Maine.

TRIP HIGHLIGHT

2 Plum Island

A barrier island off the coast of Massachusetts, Plum Island has 9 miles of wide, sandy beaches surrounded by acres of wildlife sanctuary. These are among the most pristine beaches on the North Shore, especially if you head to the furthest points on the island.

Sandy Point (www.mass. gov/dcr; ⊙dawn-8pm; ⋔), on the southern tip, is a state park that's popular for swimming, sunning and tide pooling.

Parker River Wildlife Refuge (www.fws.gov/refuge/ parker_river; car/bike & pedestrian $5/2; ⊙dawn-dusk) is the 4662-acre sanctuary that occupies the southern three-quarters of Plum Island. More than 800 species of bird, plant and animal reside in its many ecological habitats, which include beaches, sand dunes, salt pans, salt marshes, freshwater impoundments and maritime forests. Several miles of foot trails allow access to the inland area, with observation towers and platforms punctuating the trails at prime bird-watching spots. Stop at the **visitor center** (www. fws.gov/refuge/parker_river; 6 Plum Island Turnpike; ⊙9am-4pm) for information and exhibits about the refuge.

🛏 p89

The Drive ❯❯ Depart the island on the Plum Island Turnpike. After 2 miles, turn left on Ocean Ave, then left on High Rd (MA 1A). Continue south through picturesque farmland, stopping at farm stands along the way. Go through the tiny town of Newbury and picturesque Rowley, with the famous Sunday-morning Todd Farm Flea Market. Continue south into Ipswich.

---

3 Ipswich

Ipswich is one of those New England towns that are pretty today because they were poor in the past. It had no harbor and no source of waterpower for factories, so commercial and industrial development went elsewhere. As a result, Ipswich's 17th-century houses were not torn down to build grander residences. Nowadays, there are 58 existent First Period homes, including the 1677 **Whipple House** (www.ipswichmuseum.org; 1 South Village Green; adult/child $10/5; ⊙10am-4pm Thu-Sat Apr & May, 10am-4pm Wed-Sun Jun-Oct), which is open to the public. For more historic homes, pick up a map from the **Ipswich Museum** (www.ipswich museum.org; 54 S Main St; 1/3 houses $10/15; ⊙10am-4pm Thu-Sat Apr & May, 10am-4pm Wed-Sun Jun-Oct; ⋔).

🍴 p89

The Drive ❯❯ Head out of town on S Main St (MA 133) and turn left on Argilla Rd. Drive for about

MKZDILLON/SHUTTERSTOCK ©

4 miles through beautiful woods and marshland. The entrance to the Great House is on the left, while the beach is straight ahead.

④ Crane Estate

One of the longest, widest, sandiest beaches in the region is **Crane Beach** (www.thetrustees.org; Argilla Rd, Ipswich; pedestrian & cyclist $2, car weekday/weekend $25/30; ☻8am-dusk; 🛉), which has 4 miles of fine-sand barrier beach on Ipswich Bay. The beach is set in the midst of the Crane Wildlife Refuge, so the entire surrounding area is wildly

beautiful. Five miles of trails traverse the dunes.

Above the beach, on Castle Hill, sits the 1920s **estate** (www.thetrustees. org; Argilla Rd, Ipswich; house tours car/bike $15/2; ☻house 10am-4pm Tue-Sun Jun-Oct, Sat & Sun Apr, May & Dec, grounds 8am-dusk year-round; P 🛉) of Chicago plumbing-fixture magnate Richard T Crane. The 59-room Stuart-style Great House is sometimes open for tours. The lovely landscaped grounds, which are open daily, contain several miles of walking trails.

🛏 p89

The Drive » Depart by way of Argilla Rd, but turn left on Northgate Rd, which will take you back to MA 133. Turn left and continue 2.6 miles east into Essex.

⑤ Essex

The meandering Essex River shares its name with this tiny town, home to some 3500 souls. The town's proud maritime history is on display at the **Essex Shipbuilding Museum** (www.essexship buildingmuseum.org; 66 Main St; guided tours adult/child $10/5, self-guided tours $7; ☻10am-5pm Wed-Sun Jun-Oct, Sat & Sun Nov-May; 🛉).

Ipswich Crane Estate

Most of the collection of photos, tools and ship models came from local basements and attics, allowing Essex to truly preserve its history. The collection is housed in the town's 1835 school house (check out the **Old Burying Ground** behind it). The historical society also operates a museum shipyard, a section of waterfront property where shipbuilding activities have taken place for hundreds of years.

Despite centuries of maritime history, nowadays the town is more famous for its ample antique shops and succu-

lent clams. With plenty of picnic tables overlooking the namesake estuary, there is no better lunch stop.

✕ p89

The Drive ›› Continue east on MA 133, then merge onto MA 128 heading north. At the traffic circle, take the third exit to Washington St (MA 127), which circles Cape Ann. Heading up the cape's western side, the winding road follows the Annisquam River, with a long bridge over the inlet at Goose Cove. Rounding the tip of the cape, you'll pass through tiny Lanesville and Pigeon Cove before arriving in Rockport.

⑥ Rockport

Rockport is named for its 19th-century role as a shipping center for granite cut from local quarries. The stone is still ubiquitous: monuments, building foundations, pavements and piers remain as a testament to Rockport's past.

That's about all that's left of this industrial history, however. A century ago, Winslow Homer, Childe Hassam, Fitz Henry Lane and other acclaimed artists arrived, inspired by the hearty fisherfolk who wrested a hard-won but

DETOUR: ROCKY NECK ART COLONY

Start: 6 Rockport

The narrow peninsula of Rocky Neck, jutting into Gloucester Harbor, offers inspiring views of the ocean and the harbor. Between WWI and WWII, artists began renting the local fisherfolk's seaside shacks, which they used as studios. Today these same shanties, considerably gentrified, constitute the Rocky Neck Art Colony (www.rockyneckartcolony. org), home to dozens of studios and galleries. In addition to the cooperative **Gallery 53 on Rocky Neck** (53 Rocky Neck Ave; ⊙10am-6pm Sun-Thu, to 8pm Fri & Sat Jun–mid-Oct), about a dozen galleries and studios are open to visitors. There's also a couple of restaurants.

From MA 127A (at the junction with MA 128), turn left onto E Main St and right onto Rocky Neck Ave.

satisfying living from the sea. Today Rockport's main revenue source is the tourists who come to look at the artists. (The artists have long since given up looking for hearty fisherfolk because their descendants are all running B&Bs.)

The town hub is Dock Sq, recognizable by an oft-painted red fishing shack, decorated with colorful buoys. From here, **Bearskin Neck**, lined with galleries, lobster shacks and souvenir shops, juts into the harbor.

 p89

The Drive » Leave Rockport on South St (MA 127A), heading south past Delmater Sanctuary.

Now Thatcher St, the road passes the lovely Good Harbor Beach, which is a fine spot for a cool-off. Merge onto Main St as you enter Gloucester center.

---

7 Gloucester

Gritty Gloucester offers a remarkable contrast to the rest of Cape Ann. The working waterfront is dominated by marinas and shipyards, with a backdrop of fish-processing plants. This hardworking town has its own unexpected charm, which is particularly visible in the brick buildings along Main St. Nearby, the tiny **Cape Ann Museum** (www.capeannmuseum. org; 27 Pleasant St; adult/child $12/free; ⊙10am-5pm Tue-Sat, 1-4pm Sun;) is a gem – particularly for its impressive collection of paintings by Gloucester native Fitz Henry Lane. Exhibits also showcase the region's granite-quarrying industry and – of course – its maritime history.

p39, p89

Eating & Sleeping

Plum Island ②

🛏 Blue   Inn $$$

(☎855-255-2583; www.blueinn.com; 20 Fordham Way; d from $490; P ❄ 🛜 🐾) In a drop-dead-gorgeous location on a beautiful beach, this sophisticated inn is quite a surprise on unassuming Plum Island. Rooms feature high ceilings, contemporary decor, fresh white linen and streaming sunlight. Private decks, shared hot tubs and in-room fireplaces are a few of the perks – all steps from the surf. Breakfast is delivered to your room. Three-night minimum in summer.

Ipswich ③

✕ Clam Box   Seafood $$

(www.clamboxipswich.com; 246 High St/MA 133; mains $15-32; ◷11am-8pm) You can't miss this classic clam shack, just north of Ipswich center. Built in 1938, it actually looks like a clam box, spruced up with striped awnings. Folks line up out the door for crispy fried clams and onion rings – some claim they're the best in the land.

Crane Estate ④

🛏 Inn at Castle Hill   Inn $$$

(☎978-412-2555; http://innatcastlehill. thetrustees.org; 280 Argilla Rd, Ipswich; r woodland view $235-285, ocean view $395-515; P ❄ 🛜) On the beautiful grounds of the Crane Estate, this inn is an example of understated luxury, its 10 rooms each individually decorated with subtle elegance. Turndown service, plush robes and afternoon tea are some of the perks. Instead of TVs (of which there are none), guests enjoy a wraparound veranda and its magnificent views of sand dunes and salt marshes.

Essex ⑤

✕ JT Farnham's   Seafood $$

(www.jtfarnhams.com; 88 Eastern Ave; mains $16-32, sandwiches $8-12; ◷11am-8pm Mar-Dec; 🚼) When the Food Network came to Essex to weigh in on the fried-clam debate for the show *Food Feud,* the winner was JT Farnham, thanks to the crispiness of his clams. Pull up a picnic table and enjoy the amazing estuary view.

Rockport ⑥

✕ Roy Moore
Lobster Company   Seafood $$

(www.facebook.com/Roy-Moore-Lobster-Co-125287641097; 39 Bearskin Neck; lobsters $15; ◷9am-6pm Apr-Oct) This takeout kitchen has the cheapest lobster-in-the-rough on the Neck. Your beast comes on a tray with melted butter, a fork and a wet wipe for cleanup. The stuffed clams and fish cakes are also very tasty. Find a seat at a picnic table on the back patio and dig in. Don't forget to bring your own beer or wine.

Gloucester ⑦

🛏 Rocky Neck
Accommodations   Apartment $$

(☎978-381-9848; www.rockyneckaccommoda tions.com; 43 Rocky Neck Ave; r $119-250, ste $175-235; P 🛜) You don't have to be an artist to live the bohemian life in Gloucester. The colony association offers light-filled efficiencies – all equipped with kitchenettes – at the Rocky Neck Art Colony. The rooms are sweet and simple, most with beautiful views of Smith Cove. Weekly rates also available.

Berkshire Back Roads

These country roads offer a mix of cultural riches, sweet farmland and mountain scenery. In summer, enjoy music and dance in the open air; in the fall, indulge in apples straight from the orchard.

7

TRIP HIGHLIGHTS

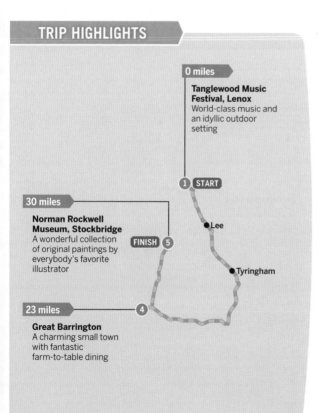

0 miles

Tanglewood Music Festival, Lenox
World-class music and an idyllic outdoor setting

1 START

30 miles

Norman Rockwell Museum, Stockbridge
A wonderful collection of original paintings by everybody's favorite illustrator

FINISH 5

●Lee

23 miles

●Tyringham

4

Great Barrington
A charming small town with fantastic farm-to-table dining

2–3 DAYS
31 MILES / 50KM

GREAT FOR...

BEST TIME TO GO

Cultural events are in full swing from mid-June to September; fall foliage is best in October.

ESSENTIAL PHOTO

Compare your photo of Main St, Stockbridge, to the Rockwell painting.

BEST FOR FOODIES

Great Barrington practically invented the locavore movement.

7

Berkshire Back Roads

Pack a picnic of farm-fresh fruit and local cheese, spread your blanket on the lush green lawns, and settle in for an evening of world-class music under the stars. Or world-class dance. Or Shakespeare. Or experimental theater. Indeed, for every day you spend hiking the hills and photographing the scenery, you can spend an evening taking in a cultural masterwork.

TRIP HIGHLIGHT

❶ Lenox

Prized for its bucolic peace, this gracious town was a summer retreat for wealthy families with surnames like Carnegie, Vanderbilt and Westinghouse. Lenox is the cultural heart of the Berkshires, and its illustrious past remains tangibly present today.

In the 19th century, writers such as Nathaniel Hawthorne and Edith Wharton set up shop here. Wharton's fabulous

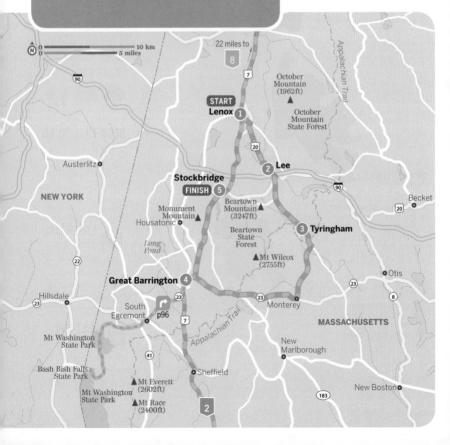

mansion, **Mount** (www. edithwharton.org; 2 Plunkett St; adult/child $20/free; ☺10am-5pm Mar-Oct, 11am-4pm Sat & Sun Nov-Feb), shows off a magnificent interior and formal gardens, demonstrating the principles that she describes in her book *The Decoration of Houses*.

About a mile west of Lenox center, **Tanglewood** (☏888-266-1200; www.tanglewood.org; 297 West St/MA 183) is the summer home of the esteemed Boston Symphony Orchestra. From June to September, these beautifully manicured grounds host concerts of pop and rock, chamber music, folk, jazz and blues, in addition to the symphony. Traditionally, the July 4 extravaganza features Massachusetts native James Taylor.

 p97

LINK YOUR TRIP

2 Fall Foliage Tour
Expand your leaf-peeping to the other New England states.

8 Mohawk Trail
For more beautiful Berkshire scenery and artistic offerings, drive north on US 7 to Williamstown.

SUMMER FESTIVALS

Aston Magna (www.astonmagna.org; tickets $30-50) Listen to Bach, Brahms and Buxtehude and other early classical music in Great Barrington during June and July.

Shakespeare & Company (☏box office 413-637-3353; www.shakespeare.org; 70 Kemble St) Shakespearean plays are performed outdoors in a bucolic context in Lenox in July and August.

Berkshire Theatre Festival (☏413-997-9444; www.berkshiretheatre.org; 83 E Main St) Stop by for experimental summer theater in an old playhouse in Stockbridge from late July through October.

Jacob's Pillow (☏413-243-9919; www.jacobspillow.org; 358 George Carter Rd, Becket; tickets $25-78) The best dance troupes of most cities can't top the stupefying and ground-breaking dance of Jacob's Pillow, which runs from mid-June through August near Lee.

Tanglewood Music Festival (☏888-266-1200; www.tanglewood.org; 297 West St/MA 183, Lenox; lawn tickets from $21; ☺late Jun-early Sep) For many, the Berkshires' most famous festival and its outstanding orchestral music are reason enough to return to Lenox each summer.

The Drive » Head out of Lenox on Walker St (MA 183), passing the historic Ventfort Hall, an impressive Jacobean Revival mansion that was a Morgan family home. One mile southeast of the center, turn right onto US 20 and drive 3 miles south, passing pretty Laurel Lake. Cross the bridge over the Housatonic River as you enter Lee.

2 Lee

Welcome to the Berkshires' towniest town, at once cute and gritty. The main street runs through the center, curving to cross some railroad tracks. On it you'll find a hardware store, a bar and a few places to eat, including a proper diner featured in a famous Norman Rockwell painting. The biggest draw to Lee is **Jacob's Pillow**, the prestigious summertime dance festival that takes place in neighboring Becket. Free Inside/Out performances are held on the outdoor Simon Stage, which has an amazing backdrop of the Berkshire hills.

 p97

The Drive » Continue east on US 20, crossing under the turnpike. Turn right on MA 102, then make an immediate left on Tyringham Rd. Hugging the Housatonic River, this scenic road passes some pretty homesteads and woodsy hillsides before entering Tyringham as Main St.

3 Tyringham

Once the home of a Shaker community (1792–1874), this tiny village enjoys a gorgeous setting in the midst of the Tyringham Valley. To get some perspective on the pastoral splendor, take a 2-mile hike over the knobs of **Tyringham Cobble** (www.thetrustees.org; Jerusalem Rd; ⊙ dawn-dusk), which offers wildflower-strewn hillsides and spectacular views.

You don't have to get out of your car to see the village's most famous attraction: the **Tyringham Gingerbread House** (Santarella; www.santarella.us; 75 Main St), an architectural fantasy designed by sculptor Henry Hudson Kitson. This fairy-tale thatched-roofed cottage is readily visible from the road, though the interior is not open to the public.

The Drive » Depart Tyringham on Main St. Turn right on Monterey Rd, passing the inviting Monterey Town Beach. Look for the old-fashioned General Store in Monterey, then head west on MA 23. Pass Beartown State Forest and Butternut Mountain as you enter Great Barrington. Continue on State Rd, cross the bridge over the Housatonic River and turn left onto Main St.

Tyringham Village

4 Great Barrington

Woolworths, diners and hardware stores have given way to galleries, boutiques and 'locavore' restaurants on Main St, Great Barrington, once named the 'best small town in America' by the Smithsonian Institution. The picturesque Housatonic River flows through the center of town, with the parallel **River Walk** (www.gbriver walk.org; ☾ sunrise-sunset Apr-Nov) offering a perfect perch from which to admire it. Access the walking path from Main St (behind Rite-Aid) or from Bridge St.

After a few hours' rest in small-town America, you might hanker for a hike in the hills. Head to **Monument Mountain** (www.thetrustees.org; US 7; parking $5; ☾ sunrise-sunset), 5 miles north. In 1850, Nathaniel Hawthorne climbed this mountain with Oliver Wendell Holmes and Herman Melville, thus sealing a lifelong friendship. You can follow their footsteps on a hike to the 1642ft summit of Squaw Peak. From the top you'll get fabulous views all the way to Mt Greylock in the northwestern corner of the state and to the Catskills in New York.

✕ 🛏 p97

The Drive ≫ Head north out of town on Main St and turn right on State St to cross the Housatonic River. Drive north on US 7, passing the pretty Fountain Pond on the right and Monument Mountain on the left. Turn left on MA 102, which is Main St, Stockbridge.

5 Stockbridge

Main St, Stockbridge, is so postcard-perfect it

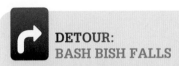

DETOUR:
BASH BISH FALLS

Start: **4** **Great Barrington**

In the southwesternmost corner of the state, near the New York state line, is **Bash Bish Falls** (www.mass.gov/locations/bash-bish-falls-state-park; Falls Rd, Mt Washington; ☺sunrise-sunset), the largest waterfall in Massachusetts. The water feeding the falls runs down a series of gorges before the torrent is sliced in two by a massive boulder perched directly above a pool. There it drops as a photogenic double waterfall. These 60ft-high falls are a popular spot for landscape painters to set up their easels. To get here from Great Barrington, take MA 23 southwest to South Egremont. Turn right onto MA 41 south and then take the immediate right onto Mt Washington Rd (which becomes East St) and continue for 7.5 miles. Turn right onto Cross Rd, then right onto West St and continue 1 mile. Turn left onto Falls Rd and follow that for 1.5 miles.

There are two trailheads. The first is for a short, steep trail that descends 300ft over the course of a quarter-mile. For a more leisurely, level hike, continue another mile over the New York state line. This 0.75-mile trail takes about 20 minutes in each direction.

looks like something out of a Norman Rockwell painting. In fact, it was depicted in the painting *Stockbridge Main Street at Christmas.* Stockbridge people and places inspired many of Rockwell's illustrations, as the artist lived here for 25 years. The **Norman Rockwell Museum** (☎413-298-4100; www.nrm.org; 9 Glendale Rd/MA 183; adult/child $20/free; ☺10am-5pm May-Oct, to 4pm Nov-Apr) displays the world's largest collection of Rockwell's original art, including the beloved *Four Freedoms* and a complete collection of *Saturday Evening Post* covers.

Norman Rockwell is the main draw, but Stockbridge was also home to Daniel Chester French in an earlier era. Sculptor of *Abraham Lincoln* at the Lincoln Memorial and *The Minuteman* in Concord, French spent his summers at **Chesterwood** (www.chesterwood.org; 4 Williamsville Rd; adult/under 13yr $20/free; ☺10am-5pm late May–mid-Oct), a 122-acre estate. His house and studio are substantially as they were when he lived here, with nearly 500 pieces of sculpture, finished and unfinished, in the studio.

✖ p97

Eating & Sleeping

Lenox ❶

✕ Nudel — American $$

(☎413-551-7183; www.nudelrestaurant.com; 37 Church St; mains $18-26; ⏱5-9:15pm) Nudel is a driving force in the area's sustainable food movement, with just about everything on the menu seasonally inspired and locally sourced. The back-to-basics approach rings through in inventive dishes, which change daily but never disappoint. Incredible flavors. Nudel has a loyal following, so reservations are recommended. The last seating is at 9:15pm.

🛏 Stonover Farm B&B — B&B $$$

(☎413-637-9100; www.stonoverfarm.com; 169 Under Mountain Rd; ste $385-585; ✳@🛜) If you're looking for a break from musty Victorians with floral wallpaper, you'll love this contemporary inn wrapped in a century-old farmhouse. The three suites in the main house groan with casual luxury. Oversized hot tubs, marble bathrooms, wine and cheese in the evening – this is pampering befitting its Tanglewood neighborhood setting. There are also two private stand-alone cottages.

Lee ❷

✕ Joe's Diner — Diner $

(☎413-243-9756; 85 Center St; mains $3.50-15; ⏱6am-4pm Mon, to 8pm Tue-Fri, to 3:30pm Sat, to 1pm Sun) There's no better slice of blue-collar Americana in the Berkshires than Joe's Diner, at the north end of Main St. Norman Rockwell's famous painting of a policeman sitting at a counter talking to a young boy, *The Runaway* (1958), was inspired by this diner. Joe's has barely changed a wink – not the bar stools and not the old-fashioned diner fare.

Great Barrington ❹

✕ Prairie Whale — Modern American $$

(www.facebook.com/PrairieWhale; 178 Main St; mains $18-30; ⏱5-10pm Mon, Thu & Fri,

11am-3pm & 5-10pm Sat & Sun) Dimly lit and atmospheric, this bar and restaurant occupies a former family home, with outdoor seating on the porch and an inventive menu. The owners are committed to using local suppliers, including sheep and laying hens from their own farm. Hand-reared farm animals and organic produce don't come cheap, however; prices are on the high side.

✕ Berkshire Co-op Market Cafe — Cafe $

(www.berkshire.coop; 42 Bridge St; sandwiches $5.50-8; ⏱8am-8pm; 🍴) You don't need to spend a bundle to eat green, wholesome and local. This cafe inside the Berkshire Co-op Market, just off Main St, has a crunchy farm-fresh salad bar, generous made-to-order sandwiches (both meat and veggie), fresh juices and fair-trade coffees.

🛏 Wainwright Inn — B&B $$

(☎413-528-2062; www.wainwrightinn.com; 518 S Main St; r $140-230; ✳🛜) Great Barrington's finest place to lay your head, this inn (c 1766) exudes historical appeal from its wraparound porches and spacious parlors to the period room decor in the nine guest rooms. Breakfast is a decadent experience. The inn is a short walk from the center of town on a busy road.

Stockbridge ❺

✕ Once Upon a Table — American $$

(☎413-298-3870; www.onceuponatablebistro.com; 36 Main St; mains lunch $10-12, dinner $15-28; ⏱11:30am-3pm & 5-8:30pm Sun-Thu, to 9pm Fri & Sat) This bright spot in the Mews shopping arcade serves upscale fare in a sunny dining room. It's the best place in town for lunch, with choices like daily-changing omelets and sophisticated sandwiches. The dinner menu features reliably delicious treats such as pecan-crusted rainbow trout and fine dessert pastries.

Mohawk Trail

New England's oldest scenic highway offers invigorating art and architecture, stimulating action and adventure, and spectacular mountain scenery – everything you need for a weekend getaway.

8

TRIP HIGHLIGHTS

43 miles

MASS MoCA
An industrial relic turned into an incredible venue for installation art

FINISH
Williamstown

5 4

24 miles

Zoar Outdoor Canopy Tours
A thrilling ride through the treetops

3

Shelburne Falls

Deerfield
START

Western Summit
Jaw-dropping views and heart-pounding hikes along the Hoosac Ridge

38 miles

2–3 DAYS
46 MILES / 74KM

GREAT FOR...

BEST TIME TO GO

Enjoy clear views and open access to sites from June to October.

ESSENTIAL PHOTO

Snap a photo of the vast three-state vista from the Western Summit.

BEST FOR SCENERY

The 19 miles from stops three to five offer hair-raising turns and astonishing views.

Berkshires Sunset near Williamstown

8 Mohawk Trail

The road winds ever upward. Suddenly, around a bend, there's a clearing in the forest and the landscape sprawls out in a colorful tapestry, yielding views across the valley and into neighboring states. Welcome to the Western Summit of the Mohawk Trail, a 63-mile stretch of scenic byway, showing off raging rivers, idyllic farms and forest-covered mountains. Drivers, beware: it's practically impossible to keep your eyes on the road.

1 Deerfield

Start your tour in **Historic Deerfield Village** (www.historic-deerfield.org; 84 Old Main St; adult/child $18/5; ⊘9:30am-4:30pm Apr-Dec), an enchanting farming settlement that has escaped the ravages of time. Old Main St now presents a noble prospect: a dozen houses dating from the 1700s and 1800s, well preserved and open to the public. The homes have been restored and furnished according to actual historical records,

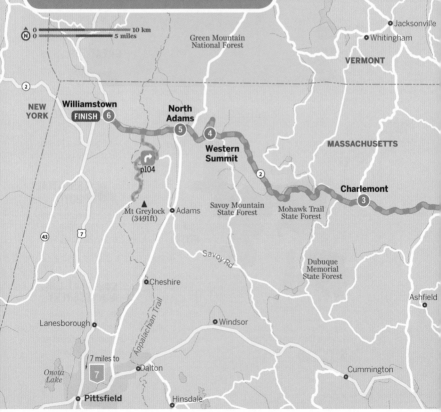

reflecting different periods in the village's history.

One block east of Old Main St, **Memorial Hall Museum** (www.americancenturies.mass.edu; 8 Memorial St; adult/child $6/3; ⏰11am-4:30pm Sat & Sun May, Tue-Sun Jun-Oct) contains lots of original artifacts from local homes, including the storied Indian House Door. This farming family's front door was hacked through during the infamous 1704 raid, when some 50 villagers were killed by French and Native American attackers.

🛏 p105

The Drive >> From Historic Deerfield Village, drive north on MA 10 (US 5) for 3 miles and turn left to head west on MA 2A. At the traffic circle, take the second exit onto the Mohawk Trail (MA 2). Turn left on Bridge St to continue into Shelburne Falls.

---

② Shelburne Falls

The main drag in this artisan community is only three blocks long — a tiny but charming stretch of turn-of-the-20th-century buildings, housing art galleries and coffee shops alongside a barber shop, a general store and an old-fashioned pharmacy. Forming the background are the forested mountains, the Deerfield River and a pair of picturesque bridges across it — one made of iron, the other covered in flowers.

Gardeners and volunteers have been maintaining the **Bridge of Flowers** (www.bridgeofflowersmass.org) since 1929. From April to October, more than 500 varieties of flowering plant, shrub and vine flaunt their colors on the 400ft-long span.

Two blocks south, the swirling of water around rocks in the Deerfield River has created an impressive collection of **glacial potholes** (Deerfield Ave) – near-perfect circular craters in the

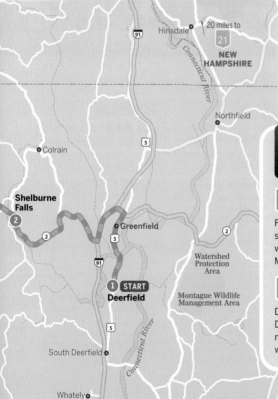

LINK YOUR TRIP

7 Berkshire Back Roads

From Williamstown, drive south on US 7 to hook up with this loop around the Massachusetts mountains.

21 Connecticut River Byway

Drive north or south from Deerfield to explore the mighty New England waterway.

river bed. There are more than 50 potholes on display, including the world's largest, which has a 39ft diameter.

✗ p105

The Drive » At the end of Bridge St, cross the metal bridge and turn right on State St, which runs parallel to the Deerfield River, and turn left on MA 2. The Mohawk Trail continues to follow the raging river, with Charlemont spread out along this road for several miles.

TRIP HIGHLIGHT

❸ Charlemont

Tucked between the Deerfield River and the Hoosac hills, tiny Charlemont is worth a stop if you're craving an adrenaline rush. This is the home of **Zoar Outdoor** (📞800-532-7483; www.zoaroutdoor.com; 7 Main St/MA 2, Charlemont; kayak $45-50, rafting $71-122, ziplining $79-94; ⏱9am-5pm daily Apr–mid-Oct, 10am-4pm Mon-Sat mid-Oct–Mar; ♿), offering canoeing, kayaking and white-water rafting on the river rapids for all skill levels, including trips for children as young as seven. Come in spring for high-water adventure or in autumn for fall-foliage brilliance.

If you prefer to keep your feet dry, the same operator runs zipling tours that let you unleash your inner Tarzan on a treetop glide above the river valley. All in all, the three-hour outing

includes three rappels, two sky bridges and 11 zips that get progressively longer. The hardest part is stepping off the first platform – the rest is pure exhilaration!

The Drive » Leaving Charlemont, you'll pass the Hail to the Sunrise statue, honoring the Five Indian Nations of the Mohawk Trail. The next stretch is the highlight of the route, as it cuts across the eponymous state forest. Continue climbing through the town of Florida, punctuated by three lookouts: the unmarked Eastern Summit, the Whitcomb Summit (the highest along the trail) and the Western Summit.

TRIP HIGHLIGHT

❹ Western Summit

Also known as Perry's Peak, the Western Summit (2100ft) shows off amazing views of the surrounding Hoosac Range. On a clear day, you can see into Vermont and even New York. The summit is topped with a ticky-tacky tourist shop, so you can buy some fudge.

You'll also find the trailhead for the **Hoosac Range** (Mohawk Trail /MA 2) just east of the gift shop. This scenic 6-mile round-

North Adams MASS MoCA

trip hike follows the ridgeline south to Spruce Hill summit, located in Savoy Mountain State Forest. Allow at least four hours for the hike; if you're pressed for time, the 1.5-mile loop to Sunset Rock is a shorter alternative.

The Drive » Back in the car, you'll find that the Mohawk Trail descends quickly, with an exhilarating spin around the Hairpin Turn to make your heart beat a little faster. Entering North Adams, the road follows the Hoosac River past vestiges of the industrial era.

TRIP HIGHLIGHT

⑤ North Adams

North Adams' beautiful and bleak 19th-century downtown seems out of sync with the rest of the Berkshires. And nestled into this industrial-era assemblage is a contemporary art museum of staggering proportions.

MASS MoCA (Massachusetts Museum of Contemporary Art; ☎413-662-2111; www.massmoca.org; 1040 Mass MoCA Way; adult/child $20/8; ⊘10am-6pm Sun-Wed, to 7pm Thu-Sat Jul & Aug, 11am-5pm Wed-Mon Sep-Jun)

sprawls over 13 acres of downtown North Adams. After the Sprague Electric Company packed up in 1985, more than $31 million was spent to modernize the property into the country's biggest art gallery, which now encompasses 222,000 sq ft and over 25 buildings, including art-construction areas, performance centers and 19 galleries. One gallery is the size of a football field, giving installation artists the opportunity to take things into a whole new dimension.

DETOUR:
MT GREYLOCK

Start 5 North Adams

Just west of downtown North Adams, look for the turn-off to Notch Rd, which will take you about 5 miles south to **Mt Greylock State Reservation** (☎413-499-4262; www.mass.gov/locations/mount-greylock-state-reservation; 30 Rockwell Rd, Lanesborough; ◷9am-4:30pm Jun-early Oct, shorter hours rest of year). In summer (mid-May to mid-October) you can drive up; otherwise, park your car at the entrance and hike 5 miles to the summit, where you will be rewarded with a 360-degree vista, taking in five states and hundreds of miles.

At 3491ft, Mt Greylock is the state's highest peak. In the 19th century, Greylock was a favorite destination for New England's nature-loving writers, including Nathaniel Hawthorne and Henry David Thoreau. Herman Melville even dedicated a novel to 'Greylock's Most Excellent Majesty.' Nowadays, it is ceremoniously topped with the 92ft-high War Memorial Tower, which you can climb (making the mountain effectively 3583ft). From May to October, you can also eat and sleep at the magnificently sited Bascom Lodge.

In addition to ever-changing, description-defying installations, there is a fascinating Sol LeWitt retrospective, on display until 2033. Little ones can always create and speculate in Kidspace, while the on-site theater space hosts music festivals, dance parties, poetry recitals and every kind of performance art imaginable.

✗ 🛏 p105

The Drive » Exiting North Adams, the Mohawk Trail crosses the Hoosac River several times before becoming Main St, Williamstown.

----

6 Williamstown

Tiny Williamstown is nestled in the heart of the Purple Valley, so named because the surrounding mountains often seem shrouded in a lavender veil at dusk. It is the quintessential college town, dominated by the marble-and-brick buildings of elite Williams College.

In addition to welcoming green spaces and academic architecture, Williamstown is home to a pair of exceptional art museums. The **Clark Art Institute** (☎413-458-2303; www.clarkart.edu; 225 South St; adult/child $20/free; ◷10am-5pm Tue-Sun Sep-Jun, daily Jul & Aug) is a gem, with wonderful paintings by French impressionists and their American contemporaries, all set amid 140 gorgeous acres of expansive lawns.

Down the road, the **Williams College Museum of Art** (☎413-597-2429; https://wcma.williams.edu; 15 Lawrence Hall Dr; ◷10am-5pm, to 8pm Thu, closed Wed Sep-May) has an impressive cache of its own. The American Collection includes substantial works by notables such as Edward Hopper, Winslow Homer and Grant Wood, to name only a few. The photography collection is also noteworthy, with images by Man Ray and Alfred Stieglitz.

✗ 🛏 p105

Eating & Sleeping

Deerfield ❶

🛏 Deerfield Inn   Inn $$$

(📞413-774-5587; www.deerfieldinn.com;
81 Old Main St; r $200-315; ❄🛜🐾) This
establishment, smack in the heart of the
historic district, has 11 rooms with various
floral decoration schemes and furnished
with antiques, housed in a grand Greek
Revival farmhouse, and a further 13 rooms
in outbuildings. Rates include a hot, hearty
breakfast and afternoon tea and cookies.
The attached restaurant, **Champney's**
(📞413-772-3087; www.champneysrestaurant.
com; mains $12-25; ⏰noon-9pm Sun-Thu, to
10pm Fri & Sat), sources many ingredients from
the surrounding farmland.

Shelburne Falls ❷

🍴 Gould's Sugar House   Breakfast $$

(www.facebook.com/GouldsSugarHouse; 570
Mohawk Trail; mains $8-12; ⏰8:30am-2pm
Mar-Apr & Sep-Nov) The standard order at this
family-run farm is fluffy pancake perfection,
drizzled with maple heaven. Other highlights
include the sugar pickles (yes, you read that
right), maple ice cream and corn fritters. While
you wait, you can watch the syrup being made.
Located right on the Mohawk Hwy, east of the
Shelburne Falls turnoff.

North Adams ❺

🍴 Public Eat & Drink   Pub Food $$

(📞413-664-4444; www.publiceatanddrink.com;
34 Holden St; mains $12-27; ⏰11:30am-10pm)
With exposed-brick walls and big windows
overlooking the street, this airy pub is the
most popular dinner spot in North Adams.
Come for an excellent selection of craft beers

and gourmet pub fare, like brie burgers, flatbread pizzas and bistro steak. Some decent
vegetarian options as well.

🛏 Porches Inn   Boutique Hotel $$$

(📞413-664-0400; www.porches.com; 231
River St; d $220-300, ste $310-420; ❄🛜🐾)
Across the street from MASS MoCA, the artsy
rooms here combine well-considered color
palettes, ample lighting and retro styling. The
accommodations are inside a row of 19th-
century houses with traditional front porches
complete with rocking chairs, perfect for
post-museum contemplation. A highlight is the
heated swimming pool and hot tub open year-
round. Rates include a cooked breakfast.

Williamstown ❻

🍴 Mezze Bistro & Bar   Fusion $$

(📞413-458-0123; www.mezzerestaurant.com;
777 Cold Spring Rd/US 7; mains $16-28; ⏰5-
9pm Sun-Thu, to 9:30pm Fri & Sat) You don't
know exactly what you're going to get at this
contemporary restaurant – the menu changes
frequently – but you know it's going to be good.
Situated on three spectacular acres, Mezze's
farm-to-table approach begins with an edible
garden right on-site. Much of the rest of the
seasonal menu, from small-batch microbrews to
organic meats, is locally sourced as well.

🛏 Maple Terrace Motel   Motel $$

(📞413-458-9677; www.mapleterrace.com; 555
Main St; d $120-200, ste $150-230; 🛜🐾) The
Maple Terrace is a simple yet cozy place on
the eastern edge of town, with family-friendly
suites equipped with kitchenettes, and spacious
gardens that make you want to linger. There's
nothing fancy going on here, but the place is
comfortable and service is warmly attentive. A
simple breakfast is included. Discounts offered
in winter and spring.

STRETCH YOUR LEGS
BOSTON

Start/Finish: Boston Common

Distance: 3 miles

Duration: Three hours

Boston is famed for its world-class museums and historical sites, but this picturesque city also offers a network of verdant parks, welcoming waterways and delightful shopping streets, making it a wonderful walking city.

Take this walk on Trips

Boston Common

Welcome to the country's oldest **public park** (btwn Tremont, Charles, Beacon & Park Sts; ⊘6am-midnight; **P** 🚻) with a convenient underground parking facility below – what foresight. A bronze plaque is emblazoned with the words of the treaty between Governor Winthrop and William Blaxton, who sold this land for £30 in 1634. The **Massachusetts State House** (☎617-727-7030; www.sec.state.ma.us; cnr Beacon & Bowdoin Sts; ⊘8:45am-5pm Mon-Fri, tours 10am-3:30pm Mon-Fri) commands a prominent position in the park's northeastern corner, while other monuments and attractions are scattered around the park.

The Walk » Follow the busy Bostonians crisscrossing the Common. Exit the park from the western side, cross Charles St and enter the tranquil Public Garden.

Public Garden

The **Public Garden** (☎617-723-8144; www.friendsofthepublicgarden.org; Arlington St; ⊘dawn-dusk; 🚻) is a 24-acre botanical oasis of Victorian flower beds, verdant grass and weeping willows, shading a tranquil lagoon. At any time of year, it is an island of loveliness, awash in seasonal blooms, gold-toned leaves or untrammeled snow. Taking a ride on the **Swan Boats** (☎617-522-1966; www.swanboats.com; adult/child $4/2.50; ⊘10am-4pm Apr-Jun, to 5pm Jul-Aug) in the lagoon has been a Boston tradition since 1877. And don't miss the famous statue **Make Way for Ducklings**, based on the beloved children's book by Robert McCloskey.

The Walk » Cross the bridge and exit the garden through the southwestern gate to Arlington St. Stroll west on swanky Newbury St, perfect for window-shopping and gallery hopping. Take a left on Clarendon St and continue to Boylston St.

Copley Square

Boston's most exquisite architecture is clustered around this stately Back Bay plaza. The centerpiece is the Romanesque-style **Trinity Church** (www.trinitychurchboston.org; 206 Clarendon St; adult/child $10/free; ⊘10am-4:30pm Tue-Sat, 12:15-4:30pm

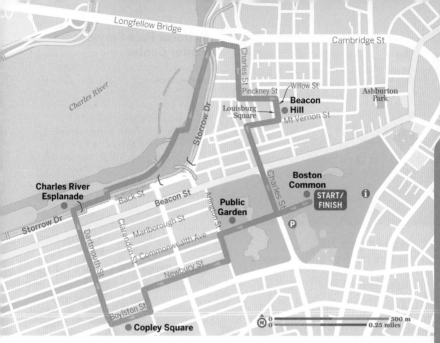

Sun Easter-Oct, shorter hours rest of year), famed for its stained-glass windows and pudding-stone facade. It's particularly lovely as reflected in the facade of the modern **John Hancock Tower** (200 Clarendon St). This assemblage faces off against the elegant neo-Renaissance **Boston Public Library** (☎617-536-5400; www.bpl. org; 700 Boylston St; ⏰9am-9pm Mon-Thu, to 5pm Fri & Sat year-round, plus 1-5pm Sun Oct-May), packed with sculpture, murals and other treasures (including books).

The Walk >> Head north on Dartmouth St, crossing the stately, dual-carriageway Commonwealth Ave, the grandest of Back Bay's grand avenues. Continue three more blocks to Back St, from where a pedestrian walkway crosses Storrow Dr to the esplanade.

Charles River Esplanade

The southern bank of the Charles River Basin is an enticing urban **escape** (www. esplanadeassociation.org;), with grassy knolls and cooling waterways. It's a perfect destination for a waterside stroll, picnic or bicycle ride. The park is dotted with public art, including an oversized bust of Arthur Fiedler,

the longtime conductor of the Boston Pops. The Hatch Memorial Shell (www. hatchshell.com) hosts free outdoor concerts and movies, including the famed July 4 concert by the Boston Pops.

The Walk >> Walk northeast along the esplanade, enjoying the breezes and views of the Charles River. It's about a half-mile to the Longfellow Bridge, where you can climb the ramp and find yourself at the top of Charles St.

Beacon Hill

With an intriguing history and iconic architecture, Beacon Hill is Boston's most prestigious address. **Charles St** is an enchanting spot for browsing boutiques and haggling over antiques. To explore further, wander down the residential streets lit with gas lanterns, admire the brick town houses decked with purple windowpanes and blooming flower boxes, and discover streets such as stately **Louisburg Square** that capture the neighborhood's grandeur.

The Walk >> Take your time strolling south along charming Charles St. For a glimpse of Louisburg Sq, walk two blocks east on Pinckney St. Then continue south to Boston Common.

STRETCH YOUR LEGS
SALEM

Start/Finish: National Park Service (NPS) Visitor Center

Distance: 2.5 miles

Duration: Two hours

A lot of history is packed into this gritty city of witches and sailors – even more than you read in the textbooks. This walk highlights the architectural gems and little-known stories that are often overlooked.

Take this walk on Trips

National Park Service Visitor Center

Start your explorations at the **NPS Visitor Center** (☎978-740-1650; www.nps.gov/sama; 2 New Liberty St; ⏰9am-5pm May-Oct, from 10am Wed-Sun Nov-Apr), which offers information on Salem. For a good overview, catch a free screening of *Where Past Is Present,* a short film about Salem history. You can also pick up a map and description of several self-guided walking tours and other area attractions.

The Walk >> From the visitor center, walk south on New Liberty St for half a block. The excellent Peabody Essex Museum sits at the corner of Essex St. Turn right and continue down Essex St.

Essex Street

The main drag in Salem is Essex St, a pedestrian mall that is lined with shops and cafes, a few historic buildings and several witch-themed attractions. The most prominent building is the **old Town Hall**, the redbrick beauty that was the seat of government in the 19th century. At the corner of Washington St stands a statue of Samantha Stephens, the spell-casting, nose-twitching beauty from the classic TV show *Bewitched*.

The Walk >> Cross Washington St and continue west on Essex St. At Summer St, turn left and walk one block south to Chestnut St.

Chestnut Street

Lovers of old houses will revel in the grand antique homes on Chestnut St, which is among the most architecturally lovely streets in the country. One of these stately homes is the **Phillips House** (www.phillipsmuseum.org; 34 Chestnut St; adult/child $8/4; ⏰11am-4pm Tue-Sun Jun-Oct), which displays the family furnishings of Salem sea captains, including a collection of antique carriages and cars.

The Walk >> Retrace your steps on Chestnut St. Cross Summer St and continue walking on

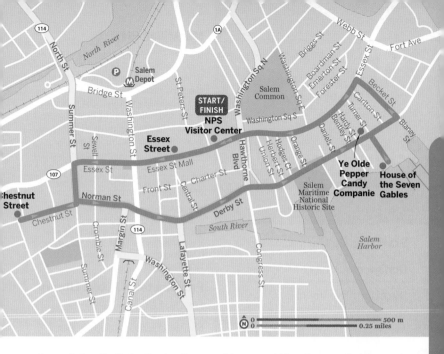

Norman St. Cross Washington St and continue walking on Derby St, passing through the heart of the Salem Maritime National Historic Site.

Ye Olde Pepper Companie

In 1806, Englishwoman Mrs Spencer survived a shipwreck en route to the New World. She arrived in Salem with nary a penny to her name, but, with a small loan, she bought a barrel of sugar and created 'Salem Gibraltar,' a candy that sated the sweet teeth of sea captains and merchants. Two centuries later, **Ye Olde Pepper Candy Companie** (☎978-745-2744; www.olde peppercandy.com; 122 Derby St; ☉10am-6pm Jul-Oct, to 5pm Nov-Jun) still uses her recipes for old-fashioned delights such as Black Jacks (flavored with blackstrap molasses) and Gibraltars (lemon and peppermint treats).

The Walk » From Derby St, turn right on Turner St and stroll to the end of this lovely residential lane.

House of the Seven Gables

'Halfway down a by-street of one of our New England towns stands a rusty wooden house, with seven acutely peaked gables facing towards various points of the compass, and a huge clustered chimney in their midst.' So wrote Nathaniel Hawthorne in his 1851 novel about the **House of the Seven Gables** (www.7gables.org; 54 Turner St; adult/child $16/11; ☉10am-7pm Jul-Oct, to 5pm Nov-Jun). The admission fee allows entrance to the site's four historic buildings, as well as the luxuriant gardens on the waterfront.

The Walk » Continue east on Derby St. Peek inside the whimsical world of metal sculpture on the corner of Blaney St before walking up Becket St. Turn left on Essex St and walk a half-mile back to the NPS Visitor Center.

STRETCH YOUR LEGS
PROVINCETOWN

Start/Finish: MacMillan Pier

Distance: 1.3 miles

Duration: Two hours

Ever since Charles Hawthorne opened the Cape Cod School of Art back in 1899, this little town at the tip of the Cape has attracted artists, writers and other creative types exploring 'alternative' lifestyles.

Take this walk on Trips

MacMillan Pier

Start your walking tour at the central pier, where fishing boats dock alongside passenger ferries and whale-watching cruisers. Before heading out take a few minutes to watch the sun over the water and reflect on the beauty of Provincetown's geography. At times it may seem like a supporting player to the fun culture the town is famous for, but without the influx of artists, drawn by the natural splendor of the area, none of the rest of it would exist.

The Walk » From MacMillan Pier, stroll east on Commercial St, dodging cyclists and tourists chasing after their kids. Keep your eyes peeled around 290 Commercial St, where you may see a renegade alley art exhibit. Then cross the street to the library.

Provincetown Public Library

Erected in 1860 as a church, this handsome belfry-topped building later became a museum, complete with a half-size replica of Provincetown's famed race-winning schooner *Rose Dorothea*. When the museum went bust, the town converted the multifunctional building to the **Provincetown Public Library** (508-487-7094; www.provincetown library.org; 356 Commercial St; 10am-5pm Mon & Fri, to 8pm Tue-Thu, 1-5pm Sat & Sun;). One catch: the boat was too big to remove, so it still occupies the upper deck, with bookshelves built around it.

The Walk » Go east on Commercial St. Grab a coffee or a snack at one of the storefronts and, when you're ready, walk up Pearl St. Cross Bradford St and continue to your next destination.

Fine Arts Work Center

Stop into the **Hudson D Walker Gallery** at the **Fine Arts Work Center** (508-487-9960; www.fawc.org; 24 Pearl St; 9am-5pm Mon-Fri), which is dedicated to fostering the type of artistic interest that first put Provincetown on the map. You can see works by past and present fellows of the center in the gallery, and when you're done with the art, check the schedule for the **Stanley Kunitz**

Common Room to see if there are any talks or presentations scheduled before continuing on.

The Walk » Return to Bradford St and turn left. Stroll for a few blocks along this backbone of Provincetown, which sees much less action than Commercial St. Bang a right on Bangs St and return to the main drag.

Provincetown Art Association & Museum

There's always something worth seeing at the **Provincetown Art Association & Museum** (PAAM; ☎508-487-1750; www. paam.org; 460 Commercial St; adult/child $10/ free; ⏰11am-5pm Sat-Thu, to 10pm Fri Jun & Sep, to 8pm Mon-Thu, to 10pm Fri, to 5pm Sat & Sun Jul & Aug, noon-5pm Thu-Sun Oct-May), which specializes in work by contemporary and classic artists who made the lower Cape their home or found the inspiration for their marvelous works here. The building itself is worth noting with its modern glass and traditional warm wood, a perfect mix of new and old Cape Cod design theory.

The Walk » Walk west on Commercial St, passing through the eclectic East End.

East End

As you walk back along Commercial St toward MacMillan Pier, you are traversing the **Provincetown East End Gallery District**. Between Bangs and Standish Sts, P-town's main drag is lined with galleries showcasing local and national (and some international) artists. Browse at your leisure, but don't miss the **Albert Merola Gallery** (☎508-487-4424; www.albertmerolagallery.com; 424 Commercial St; ⏰11am-5pm May-Sep, shorter hours rest of year), which showcases works by Provincetown artists both contemporary and from its storied artistic past. Pick up the free *Provincetown Art Guide* for a map and a complete list of galleries.

The Walk » Continue walking west on Commercial St to return to MacMillan Pier. Treat yourself to an ice cream and reflect on the great art you've experienced.

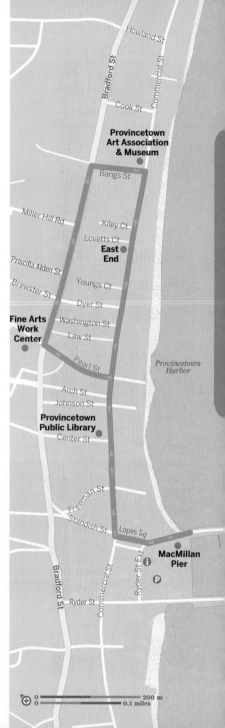

Connecticut & Rhode Island

NEW YORK'S NEIGHBOR-STATE FALLS LARGELY OFF THE TOURIST RADAR. But it shouldn't. Off the I-95, Connecticut's country roads unfurl onto a landscape punctuated by scenic lakes, woodlands and state parks, pretty, pre-Colonial villages and a patchwork of farms that form the backbone of the state's thriving farm-to-table movement.

Down the road, Rhode Island might be America's smallest state but it has clout, boasting some of the best beaches in the northeast and two impressive cities: Providence and Newport. Each is brimming with museums, architectural delights and activities galore. Old money made Rhode Island a summer playground – a tradition the nation's *nouveau-riche* seem happy to uphold. Why not join in?

Hartford Mark Twain House
SEANPAVONEPHOTO/GETTY IMAGES ©

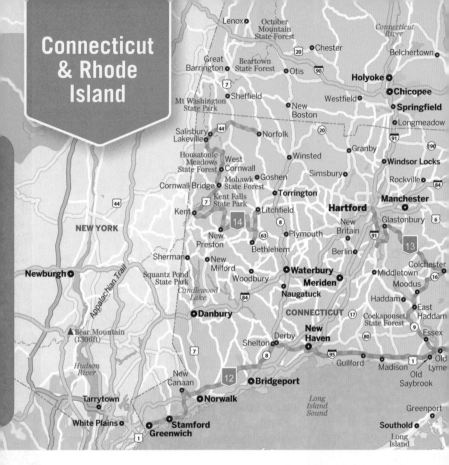

Connecticut & Rhode Island

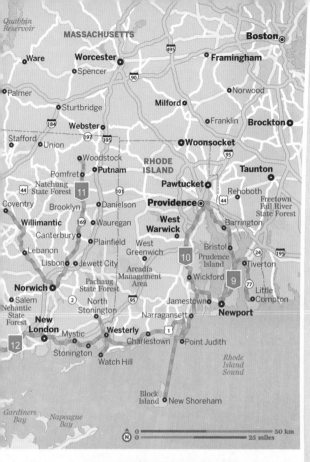

☑ DON'T MISS

Polo in Rhode Island

Enjoy polo in Portsmouth at the Glen Farm Country Estate on Trip 9

Jonathan Edwards Winery

Those in the know pick up lunch en route to this 48-acre estate overlooking the Atlantic, perfect for picnics on Trip 12

Philip Johnson Glass House

Tour Connecticut's newest National Trust Historic Site and one of the world's most famous modern houses on Trip 12

Bantam Cinema

Watch indie and foreign films in a converted red barn on the shores of Lake Bantam on Trip 14

Rhode Island Newport Polo Club

Rhode Island: East Bay

The East Bay is Rhode Island's historical heart. Tour the shoreline and follow the trail from America's humble Colonial roots in Little Compton to the industrial boomtowns of Newport and Providence.

TRIP HIGHLIGHTS

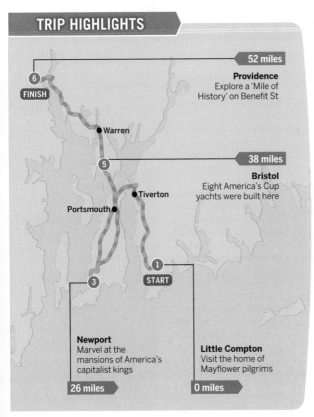

52 miles
Providence
Explore a 'Mile of History' on Benefit St

Warren

38 miles
Bristol
Eight America's Cup yachts were built here

Tiverton

Portsmouth

START

Newport
Marvel at the mansions of America's capitalist kings
26 miles

Little Compton
Visit the home of Mayflower pilgrims
0 miles

3–4 DAYS
52 MILES / 84KM

GREAT FOR...

BEST TIME TO GO

May to October for good weather and farm food.

 ESSENTIAL PHOTO

Capture the mansions and sheer cliffs along the Cliff Walk.

 BEST FOR HISTORY

Find modern America's beginnings in Little Compton.

Newport Cliff Walk

9 Rhode Island: East Bay

Rhode Island's jagged East Bay tells the American story in microcosm. Start in Little Compton with the grave of Elizabeth Pabodie (1623–1717), the first European settler born in New England. Then meander through historic Tiverton and Bristol, where slave dealers and merchants grew rich. Prosperous as they were, their modest homes barely hold a candle to the mansions, museums and libraries of Newport's capitalist kings and Providence's intelligentsia.

TRIP HIGHLIGHT

❶ Little Compton

No doubt tiring of the big-city bustle of 17th-century Portsmouth, early settler Samuel Wilbor crossed the Sakonnet River to Little Compton. His plain family home, **Wilbor House** (☎401-635-4035; www.littlecompton.org; 548 W Main Rd; adult/child $6/3; ☉1-5pm Thu-Sun Apr-Oct, 9am-3pm Tue-Fri Nov-Mar), built in 1690, still stands on a manicured lawn behind a traditional five-bar gate and tells the story of eight generations of Wilbors who lived here.

The rest of Little Compton, from the hand-hewn clapboard houses to the white-steepled **United Congregational Church**, overlooking the **Old Commons Burial Ground**, is one of the oldest and most quaint villages in all of New England. Elizabeth Pabodie, daughter of Mayflower pilgrims Priscilla and John Alden and the first settler born in New England, is buried here.

Lovely, ocean-facing **Goosewing Beach** (S Shore Rd; ☉dawn-dusk) is the only good public beach. Parking costs $10 at **South Shore Beach**, from where you can walk across a small tidal inlet.

🛏 p123

The Drive » Head north along RI 77 at a leisurely pace, enjoying the peaceful country

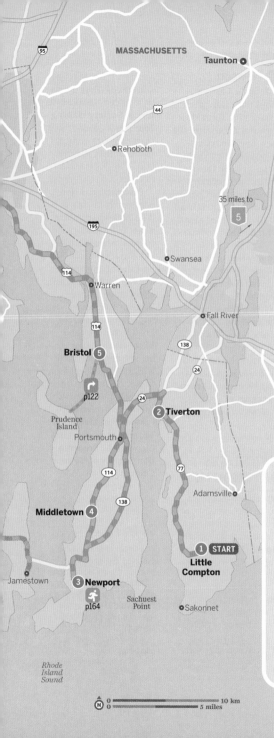

scenery of rambling stone walls and clapboard farmhouses. As you approach Tiverton, look out to your left and you'll occasionally get glimpses out to the water, which is particularly pretty in the late afternoon.

2 Tiverton

En route to Tiverton's historic Four Corners, stop in at **Carolyn's Sakonnet Vineyard** (📞401-635-8486; www.sakon netwine.com; 162 West Main Rd; 🕙11am-6pm Sun-Thu, to 8pm Fri & Sat late May–mid-Oct, 11am-5pm daily rest of year; 🅿) for free daily wine tastings and guided tours. This will set you up nicely for the gourmet treats that await in Tiverton: **Gray's Ice Cream** (📞401-624-4500; www.graysicecream.com; 16 East Rd; scoops from $3; 🕙6:30am-9pm), where over 40 flavors are made on-site daily; the gourmet deli bar at **Provender Fine**

🔗 LINK YOUR TRIP

5 **Pilgrim Trail**
Continue the historical journey in Plymouth with the Massachusetts Pilgrim Trail.

10 **Rhode Island: Coastal Culture**
Explore Rhode Island's coastal culture, heading southwest along I-95 from Providence.

Foods (☎401-624-8084; www.provenderfinefoods.com; 3883 Main Rd; items $4-18; ⊙9am-5pm Tue-Sun), where you can munch on giant cookies or forage for picnic fare; and waterfront dining at the fabulous **Boat House** (☎401-624-6300; www.boathousetiverton. com; 227 Schooner Dr; mains $18-44; ⊙11:30am-9pm; P).

Tiverton has a clutch of local artists as well as chic boutiques hawking classy, original wares including the likes of handwoven Shaker-style rugs from **Amy C Lund** (☎401-816-0000; www. aclhandweaver.com; 3964 Main Rd; ⊙10am-5pm Wed-Sat, from noon Sun).

The Drive ≫ Head north up Main St, leaving Tiverton and its green fields behind you, and merge onto the westbound RI 138/RI 24 S, which leads you directly into Newport.

TRIP HIGHLIGHT

③ Newport

Established by religious moderates fleeing persecution from Massachusetts Puritans, the 'new port' flourished to become the fourth-richest city in the newly independent colony. Downtown, the Colonial-era architecture is beautifully preserved along with notable landmarks, such as Washington Sq's **Colony House**, where Rhode Island's declaration of independence was read in May 1776.

Just off the square, the gaslights of the White Horse Tavern (p123), America's oldest tavern, still burn, and on Touro St, America's first synagogue, **Touro Synagogue** (☎401-847-4794; www.tourosynagogue.

org; 85 Touro St; adult/student/child $12/8/free; ⊙9:30am-4:30pm Sun-Fri Jul & Aug, shorter hours rest of year), still stands. Tour the past on a guided **Newport Historical Society Walking Tour** (☎401-841-8770; www. newporthistorytours.org; 127 Thames St; tours adult/child from $15/5; ⊙departures vary; ♿).

Fascinating as Newport's early history is, it struggles to compete with the town's latter-day success, when wealthy industrialists made Newport their playground and built summer houses along lantern-lined Bellevue Ave. Modeled on Italianate palazzos, French châteaux and Elizabethan manor houses, and decorated with valuable furnishings and artworks, the stately homes are now collectively referred to as the **Newport Mansions**. Tour the most outstanding with the **Preservation Society of Newport County** (☎401-847-1000; www.newportmansions.org; 424 Bellevue Ave; 5-site tickets adult/child $35/12).

✕ ⍢ p39, p123

The Drive ≫ Leave Newport by way of 10-mile Ocean Dr, which starts just south of Fort Adams and curls around the southern shore, past the grand mansions, and up Bellevue Ave before intersecting with Memorial Blvd. Turn right here for a straight shot into Middletown.

LOCAL KNOWLEDGE: POLO IN PORTSMOUTH

Drab though the urban environs of Portsmouth may seem, in-the-know locals rate Portsmouth as a family-friendly destination – not least because the polo matches hosted at Glen Farm make for a great family day out. Home to the **Newport Polo Club** (☎401-846-0200; www.nptpolo.com; 250 Linden Lane; lawn/pavilion seats $15/25; ⊙gates open 1pm), the 700-acre 'farm' was assembled by New York businessman Henry Taylor, who sought to create a gentleman's country seat in the grand English tradition. In summer, the farm is host to the club's polo matches (check the website for dates), which are a perfect way to enjoy the property and get an authentic taste of Newport high life.

Newport Touro Synagogue

4 Middletown

Flo's (📞401-847-8141; www.flosclamshacks.com; 4 Wave Ave; mains $11-22; ⏱11am-9pm Wed-Sun) jaunty red-and-white clam shack and her competition, **Anthony's Seafood** (📞401-846-9620; www.anthonysseafood.net; 963 Aquidneck Ave; mains $12-32; ⏱11am-8pm Mon-Sat, from noon Sun), would be enough reason to visit Middletown, which now merges seamlessly with Newport. But the best fried clams in town taste better after a day on **Second Beach** (Sachuest Beach; 📞401-846-6273; http://parks.middletownri.com/sachuest-aka-second-beach-and-third-beach/; Sachuest Point Rd; beach parking Mon-Fri/Sat & Sun $15/25), the largest and most beautiful beach on Aquidneck Island. Curving around Sachuest

Bay, it is backed by the 450-acre **Norman Bird Sanctuary** (📞401-846-2577; www.normanbirdsanctuary.org; 583 Third Beach Rd; adult/child $7/3; ⏱9am-5pm), which teems with migrating birds. All this driving might inspire you to check out the stunning collection of antique, luxury, hot-rod and muscle cars at the shiny new **Newport Car Museum** (📞401-848-2277; www.newportcarmuseum.org; 1847 W Main Rd; adult/child $18/8; ⏱10am-4pm; P), located just north of Middletown, in Portsmouth.

The Drive ⟩⟩ Leave Aquidneck Island via East Main Rd, which takes you north through the suburbs of Middletown and Portsmouth. After 6.5 miles, pick up the RI 114 and cross the bay via the scenic Mt Hope suspension bridge. From here it's a short 3-mile drive into Bristol.

TRIP HIGHLIGHT

5 Bristol

One-fifth of all slaves transported to America were brought in Bristol ships and by the 18th century the town was one of the country's major commercial ports. The world-class **Herreshoff Marine Museum** (📞401-253-5000; www.herreshoff.org; 1 Burnside St; adult/child $15/10; ⏱10am-5pm May-Oct; P) showcases some of America's finest yachts, including eight that were built for the America's Cup.

Local resident Augustus Van Wickle bought a 72ft Herreshoff yacht for his wife Bessie in 1895, but having nowhere suitable to moor it, he then had to build **Blithewold Mansion** (📞401-253-2707; www.blithewold.org; 101 Ferry Rd; adult/child $15/6;

121

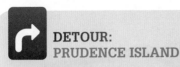

DETOUR: PRUDENCE ISLAND

Start: ❺ Bristol

Idyllic **Prudence Island** (☎401-683-0430; www. prudencebayislandstransport.com; ⏱ferries 5:45am-6pm Mon-Fri, 7:30am-6pm Sat & Sun) sits in the middle of Narragansett Bay, an easy 25-minute ferry ride from Bristol. Originally used for farming and later as a summer vacation spot for families from Providence and New York, who traveled here on the Fall River Line Steamer, the island now has only 88 inhabitants. There are some fine Victorian and beaux-arts houses near Stone Wharf, a lighthouse and a small store, but otherwise it's wild and unspoiled. Perfect for mountain biking (BYO bike), barbecues, fishing and paddling.

⏱mansion 10am-4pm Tue-Sat, to 3pm Sun Apr–mid-Oct; gardens 10am-5pm year-round; Ⓟ). The arts-and-crafts mansion sits in a peerless position on Narragansett Bay and is particularly lovely in spring, when daffodils line the shore. Other local magnates included slave trader General George DeWolf, who built **Linden Place** (☎401-253-0390; www. lindenplace.org; 500 Hope St; adult/child $10/5; ⏱10am-4pm Tue-Sat, noon-4pm Sun May-Oct & Dec, by appointment Nov & Jan-Apr; Ⓟ), famous as a film location for *The Great Gatsby*.

Bristol's **Colt State Park** (☎401-253-7482; www.riparks.com/Locations/LocationColt.html; Rte 114; ⏱dawn-dusk; Ⓟ) is Rhode Island's most scenic park, with its entire western border fronting Narragansett Bay, fringed by 4 miles of cycling trails and shaded picnic tables.

🍴 p123

The Drive » From Bristol it's a straight drive north along RI 114, through the suburbs of Warren and Barrington, to Providence. After 17 miles, merge onto I-195 W, which takes you the remaining 18 miles into the center of town.

- - - - - - - - - - - - - - - - -

TRIP HIGHLIGHT

❻ Providence

Providence, the first town of religious liberal Roger Williams' new Rhode Island and Providence Plantation colony, was established so that 'no man should be molested for his conscience sake.' A self-guided stroll along **Benefit Street** or, better still, a **Rhode Island Historical Society** (RIHS; ☎401-273-7507; www.rihs. org/walking-tours/; 52 Power St; tours adult/child $15/10; ⏱Apr-Nov) walking tour, reveals the city's rich architectural legacy. Here alone are scores of Colonial, Federal and Revival houses. Amid them you'll find William Strickland's 1838 **Providence Athenaeum** (☎401-421-6970; www.providenceathenaeum. org; 251 Benefit St; ⏱10am-7pm Mon-Thu, to 6pm Fri-Sat, 1-5pm Sun), inside which plaster busts of Greek gods and philosophers preside over a collection that dates from 1753.

Atop the hill sits **Brown University** (☎401-863-1000; www.brown.edu; 1 Prospect St), with its Gothic and beaux-arts buildings arranged around the College Green. Nearby is the **John Brown House Museum** (☎401-331-8575 ext 362; www.rihs.org/museums/john-brown-house/; 52 Power St; adult/child $10/6; ⏱tours 1:30pm & 3pm Tue-Fri, 10:30am, noon, 1:30pm & 3pm Sat Apr-Nov; Ⓟ), which should be considered a must-see for American history and architecture buffs.

End the tour with a nod toward the bronze statue of *Independent Man,* which graces the pearly white dome of the impressive **Rhode Island State House** (☎401-222-3983; www.sos.ri.gov; 82 Smith St; ⏱ self-guided tours 8:30am-4:30pm Mon-Fri, guided tours 9am, 10am, 11am, 1pm & 2pm Mon-Fri; Ⓟ).

🍴 🛏 p59, p123, p131

Eating & Sleeping

Little Compton ❶

🛏 Stone House Inn   Historic Hotel $$$

(📞401-635-2222; www.newportexperience.
com/stonehouse; 122 Sakonnet Point Rd; d from
$279; [P] 😊 ❄ 🛜) When this unashamedly
upscale inn opened its doors in 2016, Little
Compton's notoriously private elite feared it
meant the out-of-towners were coming. With
only 13 rooms (lavish as they may be), it's hardly
cause for an invasion. If you have cash and the
inclination, this is your chance to take a peek at
how the other half live.

Newport ❸

🍴 Fluke Wine Bar   Seafood $$$

(📞401-849-7778; www.flukenewport.com;
41 Bowens Wharf; mains $24-36; ⏱5-11pm
May-Oct, 5pm-10pm Wed-Sat Nov-Apr) Fluke's
Scandinavian-inspired dining room, with
blond wood and picture windows, offers an
accomplished seafood menu featuring roasted
monkfish, seasonal striped sea bass and
plump scallops. Upstairs, the Harbor View
Bar overlooking the docks and the bay, serves
rock-and-roll cocktails and beer, and pours
from an extensive wine list. Reservations are
recommended.

🍴 White Horse Tavern   American $$$

(📞401-849-3600; www.whitehorsenewport.
com; 26 Marlborough St; mains lunch $12-29,
dinner $24-42; ⏱11am-9pm Sun-Thu, to 10pm
Fri & Sat) If you'd like to eat at a 17th-century
tavern that once served as an annual meeting
place for the Colonial Rhode Island General
Assembly, try this historic, gambrel-roofed
beauty. Dinner menus might include baked
escargot, truffle-crusted Atlantic halibut or beef
Wellington. Service can be hit or miss despite
the dress code: business-casual for dinner, no
sportswear or swimwear for lunch.

🛏 Attwater   Boutique Hotel $$$

(📞401-846-7444; www.theattwater.com; 22
Liberty St; r $139-659; [P] ❄ 🛜) Newport's
newest hotel has the bold attire of a midsummer
beach party with turquoise, lime green and
coral prints, ikat headboards and snazzily
patterned geometric rugs. Picture windows and
porches capture the summer light, and rooms
come furnished with thoughtful luxuries such as
iPads, Apple TVs and beach bags.

Bristol ❺

🍴 Beehive   Cafe $

(📞401-396-9994; www.thebeehivecafe.com; 10
Franklin St; mains $7-14; ⏱7am-4pm Sun-Wed,
to 9pm Thu-Sat) There's a real buzz in Bristol
about this beehive whose busy bees buy local
wherever possible, bake their own breads
and make everything (but the ketchup) from
scratch. Best for breakfast and light lunches,
this crafty kitchen serves a limited dinner menu
from Thursday to Sunday and brews organic
coffee around the clock. Sensible pricing adds
to its appeal.

Providence ❻

🍴 Haven Brothers Diner   Diner $

(📞401-603-8124; www.havenbrothersmobile.
com; cnr Dorrance & Fulton Sts; meals $5-12;
⏱5pm-3am) Parked next to City Hall, this
Providence institution is basically a diner on
the back of a truck that has rolled into the same
spot every evening for decades. Climb up a
rickety ladder to get basic diner fare alongside
everyone from drunks to prominent politicians
and college kids pulling an all-nighter. The
murder burger comes highly recommended.

🛏 Providence Biltmore   Historic Hotel $$

(📞401-421-0700; www.providencebiltmore.
com; 11 Dorrance St; d from $189; [P] 🛜) The
granddaddy of Providence's hotels, the Biltmore
dates from the 1920s, although its 292 oversized
guestrooms and suites have been thoroughly
refurbished to a high standard, and stretch many
stories above the old city: ask for a room on a
high floor. The lobby, both intimate and regal,
nicely combines dark wood, twisting staircases
and chandeliers, harking back to a lost age.

Rhode Island: Coastal Culture

After traveling this route along the state's jagged coastline and visiting the islands floating in Narragansett Bay, you will understand why Rhode Island earned the honorable title of Ocean State.

10

TRIP HIGHLIGHTS

START ① 0 miles

Providence
Explore Rhode Island
School of Design

Wickford

③ 30 miles

Narragansett

Jamestown
Sundowners and the
best sunsets in
Rhode Island

Charlestown

Westerly

Galilee

⑦

FINISH

⑤

Watch Hill
Millionaire homes and
a yacht-studded bay

111 miles

Block Island
Best for bird-watching
and beach hopping

60 miles

4 DAYS
111 MILES / 179KM

GREAT FOR...

BEST TIME TO GO
June to September for
sun, sand and surfing.

 ESSENTIAL PHOTO
The Southeast Light
atop red clay cliffs.

 BEST FOR OUTDOORS
Block Island's 25 miles
of trails weave through
wildflowers and past
nesting birds.

Block Island Southeast Light

Rhode Island: Coastal Culture

10

Rhode Island might only take an hour to drive across but it packs 400 miles of coastline into its tiny boundaries. Much of this takes the form of white-sand beaches, arguably the finest places for ocean swimming in the northeast. There are also islands to explore, sea cliffs to stroll along and isolated lighthouses where you can frame perfect sunset shots.

TRIP HIGHLIGHT

❶ Providence

Rhode Island's capital presents visitors with some fine urban strolling, from Brown University's campus on 18th-century College Hill to the city's **Riverwalk** and the historic downtown along Weybosset St. Along the way, visit the **Rhode Island School of Design** (RISD; ☏401-454-6300; www.risd.edu; 20 N Main St; **P**), the top art school in the USA and home to the **RISD Museum of Art** (☏401-

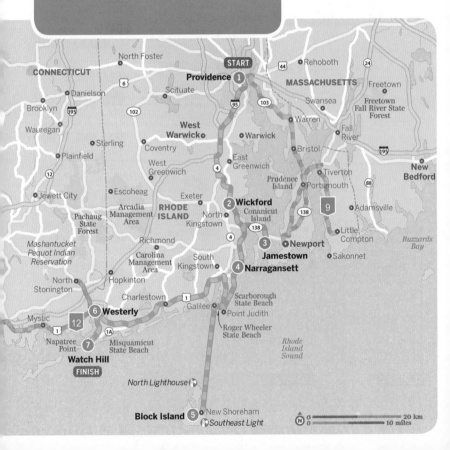

454-6500; www.risdmuseum. org; 20 N Main St; adult/under 18yr $15/free; ☺10am-5pm Tue-Sun, to 9pm 3rd Thu of month; ⓟ ♿), with its collection of Roman and Etruscan artifacts, medieval and Renaissance works, and 19th-century French paintings. RISD maintains several other fine galleries: **Sol Koffler** (📞401-277-4809; https://info. risd.edu/sol-koffler-gallery/; 169 Weybosset St; ☺noon-6pm) serves as the main exhibition space for graduate students, while **risd|works** (📞401-277-4949; www.risdworks.com; 10 Westminster St; ☺10am-5pm Tue-Sun; ♿) offers some of their work for sale.

If you're in town on the third Thursday of the month, you can catch **Gallery Night** (www.gal lerynight.org), when 23

LINK YOUR TRIP

9 **Rhode Island: East Bay**

Head east down RI 114 for a trip back in time to the earliest days of the colony.

12 **Connecticut Wine Trail**

From Westerly, drive west to Stonington on US 1 for a gourmet tour of Connecticut's vineyards and farms.

galleries and museums open their doors for free viewings.

🍴 🛏 p59, p123, p131

The Drive ⟩⟩ Leave Providence via Memorial Blvd and pick up the I-95 S. Meander through the suburbs for 1.5 miles and veer left onto RI 4 S toward North Kingstown. Exit at 7A–7B onto RI 403 east toward Quonset and after a couple of miles turn onto US 1 for Wickford.

----

② Wickford

Bypassed by the era of steamboats and train travel, Wickford's Main St and Pleasant St languished sleepily through the Industrial Revolution and are still lined with 18th-century Colonial and Federal homes, which lead down to the harbor where fishermen cast their lines off the pier. Rent kayaks from the **Kayak Centre** (www. kayakcentre.com; 9 Phillips St, Waterside Wickford; rental per 2hr from $28; ☺10am-5pm Wed-Mon) for a paddle around the bay.

Then visit the **Old Narragansett Church** (📞401-294-4357; www. stpaulswickford.org; 60 Church Lane; ☺11am-4pm Thu-Sun Jul-Aug or by appointment). It dates from 1707 and retains its box pews and upstairs gallery where plantation slaves were allowed to worship. The local artist Gilbert Scott (1755–1828), who painted the portrait of George Washington that

graces the one-dollar bill, was baptized here in the silver baptismal font.

The Drive ⟩⟩ It is a short 4-mile drive along RI 1A S from Wickford to Conanicut Island. Once you're through the Wickford suburbs, take the RI 138 ramp over the Jamestown Bridge, which affords expansive views of the bay. Once on the island, turn right down North Rd to Jamestown past the old smock windmill.

TRIP HIGHLIGHT

③ Jamestown

More rural than its prosperous neighbor, Newport, Jamestown's first inhabitants were Quaker farmers, shepherds and pirates. Captain Kidd spent considerable time here and is said to have buried his treasure hereabouts.

These days, the real treasure in Jamestown is the peace and quiet. The waterfront is undeveloped and you can walk along **Conanicus Avenue** and perch on a bench overlooking the harbor or enjoy eclectic Modern American fare on the gorgeous patio at Simpatico (p131). The **Jamestown Newport Ferry** (📞401-423-9900; www.jamestownnew portferry.com; 1 E Ferry Wharf; return adult/child $26/10; ☺May-Oct) sails to Newport with stops at Fort Adams and Rose Island. It is the best deal going for a harbor tour.

At the southernmost tip of Conanicut Island is **Beavertail State Park** (401-423-9941; www.riparks.com/Locations/LocationBeavertail.html; Beavertail Rd; ☼dawn-dusk; P), where you can enjoy one of the best vistas – and sunsets – in the Ocean State. Many vacationers bring lawn chairs, barbecues and picnics, and spend all day enjoying the walking trails and cliff-top views. At the point, picturesque 1749 **Beavertail Light** (☎401-423-3270; www.beavertaillight.org; Beavertail Rd; donations welcome; ☼10am-4:30pm Jun-Sep; P), one of the oldest along the Atlantic coast, still signals ships into Narragansett Bay.

✗ p131

The Drive » Leaving Conanicut Island, head south along the scenic route RI 1A, along which you'll enjoy woodsy roads around Saunderstown and glimpses of the bay as you skirt the shoreline south of Narragansett Pier.

SHOBEIR ANSARI/GETTY IMAGES ©

❹ Narragansett

Scarborough State Beach (☎401-789-2324; www.riparks.com/Locations/LocationScarborough.html; 970 Ocean Rd; parking Mon-Fri/Sat & Sun $12/14; ☼dawn-dusk May-Oct; P), just south of Narragansett Pier, is one of the state's biggest beaches and is considered by many to be the best.

A few miles further south is **Galilee**, the departure point for the **Block Island Express** (☎860-444-4624; www.goblockisland.com) to Block Island. Sometimes called Point Judith in ferry schedules, Galilee is a workaday fishing town. Arrive in time and eat at dockside **Champlin's Seafood** (☎401-783-3152; 256 Great Rd, Point Judith; mains

FANTASTIC UMBRELLA FACTORY

A collection of 19th-century farm buildings and unkempt gardens, the **Fantastic Umbrella Factory** (☎401-364-6616; www.fantasticumbrellafactory.com; 4820 Old Post Rd, Charlestown; ☼10am-6pm), a former commune, got its start as one of Rhode Island's strangest stores in 1968. You can find almost anything in a series of shacks filled with gift items, flowers, toys, handmade jewelry and hemp clothing. Exotic birds and farm animals walk all over the place, much to the delight of children.

Jamestown Waterfront

$10-26; ⏰11am-9pm summer, shorter hours off-season), where they haul the fish right out of the bay onto your plate.

Further south still, the **Roger W Wheeler State Beach** (📞401-789-3563; www.riparks.com/Locations/LocationRogerWheeler.html; 100 Sand Hill Cove Rd; parking Mon-Fri/Sat & Sun $12/14; 🅿️🚻) is a good spot for families with small children. Not only does it have a playground and other facilities, but it also has a very gradual drop-off and little surf. All-day parking in Galilee costs $10 in any of the several lots.

🛏️ p131

The Drive » Car-and-passenger ferries and fast catamarans run from Galilee State Pier, Point Judith, to Old Harbor, Block Island, daily in off-season (October to May). In the busy summer season (June to September) boats depart almost hourly.

TRIP HIGHLIGHT

⑤ Block Island

From the deck of the ferry you'll see a cluster of mansard roofs and gingerbread houses rising picturesquely from **Old Harbor**, Block Island's main center of activity.

Beyond here, the island's attractions are simple. Stretching for several miles to the north of Old Harbor is the 3-mile **State Beach** (www.blockislandinfo.com/maps/beaches-parks-map; 🅿️), which is long enough to find a quiet spot even on a busy day. Otherwise, bike or hike around the island's rolling farmland, pausing to admire the island's lighthouses: **Southeast Light** (📞401-466-5009; 122 Mohegan Trail, New Shoreham; ⏰10am-4pm Jun-Jan; 🅿️), set dramatically atop 200ft red clay cliffs, and **North Lighthouse** (Corn Neck Rd, New Shoreham; ⏰museum

LOCAL KNOWLEDGE: ALLIE'S

Poll a couple of Rhode Islanders for the state's best souvenir, and one of them will probably say a treat from **Allie's Donuts** (📞401-295-8036; 3661 Quaker Lane, North Kingstown; ⏰5am-3pm Mon-Fri, 6am-1pm Sat & Sun). Allie has been turning out hot-to-trot homemade doughnuts from her roadside shack on RI 2 for more than 40 years and Rhode Islanders travel from across the state to take them away by the dozen ($7.20). Light as air, they are filled and topped with delectable condiments such as flaked coconut, chocolate and lemon cream, and cherry jelly.

10am-4pm Tue-Mon Jun-Sep; 🅿), which stands at the end of a long sandy lane lined with beach roses. In spring and fall, when migratory species fly south along the Atlantic Flyway, bird-watching opportunities abound and if you're traveling with kids or just like a good treasure hunt yourself, take part in the unique **Glass Float Project** (www.glassfloat project.com).

Hire bikes from **Island Moped and Bike Rentals** (📞401-466-2700; www. bimopeds.com; 41 Water St, Old Harbor; per day bikes/mopeds from $20/45; ⏰9am-8pm May-Oct).

✕ 🛏 p131

The Drive » Take the ferry back to Galilee and follow the signs to the main interstate RI 1. This 20-mile stretch of highway to Westerly is pleasant enough, lined with thick woods and plenty of opportunities to detour to various beaches.

---

6 Westerly

Westerly sits on Rhode Island's western border, sharing the banks of the Pawcatuck River with Connecticut. In the 19th century it was a town of some wealth, thanks to its high-grade granite quarries. That heyday is long gone, although local **Misquamicut State Beach** (📞401-322-8910; www.riparks.com/Locations/LocationMisquamicut.html; 257 Atlantic Ave; parking Mon-Fri/Sat & Sun $12/14; ⏰dawn-dusk May-late Oct) still draws weekending crowds who favor its scenic situation on Winnapaug Pond. Nearby is the old-fashioned amusement resort of **Atlantic Beach Park** (📞401-322-0504; www. atlanticbeachpark.com; 321 Atlantic Ave; ⏰dawn-dusk May-late Oct; 👶), which offers miniature golf, wave rides, batting cages and the like.

✕ 🛏 p131

The Drive » It's a short and scenic 2-mile drive south down RI 1A from the center of Westerly to the heady heights of mansion-clad Watch Hill. Along the way, enjoy views over Little Narragansett Bay across landscaped lawns and gardens.

- - - - - - - - - - - - - - - - - - -

TRIP HIGHLIGHT

7 Watch Hill

The wealthy summer colony of Watch Hill, with its huge Queen Anne summerhouses, occupies a spit of land at the southwestern tip of Rhode Island.

Visitors spend their time at **East Beach** (Bluff Ave), which stretches for several miles from Watch Hill lighthouse all the way to Misquamicut. (The public access to the beach is on Bluff Ave near Larkin Rd.) For children, an ice-cream cone and a twirl on the **Flying Horses Carousel** (151 Bay St; rides $1; ⏰11am-9pm Mon-Fri, from 10am Sat & Sun May-Oct; 👶) provide immediate gratification. The antique carousel dates from 1883 and its horses, suspended on chains, really do appear to 'fly' when the carousel spins.

For a leisurely beach walk, the half-mile stroll to the **Napatree Point Conservation Area** (📞401-315-5399; www. thewatchhillconservancy.org/napatree.html; Fort Road) is unbeatable with the Atlantic on one side and yacht-studded Little Narragansett Bay on the other.

Eating & Sleeping

Providence ❶

✕ Al Forno   Italian $$$

(☎401-273-9760; www.alforno.com; 577 S
Main St; mains $18-40; ⏱5-10pm Tue-Sat; ℗)
Our most recent visit featured scallops with
blackened bacon so perfect that they were
celestial. Also enjoy wood-grilled leg of lamb,
handmade *cavatelli* with butternut squash and
prosciutto, and incredible desserts. Budget-
minded folks can order wood-fired pizzas ($20)
big enough for two to split. Make a reservation.

⇌ Renaissance
Providence Hotel   Historic Hotel $$

(☎401-276-0010; www.renaissance-hotels.
marriott.com/renaissance-providence-
downtown-hotel; 5 Ave of the Arts; d from $237;
℗ ✳ 🛜) Built as a Masonic temple in 1929,
this monster stood empty for 77 years before it
opened as a hotel in 2007. Some rooms overlook
the Rhode Island State House (p122) and are
decorated in forceful colors that attempt, with
limited success, to evoke Masonic traditions.

Jamestown ❸

✕ Simpatico Jamestown   American $$

(☎401-423-2000; www.simpaticojamestown.
com; 13 Narragansett Ave; mains $18-24;
⏱5-9pm Tue-Sat) Sample the likes of shrimp
paella, comfort chicken and citrus-barbecued
pork tenderloin from a menu that includes
seafood, but is not limited to it. Simpatico has
a wonderfully romantic yet casual ambience,
especially when dining alfresco under the fairy
lights on the split-level patio.

Narragansett ❹

⇌ Fishermen's
Memorial State Park   Campground $

(☎401-789-8374; www.riparks.com/Locations/
LocationFishermens.html; 1011 Point Judith Rd;
tent sites RI residents/nonresidents $14/20;
⏱May-Oct; ℗) So popular that many families
return year after year to the same site. There
are only 180 tent sites at Fishermen's, so

it's wise to reserve early by requesting the
necessary form from the park management or
the Division of Parks & Recreation.

Block Island ❺

✕ Eli's   Modern American $$$

(☎401-466-5230; www.elisblockisland.com; 456
Chapel St, Old Harbor; mains $19-32; ⏱6-10pm
Fri-Sun; 🅟) The locally caught sea-bass special
(tender fillets over scallions, grapes and beans)
tastes so fresh and mildly salty and sweet that
its memory will haunt you for weeks. For real.
The room is cramped, crowded and casual with
lots of pine wood and some well-conceived art.

⇌ Sea Breeze Inn   Inn $$

(☎401-466-2275; www.seabreezeblockisland.
com; 71 Spring St, New Shoreham; d with/without
bath from $230/95; ℗ 🛜) Some rooms in these
charming cottages have views over a tidal pond
and the ocean beyond. Others face inward toward
a country garden. Inside, airy rooms have rustic
furnishings, cathedral ceilings, and no electronic
distractions such as TVs and clocks. Breakfast
comes in a basket, which can be enjoyed on the
porch. Open April to September.

Westerly ❻

✕ St Clair's Annex   Ice Cream $

(☎401-348-8407; www.stclairannexrestaurant.
com; 141 Bay St; cones from $3; ⏱8am-9pm May-
Oct; 🅟) This ice-cream shop has been run by
the same family since 1887, and features several
dozen flavors of homemade ice cream. On top of
traditional light breakfast fare (omelets and the
like), it serves seaside specialties such as lobster
rolls, hot dogs and lemonade.

⇌ Margin St Inn   B&B $$

(☎401-348-8710; www.marginstreetinn.
com; 4 Margin St; d from $225; ℗ 😀 🛜) This
handsome historic home (well, two homes
actually) has been converted into a classy
B&B with 10 fresh, beautifully furnished rooms
spread across the two houses and their pretty
gardens. There's not an air of stuffiness or
floral chintz about the place. It's the closest
accommodation to downtown Westerly.

Quiet Corner

Known as 'the last green valley' between Boston and Washington, Connecticut's Quiet Corner offers lovely rural scenery, as well as a couple of top wineries, cheese and beer crafters, farmland and parkland, Colonial history and abiding peace far from the tailgaters on I-95 and I-84.

11

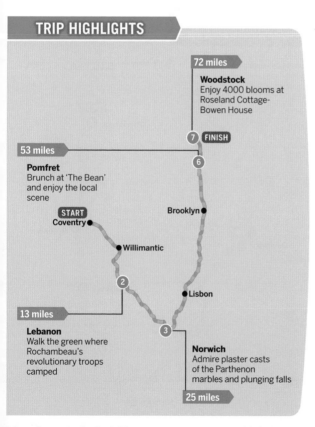

The Quiet Corner has the distinction of nurturing state hero Nathan Hale, the patriot-spy from Coventry whose only regret was that he had 'but one life to lose for his country,' and state heroine, abolitionist and Canterbury school teacher Prudence Crandall. Take this trip for a glimpse of New England past, when Washington plotted revolution on Lebanon's Green, and where today, local farms continue to welcome visitors with small-town friendliness.

❶ Coventry

Begin where it all began, at the **Nathan Hale Homestead** (☎860-742-6917; www.ctlandmarks.org; 2299 South St; adult/under 6yr $12/free; ☺noon-4pm Sat & Sun May & Oct, noon-4pm Thu-Sun, Jun-Sep) on the edge of the **Nathan Hale State Forest**. Nathan, whose five brothers also served in the Revolutionary War, was already in the Continental Army when his father built this rather fine red clapboard farmhouse in 1776. Inside, period furnishings re-create

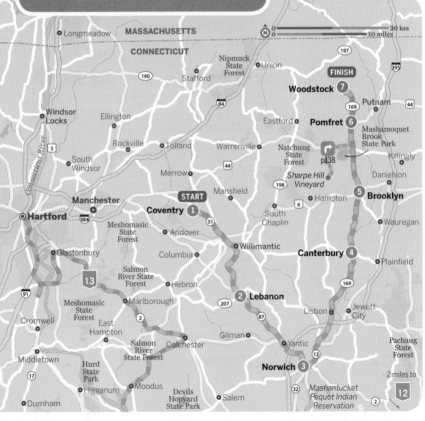

the domestic life of the early colony, along with a display of memorabilia of the schoolteacher turned patriot who was eventually pegged as a spy by the British and hanged at the age of 21. There are also tours of the heirloom gardens, guided walks around the 450-acre estate, Colonial cooking demonstrations and fall lantern tours.

📖 p139

The Drive ›› Sweep round Lake Wangumbaug, past the Nathan Hale Cemetery and onto CT 31, which soon merges with CT 32 southwards. Loop through industrial Willimantic, once home to the American Thread Company and known as 'Thread City,' and stop for barbecued ribs or a brew at 'The Willi' if you're hungry. Cross the bridge, adorned with its giant bullfrogs.

LINK YOUR TRIP

12 Connecticut Wine Trail

Meander south down CT 2 to the Jonathan Edwards Winery in North Stonington and join the Connecticut Wine Trail.

13 Lower River Valley

From hills and meadows to the banks of the Connecticut River, pick up the Byway at Springfield and travel north along its course.

sitting atop concrete spools of thread, and pick up CT 289 south to Lebanon.

- - - - - - - - - - - - - - - - - -

TRIP HIGHLIGHT

2 Lebanon

The best way to get acquainted with Lebanon's mile-long historic **Green** is to take a stroll around it on the walking path. On the eastern side, the butter-yellow **Jonathan Trumbull Jr House** (780 Trumbull Hwy; ⊙ noon-4pm Sat & Sun mid-May–mid-Oct; P) was home to Washington's military secretary, who hosted the great general in front of its eight fireplaces in March 1781. On the southwestern side of the Green you'll find **Governor Jonathan Trumbull House** (☏860-642-6100; www.govtrumbullhousedar. org; 169 West Town St; by donation; ⊙10am-5pm Sat, 1-5pm Sun May 15–Oct 15; P), the home of Trumbull's father, governor of Connecticut and the only Colonial governor to defy the Crown and support the War of Independence.

Next door, the strange little Palladian clapboard is actually the **Wadsworth Stable**, where Washington's horse overnighted. A little beyond that is the two-room **Revolutionary War Office** (www.lebanontownhall. org; 149 West Town St; by donation; ⊙ noon-4pm Sat & Sun Memorial Day–Labor Day), where Washington met with Trumbull and the

Comte de Rochambeau to coordinate military strategy.

The Drive ›› Pick up CT 87 and head south along its leafy route, straight into Norwich. It's a short 11-mile drive.

- - - - - - - - - - - - - - - - - -

TRIP HIGHLIGHT

3 Norwich

Money from the Quiet Corner's mills flowed into Norwich, accounting for the handsome Victorian houses set around the **Norwichtown Green**, the gorgeous Second Empire **City Hall** and the unique Romanesque Revival **Slater Memorial Museum** (☏860-887-2506; www.slater museum.org; 108 Crescent St; adult/child $3/2; ⊙9am-4pm Tue-Fri, 1-4pm Sat & Sun), designed by Stephen Earle in 1886.

The museum was commissioned by William Slater, an educated and well-traveled man who aspired to make the great art of the classical and Renaissance periods accessible to Norwich's citizens. With this in mind, he commissioned the 227 plaster casts that fill the museum's beaux-arts interior on his grand tour in 1894–95. Ranging from the Parthenon Marbles to Michelangelo's *Pieta,* the casts were created via a now-illegal process from molds of the original. Visit the exhibit of Slater's grand tour before heading into the museum, which still

forms part of the Norwich Free Academy.

Just about a mile away, a crucial cog in the town's industrial history and Native American legend, **Yantic Falls** (Indian Leap; 210 Yantic St), awaits your visit.

🛏 p139

The Drive ›› From the Norwichtown Green, head down Washington St and Broadway, past grand Victorian mansions and the architecturally noteworthy City Hall, before picking up N Main St and heading out of town in a northeasterly direction to pick up the National Scenic Byway CT 169. Once en route, the scenery quickly becomes picturesque following low stone walls into deeply rural Canterbury.

- - - - - - - - - - - - - - - - - - -

❹ Canterbury

Tiny Canterbury was at the forefront of the abolitionist cause some 30 years before the Civil War, thanks to Baptist schoolmistress Prudence Crandall. The **Prudence Crandall House Museum** (📞860-546-7800; www.friendsofprudencecrandallmuseum.org; 1 South Canterbury Rd; adult/child $6/free; 🕙10am-4pm Thu-Sun May-Nov) was the site of an academy that Crandall opened in 1831.

When Crandall later accepted Sarah Harris, the daughter of a free African American farmer, among her students in the fall of 1832, many prominent townspeople withdrew their daughters from the school in protest. Rather than give in, Crandall changed her admissions policy and offered schooling to the free African American community. By April 1833, some 20 girls from Boston, Providence, New York and Philadelphia had enrolled. This caused

Norwich Slater Memorial Museum

an angry backlash; the school was vandalized, its well poisoned and, in July, Prudence was arrested. When the case against her was finally dismissed on September 9, 1834, the school was set on fire and Prudence reluctantly closed its doors.

The Drive ⟩⟩ Leaving Canterbury's clapboard homesteads behind you, continue north on CT 169 to Brooklyn. To your right, sweeping views across paddocks and the distant valley open up and the country road is lined with farmyards and historic Dutch barns.

----

⑤ Brooklyn

By the time you hit Brooklyn, you're in the heart of the Quiet Corner, where admiring the scenery and stopping in at local farms and ice-cream stalls is the main activity.

First stop is the **Creamery Brook Bison Farm** (☏860-779-0837; www.creamerybrookbison. net; 19 Purvis Rd; ⊙hours vary), where you can take the equivalent of a Quiet Corner safari among the bison herd before stocking up at the farm shop: phone ahead so

staff know you're coming. Next, hit the **Grassland Bird Conservation Center** (Connecticut Audubon Center at Pomfret; www. ctaudubon.org; 218 Day Rd, Pomfret Center) on the way into Pomfret for hiking and birding along the rolling hills.

The Drive ⟩⟩ On your way out of Brooklyn, you'll pass the access road to the Golden Lamb Buttery (sadly closed, but the sign is still there) on your left. Continue along CT 169, beneath the leafy canopy that creates the impression of driving through a verdant green tunnel. You'll pass fruit orchards on your right, which belong to

137

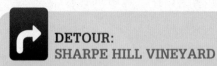

DETOUR:
SHARPE HILL VINEYARD

Start: **6** **Pomfret**

In nearby Abington, up a winding country road buried deep in the forest, you'll find the Quiet Corner's most scenic vineyard, **Sharpe Hill** (☎860-974-3549; http://sharpehill.com; 108 Wade Rd, Pomfret; tastings $10-15; ☺11am-5pm Fri-Sun). It's also arguably Connecticut's finest vineyard, with over 250 medals for its signature chardonnay Ballet of Angels and its St Croix cabernet franc. To appreciate the beautiful setting, consider spending the day here, walking up through the vineyard for spectacular views, tasting wine on the patio and then sitting down to a gourmet farm-to-table lunch or dinner in the gracious Fireside Tavern. Worthwhile, too, is a detour to Cato Corner Farm (p152) for some excellent cheese to go with that wine.

Lapsley Orchard farm, where you can PYO in season.

- - - - - - - - - - - - - - - - - -

TRIP HIGHLIGHT

6 Pomfret

With its expansive Colonial homes and hearty restaurants, Pomfret is considered the heart of the Quiet Corner, and is where many visitors choose to base themselves. 'The Bean' will amaze you with its filling grub and superb acoustic jams.

Farming lives on in the vineyards, nurseries and orchards that surround Pomfret, while legends live on in **Mashamoquet Brook State Park** (☎860-928-6121; www.ct.gov; 147 Wolf Den Dr, Pomfret Center; campsites $24). Here, local hero Israel Putnam, who led the troops at Bunker Hill in Boston, is said to have crawled into the den of a she-wolf that was ravaging local sheep, and shot it.

To follow in his footsteps, take the trail past the campground to Wolf Den. You can then continue on a 5-mile loop through thick woodland. Take a swimming costume along if you fancy bathing in the shallow pond.

✗ p139

The Drive » The final stretch of CT 169 from Pomfret to Woodstock continues past farmland and the Roseland Lake, up through the modern buildings and grassy playing fields of South Woodstock, before arriving in Woodstock proper.

- - - - - - - - - - - - - - - - - -

TRIP HIGHLIGHT

7 Woodstock

Roseland Cottage (Bowen House; ☎860-928-4074; www.historicnewengland.org; 556 CT 169; adult/student $10/5; ☺11am-4pm Wed-Sun Jun 1–Oct 15) is proof that wealthy Americans had fancy summer homes even in the mid-1800s.

Beautifully preserved, this lovely Gothic Revival house sports pointed arches, crockets and stained-glass windows.

The garden is also a historic treasure, laid out according to the 1850 plan with some 4000 blooms bordered by formal boxwood parterres. Other follies include an aviary, a summerhouse, an icehouse and a vintage bowling alley.

After a stroll around the garden, head down to **Woodstock Orchards** (☎860-928-2225; 494 CT 169; ☺9am-6pm) for a glass of fresh cider and to stock up on apples and berries before heading home. If you're in town around Labor Day, be sure to check out the enormous **Woodstock Fair** (www.woodstockfair.com; 281 CT 169; adult/child $12/free; ☺early Sep; 🚻).

✗ 🛏 p139

Eating & Sleeping

Coventry ➊

🛏 Daniel Rust House   B&B $$

(📞860-742-0032; www.thedanielrusthouse.
com; 2011 Main St; d $120-185; 🅿 😊 🛜)
Serving travelers since 1800, the four period
rooms here brim with history. The finest is the
Anna White room with its antique canopy bed,
although the Mary Rose has a secret closet that
was used to hide enslaved people traveling to
freedom on the Underground Railroad.

Norwich ➌

🛏 Spa at Norwich Inn   Inn $$$

(📞860-425-3500; www.thespaatnorwichinn.
com; 607 West Thames St; d/ste from $205/305;
🅿 🛜 🏊) Set in 42 acres of woodland near
the Public Golf Course, Norwich's elegant
Georgian spa offers 36 treatment rooms, indoor
and outdoor pools, tennis and golf. Be sure to
book a room in the main house overlooking the
flowering gardens.

Pomfret ➏

🍴 Vanilla Bean Cafe   Modern American $

(www.thevanillabeancafe.com; 450 Deerfield Rd;
mains $6.50-16; 🕗7am-3pm Mon-Thu, to 8pm Fri
& Sat, 8am-4pm Sun; 🚶) Families, cyclists and
Sunday drivers regularly make the pilgrimage to
'The Bean' for creative casual dining, live music
(including open mikes and well-known folkies)
and artful surroundings. The acoustic balance
of the room and local artwork can't help but get
your head right.

🍴 We-Li-Kit Ice Cream   Ice Cream $

(📞860-974-1095; www.welikit.com; 728
Hampton Rd, Pomfret Center; scoops from

$3.50; 🕗11am-8pm Apr-Oct; 🚶) Sit at trestle
tables and slurp sundaes and housemade, farm-
fresh ice cream with holidaymakers and locals.
There's a bunch of wacky and wonderful flavors
to choose from.

Woodstock ➐

🍴 Soleil and Suns Bakery   Bakery $

(www.facebook.com/SoleilBakeryLLC; 35 CT
171; pastries & cupcakes $2.50-5, whole pies &
cakes $20-25; 🕗7am-6pm) Quiet Cornerners
from miles around love Bill Beausoleil's loaves,
including Asiago cheese, cranberry-pecan,
cinnamon-raisin and garlic cheddar. English
toasting buns were created here, and there are
rows of cannoli, cream puffs and cupcakes for
the sweet-toothed among ye.

🍴 Sweet Evalina's   Cafe $

(📞860-928-4029; www.sweetevalinas.com;
688 CT 169; grinders $8-10, pizzas $14-18;
🕗9am-9pm) Serving up comfort food for
two decades, this roadside stand features
housemade doughnuts and pies, popular
pizzas (including one with clams, scallops and
shrimp) and some very edible but low-cost
grinders. They even have an electric car
charging station.

🛏 Inn at Woodstock Hill   Inn $$$

(📞860-928-0528; www.woodstockhill.com;
CT 169 & Plaine Hill Rd; r from $190; 🅿 ❄ 🛜)
The Bowen family has owned this property,
now a smart 21-room inn with its own vegetable
garden and a beautiful sitting room/library,
since 1816. Some rooms have fireplaces and
four-poster beds, and you'll be spoiled by the
dining room, which serves up fresh American-
European fare like heritage pork chops.

Connecticut Wine Trail

Connecticut has established itself as a serious wine-growing region. Combine this vineyard tour of some of the best producers with gourmet dining in Greenwich and New Haven's stellar galleries.

12

TRIP HIGHLIGHTS

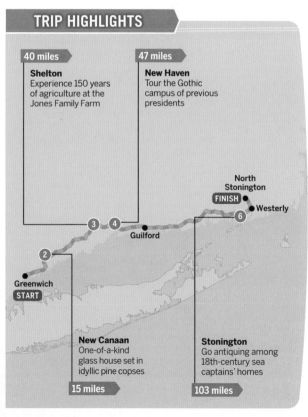

40 miles

Shelton
Experience 150 years of agriculture at the Jones Family Farm

47 miles

New Haven
Tour the Gothic campus of previous presidents

North Stonington
FINISH
● Westerly

6

3 **4**
● **Guilford**

2

● **Greenwich**
START

New Canaan
One-of-a-kind glass house set in idyllic pine copses
15 miles

Stonington
Go antiquing among 18th-century sea captains' homes
103 miles

5 DAYS
132 MILES / 212KM

GREAT FOR...

BEST TIME TO GO
August to October for the grape harvest.

ESSENTIAL PHOTO
Philip Johnson's glass cube amid the trees.

BEST FOR OUTDOORS
Picnicking at the Jonathan Edwards Winery.

New Haven Yale University

12 Connecticut Wine Trail

Starting on Connecticut's moneyed Gold Coast, this tour wends its way between vineyards to encompass the compact downtown of Greenwich, with its high-end shops and notable museums; Philip Johnson's radical mid-century modern Glass House in New Canaan; and New Haven's neo-Gothic turrets. At its northern reaches Stonington's 19th-century sea captains' homes cluster amid maritime vineyards, which produce some of the state's finest drops.

1 Greenwich

In the early days, Greenwich was home to farmers and fishers who shipped oysters and potatoes to nearby New York. But with the advent of passenger trains and the first cashed-up commuters, the town became a haven for Manhattanites in search of country exclusivity. Along **Greenwich Avenue**, high-end boutiques and gourmet restaurants line the route where the town's trolley once traveled.

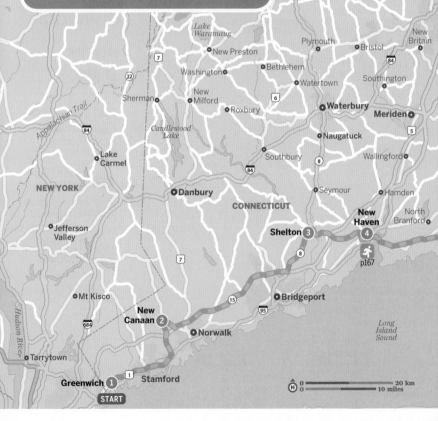

One of Greenwich's wealthiest 19th-century inhabitants was Robert Moffat Bruce, a textile tycoon who lived in what is now the **Bruce Museum** (203-869-0376; www.brucemuseum.org; 1 Museum Dr; adult/student & senior $10/8, Tue free; 10am-5pm Tue-Sun). Now a variety of galleries house a natural science collection and a permanent display of impressionist works by the Cos Cob art colony, as well as hosting more than a dozen art exhibits a year.

 p147

The Drive » Head northeast along I-95, paralleling US 1, the old Boston–New York post road, until you come to the steel-and-glass towers of metropolitan Stamford. Then take exit 9 onto CT 106 and head inland through the suburbs to New Canaan.

TRIP HIGHLIGHT

2 New Canaan

The only Gold Coast town without a shoreline, New Canaan is

LINK YOUR TRIP

1 Coastal New England

From Stonington, continue north along I-95 across the Jamestown Bridge to Newport for more salty coastal scenery.

11 Quiet Corner

Continue north along scenic CT 169 to Canterbury for a laid-back tour of the Quiet Corner.

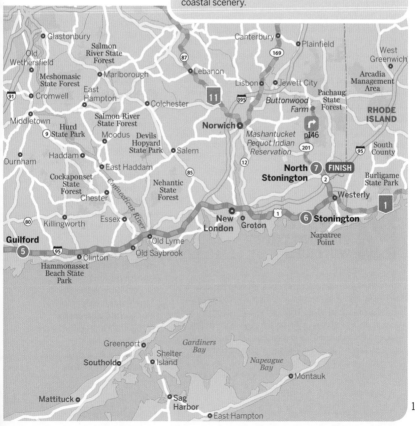

characterized by large clapboard houses, grand Georgian mansions and, unusually, one of the most famous modern houses in the world: the 1949 **Philip Johnson Glass House** (866-811-4111; www.theglasshouse.org; 199 Elm St, New Canaan; tours from $25; ⊘9:30am-5:30pm Thu-Mon May 1–Nov 30, last tour 2pm). This icon of mid-century modern architecture, set in a dappled wood on 47 acres, was the home of the late Pritzker Prize–winner Philip Johnson, and his art collector partner, David Whitney.

Almost totally transparent, the house offers stunning views of the autumnal countryside and Johnson's intriguing collection of contemporary art. Guided tours must be reserved; visitors assemble at the visitor center across the street from the New Canaan train station. In addition to the house, the tour includes a look at Da Monsta, the concrete-

and-Styrofoam gatehouse to the property.

✕ p147

The Drive » Leave bucolic New Canaan via CT 123 S and after 2 miles merge with the CT 15. Head north toward New Haven, skirting the suburbs of Norwalk, Westport and Trumbull, then take exit 8 onto CT 8 toward Waterbury. After 6 miles you'll arrive in Shelton.

- - - - - - - - - - - - - - - - - -

TRIP HIGHLIGHT

❸ Shelton

Nestled in the White Hills of Shelton you'll find the 150-year-old, 400-acre **Jones Family Farm** (📞203-929-8425; www.jonesfamilyfarms.com; 606 Walnut Tree Hill Rd, Shelton; ⊘picking 8am-5:30pm Mon-Sat, wine tastings 11am-5:30pm Sun), home of one of the premier wineries in the state. Jones Winery is known for using its own grapes and those from local vineyards. The vineyard's founder and resident winemaker, Jamie Jones, is now the sixth generational family

member to operate the farm.

Aside from the winery and tasting room there's berry picking in summer, a Heritage Farm Hike in June, pumpkins and hayrides in fall and, of course, Christmas trees in November and December. You can also sign up for cooking classes and wine-education suppers at the Harvest Kitchen studio. Check the website for details.

The Drive » Rejoin CT 8 and cross the Housatonic River before taking exit 15 onto CT 34. After less than a mile, take the ramp onto CT 15 N, which weaves through New Haven's exclusive golf greens for 4 miles. Then take exit 59 onto CT 69 S, which takes you right into the center of New Haven.

- - - - - - - - - - - - - - - - - -

TRIP HIGHLIGHT

❹ New Haven

New Haven is home to America's third-oldest university, Yale, and its leafy green is bordered by graceful Colonial buildings, statehouses and churches. The 1816 **Trinity Church** resembles England's Gothic York Minster, while the Georgian-style, 1812 **Center Church on the Green** is a fine example of New England Palladian. But nowhere is the city's history more palpable than at **Yale University** (📞203-432-2300; www.yale.edu/visitor; 149 Elm St).

Pick up a free map of the campus from **Yale**

TOP TIP:
FINDING THOSE WINERIES

It's worth bearing in mind that most wineries are tucked away down country roads, and finding your way can often be a challenge. A useful resource is the **Connecticut Wine Trail** (www.ctwine.com) brochure, which covers all the wineries in the state along with detailed driving directions. Ambitious vinophiles can get their 'passport' stamped at each vineyard and be eligible for prizes.

Stonington Saltwater Farm Vineyard

University Visitor Center
(📞203-432-2300; http://
visitorcenter.yale.edu; 149 Elm
St; 🕘9am-4:30pm Mon-Fri,
11am-4pm Sat & Sun) and
take a stroll around the
stately buildings, where
alumni such as Presidents William H Taft,
George HW Bush and Bill
Clinton once studied.

In more recent years,
New Haven has also built
a reputation for itself as
an arts mecca.

✕ 🛏 p39, p59, p147

The Drive » The 14-mile
drive east from New Haven to
Guilford is easy but uneventful.
The highlight is crossing the
New Haven harbor bridge
before rejoining I-95 through
the conurbations of East Haven
and Branford before reaching
Guilford.

- - - - - - - - - - - - - - - - -

❺ Guilford

In the historic seaside town of Guilford,
Bishop's Orchards

Winery (📞203-453-2338;
www.bishopsorchards.com;
1355 Boston Post Rd/US 1;
🕘8am-6:30pm Mon-Sat,
10am-5:30pm Sun; 👶) has
been serving shoreline
communities with fresh
produce since 1871. Much
more than just a winery,
Bishop's is also a pick-
your-own farm, where
berries, peaches, pears,
apples and pumpkins
can be picked from June
through October. The
rich variety of produce
means the Bishop's **mar-
ket** (open year-round)
is one of the best in the
area. If you have kids,
they'll get a kick out of
the llamas, alpacas and
grazing goats.

The coastline around
Guilford is wonderful,
but much of it is built
up. However, the nearby
**Hammonasset Beach
State Park** (📞203-245-
2785; www.ct.gov; 1288 Boston
Post Rd, Madison; weekdays/

weekends $15/22; 🕘8am-
sunset; 🅿) provides a
1100-acre oasis, with
a 2-mile pine-backed
beach, boardwalk trails
and excellent facilities for
camping, picnicking and
swimming.

✕ p147

The Drive » Leave I-95 and
pick up the old post road, US 1.
This takes you through genteel
Madison to the marshy doorstep
of Hammonasset Beach State
Park. Stop for a stroll or a
picnic, then continue on US 1 for
another 6 miles before rejoining
I-95 for the remaining 28 miles
to Stonington.

- - - - - - - - - - - - - - - - -

TRIP HIGHLIGHT

❻ Stonington

Stonington is one of the
most appealing towns
on the Connecticut
coast. Compactly laid
out on a peninsula, the
town offers complete
streetscapes of 18th- and
19th-century houses,

DETOUR:
BUTTONWOOD FARM

Start: ❼ **North Stonington**

Beginning as early as mid-July, an astonishing number of interactive corn mazes begin cropping up on farms throughout New England. Travel north up CT 201 and you can get lost in the themed maze at **Buttonwood Farm** (☎860-376-4081; www. buttonwoodfarmicecream.com; 471 Shetucket Turnpike/CT 165, Griswold; cones $5; ☺1-9pm Mon-Fri, noon-9pm Sat & Sun Mar-Oct; 👶), pick pumpkins from their patches, take hayrides and finish up with some of the farm's delicious homemade ice cream. In October, the maze is also open for nighttime adventures – if you dare!

---

many of which were once sea captains' homes.

The main thoroughfare, **Water Street**, features shops selling antiques and Quimper porcelain, colorfully painted dinnerware handmade in France since the 17th century. At the southern end is the 'point,' with a park, a lighthouse and a tiny beach.

Situated on Stonington's south-facing slopes, **Stonington Vineyards** (☎860-535-1222; www. stoningtonvineyards.com; 523 Taugwonk Rd; tastings/tours $12/free; ☺11am-4pm; P) produces some of the state's finest table wines, thanks to its glacial soils and maritime climate not unlike that of Bordeaux in France. As a result, you can expect creamy chardonnays and award-

winning cabernet franc. It may also be worth your while to wet your whistle at the recommended **Saltwater Farm Vineyard** (☎860-415-9072; www.saltwaterfarmvineyard. com; 349 Elm St; tastings $10; ☺11am-5pm Wed & Thu, to 3pm Fri-Sun), on the way out of town on Route 1.

🍴 🛏 p147

The Drive » Exit Stonington on US 1, which takes you through some very pretty rural countryside lightly dotted with handsome country homes. At Westerly, turn northward on US 2 for a further 5 miles, before turning right on Main St and heading into North Stonington.

- - - - - - - - - - - - - - - -

❼ North Stonington

Heading northward away from the coast, you arrive at one of the most picturesque and sceni-

cally situated vineyards on the tour, the **Jonathan Edwards Winery** (☎860-535-0202; www.jedwardswinery.com; 74 Chester Maine Rd, North Stonington; 7 wine tastings $15; ☺11am-5pm daily May-Dec, Wed-Sun Jan-Apr; P) in North Stonington. Housed in a lovingly renovated dairy barn on a hilltop overlooking the Atlantic, it is the perfect spot for a late-afternoon BYO picnic and wine tasting.

In winter, oenophiles warm themselves around the stone fireplace in the wood-paneled tasting room, while the knowledgeable and enthusiastic staff talk through a variety of wines, both from the Connecticut coast and the Edwards vineyards in Napa, CA.

Eating & Sleeping

Greenwich ❶

✕ Meli-Melo — Crêpes $

(☎203-629-6153; www.melimelogreenwich.com; 362 Greenwich Ave; crepes $8-17; ⏰7am-10pm Mon-Fri) For a quick and delicious bite, you can't do better than Meli-Melo. It serves salads, soups and sandwiches, but its specialty is undoubtedly buckwheat crepes. Try a wild combination like smoked salmon, chive sauce, lemon and daikon ($11). The French onion and French lentil soups are also recommended.

New Canaan ❷

✕ Solé — Italian $$

(☎203-972-8887; www.zhospitalitygroup.com/sole; 105 Elm St; mains $17-28; ⏰11:30am-10pm) Sit at the marble-topped bar with a glass of pinot grigio and watch the chef prepare wood-fired pizzas and northern Italian dishes, such as Tuscan bread salad or handmade potato gnocchi with sausage, mushrooms and basil.

New Haven ❹

✕ Union League Café — French $$$

(☎203-562-4299; www.unionleaguecafe.com; 1032 Chapel St; mains $23-38; ⏰11:30am-9:30pm Mon-Fri, 5-10pm Sat) An upscale French bistro in the historic Union League building. Expect continental classics like *cocotte de joues de veau* (organic veal cheeks with sautéed wild mushrooms; $25) along with nouvelle cuisine. If your budget is tight, try a sinful dessert like *crêpe soufflé au citron* (lemon crepes) washed down with a glass from the exquisite wine list.

✕ Pantry — American $

(☎203-787-0392; 2 Mechanic St; breakfast $11-24; ⏰7am-2pm Mon-Sat, 8am-3pm Sun) The secret is out about New Haven's ah-mazing little breakfast-lunch joint. You'll most likely have to line up then rub shoulders with a bunch of hungry students (who'd probably rather we kept this one to ourselves), but persevere if you can: you won't find a better-value, more drool-worthy breakfast for miles. Take your pick: it's *all* good.

🛏 Austin Street
Inn & Gallery of Art — Boutique Hotel $$

(☎203-387-1699; www.austinstreetinn.net; 9 Austin St, Westville Village; r from $179; P 🛜) A hotel that's a work of art, and vice versa, the Austin features parlors done in tasteful blue/green and cranberry/ochre accents, a welcoming hearth and local art on the walls. Four comfy rooms can be enhanced by also renting one of the adjoining parlors. Convenient to two lovely parks: Edgewood and West Rock Ridge State Park.

Guilford ❺

✕ The Place Restaurant — Seafood $$

(☎203-453-9276; www.theplaceguilford.com; 901 Boston Post Rd/US 1; mains $12-20; ⏰5-9pm Mon-Fri, 1-10pm Sat, noon-9pm Sun May-Sep, weekends only Oct) Drive in, snag a tree stump for a stool, crack open the cold beer or wine you've brought with you and order up a feast of littleneck clams, lobsters and charred corn on the cob from the open-air firepit. Cash only.

Stonington ❻

✕ Noah's — Cafe $$

(☎860-535-3925; www.noahsfinefood.com; 113 Water St; mains $12-27; ⏰7:45am-9pm Tue-Sun; 👶) Noah's is a popular, informal place, with two small rooms topped with original stamped-tin ceilings. It's famous for its seafood (especially chowder and scallops) and pastries, like the mouthwatering apple-spice and sour-cream coffee cakes. Lunchtime is a family-friendly affair, while dinner is more formal. Book ahead at weekends.

🛏 Inn at Stonington — Inn $$$

(☎860-535-2000; www.innatstonington.com; 60 Water St; d from $290-490; P ❄ @ 🛜) Offering an easy sophistication, this romantic inn continues to stay at the top of its game. From windows overlooking Stonington Harbor you can watch the sunrise or yachties tying up at the hotel dock of an evening. Elegant, country-style rooms feature plump sofas, four-poster beds, soaking tubs and fireplaces. Bikes, kayaks, free beach access and massages are available.

Lower River Valley

From its spring-fed source near the Canadian border, the Connecticut River cuts a 410-mile trail southeast. Tour the valley for a glimpse of the state's first settlers and holidaying industrialists.

13

TRIP HIGHLIGHTS

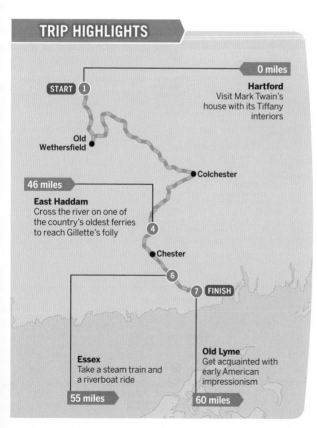

0 miles

Hartford
Visit Mark Twain's house with its Tiffany interiors

START 1

Old Wethersfield ●

● Colchester

46 miles

East Haddam
Cross the river on one of the country's oldest ferries to reach Gillette's folly

4

● Chester

6

7 **FINISH**

Essex
Take a steam train and a riverboat ride

55 miles

Old Lyme
Get acquainted with early American impressionism

60 miles

**4 DAYS
60 MILES / 97KM**

GREAT FOR...

BEST TIME TO GO
September to February for cruising and eagle-spotting.

ESSENTIAL PHOTO

William Gillette's ruined Gothic folly.

BEST FOR FAMILIES

Enjoy the summer steam train in Essex.

East Haddam Gillette Castle

13 Lower River Valley

Once the engine of 19th-century commerce, the Connecticut River – New England's longest waterway – now enchants visitors with its historic towns, artist colonies, nature conservancies and gracious country inns. River cruises and steam train rides allow for authentic glimpses into provincial Connecticut life. Even Hartford, the state capital, is rediscovering the river these days with new parks and walkways landscaped along its banks.

TRIP HIGHLIGHT

1 Hartford

Despite the exodus of the insurance companies that earned Hartford its reputation as the 'filing cabinet of America,' those passing through will be surprised at how much the city has to offer. The standout **Wadsworth Atheneum** (☎860-278-2670; https://thewadsworth.org; 600 Main St; adult/child $15/free; ⊙11am-5pm Wed-Fri, 10am-5pm Sat & Sun) houses 40,000 pieces of art in a castlelike Gothic

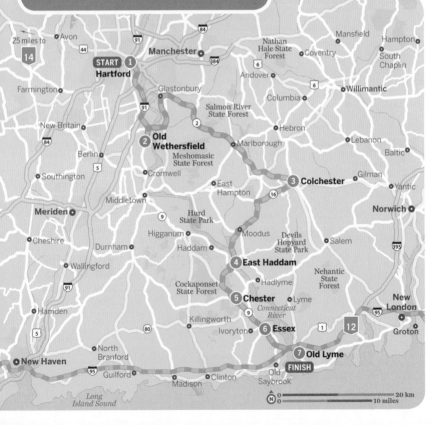

Revival building. These include some by Hartford native Frederic Church, alongside 19th-century impressionist works and a small but outstanding collection of surrealist art.

Other notable sites include **Mark Twain House** (☑860-247-0998; www.marktwainhouse.org; 351 Farmington Ave, parking at 385 Farmington Ave; guided house tours adult/child $20/11, living history/ghost tours $25/12, museum only $6; ☺9:30am-5:30pm, closed Tue Jan & Feb; **P**), where novelist Samuel Langhorne Clemens (1835–1910) spent 17 years of his life writing the *Adventures of Tom Sawyer* and *Huckleberry Finn*. Architect Edward Tuckerman Potter embellished the house with turrets and gables, and some of the

interiors were styled by Louis Comfort Tiffany. Next door to the Twain house is **Harriet Beecher-Stowe Center** (☑860-522-9258; www.harrietbeecherstowe.org; 77 Forest St; adult/child $16/10; ☺9:30am-5pm Mon-Sat, noon-5pm Sun; **P**). Built in 1871, the house reflects Stowe's ideas about decorating and domestic efficiency, which she expressed in her bestseller *American Woman's Home*. Stowe is most famous for her antislavery book, *Uncle Tom's Cabin*.

✕ ⫘ p155

The Drive » Exit Hartford along Capitol Ave and Hudson, and merge onto the Colin Whitehead Hwy. Join I-91 S for a short 3.5-mile drive through Hartford's suburbs before taking exit 26 for Old Wethersfield.

- - - - - - - - - - - - - - - -

❷ Old Wethersfield

A quick jaunt down I-91 will bring you to the historic district of Old Wethersfield. Despite sitting in the larger Hartford suburbs, Old Wethersfield is a living monument to the past, perfectly preserved for more than 375 years. Wander around and you'll find hundreds of historic homes, as well as a number of interesting museums. The best way to get your bearings, however, is to start at the **Wethersfield Museum** (☑860-529-7656; www.wet

hersfieldhistory.org; 200 Main St, Wethersfield; ☺10am-4pm Tue-Sat, 1-4pm Sun).

The Drive » Accommodations in Hartford and Old Wethersfield tend to be underwhelming, expensive and business oriented. It's far better to push on across the river, via CT 3 N. The pretty, historic town of Glastonbury (p155) has some great B&B options. From there, continue along CT 2 toward Colchester.

- - - - - - - - - - - - - - - -

❸ Colchester

Rural Colchester, with its grazing fields and serried ranks of vines, is a certified Community Wildlife Habitat and listed on the National Register of Historic Places. However, the real reason to come to Colchester is so you can visit **Cato Corner Farm** (☑860-537-3884; www.catocornerfarm.com; 178 Cato Corner Rd; ☺10am-4pm Fri-Sun), where mother-and-son cheese makers Elizabeth and Mark craft dozens of aged farmhouse cheeses with raw milk from their herd of Jersey cows. Many of the cheeses, such as the Dairyere (a firm washed-rind cheese), are prizewinners.

Near the cheese shop is the notable **Priam Vineyards** (☑860-267-8520; www.priamvineyards.com; 11 Shailor Hill Rd; ☺11am-6pm Wed-Sun mid-Mar–Dec), a 24-acre, solar-powered, sustainable vineyard growing French and American varieties,

LINK YOUR TRIP

12 Connecticut Wine Trail

Travel west to Guilford along I-95 for a taste of Connecticut's cabernet sauvignon and New Haven culture.

14 Litchfield Hills Loop

Head into the hills on US 44 for bucolic rural views, market towns and gourmet eats.

such as cabernet sauvignon, riesling, merlot, Cayuga and St Croix. In summer, visitors can take self-guided tours of the vineyards, picnic amid the vines and even enjoy live music concerts.

The Drive ⟫ Leaving the interstate, turn southwest along Middletown Rd (CT 16) through farmland and alongside Babcock Pond until you reach CT 149, where you turn left and head directly south back toward the river. This part of the drive passes pleasantly through rural communities and historic towns along tree-lined roads.

TRIP HIGHLIGHT

④ East Haddam

Looming on one of the Seven Sisters hills just above East Haddam is **Gillette Castle** (☎860-526-2336; www.ct.gov; 67 River Rd; grounds free, castle tours adult/child $6/2; ⊙ castle 11am-5pm late May–early Sep, weekends Nov-Dec, grounds 8am-dusk year-round; [P]), a turreted mansion made of fieldstone. Built in 1919 by eccentric actor William Gillette, who made his fortune in the role of Sherlock Holmes, the folly is modeled on the medieval castles of Germany's Rhineland and the views from its terraces are spectacular. The surrounding 125 acres are a designated state park and open year-round but the interior is only open

for tours from late May through September (and on special holiday weekends in November and December).

With residents such as Gillette and banker William Goodspeed, East Haddam became a regular stopover on the summer circuit for New Yorkers, who traveled up on Goodspeed's steamship. To entertain them, he built the **Goodspeed Opera House** (☎860-873-8668; www.goodspeed. org; 6 Main St; tickets $29-85, tours adult/child $5/1; ⊙ performances Wed-Sun Apr-Dec) in 1876. It's now

dedicated to preserving and developing American musicals, and you can still enjoy your intermission drinks on the balcony overhanging the river.

The Drive ⟫ From East Haddam, cross the Connecticut River via the steel swing bridge and meander southeast through rural countryside for about 5 miles before merging with I-9 S toward Old Saybrook. After 1.5 miles, take exit 6 for Chester.

⑤ Chester

Cupped in the valley of Pattaconk Brook, Chester is one of the most

Essex Essex Steam Train

charming river towns along the Connecticut River. Its quaint Main St is lined with good restaurants and thriving galleries and workshops, and most visitors come to simply browse the antique shops and indulge in some fine dining.

The town's new brewpub, **Little House Brewing Co** (www.little housebrewing.com; 16 Main St; ☺3-8pm Wed & Thu, 2-9pm Fri, noon-9pm Sat, noon-6pm Sun), offers a respite from road stress, but if you're seeking caffeination, drop in to have a coffee at local provender **Simon's Mar-**

ketplace (☎860-526-8984; www.simonsmarketplaceches ter.com; 17 Main St; items from $4; ☺8am-6pm; 🖉 🚹) and pick up some tasty deli treats.

✖ p155

The Drive ›› Rejoin I-9 for the short 6-mile hop to Essex.

TRIP HIGHLIGHT

6 Essex

Handsome, tree-lined Essex, established in 1635, features well-preserved Federal-period homes, legacies of rum and tobacco fortunes made in the 19th century. Today

the town prides itself on the oldest-known continuously operating waterfront in the country. That and the **Connecticut River Museum** (☎860-767-8269; www.ctrivermuseum.org; 67 Main St; adult/child $10/6; ☺10am-5pm, closed Mon Oct-May; P 🚹), next to the Steamboat Dock, where exhibits recount the area's history, including a replica of the world's first submarine, the *American Turtle,* built by Yale student David Bushnell in 1776.

The best way to experience the river is to take the **Essex Steam Train &**

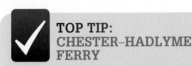

TOP TIP:
CHESTER–HADLYME FERRY

In summer you can cross the Connecticut River on the **Chester–Hadlyme Ferry** (www.ctvisit.com/listings/chesterhadlyme-ferry; car/pedestrian $6/2; ⊙7am-6:45pm Mon-Fri, 10:30am-5pm Sat & Sun Apr-Nov). The five-minute river crossing on the *Selden III* is the second-oldest ferry service in America, beginning in 1769. The ferry ride affords great views of Gillette Castle and is a fun way to link up with the Essex Steam Train, which runs between Chester and Essex.

Riverboat Ride (☑860-767-0103; www.essex steamtrain.com; 1 Railroad Ave; adult/child $20/10, incl cruise $30/20; ⊙daily May-Oct, seasonal events year-round; 🚂), which transports you to Deep River on a steam train and then runs you up to the Goodspeed Opera House at East Haddam in a riverboat. The train trip takes about an hour; with the riverboat ride, the excursion takes 2½ hours. In February look out for **eagle-watching cruises** (Connecticut Audubon; ☑860-575-4317; www.ctaudubon.org; Eagle Landing State Park, Haddam; $45; ⊙Apr), as bald eagles migrate to winter in the river valley.

🛏 p155

The Drive » For the final leg of the trip, rejoin I-9 for an uneventful drive south. Just the other side of the highway, Ivoryton offers some good accommodation options. Leave I-9 at exit 70 onto CT 156 E, which will loop round onto Shore Rd. Then follow the signs into Old Lyme.

- - - - - - - - - - - - - - - - - -

TRIP HIGHLIGHT

7 Old Lyme

Since the early 20th century, Old Lyme has been the center of the Lyme Art Colony, which embraced and cultivated the nascent American impressionist movement. Numerous artists, including William Chadwick, Childe Hassam, Willard Metcalfe and Henry Ward Ranger, came here to paint, staying in the mansion of local art patron Florence Griswold.

Her house, which her artist friends decorated with murals (often in lieu of paying rent), is now the **Florence Griswold Museum** (☑860-434-5542; www.florencegriswoldmuseum.org; 96 Lyme St; adult/student/child $10/$8/free; ⊙10am-5pm Tue-Sat, 1-5pm Sun; 🅿) and contains a fine selection of both impressionist and Barbizon paintings. The estate consists of her Georgian-style house, the Krieble Gallery, the Chadwick studio and Griswold's beloved gardens.

🛏 p155

Eating & Sleeping

Hartford ❶

✕ Trumbull Kitchen
Modern American $$

(www.maxrestaurantgroup.com/trumbull; 150 Trumbull St; mains $13-30; ⊗ noon-11pm Mon-Sat, 4-10pm Sun) TK's smart-yet-casual fine-dining atmosphere awaits, with excellent service and a wonderfully executed, diverse menu. Drop in for a cocktail and some fabulous appetizers, or save that appetite for fish, chicken, burgers and steak, freshly prepared and presented like works of art: dressed-up comfort food.

✕ Bear's Smokehouse
Barbecue $$

(☎860-724-3100; www.bearsbbq.com; 89 Arch St; mains $10-20; ⊗11am-9pm) Locals love this wood-smoked Kansas-style barbecue famed for brisket, baby back ribs and pulled pork, and some kick-ass sides: collard greens, broccoli salad and mac 'n' cheese. Carnivores will dig the Moink balls (a little bit of 'moo' crossed with a little bit of 'oink'): bacon-wrapped meatballs with your choice of sauce.

⌂ Goodwin
Boutique Hotel $$$

(☎860-246-1881; www.goodwinhartford.com; 1 Haynes St; r from $359) This historic building reopened with a bang in 2017, redone in modern New York chic. The Queen Anne terra-cotta facade exudes the building's 19th-century origins while the inside oozes 21st-century cool. Convenient to the downtown scene, the Goodwin gives you no reason to leave the premises with its own charming bar-restaurant Porrón and Piña, managed by chef Tyler Anderson.

Glastonbury ❷

✕ Plan B
Burgers $$

(☎860-430-9737; www.burgersbeerbourbon. com; 120 Hebron Ave; mains $8-16; ⊗11:30am-midnight) The Glastonbury branch of this northeast burger chain is a rowdy joint with a cabinet of bourbon behind the bar, televised football games and red-leather booths. The burgers are 100% organic beef and come in a bewildering array of options. Try 'Three Shrooms,' with truffle mayo.

⌂ Connecticut River Valley Inn
B&B $$$

(☎860-633-7374; www.crvinn.com; 2195 Main St; d from $220; P ❈ ☎) This large Colonial clapboard sits proudly on Glastonbury's Main St and offers five handsome bedrooms, artfully decorated by host Pat Brubaker. The best bit is the sumptuous homemade breakfast, which features muffins and lavender scones, pancakes and hot salmon quiche.

Chester ❺

✕ River Tavern
Bistro $$$

(☎860-526-9417; www.rivertavernrestaurant. com; 23 Main St; lunches $12-22, meals $20-34; ⊗11:30am-2:30pm & 5-9pm Sun-Thu, to 10pm Fri & Sat) This popular wood-accented bistro with a bar and dining-room menu dishes up impeccable food. The menu changes, but if it's in season you should definitely order shad, caught from the Connecticut River. Save room for Toshi's made-to-order date pudding with dark rum caramel sauce – order ahead.

Essex ❻

⌂ Griswold Inn
Inn $$

(☎860-767-1776; www.griswoldinn.com; 36 Main St; d/ste from $195/240; P ☎) The 'Gris' is one of the country's oldest continually operating inns, Essex' physical and social centerpiece since 1776. The buffet-style Hunt Breakfast (11am to 1pm Sunday) is a tradition dating from the War of 1812, when British soldiers occupying Essex demanded to be fed.

Old Lyme ❼

⌂ Bee & Thistle Inn
Inn $$

(☎860-434-1667; www.beeandthistleinn.com; 100 Lyme St; r $150-289; P ☎) Occupying a handsome, Dutch Colonial farmhouse dating from 1756, this classy establishment has beautiful, well-tended gardens that stretch down to the Lieutenant River. Most of its 11 plush, well-appointed rooms feature abundant antiques and a canopy or four-poster bed.

Litchfield Hills Loop

14

The Litchfield Hills offer rolling, single-lane roads that pass sparkling lakes, enchanting forests, roaring waterfalls, must-stop farm stands and Colonial farmhouses. Take your time, enjoy the scenery and mind the curves.

TRIP HIGHLIGHTS

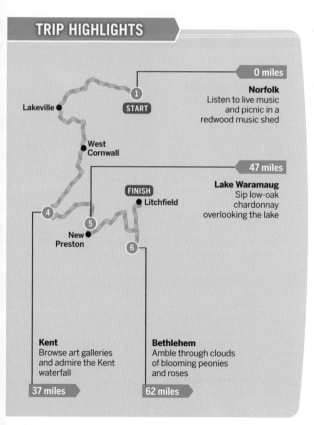

0 miles

Norfolk
Listen to live music and picnic in a redwood music shed

47 miles

Lake Waramaug
Sip low-oak chardonnay overlooking the lake

Kent
Browse art galleries and admire the Kent waterfall
37 miles

Bethlehem
Amble through clouds of blooming peonies and roses
62 miles

5 DAYS
77 MILES / 123KM

GREAT FOR...

BEST TIME TO GO
August to October for harvest bounty.

 ESSENTIAL PHOTO
Cornwall's picturesque covered bridge over the Housatonic.

 BEST FOR FOODIES
Dine in style in Litchfield and Bantam.

West Cornwall Covered Bridge

157

14 Litchfield Hills Loop

With scenery to match the Green Mountains of Vermont, pre-Colonial villages worthy of any movie set, and the finest food, culture and music in Connecticut, the Litchfield Hills attract a sophisticated crowd of weekending Manhattanites. But its hardwood forests, dappled river valleys, covered bridges, waterfalls, lakes and abundant fall fairs also offer endless possibilities for intrepid walkers, anglers, antiquers and history buffs.

TRIP HIGHLIGHT

❶ Norfolk

Norfolk's bucolic scenery and cool summers have long attracted prosperous New Yorkers. They built many of the town's fine mansions, its well-endowed Romanesque Revival library and its arts-and-crafts-style town hall, now the **Infinity Music Hall & Bistro** (☎866-666-6306; www.infinityhall.com; 20 Greenwoods Rd W/CT 44; ticket prices vary; ☺box office 11am-9pm Wed-Sun).

Most opulent of all was **Whitehall**, the summer estate of Ellen and Carl Battell Stoeckel, passionate (and moneyed) music lovers who established the **Norfolk Chamber Music Festival** (☎860-542-3000; www.norfolkmusic.org; 20 Litchfield Rd; tickets $25-100; ☺Jul-Aug). These extravagant affairs – the couple thought nothing of recruiting a 70-piece New York philharmonic orchestra and paying for a special train to transport it to their festival – were among the most popular summer events in New England. On her death in 1939, Ellen Stoeckel bequeathed the redwood 'Music Shed' to Yale University Summer School of Music, ensuring the tradition continues.

The Drive » Head west along the main, forest-lined route US

44 for Lakeville's twin town of Salisbury. From here it's a short, 1-mile drive along historic Main St to Lakeville's town center.

- - - - - - - - - - - - - - -

❷ Lakeville

The rolling farmland in this quiet and remote corner of the Litch-field Hills is home to millionaires and movie luminaries such as Meryl Streep. The Rockefel-lers favored the famous Hotchkiss preparatory school, and in Lakeville, Paul Newman raced the **Lime Rock Race Track** (www.limerock.com; 497 Lime Rock Rd/CT 112; ⏱Mar-Nov), which he thought was the most beautiful racing track in America. Today the seven-turn, 1.5-mile circuit hosts vintage and historic automobile races, along with regular stock-car races.

Otherwise, head to the peaks of **Bear Mountain**

LINK YOUR TRIP

❷ Fall Foliage Tour
Head north on CT 7 for leaf-peeping, walking and zip-lining in Massachusetts, Vermont and New Hampshire.

13 Lower River Valley
From Woodbury, take CT 84 for Mark Twain's hometown of Hartford and a leisurely drive down the Connecticut River Valley.

LOCAL KNOWLEDGE: BANTAM CINEMA

Locals know that one of the best things to do on rainy days is book in to see a film at the **Bantam Cinema** (☑860-567-0006 showtimes, 860-567-1916 box office; www.bantamcinema.com; 115 Bantam Lake Rd/CT 209, Bantam). Housed in a converted red barn on the shores of Lake Bantam, it's the oldest continuously operating movie theater in Connecticut and is a real Litchfield experience. The well-curated screenings focus on independent and foreign films, and the 'Meet the Filmmaker' series features guest directors, actors and producers, many of whom live here.

or **Lion's Head** for eye-popping panoramas. Part of the Appalachian National Scenic Trail (www.appalachiantrail.com), you'll find the trailheads leading off Rte 41.

🛏 p163

The Drive » Exit Lakeville south on Sharon Rd before picking up the CT 112 E past the Lime Rock Race Track. From here, the drive swoops south through rolling farmland, dotted with big red-and-white barns and stables. After 5 miles, turn south on US 7 into West Cornwall.

- - - - - - - - - - - - - - - - -

❸ West Cornwall

The village of West Cornwall is just one of six Cornwall villages in Connecticut, but it is the most famous thanks to its picturesque **covered bridge**. The bridge was known as the 'Kissing Bridge,' because horse-drawn carriages were able to slow down to a steady trot inside, thus

allowing their passengers a brief bit of alone time.

Otherwise, the area attracts nature-lovers and birders who come to hike, fish and boat on the Housatonic River. In winter, nearby **Mohawk Mountain Ski Area** (☑860-672-6100; www.mohawkmtn.com; 46 Great Hollow Rd) is the largest ski resort in the state, with 24 slopes and trails.

The Drive » The 14-mile drive south along US 7 to Kent from West Cornwall is the most scenic stretch of the trip, especially in fall, when the thickly forested hillsides are ablaze. The road runs parallel to the Appalachian Trail and Housatonic River for most of the way, offering lots of opportunities to stop and stretch your legs along the river.

- - - - - - - - - - - - - - - - -

TRIP HIGHLIGHT

❹ Kent

The area around Kent presents some of the loveliest rural scenery in the hills. At **Kent Falls State Park** (462 Kent Cornwall Rd/ CT 7; Mon-Fri free, Sat & Sun

$15; ☺8am-sunset), a waterfall tumbles 250ft over the rocky hillside. Hike the easy trail to the top, or just settle into a sunny picnic spot. Nearby, the **Sloane-Stanley Museum** (☑860-927-3849; www.ericsloane.com/museum.htm; 31 Kent Cornwall Rd; adult/child $8/5; ☺10am-4pm Wed-Sun May-Oct) houses a barn full of early American tools, collected by artist and author Eric Sloane, who painted the cloud-filled sky mural at the Smithsonian Air and Space Museum in Washington, DC. In autumn, the adjacent **Connecticut Industrial Museum** (☑860-927-0050; www.ctamachinery.com; 31 Kent Cornwall Rd; suggested donation adult/child $3/1.50; ☺10am-4pm Wed-Sun May-Oct; 🚹) is a fun, mostly outdoor child-friendly attraction with all manner of steam-powered locomotives. One inventive sculptor has turned his yard into a public art space called **Sculpture-dale** (☑860-927-3429; www.deniscurtissculptor.com; 3 Carter Rd, cnr Kent Cornwall Rd/US 7; ☺7am-dusk).

Worth a detour before heading east out of town is a drive further south to Bulls Bridge, the area's other drivable covered bridge.

🍴🛏 p163

The Drive » Take the CT 341 eastward out of Kent, climbing up out of the valley through more forested hills. After 10

Lake Waramaug View through trees

miles, turn south toward Warren along CT 45. After a further 1.6 miles, Lake Waramaug will peek between the trees on your left.

TRIP HIGHLIGHT

⑤ Lake Waramaug

Of the dozens of lakes and ponds in the Litchfield Hills, Lake Waramaug stands out. As you make your way around the northern shore of the lake on North Shore Rd, you'll come to the **Hopkins Vineyard** (☎860-868-7954; www.hopkinsvineyard.com; 25 Hopkins Rd, New Preston; tastings $12; ⏰10am-5pm Mon-Fri, to 7pm Sat, 11am-6pm Sun May-Dec, 10am-5pm Fri-Sun Jan-Feb, 10am-5pm Wed-Sun Mar & Apr). The wines here are made mostly from French American hybrids and the low-oak chardonnay frequently wins awards. The vineyard hosts wine tastings, and the view

from the bar is worth the trip, particularly when the foliage changes in the fall. Be sure to arrive well before closing time for a tasting, and call ahead during the low season.

 p163

The Drive ›› Leaving Lake Waramaug along North and East Shore Rd, turn left onto US 202 toward Bantam. At Lake Bantam, take CT 209 and 109 around the western and southern edges of the lake and after 3.5 miles turn right onto CT 61 S into Bethlehem.

↱ DETOUR: WOODBURY

Start: ⑥ Bethlehem

At the southern border of the Litchfield Hills, Woodbury is justifiably famous as the 'antiques capital' of Connecticut, boasting over 30 dealerships and 20 stores along historic Main St. Woodbury Antiques Dealers Association (www.antiqueswoodbury.com) publishes an online guide. While you're in Woodbury, don't forget to stop by the **Good News Cafe** (☎203-266-4663; www.good-news-cafe.com; 649 Main St S/US 6; mains $14-22; ⏰11:30am-10pm Mon & Wed-Sat, noon-10pm Sun; 🅿🚻). Run by Carole Peck, considered the Alice Waters of the East Coast, the cafe is a magnet for celebrities and lovers of fine food who come for the locally sourced farm produce and inventive, seasonal menus.

LOCAL KNOWLEDGE: WATERBIRDS

The **Livingston Ripley Waterfowl Conservancy** (☎860-567-2062; www.lrwc.net; 55 Duck Pond Rd, Litchfield; adult/senior/child $10/8/5, guided tours additional $30-50; ⏰10am-4pm Fri-Sun May 1–Nov 30; 🚻), home to former director of Yale's Peabody Museum and later a Smithsonian bigwig, S Dillon Ripley, hosts a collection of more species of waterbird (from around the world) than nearly any facility in the US. There's also a resident falconer and some spooky birds of prey, and even African cranes cavort around the expansive property.

TRIP HIGHLIGHT

⑥ Bethlehem

Bethlehem is Connecticut's 'Christmas Town' and every year thousands of visitors come for the **Christmas Fair** (https://christmastownfestival.com; Town Green; ⏰Dec) and to have their Christmas mail hand-stamped in the village post office.

The town's religious history extends to the founding of the first theological seminary in America by local resident Reverend Joseph Bellamy. His home, the **Bellamy-Ferriday House & Garden** (☎203-266-7596; www.ctlandmarks.org; 9 Main St N; adult/child $8/4; ⏰noon-4pm Thu-Sun May-Sep, noon-4pm Sat & Sun Oct), a 1750s clapboard mansion, is open to the public and is a treasure

trove of delftware, Asian art and period furnishings. Equally exquisite is the garden, the design of latter-day owner Caroline Ferriday, who designed it to resemble an Aubusson Persian carpet. Its geometrical box hedges are in-filled with frothing peonies, lilacs and heirloom roses.

The Drive » The final drive north to Litchfield passes through more bucolic scenery, dotted with country farmhouses and past the shores of Lake Bantam. Head north out of Bethlehem along CT 61, past the Bellamy-Ferriday House & Garden, then connect to CT 63 via Old Litchfield Rd, for a straight run into town.

⑦ Litchfield

The centerpiece of the region is Connecticut's best-preserved late-18th-century town. Founded in 1719 Litchfield

prospered as a main thoroughfare between New York and Boston. The town itself converges on a long oval green, and is surrounded by swaths of protected land. In late July or early August the **Litchfield Jazz Festival** (www.litchfieldjazzfest.com; Goshen Fair Grounds; ⏰Jul or Aug), in nearby Goshen, draws a thousands-strong crowd.

Walk down **North Street** and **South Street** (with a free walking tour sheet from the information kiosk) and admire the great mansions. Washington slept at the **Sheldon Tavern** on North St on his way to confer with General Rochambeau. Down the street, **Bull House** was home to Ludlow Bull, the American Egyptologist who participated in the discovery of Tutankhamen's gold-filled tomb. On South St, New Jersey judge Tapping Reeve founded America's first law school, the **Litchfield Law School** (☎860-567-4501; www.litchfieldhistoricalsociety.org; 82 South St/CT 63; ⏰11am-5pm Tue-Sat, 1-5pm mid-Apr–Nov), in 1775. Admission to the small **Litchfield History Museum** (☎860-567-4501; 7 South St; ⏰11am-5pm Tue-Sat, 1-5pm Sun mid-Apr–Nov) is included in the ticket.

🍴 p163

Eating & Sleeping

Lakeville ❷

🛏 Inn at Iron Masters   Motel $$

(📞860-435-9844; www.innatironmasters.com; 229 Main St/US 44; d from $159; P 🌐🎛🛜🎛) At first glance the one-story Inn at Iron Masters, in Lakeville, looks suspiciously like a Florida motel, but the rooms are slightly more elegant, the grounds feature gardens and gazebos, and there's a large common fireplace for chilly evenings. Efficient, if not B&B charming, it'll do in a pinch.

Kent ❹

✗ J.P. Gifford Market   Modern American $

(📞860-592-0200; www.jpgifford.com/kent; 12 N Main St; mains $10-12; 🕖7am-6pm Mon-Sat, to 3pm Sun) Gifford has expanded to two Litchfield locations, and the Kent market is a handy spot to get all-day breakfast burritos and intriguing sandwiches like the Chicken Cutlet Apple Melt. They also offer a few variations on the traditional burger and noodle bowls, all for a pretty decent price.

✗ Fife 'n' Drum   Diner $$

(📞860-927-3509; www.fifendrum.com; 53 Main St; mains $8-24; 🕦11:30am-10pm Mon-Sat, to 3pm Sun; P) If you're a fan of 1950s Americana, you'll love this dark woodsy restaurant-cum-diner-cum-bar attached to an inn of the same name. It's delightfully olde-worldly, serving hearty comfort food to get you through a day's driving around the Litchfield Hills, or to put you to sleep (if you're the lucky one in the passenger seat) for said day's driving.

🛏 Starbuck Inn   Inn $$$

(📞860-927-1788; www.starbuckinn.com; 88 N Main St; d $220-250) A B&B with a modern twist, including central air-conditioning and cable TV. Peter Starbuck, your host, makes sure you get a freshly prepared breakfast every day, sometimes featuring the house's famed blueberry pancakes. A lovingly prepared high tea is served at 4pm, and you're walking distance from all of Kent's shops and attractions.

Lake Warramaug ❺

✗ Community Table   Modern American $$$

(Ct; 📞860-868-9354; http://communitytablect.com; 223 Litchfield Turnpike/US 202, Washington; brunch $22-28, mains $26-42; 🕔5-9:30pm Sat, 10am-2pm & 3:30-9pm Sun; P) The name of this Scandinavian-inspired restaurant comes from the 300-year-old black-walnut table, where you can sit down to Sunday brunch. The modern American menu is locally sourced.

🛏 Hopkins Inn   Inn $$

(📞860-868-7295; www.thehopkinsinn.com; 22 Hopkins Rd, Warren; r $140-150, without bath $130, apt $160-250; 🕒closed Monn; P 🌐🎛) The 19th-century Hopkins Inn boasts a well-regarded restaurant with Austrian-influenced country fare (the chef whips up a mean schnitzel and mouthwatering pastries) and a variety of lodging options, from simple rooms with shared bathrooms to lake-view apartments. Whatever the season, there's something magical about sitting on the porch gazing upon Lake Waramaug and the hills. In the winter months the restaurant closes and the Hopkins becomes more of a B&B.

Litchfield ❼

✗ Peaches 'N Cream   Ice Cream $

(📞860-496-7536; www.peachesncreamicecream.com; 632 Torrington Rd; scoops $3; 🕛noon-9pm) This old-fashioned ice-cream parlor on the road to Torrington has been serving up homemade ice cream for decades. Seasonal flavors include the eponymous peaches 'n' cream, cashew cream, maple walnut and Kahlúa chocolate.

✗ West Street Grill   American $$$

(📞860-567-3885; www.weststreetgrill.com; 43 West St; mains $25-40; 🕦11:30am-9pm Wed-Sun) A Parisian-style bistro on Litchfield's historic green, this is one of the state's top restaurants. Over the years its inventive modern American cooking has earned it nods from *Gourmet* magazine and the *New York Times*. The Asian chicken salad with cabbage and mango is a crunchy delight.

STRETCH YOUR LEGS
NEWPORT

Start/Finish: International Tennis Hall of Fame

Distance: 4 miles

Duration: 3½ hours

Newport's status as a summer resort stretches back to the 19th century, when America's wealthiest industrialists erected mansions along Bellevue Ave. Admire their extravagant summer 'cottages,' which still line Newport's cliff tops, on this walk.

Take this walk on Trips

International Tennis Hall of Fame

To experience something of the 19th-century American aristocracy's approach to leisure, visit the **International Tennis Hall of Fame** (☏401-849-3990; www.tennisfame.com; 194 Bellevue Ave; adult/child $15/free; ◷10am-5pm Sep-Jun, to 6pm Jul & Aug, closed Tue Jan-Mar). It lies inside the Newport Casino building (1880), which served as a summer club for Newport's wealthiest residents. If you've brought your whites, playing on one of its 13 grass courts ($160 for one or two people per 90 minutes) is a delightful throwback to earlier times; otherwise, have a drink lawnside at the **La Forge Casino Restaurant**.

The Walk » Stroll along lantern-lined Bellevue Ave past Newport's first 'cottage,' the Elizabethan folly of Kingscote on the right. Further on you'll pass the National Museum of American Illustration on the left, before arriving at Rosecliff.

Rosecliff

Further down Bellevue Ave stands the impressive **Rosecliff** (☏401-847-1000; www.newportmansions.org; 548 Bellevue Ave; adult/child $17.50/8; ◷9am-4pm Apr–mid-Oct, hours vary mid-Oct–Mar; Ⓟ), built for Mrs Hermann Oelrichs, an heiress of the Comstock Lode silver discovery. Designed to look like the Grand Trianon at Versailles, its palatial ballroom and landscaped grounds quickly became the setting for some enormous parties. In June the **Newport Flower Festival** is held here.

The Walk » Continue straight along Bellevue Ave to reach Rough Point. In quick succession you'll pass the Astor's stucco mansion, Beechwood, on the left, along with William Vanderbilt's garishly opulent Marble House, with its white marble driveway and grand porte cochere.

Rough Point

While the splendor of the grounds alone is worth the price of admission to **Rough Point** (☏401-849-7300; www.newportrestoration.org/roughpoint/; 680 Bellevue Ave; adult/child $25/free; ◷9:30am-2pm

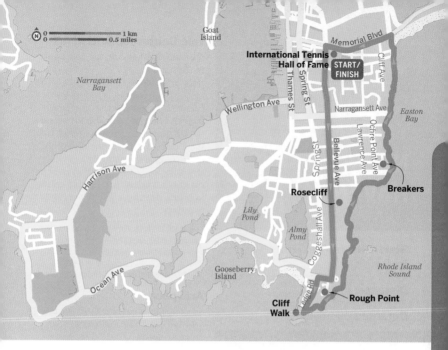

Thu-Sun Apr–early May, 9:30am-3:30pm Tue-Sun early May–early Nov; **P**), this faux-English manor house also contains Doris Duke's impressive art holdings, including medieval tapestries, furniture owned by French emperors, Ming-dynasty ceramics, and paintings by Renoir and Van Dyck. The house sits in a peerless location right on the point.

The Walk » To access the start of the Cliff Walk at Bailey's (Reject's) Beach, head right down to the end of Bellevue Ave. Before the avenue starts to merge with Ocean Ave, take a left down Ledge Rd to the trailhead.

Cliff Walk

In 1975, eager to protect their privacy, Newport's mansion owners sought to close **Cliff Walk** (www.cliffwalk.com; Memorial Blvd), the public footpath that snakes along the cliff top overlooking their front lawns. The move was prevented by local fishers and the 3.5-mile path was designated a National Recreation Trail. The best section runs from Ledge Rd near Rough Point to the Forty Steps

(each one named for someone lost at sea) on Narragansett Ave.

The Walk » Head down Ledge Rd, from Bellevue Ave, and pick up the Cliff Walk trail. The views are spectacular. The stretch between Ruggles Ave and Narragansett Ave is the most scenic, passing the Breakers, Vineland and French Gothic Ochre Court.

Breakers

Built at the behest of Cornelius Vanderbilt II, the **Breakers** (☎401-847-1000; www.newportmansions.org; 44 Ochre Point Ave; adult/child $24/8; ◷9am-5pm Apr–mid-Oct, hours vary mid-Oct–Mar; **P**) is the most magnificent of the Newport mansions. A 70-room Italian Renaissance mega-palace, it was inspired by 16th-century Genoese palazzi, and over 200 craftspeople were engaged to complete the lavish marquetry, mosaics and ornate sculptural details.

The Walk » Exit Cliff Walk up the Forty Steps, which brings you to Narragansett Ave. From here, it's a short walk back to Bellevue Ave. Turn right to return to the start and the International Tennis Hall of Fame for a drink.

STRETCH YOUR LEGS
NEW HAVEN

Start/Finish: Yale Center for British Art

Distance: 1.8 miles

Duration: 2½ hours

White-steepled churches, Colonial Revival buildings and neo-Gothic turrets form the stage-set for this exploration of New Haven's thriving arts scene, which includes Revolutionary canvases, rare manuscripts, community craftwork and avant-garde visual arts.

Take this walk on Trips

Yale Center for British Art

A Chapel St landmark, the **Yale Center for British Art** (☏203-432-2800; www.ycba. yale.edu; 1080 Chapel St; ⊕10am-5pm Tue-Sat, noon-5pm Sun) was Louis Kahn's last commission and is the setting for the largest collection of British art outside the UK. Spanning three centuries from the Elizabethan era to the 19th century, and arranged thematically as well as chronologically, the collection gives an insight into British art, life and culture in prints, drawings, watercolors and paintings.

The Walk » This half-mile walk takes you past the New Haven Green. The Center Church's white spire is visible above the trees and the Gothic Revival Trinity Church is on your left. After Temple St, take the second right onto Orange St.

ArtSpace

Specializing in contemporary visual arts and community outreach, non-profit **Artspace** (☏203-772-2709; www. artspacenh.org; 50 Orange St; ⊕noon-6pm Wed-Sat) organizes the annual **City-Wide Open Studios** (www.cwos.org; ⊕Oct) each fall. During the event it is possible to take a peek inside the workspaces of some of New Haven's up-and-coming artists. Check out the website for exact details.

The Walk » Retrace your steps to Church St and stroll northeast beside the green. On your right you'll pass the Federal Courthouse, the turreted City Hall and the Amistad Memorial. Continue onto Whitney Ave and then turn right on Audubon St.

Creative Arts Workshop

New Haven's Audubon Arts District is located between Whitney and Orange Sts. In its midst is the **Creative Arts Workshop** (☏203-562-4927; www.creative artsworkshop.org; 80 Audubon St; classes & workshops from $90; ⊕9am-7pm Mon-Thu, to 5pm Fri, to noon Sat), a visual arts studio that operates both as a cultural resource center and as an art school. Classes are available.

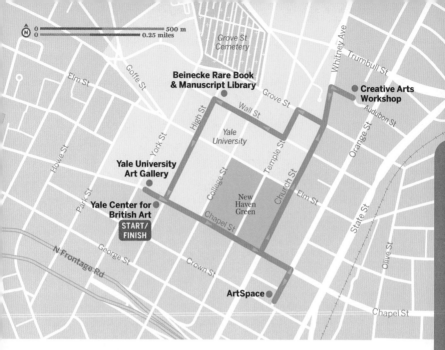

In June, the workshop and the art district are abuzz with activity, hosting events for the two-week-long **International Festival of Arts & Ideas** (www.artidea.org; ⊘Jun).

The Walk » Return to Whitney Ave, walk south and turn right on Grove St. Walk one block beside Timothy Dwight College, go left down Temple St and then right down Wall St. From here it's a pleasant tree-lined walk to Beinecke Plaza.

Beinecke Rare Book & Manuscript Library

On your stroll back, swing past the **Beinecke Rare Book & Manuscript Library** (☎203-432-2977; www.library.yale.edu; 121 Wall St; ⊘10am-7pm Mon, 9am-7pm Tue-Thu, 9am-5pm Fri). This extraordinary piece of architecture is the largest building in the world designed for the preservation of rare manuscripts. The windowless cube has walls of Danby marble, which subdue the effects of light, while inside glass towers display sculptural shelves

of books, including one of only 48 surviving Gutenberg Bibles (1455).

The Walk » Exit Beinecke Plaza westward onto High St. Walk southwest, passing Sterling Memorial Library on your right, and Dwight Hall on your left. At Chapel St, turn right and you'll find the modern exterior of the art gallery on your right.

Yale University Art Gallery

The oldest university art museum in the country, **Yale University Art Gallery** (☎203-432-0600; http://artgallery.yale.edu; 1111 Chapel St; ⊘10am-5pm Tue-Fri, to 8pm Thu, 11am-5pm Sat & Sun) was opened in 1832 with Colonel John Trumbull's collection of paintings depicting the American Revolution. Now it is home to 185,000 objects, including paintings, sculpture, silverware and artifacts from as far afield as Asia, South America and Africa.

The Walk » From the Yale University Art Gallery you can see the Yale Center for British Art across the street, where you started your walk.

Vermont

IF YOUR IDEA OF THE PERFECT ROAD TRIP involves slow-paced meandering through verdant countryside, Vermont may feel like paradise. Mountain ridges and narrow country roads ensure an ever-present sense of adventure as you zigzag through one of America's most uniformly bucolic landscapes. The Green Mountain State's eclectic allure combines outdoor adventure, photogenic villages and locavore eating – along with quirky claims to fame like the USA's highest per-capita concentration of microbreweries, public libraries and covered bridges. Newcomers invariably notice something different when they cross the state line. Perhaps it's the lack of billboards, or the enduring philosophy that 'small is beautiful,' but it's also Vermont's independent-minded, creative spirit – from politicians who eschew traditional party labels to world-class theater artists and cult-status brewers.

Mount Equinox View over Vermont mountains
RVCL ROB/SHUTTERSTOCK ©

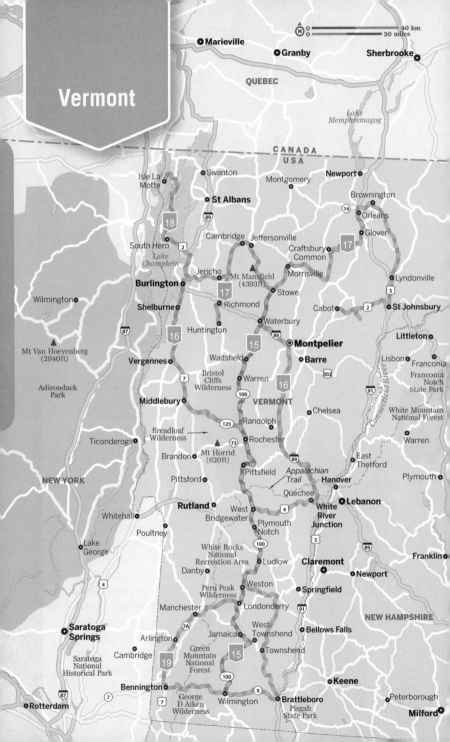

Stowe Fall foliage

DON'T MISS

Ben & Jerry's Factory Tour

Find out how two high-school pals created America's best-known ice cream on Trip 15

Boyden Valley Winery

Sip traditional varietals or maple-infused fruit wine at this celebrated winery with a gorgeous mountain backdrop on Trip 16

Stowe

Vermont's most stunning mountain village: a mix of traditional New England architecture in an awe-inducing setting. Visit on Trip 15

Magic Hat Brewery

Take an 'Artifactory' tour at Vermont's most creative microbrewery then sample the wares on Trip 18

Shelburne Museum

Learn about Vermont farm life and get a healthy dose of Americana on Trip 18

Classic Trip

Vermont's Spine: Route 100

15

Idyllic green landscapes, charming villages and scoops of America's most famous ice cream make this one of New England's most iconic road trips.

TRIP HIGHLIGHTS

130 miles — **9 FINISH**

Stowe
A postcard-worthy
New England village
nestled in the Green
Mountains

8 — **122 miles**

● Waitsfield

Ben & Jerry's Factory
Watch how they make
Chunky Monkey and
Cherry Garcia

Rochester ●

67 miles — **5**

Killington
Zip up the gondola for
awe-inducing
mountain views

● West
Bridgewater

3 — **38 miles**

Weston
Hit the state's most
famous country store

Wilmington ●
START

3–4 DAYS
130 MILES / 209KM

GREAT FOR...

BEST TIME TO GO

May to October for
snow-free roads and
sun-filled days.

 **ESSENTIAL
PHOTO**

The 360-degree views
from the K1 Gondola
above Killington.

 **BEST FOR
FAMILIES**

Poking around the
Weston country store
and taking a Ben &
Jerry's Factory tour.

Classic Trip

15 Vermont's Spine: Route 100

Spanning the state from bottom to top, Vermont's revered Route 100 winds past the Northeast's most legendary ski resorts and through some of New England's prettiest scenery, with the verdant Green Mountains always close at hand. This drive takes you on a slow meander through the state, though you might speed up in anticipation of the Ben & Jerry's Factory tour beckoning on the final stretch of road.

① Wilmington

Chartered in 1751, Wilmington is the winter and summer gateway to Mt Snow, one of New England's best ski resorts and an excellent summertime mountain-biking and golfing spot. There are no main sights per se, but the **Historic District** on W Main St is a prime example of 18th- and 19th-century architecture and is chock-full of restaurants and boutiques; the bulk of the village is on the National Register of Historic Places. This is an excellent base where you can stay overnight and grab a bite before your journey up north.

✖ p181

The Drive ›› Ski country (look for Mt Snow on your left) gives way to sleepy hamlets as you drive 26 miles north on VT 100 to the village of Jamaica.

② Jamaica

A prime dose of rural Vermont, with a country store and several antique shops, this artsy community tucked into the evergreen forest is also home to **Jamaica State Park** (☎802-874-4600; www.vtstateparks.com/jamaica.html; 48 Salmon Hole Lane; day use adult/child $4/2, campsites $20-22, lean-tos $27-29; ☺early May–mid-Oct), the best place in Vermont for riverside camping. The annual **Whitewater Weekend** held here in late September draws kayaking enthusiasts

from all over New England to pit their skills against the rampaging West River. There's good swimming right in the heart of the campground, and walkers can also head 3 miles upstream along a 19th-century railway bed to **Hamilton Falls**, a 50ft ribbon of water cascading into a natural swimming hole.

The Drive ›› Continue north 17 miles on VT 100 to Weston.

TRIP HIGHLIGHT

③ Weston

Picturesque Weston is home to the **Vermont Country Store** (☎802-824-3184; www.vermontcountrystore.com; 657 Main St/VT 100, Weston; ☺8:30am-7pm Jul–mid-Oct, 9am-6pm

rest of year), founded in 1946 and still going strong under the Orton family's ownership, four generations later. It's a time warp from a simpler era, when goods were made to last and quirky products with appeal had a home. The eclectic mix filling the shelves today ranges from the genuinely useful (cozy old-fashioned flannel nighties) to the nostalgic (vintage tiddlywinks and the classic 1960s board-game Mystery Date) to the downright weird (electronic yodeling pickles, anyone?). For a midtrip pick-me-up, prowl through their vast array of traditional penny-candy jars and enjoy free tastes of Vermont cheeses, cookies and other temptations.

The Drive » Continue north on VT 100. At Plymouth Union, veer off to the right onto VT 100A for about a mile until you reach Plymouth Center. The total drive is 22 miles.

LINK YOUR TRIP

16 Cider Season Sampler

From Killington, head west on US 4 to enjoy fall's delicious delights.

19 Southern Vermont Loop

In Weston, branch off onto this circle tour of southern Vermont..

Classic Trip

---

❹ Plymouth

Gazing across the high pastures of Plymouth, you feel a bit like Rip Van Winkle – only it's the past you've woken up to. President Calvin Coolidge's boyhood home looks much as it did a century ago, with houses, barns, a church, a one-room schoolhouse and a general store gracefully arrayed among old maples on a bucolic hillside. At Plymouth's heart is the preserved **President Calvin Coolidge State Historic Site** (📞802-672-3773; www.historicsites. vermont.gov; 3780 Rte 100A, Plymouth Notch; adult/child $10/2; ⏱10am-5pm late May–mid-Oct). The village's streets are sleepy today, but the museum tells a tale of an earlier America filled with elbow grease

and perseverance. Tools for blacksmithing, wood-working, butter making and hand laundering are indicative of the hard work and grit it took to wrest a living from Vermont's stony pastures. As a boy, Calvin hayed with his grandfather and kept the woodbox filled.

Cofounded by Coolidge's father, **Plymouth Artisan Cheese** (📞802-672-3650; www.plymouth artisancheese.com; 106 Messer Hill Rd; ⏱10am-5pm Jun-Oct, to 4pm Nov-May) still produces a classic farmhouse cheddar known as granular curd cheese. Its distinctively sharp tang and grainy texture are reminiscent of the wheel cheese traditionally found at general stores throughout Vermont. Panels downstairs tell the history of local cheese making, while a museum upstairs displays cheese-making equipment from another era.

ROBERT FROST'S VERMONT

In 1920 Robert Frost (1874–1963) moved from New Hampshire to Vermont seeking 'a better place to farm and especially grow apples.' For almost four decades, Frost lived in the Green Mountain State, growing apples and writing much of his poetry in a log cabin in **Ripton**, a beautiful hamlet set in the Green Mountains 12 miles west of VT 100, where he kept a summer home. Today, tiny Ripton and the surrounding area in the Green Mountain National Forest have been officially designated **Robert Frost Country**.

The Drive ⟫ Drive back along VT 100A and turn right to return to VT 100 N. The drive is 13 miles.

TRIP HIGHLIGHT

❺ Killington

The largest ski resort in the east, Killington spans seven mountains, highlighted by 4241ft **Killington Peak**, the second highest in Vermont. It operates the largest snow-making system in North America and its numerous outdoor activities – from skiing and snowboarding in winter to mountain biking and hiking in summer – are all centrally located on the mountain. **Killington Resort** (📞info 800-734-9435, reservations 800-621-6867; www.killington. com; 4763 Killington Rd; lift tickets adult/child/senior $124/95/105), the East Coast's answer to Vail, runs the efficient **K1-Express Gondola**, which in winter transports up to 3000 skiers per hour in heated cars along a 2.5-mile cable – it's the highest lift in Vermont. In summer and fall it whisks you to impeccable vantage points above the mountains: leaf-peeping atop the cascading rainbow of copper, red and gold in foliage season is truly magical.

The Drive ⟫ Enter the idyllic valley of the White River as you drive 24 miles north on VT 100 to Rochester.

DETOUR:
MIDDLEBURY & LINCOLN GAPS

Start: **6** **Rochester**

The 'gap roads' that run east–west over the Green Mountains offer some of the most picturesque views in Vermont. Ready to explore? Four miles north of Rochester, in Hancock, scenic VT 125 splits west off VT 100 and climbs over **Middlebury Gap**. Stops to look out for as you make the 15-mile crossing from Hancock to East Middlebury include beautiful **Texas Falls** (3 miles from Hancock), Middlebury Gap (6 miles) and the **Robert Frost Interpretive Trail**, an easygoing loop trail enlivened by plaques featuring Frost's poetry (10 miles). For a scenic loop back to the main route, continue west on VT 125 to East Middlebury, then take VT 116 north. Soon after crossing through the pretty village of **Bristol**, turn right on Lincoln Gap Rd and follow it 14 miles east to rejoin the main route at Warren. The return trip also offers some nice stops. As you turn onto Lincoln Gap Rd, look for the parked cars at **Bartlett Falls**, where the New Haven River's raging waters cascade into one of Vermont's most pristine swimming holes. Later, after a crazy-steep climb (partly unpaved) to **Lincoln Gap**, stop at the 2428ft summit for lovely views and some nice trails, including the 5-mile round trip to the 4000ft summit of **Mt Abraham**.

6 Rochester

This unassuming blink-and-you'll-miss-it town, with a vast village green lined by well-maintained, historic New England homes, is worth a stop to experience rural Vermont life minus the masses of tourists in other towns along VT 100.

Stop in at **Sandy's Books & Bakery** (☏802-767-4258; www.facebook.com/sandysbooksandbakery; 30 N Main St; baked goods & light meals $3-10; ☟7:30am-6pm Mon-Sat, to 3pm Sun; 🛜), a cafe, bookstore and popular local hang-out. With homemade everything – granola, bagels, whole-wheat bread – Sandy's serves up mean dishes such as spinach-and-egg-filled biscuits, spanako-pita, salads and soups.

Tables are scattered between bookshelves, so it's a great spot for a java break and a browse of the new and used books (or the locally made Vermont soap). We dare you to resist the cookies.

🛏 p181

The Drive » Continue north on VT 100. Roughly 10 miles past Rochester, a pullout on the left provides views to Moss Glen Falls. A mile or so later, the small ponds of Granville Gulf comprise one of the state's most accessible moose-watching spots. About 5 miles further north, turn right onto Covered Bridge Rd and cross the bridge into Warren village.

7 Warren

This sweet village is the southern gateway into Vermont's picturesque Mad River Valley. The river is popular with swimmers and kayakers, while the surrounding mountains are a mecca for skiers, who flock to the slopes at nearby **Sugarbush** (☏802-583-6300; www.sugarbush.com; 102 Forrest Dr; adult/child lift tickets $97/77) and **Mad River Glen** (☏802-496-3551; www.madriverglen.com; VT 17, Waitsfield; lift tickets adult/child $89/72).

Stop in at the Warren Store (p181) in the village center, an animated community hang-out with wavy 19th-century wood floors, a deli serving gourmet sandwiches and pastries, and a front porch ideal for sipping coffee while poring over the *New York Times*. The store upstairs sells an eclectic mix of jewelry, toys, Vermont casual clothing

BRIAN S/SHUTTERSTOCK ©

ALLARD ONE/SHUTTERSTOCK ©

WHY THIS IS A CLASSIC TRIP
GREGOR CLARK, WRITER

After 20-plus years living in Vermont, I'm still smitten with VT 100. No other route so fully captures Vermont's four-season beauty, from the Green Mountains' fall colors to the Mad River's ski areas and sculpted-rock swimming holes; from the lonely moose country near Granville to the cozy village feel of Weston. For an unforgettable add-on, climb VT 108 from Stowe through Smugglers Notch at trip's end.

Above: Vermont Country Store, Weston
Left: Ben & Jerry's Factory, Waterbury
Right: Killington Resort

and knickknacks, while the sundeck below overlooks a pretty swimming hole framed by sculpted granite rocks.

✗ ⊨ p181

The Drive » Continue north 20 miles on VT 100 through pretty farm country to Waterbury, then follow signs for Stowe, crossing the overpass over I-89 to reach Ben & Jerry's.

TRIP HIGHLIGHT

❽ Ben & Jerry's Factory

No trip to Vermont would be complete without a visit to **Ben & Jerry's Factory** (📞802-882-2047; www.benjerry.com/about-us/factory-tours; 1281 VT 100, Waterbury; adult/under 13yr $4/free; ⏰9am-9pm Jul–mid-Aug, shorter hours rest of year; ♿), the biggest production center for America's most famous ice cream. Sure, the manufacturing process is interesting, but a visit here also explains how school pals Ben and Jerry went from a $5 ice-cream-making correspondence course to a global enterprise, and offers a glimpse of the fun, in-your-face culture that made these frozen-dessert pioneers so successful. You're treated to a (very) small free taste at the end – for larger doses head to the on-site scoop shop.

Quaintly perched on a knoll overlooking the parking lot, the Ben & Jerry's Flavor Graveyard's neat rows of headstones pay silent tribute to

flavors that flopped, like Makin' Whoopie Pie and Dastardly Mash. Each memorial is lovingly inscribed with the flavor's brief life span on the grocery store of this earth and a tribute poem. Rest in peace, Holy Cannoli (1997–98)! Adieu, Miss Jelena's Sweet Potato Pie (1992–93)!

The Drive » Wipe that icecream smile off your face and replace it with an ear-to-ear grin as you continue 9 miles up VT 100 to the legendary ski village of Stowe.

9 Stowe

In a cozy valley where the West Branch River flows into the Little River and mountains rise to the sky in all directions, the quintessential Vermont village of Stowe (founded in 1794) bustles quietly. Nestled in the Green Mountain National Forest, the highest point in Vermont, Mt Mansfield (4393ft) towers in the background, juxtaposed against the pencil-thin steeple of Stowe's Community Church, creating *the* classic Vermont picture-postcard scene.

With more than 200 miles of cross-country ski trails, some of the finest mountain biking and downhill skiing in the east and world-class hiking, this is a natural mecca for adrenaline junkies and active families. If shopping and cafe-hopping are more your style, the village center also makes a delightful spot for a leisurely stroll. In addition to winter snow sports, **Stowe Mountain Resort**

(📞802-253-3000; www. stowe.com; 5781 Mountain Rd; lift ticket adult $85-115, child $72-98) opens from spring through to fall with gondola sky rides, an alpine slide and a scenic auto toll road that zigzags to the top of Mt Mansfield.

If *The Sound of Music* is one of your favorite things, the hilltop Trapp Family Lodge boasts sprawling views and oodles of activities, such as hiking, horse-drawn sleigh and carriage rides, lodge tours detailing the family history (often led by a member of the Trapp family), summer concerts on their meadow and some frothy goodness at the nearby **Von Trapp Bierhall** (📞802-253-5750; www.vontrappbrewing.com/ bierhall.htm; 1333 Luce Hill Rd; mains $13-31; ⏲11:30am-9pm).

🍴 🛏 p181

DETOUR:
VERMONT ICELANDIC HORSE FARM

Start: 7 Warren

Icelandic horses are one of the oldest, and some say most versatile, breeds in the world. They're also friendly and unbelievably affectionate creatures, and are fairly easy to ride even for novices – they tend to stop and think (rather than panic) if something frightens them. The **Vermont Icelandic Horse Farm** (📞802-496-7141; www. icelandichorses.com; 3061 N Fayston Rd, Waitsfield; 1-3hr rides $60-120, full day incl lunch $220, multiday treks $675-1695; ⏲by appointment; 🐴), 3 miles west of VT 100 (where the tarmac ends and becomes a dirt road), takes folks on one- to three-hour or full-day jaunts year-round; it also offers two- to five-day inn-to-inn treks (some riding experience required). The farm also runs **Mad River Inn** (📞802-496-7900; www.madriverinn.com; 243 Tremblay Rd, Waitsfield; r $115-150; 🅿🛜), a pleasant inn a short trot away. Head 9 miles north of Warren on VT 100 and follow the signs to the horse farm.

Eating & Sleeping

Wilmington ❶

✗ Folly   Bistro $$$

([☎]802-464-1333; www.vtfolly.com; 33 W Main St; mains $25-35; [🕐]5:30-9pm Fri-Sun) Book ahead for this fabulous little bistro, which only opens three nights a week. The inspired menu changes weekly, drawing on a diversity of ingredients and international influences – from quail to octopus to wild mushrooms, and from Alpine to Italian to South American – but delivering consistently interesting, delicious and beautifully presented results.

Rochester ❻

⌂ Liberty Hill Farm   B&B $$

([☎]802-767-3926; www.libertyhillfarm.com; 511 Liberty Hill Rd; r incl dinner & breakfast per adult/teen/child $139/75/65) With its magnificent red barn and White River Valley panoramas, this working farm just south of Rochester is a Vermont classic. Overnight stays include dinner and breakfast, served family-style and making ample use of produce from the on-site garden. Other highlights include lounging on the front porch, getting to know the farm animals and sampling the farm's ultrafresh dairy products.

Warren ❼

✗ Warren Store   Sandwiches $

([☎]802-496-3864; www.warrenstore.com; 284 Main St; sandwiches & light meals $5-9; [🕐]7:45am-7pm) This atmospheric country store serves the area's best sandwiches along with delicious pastries and breakfasts. In summer, linger over coffee on the front porch, or eat on the deck overlooking the waterfall, then descend for a cool dip among river-sculpted rocks.

⌂ Inn at Round Barn Farm   Inn $$$

([☎]802-496-2276; www.theroundbarn.com; 1661 E Warren Rd, Waitsfield; r $179-359; [🛜][❄]) This place gets its name from the adjacent 1910 round barn – among the few authentic examples remaining in Vermont. The decidedly upscale inn has antique-furnished rooms with mountain views, gas fireplaces, canopy beds and antiques. All overlook the meadows and mountains. In winter guests leave their shoes at the door to preserve the hardwood floors. The country-style breakfast is huge.

Stowe ❾

✗ Hen of the Wood   Modern American $$$

([☎]802-244-7300; www.henofthewood.com; 92 Stowe St, Waterbury; small plates $12-15, mains $22-35; [🕐]5-9pm Tue-Sat) Arguably the finest dining in Northern Vermont, this chef-driven restaurant, set in a historic grist mill in Waterbury, gets rave reviews for its innovative farm-to-table cuisine. The ambience is as fine as the food, which features seasonal ingredients such as wild mushrooms and densely flavored dishes like smoked duck breast or sheep's-milk gnocchi.

⌂ Trapp Family Lodge   Lodge $$$

([☎]802-253-8511; www.trappfamily.com; 700 Trapp Hill Rd; r $175-425, ste $275-750; [@][🛜][❄][🐕]) This hilltop lodge 3km above town boasts Stowe's most dramatic setting. The Austrian-style chalet, built by Maria von Trapp of *The Sound of Music* fame (note the family photos lining the walls), houses 96 traditional lodge rooms, many newly renovated and most with balconies affording lovely mountain vistas. Alternatively, rent one of the cozy villas or guesthouses scattered across the property.

Cider Season Sampler

Early fall in Vermont is radiant, with farm stands overflowing and colorful leaves ablaze. Fresh-pressed cider, pick-your-own berries, craft breweries and a thriving locavore movement make this an epicure's delight.

16

TRIP HIGHLIGHTS

Cambridge

Burlington

5

93 miles

Montpelier

Shelburne
Hop in a wagon and take a farm tour

Middlebury

3

1 START/ FINISH

Bridgewater Corners
Decide if Long Trail is your favorite Vermont craft beer

15 miles

Quechee
Stare down at Vermont's version of the Grand Canyon

0 miles

3–4 DAYS
229 MILES / 369KM

GREAT FOR...

BEST TIME TO GO
August to October – apple-picking is at its prime.

ESSENTIAL PHOTO

Shelburne Farms orchards in the late-afternoon light.

☑ **BEST FOR FOODIES**

Award-winning cheddar and crisp apples from Shelburne Farms, or divine meals with a waterfall view at Simon Pearce.

Middlebury Apple orchard

183

16 Cider Season Sampler

When most people think 'Vermont food and drink,' beer or maple syrup come to mind. But these days, vineyards, makers of craft cider and locavore restaurants are also sprouting up around the state. Chefs, farmers and communities have begun working together in mutually supportive ways, revitalizing local culture as they build on Vermont's deep agricultural roots. Fall, with its blaze of colors, is the best time to embrace the bounty.

TRIP HIGHLIGHT

1 Quechee

Vermont's tongue-in-cheek answer to the Grand Canyon, the **Quechee Gorge** is a 163ft-deep scar that cuts about 3000ft along the Ottauquechee River. View it from the bridge or work off those pancake breakfasts with a hike to the bottom – the 15-minute descent through pine forest is beautiful, following a trail on the south side of US 4.

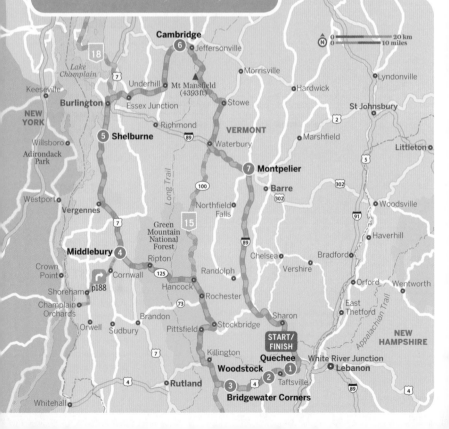

In downtown Quechee Village, make a beeline for **Simon Pearce Glass** (☎802-295-2711; www.simon pearce.com; 1760 Quechee Main St; ⊕10am-9pm), in the old woolen mill cantilevered out over the Ottauquechee River. Pearce, an Irish glassblower, immigrated to Quechee in 1981, drawn by a vision of running his entire operation self-sufficiently with hydropower. Three decades later, he's built a small empire. His flagship Quechee store displays pottery and glassware and offers glassblowing demonstrations daily.

 p189

The Drive » Follow US 4 west for 7 miles to Woodstock.

 LINK YOUR TRIP

15 Vermont's Spine: Route 100

Connect to VT 100 from Cambridge via mountain-hugging VT 108 through Smugglers Notch.

18 Lake Champlain Byway

In Shelburne you can connect with this scenic journey up through Vermont's Champlain Islands.

VERMONT FRESH NETWORK

Fresh local food is never far away in the Green Mountain State, thanks to the Vermont Fresh Network (www.vermontfresh.net), a partnership between the state's restaurants and farmers. Restaurants commit to supporting local producers by buying direct from the farm, while 'farmers dinners' throughout the year allow diners to meet the people who put the food on their table. For a full list of participating restaurants and upcoming events, see their website.

---

2 Woodstock

Chartered in 1761, Woodstock has been the highly dignified seat of scenic Windsor County since 1766. The townspeople built grand Federal and Greek Revival homes surrounding the oval village green, and four of Woodstock's churches can claim bells cast by Paul Revere. Senator Jacob Collamer, a friend of Abraham Lincoln's, once observed, 'The good people of Woodstock have less incentive than others to yearn for heaven.'

Billings Farm & Museum (☎802-457-2355; www.billingsfarm.org; 69 Old River Rd; adult/child $16/8; ⊕10am-5pm daily Apr-Oct, to 4pm Sat, Sun & holidays Nov-Feb; ☒) employs a mix of 19th- and 20th-century methods. Visitor activities are seasonal, from horse and sleigh rides and afternoon milking of cows to demonstrations

of strawberry shortcake made in a cast-iron stove.

At the adjacent **Marsh-Billings-Rockefeller National Historical Park** (☎802-457-3368; www.nps. gov/mabi; 54 Elm St; mansion tours adult/child $8/free, trails & carriage roads free; ⊕ visitor center & tours 10am-5pm late May-Oct, trails & carriage roads year-round), a 20-mile network of carriage paths and trails wind through the beautifully conserved fields and forests surrounding Mt Tom. The centerpiece is a 19th-century mansion once owned by early American conservationist George Perkins Marsh and members of the Rockefeller family. Combined tickets with the Billings Farm & Museum are available.

 p139, p189

The Drive » Drive west on US 4 for 8 miles to Bridgewater Corners, following the curve of the Ottauquechee a few miles upstream.

TRIP HIGHLIGHT

❸ Bridgewater Corners

Just off the road on the left, **Long Trail Brewing Company** (☎802-672-5011; www.longtrail.com; 5520 US 4 at VT 100A; ☺10am-7pm) is one of Vermont's leading producers of craft beer. On a sunny day, it's delightful to sit in its riverside beer garden, modeled after Munich's Hofbrauhaus. Inside is a cozy beer hall that's great for sampling brews. Check out the self-guided brewery tour on the 2nd floor – panels on the small observation platform explain the beer-making process unfolding on the floor below.

The Drive » Take US 4 for 12 miles west through Killington, then head north 23 miles on VT 100 to Hancock. From here, scenic VT 125 snakes 20 miles west over the Green Mountains into Middlebury.

❹ Middlebury

Middlebury's original claim to fame was its prestigious liberal-arts college, founded here in 1800. The pretty campus, dotted with buildings constructed of local marble and gray limestone, makes for a pleasant stroll, as does the pedestrian bridge along the base of Otter Creek Falls in the heart of town.

Surrounded by fertile farm and orchard land, Middlebury is also a leader in Vermont's locavore movement and a major producer of craft beer and cider. On Wednesdays and Saturdays in summer, head down to the Marble Works, near the falls, to revel in the cornucopia of organic produce at the twice-weekly **farmers market**. Just under 2 miles north, you can stop at **Wood-**

Quechee Quechee Gorge

chuck Cidery (📞802-385-3656; www.woodchuck.com/ciderhouse; 1321 Exchange St; 🕐11am-6pm Wed-Fri, to 5pm Sat & Sun), Vermont's largest producer of hard cider, for tastes ($3 gets you any four flavors from their dozen-plus lineup), or hop on over to **Otter Creek Brewing** (📞802-388-0727; www.ottercreek brewing.com; 793 Exchange St; 🕐11am-6pm Sat-Thu, to 7pm Fri), where you can watch the brewers at work while enjoying lunch and a four-beer sampler in the adjacent brewpub. If wine tasting is more your thing, continue 2 miles north on US 7 to

New Haven's Lincoln Peak Vineyard (www.lincolnpeakvineyard.com), one of the finest wineries in the state.

 p189

The Drive » Head north 27 miles on US 7 into Shelburne, then take Harbor Rd 1.6 miles northwest to Shelburne Farms.

- - - - - - - - - - - - - - - -

TRIP HIGHLIGHT

⑤ Shelburne

In 1886 William Seward Webb and Lila Vanderbilt Webb built a little place for themselves on Lake Champlain. The 1400-acre farm, designed by landscape architect Frederick Law Olmsted (who

also designed New York City's Central Park), was both a country house for the Webbs and a working farm. These days, the century-old estate and National Historic Landmark exists as Shelburne Farms (p205), a working farm and environmental education center.

Tours in a truck-pulled open wagon are a barrel of fun: you can admire the buildings (inspired by European Romanticism), observe cheese-making and learn about maple syrup and mustard production. Hikers can meander the walking trails and kids

DETOUR: CHAMPLAIN ORCHARDS

Start: ❹ **Middlebury**

Wide-open farm country cascades toward Lake Champlain as you detour 16 miles southwest from Middlebury along VT 30 and VT 74 to **Champlain Orchards** (☎802-897-2777; www.champlainorchards. com; 3597 VT 74 W, Shoreham; ☺9am-5pm; 🚻). Here you can pick two dozen varieties of apples – including many New England heirloom varieties – or watch the pressing and bottling of ultrafresh cider. The orchard is famous for its free 'while-you-pick' acoustic concerts and an annual October harvest celebration.

love the animals in the children's farmyard. In mid-September, drop by and celebrate autumn traditions at the annual **Harvest Festival**, featuring hay rides, a hay-bale maze, music and antique farm machines.

🛏 p205

The Drive ≫ Head north on US 7 through Burlington. Hop on VT 15, then VT 128 and VT 104 to Cambridge. The drive is 35 miles.

- - - - - - - - - - - - - - -

❻ Cambridge

Tucked into the stunningly beautiful Lamoille River valley at the foot of Mt Mansfield, **Boyden Valley Winery** (☎802-644-8151; www.boydenvalley. com; 64 VT 104; ☺10am-6pm Tue-Sat May-Oct, to 5pm Tue-Sat Nov & Dec, to 5pm Thu-Sat Jan-Mar) is one of Vermont's leading producers of dessert wines. Savor

the views and check out the award-winning Gold Leaf, a Vermont-inspired concoction that uses maple syrup straight from the farm combined with local apples.

The Drive ≫ For spectacular mountain scenery, take VT 108 south through Smugglers Notch to Stowe, then pick up VT 100 south to Waterbury and hop on I-89 east to Montpelier. The drive is 42 miles.

- - - - - - - - - - - - - - -

❼ Montpelier

With 9000 residents, Montpelier is America's smallest capital city and the only one without a McDonald's. It's home to the prestigious **New England Culinary Institute** (NECI; www.neci.edu) – stop for a dose of Vermont history paired with fine food.

Adjacent to the gold-domed **State House**

(☎802-828-1411; www. vtstatehousefriends.org; 115 State St; ☺guided tours 10am-3:30pm Mon-Fri, 11am-2:30pm Sat Jul–mid-Oct, 9am-3pm Mon-Fri mid-Oct–Jun), whose front doors are guarded by a massive statue of American Revolutionary hero Ethan Allen, is **Vermont History Museum** (☎802-828-2291; www.vermonthistory.org/visit/vermont-history-museum; 109 State St; adult/child $7/5; ☺10am-4pm Tue-Sat). Its award-winning 'Freedom and Unity' (the state motto) exhibit shows 400 years of Vermont history. From your first steps into an Abenaki wigwam, you're asked to consider the true meaning of this phrase. Controversies aren't brushed under the rug: a short film presents the early-20th-century debate over women's suffrage alongside footage from the 1999 statehouse hearings where citizens voiced support for or opposition to civil unions. In a very Vermontish way, you're invited to ponder issues on your own regardless of any party line. The panoply of voices and imaginative presentation keep this exhibit fun and lively.

✗ 🛏 p189

The Drive ≫ From Montpelier, a straight 54-mile shot down I-89 returns you to your starting point at Quechee.

Eating & Sleeping

Quechee ❶

✗ Simon Pearce Restaurant
Modern American $$$

(☎802-295-1470; www.simonpearce.com; 1760 Quechee Main St; mains lunch $14-19, dinner $23-33; ⏱11:30am-2:45pm & 5:30-9pm) Few views in Vermont compare with those from the window tables overlooking spectacular Ottauquechee Falls in Simon Pearce's dining room, suspended over the river in a converted brick mill. Local ingredients are used to fine effect in salads, cheese plates and dishes such as braised lamb shoulder or cider-brined chicken. The restaurant's stemware is hand-blown in the adjacent glass workshop (p185).

Woodstock ❷

✗ Mon Vert Cafe
Cafe $

(☎802-457-7143; www.monvertcafe.com; 28 Central St; breakfast $7-13, lunch $9-11; ⏱7:30am-5:30pm Mon-Thu, to 6:30pm Fri & Sat, 8am-5:30pm Sun) Pop into this cheerful two-level cafe for croissants, scones, egg sandwiches and maple lattes in the morning, or settle in on the front patio for salads and panini at lunchtime. A large map of Vermont and New Hampshire highlights the multitude of farms and food purveyors that provide the restaurant's locally sourced ingredients.

Middlebury ❹

✗ American Flatbread
Pizza $$

(☎802-388-3300; www.americanflatbread. com/restaurants/middlebury-vt; 137 Maple St; flatbreads $9-25; ⏱5-9pm Tue-Sat) In a cavernous marble-block building with a bustling bar and blazing fire that keeps things cozy in winter, this is one of Middlebury's most beloved

eateries. The menu revolves around farm-fresh salads and custom-made flatbreads (don't call it pizza or they'll come after you with the paddle) topped with locally sourced organic cheeses, meat and veggies, accompanied by Vermont microbrews.

⭗ Swift House Inn
Inn $$

(☎802-388-9925; www.swifthouseinn.com; 25 Stewart Lane; r $165-299; 🐾) Two blocks north of the town green, this grand white Federal mansion (1814) is surrounded by formal lawns and gardens. Luxurious standard rooms in the main house and adjacent carriage house are supplemented by suites with fireplaces, sitting areas and hot tubs. Other welcome luxuries include a steam room and sauna, a cozy pub, a library and a sun porch.

Montpelier ❼

✗ Three Penny Taproom
Pub Food $

(☎802-223-8277; www.threepennytaproom. com; 108 Main St; burgers $6-14, mains $9-16; ⏱kitchen 11am-9pm Mon-Thu, to 10pm Fri & Sat, to 4pm Sun, bar to midnight Mon-Thu, to 2am Fri & Sat, to 6pm Sun) Pouring two dozen microbrews from Vermont and beyond, this pub is a perennial late-night favorite. It's also popular for its pub grub: grilled cheese and soup, Greek quinoa salad, fish and chips, and the budget-saving 'flatty,' a 2oz burger with Vermont cheddar and a half order of fries.

⭗ Inn at Montpelier
Inn $$

(☎802-223-2727; www.innatmontpelier.com; 147 Main St; r $170-300; ✴🐾) This first-rate inn made up of two refurbished Federal houses sits smack in the heart of town. All the rooms are luxuriously furnished, including some deluxe units with ornamental fireplaces. The wraparound veranda makes a delightful spot to enjoy the included homemade continental breakfast or a lazy afternoon of reading.

Northeast Kingdom to Camel's Hump

17

From Vermont's sparsely populated 'Northeast Kingdom' to the dramatic beauty of the Green Mountains' highest peaks, this back-road ramble through northern Vermont mixes off-the-beaten-track treasures with iconic villages and scenery.

TRIP HIGHLIGHTS

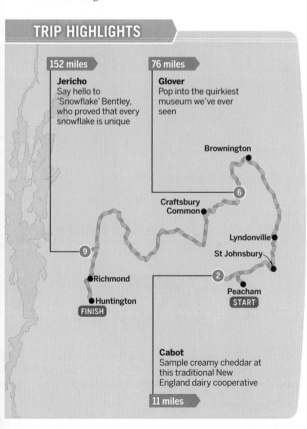

152 miles

Jericho
Say hello to 'Snowflake' Bentley, who proved that every snowflake is unique

76 miles

Glover
Pop into the quirkiest museum we've ever seen

Brownington

6

Craftsbury
Common

Lyndonville

St Johnsbury

9

Richmond

2

Peacham
START

Huntington
FINISH

Cabot
Sample creamy cheddar at this traditional New England dairy cooperative

11 miles

3–4 DAYS
169 MILES / 272KM

GREAT FOR...

BEST TIME TO GO

May to October for warmish weather and snow-free roads.

ESSENTIAL PHOTO

Snap the papier-mâché creatures at the Bread & Puppet Museum.

BEST FOR OUTDOORS

Enjoy stunning vistas of bucolic rolling hills and peaceful, sparsely populated countryside.

17

Northeast Kingdom to Camel's Hump

Some say this is the real Vermont: historic villages frozen in time, narrow mountain passes and expanses of farmland stretching out to lush, maple-covered mountains. A word of warning: this trip is full of curves, lesser-known attractions and dirt roads without phone service. Translation? This trip is perfect for spontaneous explorers ready to embrace Vermont's quirky spirit of off-the-radar backroad adventure.

❶ Peacham

Surrounded by a dreamy landscape of high pastures and stone walls, Peacham is one of Vermont's quintessential historic villages. Originally a stop on the Bayley–Hazen Military Rd – intended to help Americans launch a sneak attack on the British during the Revolutionary War – Peacham today retains a sleepy, lost-in-time quality. Take a self-guided **walking tour** using the free brochure from the town

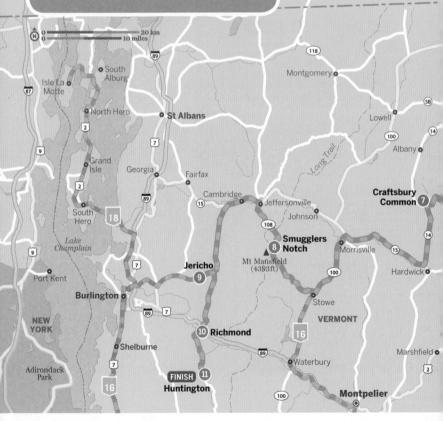

library, or browse the antiques and handicrafts at the **Peacham Corner Guild**.

The Drive ⟫ Head northwest over the mountains on unpaved Mack Mountain Rd; 7 miles out, a quick drive west on US 2 brings you to Danville Hill Rd, which plunges steeply down to Cabot. The drive is 11 miles.

TRIP HIGHLIGHT

❷ Cabot

Despite its nationwide distribution network, **Cabot Creamery** (☏800-837-4261; www.cabotcheese. coop; 2878 Main St; ⏱9am-

5pm mid-May–Oct, 10am-4pm Nov & Dec, 10am-4pm Mon-Sat Jan–mid-May) remains basically true to its roots as a New England dairy cooperative. A video tour of the creamery gives you a look at the cheese-making process (not to mention high-tech machinery painted like Holstein cows), after which you can pig out to your heart's content in the sample room.

The Drive ⟫ Backtrack 3.5 miles up Danville Hill Rd, then follow US 2 east for 14 miles into St Johnsbury.

----

❸ St Johnsbury

Home to America's oldest art gallery (founded in 1871) still preserved in its original layout, the **St Johnsbury Athenaeum** (☏802-748-8291; www. stjathenaeum.org; 1171 Main St; $5 donation requested; ⏱10am-5:30pm Mon, Wed & Fri, noon-7pm Tue & Thu, 10am-3pm Sat) is built around its crown jewel, Albert Bierstadt's 10ft-by-15ft painting *Domes of the*

Yosemite. The rest of the collection consists of works by such Hudson River School painters as Asher B Durand, Worthington Whittredge and Jasper Cropsey.

 p197

The Drive ⟫ Take exit 23 off I-91 north in Lyndonville, then continue north on US 5 and VT 5A to Lake Willoughby, 27 miles away.

----

❹ Lake Willoughby

Sandwiched between Mt Hor and Mt Pisgah, whose cliffs plummet more than 1000ft to the waters below, this stunningly beautiful glacial lake resembles a landlocked fjord. To appreciate the dramatic scenery, head for the good swimming beach at the lake's northern tip, or climb to one of the surrounding summits. The **South Trail** to Mt Pisgah (3.4 miles, three-hour round trip) and the easier **Herbert Hawkes Trail** to Mt Hor (1.9 miles, 1½-hour round trip) both begin just

Irasburg
⑤ **Brownington**
Orleans
Lake ④
Willoughby
Glover ⑥
p194
Hill Farmstead Brewery
Lyndonville
Cabot ②
St Johnsbury ③
① **Peacham**
START
Mcindoe Falls

LINK YOUR TRIP

16 **Cider Season Sampler**

After Craftsbury Common, join the Cider Season Sampler trip in Cambridge for a taste of Vermont's harvest season.

18 **Lake Champlain Byway**

After hitting Richmond, hop on I-89 north to Burlington for a trip along pristine islands and jagged shorelines.

south of the great cleft along Lake Willoughby's southern shore.

The Drive >> Head briefly north of the lake on VT 5A, then turn left onto Schoolhouse Rd, continuing west into Brownington. The drive is 7 miles.

⑤ Brownington

Brownington's well preserved but little-visited **Old Stone House Museum** (☎802-754-2022; www. oldstonehousemuseum.org; 109 Old Stone House Rd; adult/ child $10/5; ⊙11am-5pm Wed-Sun mid-May–mid-Oct) is just one of many lovely 19th-century buildings reposing under the shade of equally ancient maple trees. The museum pays tribute to educational trailblazer Alexander Twilight, the USA's first African American college graduate, who built

Brownington's boarding school and ran it for decades.

The Drive >> Take VT 58 west, I-91 south and VT 16 south to Glover (13 miles), then turn left onto VT 122 and look for the Bread & Puppet Museum on your left within less than 1 mile.

TRIP HIGHLIGHT

⑥ Glover

A bright-turquoise school bus parked across from a barn with painted letters proclaiming 'Cheap Art Store' is your sign that you've stumbled upon the **Bread & Puppet Museum** (☎802-525-3031; www. breadandpuppet.org/museum; 753 Heights Rd; donations welcome; ⊙10am-6pm Jun-Oct, self-serve access only Nov-May). For nearly 50 years, the internationally renowned Bread & Puppet Theater has been staging politically

charged, avant-garde satirical spectacles starring gigantic papier-mâché puppets (some up to 20ft tall) borne through the fields on the company's hilltop farm. Vermont performances take place on weekends in July through August.

When no show is going on (the troupe tours nationally and internationally outside summer), visit the museum in the cavernous old barn and admire freakishly impressive angels, devils, horses and other fantastic creatures from past performances, hauntingly crammed over two stories. Oh, and about that name? The troupe bakes bread and shares it with the audience at each performance to create a sense of community.

🛏 p197

DETOUR:
HILL FARMSTEAD BREWERY

Start: ⑥ Glover

You know you're getting close when the asphalt disappears and you haven't had a phone signal for 30 minutes. Down two dirt roads in the middle of nowhere, **Hill Farmstead Brewery** (☎802-533-7450; www.hillfarmstead.com; 403 Hill Rd, Greensboro; ⊙noon-5pm Wed-Sat) is, well, a farm on a hill, with a garage that holds a brewery that has repeatedly been voted best in the world. Production is limited to 150,000 gallons per year, and the output rarely leaves the state, yet Hill Farmstead has a cult following for its small-batch brews. Produced by Shaun Hill, who's known for his creative concoctions and uncompromising adherence to quality, many of the beers have names based on the Hill family: Damon, a bourbon-barrel-aged Russian Imperial Stout, is the namesake of Shaun's childhood dog; the hoppy IPA, Edward, is named after Shaun's grandfather. Bitter, malty, spicy – friendly staff will guide you to your favorite at the adjacent taproom.

Jericho Old Red Mill

The Drive » Return to Glover and take VT 16 south for 2 miles, then head 13 miles west on Shadow Lake Rd, E Craftsbury Rd and S Craftsbury Rd into Craftsbury Common.

⑦ Craftsbury Common

Welcome to Craftsbury Common, where you'll find one of Vermont's most impressive village greens. White clapboard buildings surround a rectangular lawn that hasn't changed one iota since the mid-19th century. Nearby, the community-owned Craftsbury General Store (p197) has a well-stocked deli and a nice array of Vermont-made products, while the **Craftsbury Outdoor Center** (✆802-586-7767; www.craftsbury.com; 535 Lost Nation Rd; trail pass adult/child $10/5, ski/bike rental per day $15/40; ☺8:30am-5pm; ⚑)

offers year-round outdoor activities (skiing, biking, running, kayaking, canoeing and stand-up paddleboarding) on its 80 miles of trails and Big Hosmer Pond.

✗ p197

The Drive » Take VT 14 south past Hardwick, then follow VT 15 west to Morrisville, looking on your left for the Fisher Covered Railroad Bridge, one of America's last covered railroad bridges. At Morrisville, turn south to Stowe on VT 100, then climb 9 miles up VT 108 to Smugglers Notch. The drive is 36 miles.

⑧ Smugglers Notch

Tucked beneath Mt Mansfield (Vermont's highest peak; 4393ft), Smugglers Notch is Vermont's narrowest and most visually stunning paved mountain pass. As you crest the notch, the painted center line disappears in deference

COVERED BRIDGES OF MONTGOMERY

A 20-mile drive north from Johnson via VT 100C and VT 118 takes you to the covered-bridge capital of Vermont. In an idyllic valley at the confluence of multiple watersheds, the twin villages of Montgomery and Montgomery Center share seven spans crisscrossing the local rivers. Especially beautiful – though challenging to find – is remote **Creamery Bridge** just off Hill West Rd, which straddles a waterfall with a swimming hole at its base.

LOCAL KNOWLEDGE: KINGDOM TRAILS

In 1997 a group of dedicated locals linked together 200-plus miles of single and double tracks and dirt roads to form the Northeast Kingdom's astounding, award-winning **Kingdom Trails network** (📞802-626-0737; www.kingdomtrails.com; 478 VT 114, East Burke; day pass adult/child $15/7; ⏰8am-5pm Sat-Thu, to 6pm Fri May-Oct; 🚴). Passing through century-old farms and soft forest floors dusted with pine needles, it offers one of New England's best mountain-biking experiences. In winter, the trails are ideal for cross-country skiing, snowshoeing and fat biking. Buy passes at the Kingdom Trails Welcome Center on VT 114 in East Burke, 5 miles east of I-91.

to a fairy-tale landscape of encroaching cliffs and boulders that squeeze the roadway down to a scant lane and a half. It's the trailhead for numerous (uphill!) hikes, including the scenic 1.2-mile scramble through the boulders to pretty **Sterling Pond**.

 p197

The Drive » Descend through pretty mountain scenery along VT 108 to Jeffersonville, where you'll take VT 15 west for 24 miles to Jericho.

- - - - - - - - - - - - - - - -

9 Jericho

Jericho's photogenic **Old Red Mill** (📞802-899-3225; www.jerichohistoricalsociety.org/the-old-red-mill.html; 4a Red Mill Dr; ⏰10am-5pm Mon-Sat Apr-Dec, 11:30am-4pm Sun Apr-Jun & Sep-Dec) sits astride the Browns River gorge. Inside the mill, a

nice display of Vermont crafts shares space with a free museum showcasing the captivating microphotography of native son 'Snowflake' Bentley, who provided groundbreaking evidence that no two snowflakes are identical. Out back, the **Browns River Trail** traverses a soft carpet of evergreen needles to a little sandy beach with big boulders and a deep pool for swimming.

The Drive » Return 2 miles east on VT 15, then take Browns Trace Rd 8 miles south through Jericho Center into Richmond.

- - - - - - - - - - - - - - - -

10 Richmond

Straddling the shores of the Winooski River, this pleasant village is worth a stop for its early-19th-century **Old Round**

Church (📞802-434-3654; www.oldroundchurch.com; 25 Round Church Rd; donations welcome; ⏰10am-4pm Sat & Sun late May–mid-Jun, daily mid-Jun–mid-Oct), one of Vermont's most noteworthy structures. The graceful 16-sided edifice, used by multiple congregations over the years, is as elegant inside as outside.

The Drive » The main road (Huntington Rd) curves west just beyond the Old Round Church, then turns south toward Huntington, 7 miles away. In July and August, consider a brief detour off-route to Owl's Head Blueberry Farm, a scenic spot to pick your own berries.

- - - - - - - - - - - - - - - -

11 Huntington

Huntington's gorgeous valley is presided over by Vermont's most distinctively shaped peak, **Camel's Hump** (known to early French explorers as 'Le Lion Couchant' for its resemblance to a sleeping lion). It remains one of the state's wildest spots – the only significant Vermont peak not developed for skiing – and the summit is a hiker's dream: from Huntington Center, head east 3 miles, dead-ending at the trailhead for the 6-mile **Burrows to Forest City loop**. After climbing through forest, the final ascent skirts rock faces above the tree line, affording magnificent views.

Eating & Sleeping

St Johnsbury ❸

✖ Kingdom Taproom   Pub Food $
(📞802-424-1355; www.kingdomtaproom.com; 397 Railroad St; mains $8-16; 🕙noon-10pm Tue-Thu, to midnight Fri & Sat, to 8pm Sun)
You'll find the Northeast Kingdom's largest selection of microbrews on tap at this pub in the heart of St Johnsbury. A bevy of beers from Vermont and beyond, including selections from neighboring New Hampshire and Québec, come accompanied by mac 'n' cheese, soups, salads, flatbreads and sandwiches.

🛏 Inn at Mountain View Farm   Inn $$
(📞802-626-9924; www.innmtnview.com; 3383 Darling Hill Rd, East Burke; r $215-245, ste $295-375; ❄️📶) Built in 1883, this spacious, elegant farmhouse is set on a hilltop with stunning views, surrounded by 440 acres that are ideal for mountain biking, cross-country skiing or simply taking a long stroll on the hillside. There's also an on-site animal sanctuary, which is a rescue center for large farm animals; guests are encouraged to visit. Room prices include breakfast and afternoon tea.

Glover ❻

🛏 Rodgers Country Inn   Inn $
(📞802-525-6677; www.rodgerscountryinn.com; 582 Rodgers Rd, West Glover; s/d $70/80, cabin per week $600) Not far from Shadow Lake's shores, Jim and Nancy Rodgers offer five guest rooms in their 1840s farmhouse, plus a secluded cabin sleeping up to six. Relax on the front porch and read, or take a stroll on this 350-acre former dairy farm. At this inn you can really feel what it's like to live in rural Vermont.

Craftsbury Common ❼

✖ Craftsbury General Store   American $

(📞802-586-2440; www.craftsburygeneralstore.com; 118 S Craftsbury Rd; sandwiches

$7-10; 🕙7am-8pm) Attached to Craftsbury village's post office, this community-owned store serves sandwiches, pizzas and tasty deli treats. Don't miss the Wednesday-evening Globetrotting Dinners (4pm to 8pm), featuring cuisine from a different country every week.

Smugglers Notch ❽

✖ Pie-casso   Pizza $$

(📞802-253-4411; www.piecasso.com; 1899 Mountain Rd, Stowe; mains $9-24; 🕙11am-9pm Sun-Thu, to 10pm Fri & Sat) Best known for its ample pizzas, from the sausage-and-pepperoni-packed Heart Stopper to the veggie-laden Vienna, family-friendly Pie-casso also serves up everything from eggplant Parmesan subs to fettuccine Alfredo and penne with pesto. Gluten-free crusts using flour from the nearby West Meadow Farm are also available.

🛏 Green Mountain Inn   Inn $$$
(📞802-253-7301; www.greenmountaininn.com; 18 Main St, Stowe; r/ste/apt from $169/239/259) The Stowe Recreation Path (www.stowerec.org/parks-facilities/rec-paths/stowe-recreation-path) unfurls just a few steps from this 180-year-old redbrick inn, which sits in the heart of downtown Stowe. How best to relax? Settle into a rocking chair on the front porch, enjoy afternoon cookies and tea, then head to the spa. The 104 rooms are classically decorated and come in a variety of configurations.

🛏 Smugglers' Notch State Park   Campground $
(📞802-253-4014; www.vtstateparks.com/smugglers.html; 6443 Mountain Rd; tent sites $20-22, lean-tos $27-29; 🕙mid-May–mid-Oct) This 35-acre park, 8 miles northwest of Stowe, is perched up on the mountainside. There are 20 tent sites (mostly walk-in), and 14 lean-tos.

Lake Champlain Byway

Vermont's 'Great Lake' offers delights from the semi-urban sophistication of Burlington – Vermont's largest and prettiest city – to the tranquil Champlain Islands, stretching like stepping stones to the Canadian border.

TRIP HIGHLIGHTS

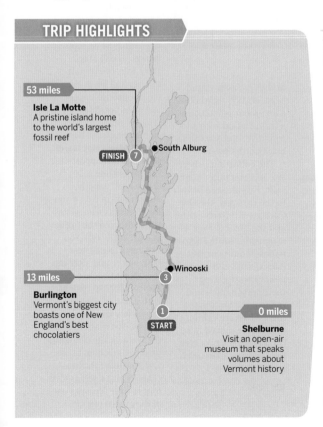

53 miles

Isle La Motte
A pristine island home to the world's largest fossil reef

FINISH 7 ● South Alburg

13 miles

Burlington
Vermont's biggest city boasts one of New England's best chocolatiers

3 ● Winooski

1
START

0 miles

Shelburne
Visit an open-air museum that speaks volumes about Vermont history

1–2 DAYS
53 MILES / 85KM

GREAT FOR...

BEST TIME TO GO

June to October for long, summery days and abundant leaf-peeping opportunities.

ESSENTIAL PHOTO

Water's edge on Isle La Motte.

BEST FOR FOODIES

Sample the state's most famous beer export and indulge in Burlington's vibrant restaurant scene.

18 Lake Champlain Byway

Between the Green Mountains and the Adirondacks, beautiful Lake Champlain is the defining feature of northwest Vermont's landscape. Survey the lake from the historical museum in Shelburne and the waterfront in Burlington, then set off to the Champlain Islands, a 27-mile ribbon of largely undeveloped isles where simpler pleasures prevail: boating, apple-picking, wine-tasting, or rambling along sleepy farm roads and interisland causeways.

TRIP HIGHLIGHT

1 Shelburne

Feast your eyes on the impressive array of 17th- to 20th-century American artifacts – folk art, textiles, toys, tools, carriages and furniture – spread over the 45-acre grounds and gardens at **Shelburne Museum** (📞802-985-3346; www.shelburnemuseum.org; 6000 Shelburne Rd/US 7; adult/child $25/14 May-Oct, $10/5 Nov-Apr; ⏰10am-5pm daily May-Dec, Wed-Sun Jan-Apr; ♿). This remarkable place is set up as a mock village, with 150,000 objects housed in 39 buildings. Highlights include a full-size covered bridge, a classic round barn, an 1871 lighthouse, a one-room schoolhouse, a train station with a locomotive, and a working blacksmith's forge.

The collection's sheer size lets you tailor your visit. Families are drawn to the carousel, the Owl Cottage children's center and the *Ticonderoga* steamship, while aficionados of quilts or, say, duck decoys can spend hours investigating their personal passion. Indeed, the buildings themselves are exhibits. Many were moved here from other parts of New England to ensure their preservation.

🛏 p205

The Drive 》 Head north on US 7 for 4 miles until you reach South Burlington.

2 South Burlington

One of the pioneers – and among the most famous – of Vermont's microbreweries is **Magic Hat Brewery** (📞802-658-2739; www.magichat.net; 5 Bartlett Bay Rd; ⏰11am-7pm Mon-Sat, noon-5pm Sun), which started brewing in 1995. The 'Artifactory' exudes an infectious creative energy, with over 20 varieties flowing from four dozen taps.

Guided 30-minute tours take you through the history of Vermont breweries and Magic Hat's role, how it makes its beer and keeps the environmental impact as low as possible, and its involvement in the community (such as the annual **Magic Hat Mardi Gras** and its support of the performing arts). Guides will happily answer any question you have, such as who writes the sayings on the inside of each bottle cap. You can enjoy free tastes both before and after the tour. Must-tries are the trademark No 9 (pale ale with a hint of apricot), Circus Boy (lemongrass-infused Hefeweizen) and the whimsically changing lineup of seasonal brews and 'Reclusive Rarities.' (There's also a self-guided tour in case you miss one of the guided ones.)

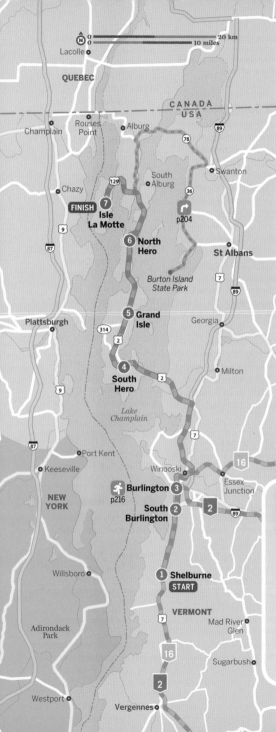

The Drive ⟫ Continue north on US 7 for 4 miles to Burlington.

- - - - - - - - - - - - - - - -

TRIP HIGHLIGHT

❸ Burlington

Perched above glistening Lake Champlain, Vermont's largest city would be small in most other states. Yet Burlington's diminutive size is one of its charms, with an easily walkable downtown and a gorgeous, accessible lakefront. With the University of Vermont (UVM) swelling the city (by 13,000 students) and a vibrant cultural and social life, Burlington has a spirited, youthful character. And when it comes to nightlife, this is Vermont's epicenter.

Just before you reach the city center, a chocolate stop is in order. The aroma of rich melted cocoa is intoxicating as you enter the gift shop next to the glass

🔗 LINK YOUR TRIP

2 **Fall Foliage Tour**
In Burlington, branch off to discover New England's blazing fall colors.

16 **Cider Season Sampler**
In Shelburne, hook up to the fall food-and-drink-filled loop.

201

wall overlooking the small factory at **Lake Champlain Chocolates** (☎802-864-1807; www.lakechamplainchocolates.com; 750 Pine St; ⏰9am-6pm Mon-Sat, 11am-5pm Sun). Take the tour to get the history of the chocolatier and ample samples to taste-test the gooey goodness. Oh, and this shop is the only one with factory-seconds shelves containing stacks of chocolate at a discount. It tastes the same as the pretty stuff but for cosmetic reasons can't be sold at regular price. The cafe serves coffee drinks and its own luscious ice cream.

✗ ▤ p49, p205

The Drive » Cast off for the Champlain Islands, cruising 10 miles north of Burlington on I-89 to exit 17, then west on US 2 for 9 miles. After Sand Bar State Park – a great picnic

and swimming spot – cross the causeway and look for the photo-perfect parking island halfway across.

---

❹ South Hero

Settle into the slower pace of island life at **Allenholm Orchards** (☎802-372-5566; www.allenholm.com; 111 South St; ⏰9am-5pm late May–Christmas Eve; 🖐), just outside the town of South Hero; grab a creemee (that's Vermont-speak for soft-serve ice cream) or pick a few apples for the road ahead. About 3 miles west is **Snow Farm Vineyard** (☎802-372-9463; www.snowfarm.com; 190 W Shore Rd; ⏰11am-5pm daily May-Oct, to 4pm daily Nov & Dec, to 4pm Sat & Sun Jan-Apr), Vermont's first vineyard, which boasts a sweet tasting room tucked away down a dirt road (look for

the signs off US 2). Sample its award-winning whites or have a sip of ice wine in the rustic barn (three tastes are free), or drop by on Thursday summer evenings at 6:30pm for the free **concert series** on the lawn next to the vines – you can expect anything from jazz to folk to rock.

The Drive » Continue north on US 2 for 8 miles.

---

❺ Grand Isle

The **Hyde Log Cabin** (☎802-372-4024; 228 US 2; adult/child $3/free; ⏰11am-4pm Fri-Sun late May–mid-Oct; 🐾), the oldest (1783) log cabin in Vermont and one of the oldest in the USA, is worth a short stop to see how settlers lived in the 18th century and to examine traditional household artifacts from Vermont.

▤ p205

The Drive » Continue north on US 2 for another 8 miles.

---

❻ North Hero

Boaters for miles around cast anchor at popular general store **Hero's Welcome** (☎802-372-4161; www.heroswelcome.com; 3537 US 2; ⏰6:30am-7pm Mon-Fri, from 7am Sat & Sun mid-Jun–early Sep, shorter hours rest of year). The store's amusing wall display of 'World Time Zones' – four clocks showing identical hours for Lake Champlain's

---

LOCAL KNOWLEDGE: CHAMPLAIN'S LOVABLE LAKE MONSTER

Dinosaur relic or Ice Age proto-whale? Tree trunk? Really really big fish? Lake Champlain's legendary lake monster – nicknamed 'Champ' – has long fascinated local residents. Known to the Abenaki as Tatoskok, Champ was even sighted by French explorer Samuel de Champlain back in the early 17th century. Indulge your curiosity at the Champ display in Burlington's **Echo Leahy Center for Lake Champlain** (☎802-864-1848; www.echovermont.org; 1 College St; adult/child $14.50/11.50; ⏰10am-5pm; 🖐). For a more dependable sighting, attend a Vermont Lake Monsters baseball game, where a lovable green-costumed Champ mascot dances on the dugout roof between innings.

Burlington Vermont's largest city

DETOUR:
BURTON ISLAND
STATE PARK

Start: ❻ **North Hero Island**

For a deeper immersion in Lake Champlain's natural beauty, spend a night or two camping at **Burton Island State Park** (☏802-524-6353; www.vtstateparks.com/burton.html; 2714 Hathaway Point Rd, St Albans; day use adult/child $4/2, campsite/lean-to $20/39; ☺late May-late Sep; ⛺), in the middle of the lake. Between Memorial Day and Labor Day, the *Island Runner* ferry (10 minutes) shuttles campers and their gear across a narrow channel from the mainland near St Albans to this pristine, traffic-free island with over two dozen lakefront lean-tos and campsites. Park facilities include boat rentals, a nature center with daily kids' activities and a store selling breakfast, lunch and groceries; the sign outside ('No shoes, no shirt, no problem!') epitomizes the island's laid-back vibe. It's an easy 45-minute loop around the lake from North Hero to the ferry dock at Kill Kare State Park. Head 10 miles north on US 2 and then 10 miles east on VT 78 to get to Swanton; from there drive 10 miles south on VT 36 and turn right onto Hathaway Point Rd for the final 2.5 miles.

North Hero, South Hero, Grand Isle and Isle La Motte – reflects the prevailing island-centric attitude. Pick up a souvenir, grab a sandwich or coffee and snap some pics on the outdoor terrace overlooking the boat landing.

🛏 p205

The Drive » From US 2, head west 4 miles on VT 129 to historic Isle La Motte.

TRIP HIGHLIGHT

❼ Isle La Motte

Pristine Isle La Motte is one of the most historic of the Champlain Islands. Signs along its western shore signal its tradi-

tional importance as a crossroads for Native Americans and commemorate French explorer Samuel de Champlain's landing here in 1609.

Tool around the loop road hugging the coast, stopping at **St Anne's Shrine** (☏802-928-3362; www.saintannesshrine.org; 92 St Anne's Rd; ☺shrine mid-May–early Oct, grounds year-round) on the site of Fort St Anne, Vermont's oldest settlement. (Though it is welcoming to all, this is a religious place, so be respectful of those who come to pray.) The site features a striking granite statue of Samuel de Champlain, and its waterfront has spectacular views and a large picnic area.

Isle La Motte is also home to the 20-acre **Fisk Quarry Preserve** (www.ilmpt.org; W Shore Rd; ☺dawn-dusk), the world's largest fossil reef, 4 miles south of St Anne's Shrine. Half a million years old, the reef once provided limestone for Radio City Music Hall and Washington's National Gallery. Interpretive trails explain the history of the quarry.

Eating & Sleeping

Shelburne ❶

🛏 Inn at Shelburne Farms   Inn $$$

(📞802-985-8498; www.shelburnefarms.org/
staydine; 1611 Harbor Rd; r $270-530, without
bath $160-230, cottages & houses $270-850;
⏰ early May-late Oct; 🛜) One of New England's
top 10 places to stay, this inn, 7 miles south
of Burlington off US 7, was once the summer
mansion of the wealthy Webb family. It has rooms
in the welcoming country manor house by the
lakefront, as well as four independent, kitchen-
equipped cottages and guesthouses across the
property. Relive the Webbs' opulent lifestyle by
taking tea (served every afternoon) or eating
in the inn's fabulous restaurant (dinner mains
$28 to $36; most of the menu is built around
produce from the surrounding 1400-acre farm).
Or chill out playing billiards or relaxing in one of
the common areas. The hiking trails, architect-
designed barns and vast grounds (see p187) are
also worthy of several hours' exploration.

Burlington ❸

✗ Penny Cluse Cafe   Cafe $

(📞802-651-8834; www.pennycluse.com;
169 Cherry St; mains $6-14; ⏰6:45am-3pm
Mon-Fri, from 8am Sat & Sun) This ever-popular
downtown eatery serves pancakes, biscuits and
gravy, omelets and tofu scrambles, along with
sandwiches, tacos, salads and delightful drinks
ranging from smoothies to Bloody Marys. Don't
miss its decadent Bucket-o-Spuds (home-fried
potatoes with cheddar, salsa, sour cream and
scallions) and *chiles rellenos* – among the best
you'll find anywhere east of the Mississippi.
Expect an hour's wait on weekends.

✗ Revolution
Kitchen   Vegan, Vegetarian $$

(📞802-448-3657; www.revolutionkitchen.
com; 9 Center St; mains $14-18; ⏰5-9pm
Tue-Thu, to 10pm Fri & Sat; ✈) Vegetarian fine
dining? And romantic atmosphere to boot?
Yep, they all come together at this cozy brick-
walled restaurant that makes creative use of
Vermont's abundant organic produce. Asian,
Mediterranean and Latin American influences
abound in house favorites like Revolution tacos,
crispy seitan piccata and the laksa noodle pot.
Most items are (or can be adapted to be) vegan.

Citizen Cider   Microbrewery

(📞802-497-1987; www.citizencider.com; 316 Pine
St; ⏰11am-10pm Mon-Sat, to 7pm Sun) Tucked
into an industrial-chic building with painted
concrete floors and long wooden tables, this
homegrown success story uses apples trucked in
from Vermont orchards to make its ever-growing
line of hard ciders. Taste test a flight of five for
$7, including favorites such as the ginger-and-
lemon-peel-infused Dirty Mayor, or go for one of
the inventive cider-based cocktails.

🛏 Willard Street Inn   Inn $$

(📞802-651-8710; www.willardstreetinn.com;
349 S Willard St; r $155-305; 🛜) Perched on a
hill within easy walking distance of UVM and
the Church Street Marketplace (p216), this
mansion, fusing Queen Anne and Georgian
Revival styles, was built in the late 1880s. It has
a fine-wood and cut-glass elegance, yet radiates
a welcoming warmth. Many of the guest rooms
overlook Lake Champlain.

Grand Isle ❺

🛏 Grand Isle State Park   Campground $

(📞802-372-4300; www.vtstateparks.com/
grandisle.html; 36 E Shore South; tent & RV sites
$20-22, lean-tos $27-29, cabins $50; ⏰mid-
May–mid-Oct) Vermont's most popular state-
park campground straddles a pretty stretch of
Lake Champlain waterfront, with 115 tent and
RV sites, 36 lean-tos and four cabins.

North Hero ❻

🛏 North Hero House   Inn $$

(📞888-525-3644; www.northherohouse.com;
3643 US 2; r $125-250, ste $295-350; 🛜) This
country inn directly opposite Lake Champlain
entices guests with quilt-filled rooms, private
porches and four-poster beds. Eating options
include a main dining room serving New
American cuisine, the casual Oscar's Oasis pub
and the waterfront Steamship Pier Bar & Grill,
where you can enjoy kebabs, burgers, lobster
rolls and cocktails smack on the pier.

Southern Vermont Loop

19

Crisscross the Green Mountains for a taste of southern Vermont, from Brattleboro's artsy counterculture to Bennington's white-steepled Colonial heritage – with some of Vermont's prettiest small villages thrown in.

TRIP HIGHLIGHTS

63 miles

Manchester
Shop your heart out at the foot of beautiful Mt Equinox

104 miles

Grafton
Travel back in time to one of Vermont's prettiest historic villages

Weston

6

8

Townshend

2

Wilmington

Brattleboro
START/ FINISH

Bennington
Find out why Bennington was crucial to the American Revolution

40 miles

**2–3 DAYS
131 MILES / 211KM**

GREAT FOR...

BEST TIME TO GO

May to October for great weather and autumnal colors.

ESSENTIAL PHOTO

Quintessential New England beauty of Grafton's clapboard homes, covered bridges and venerable old brick inn.

✓ **BEST FOR OUTDOORS**

Trails on the Hildene grounds, the Lincoln family estate.

Bennington Bennington Battle Monument

Tidy white churches and inns surround village greens throughout historic southern Vermont, a region that's home to several towns that predate the American Revolution. This scenic loop takes in all the region's highlights: history-rich Bennington, the picture-postcard villages of Grafton and Weston, upscale Manchester, the imposing peak of Mt Equinox, the old stone home of Robert Frost and the opulent mansion of Abraham Lincoln's descendants.

1 Brattleboro

Perched at the confluence of the Connecticut and West Rivers, Brattleboro is a little gem packed with independent shops, eateries and cultural venues such as the **Latchis Theater** (☎802-246-2020; http://theater.latchis.com; 50 Main St) and the **Brattleboro Museum & Art Center** (☎802-257-0124; www.brattleboromuseum. org; 10 Vernon St; adult/child $8/free; ⏱11am-5pm Wed-Mon), housed in the town's 1915 former train station. An energetic mix

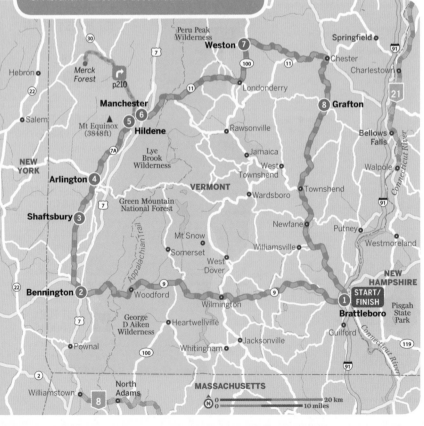

of aging hippies and the latest crop of pierced and tattooed hipsters fuels the town's sophisticated eclecticism, keeping the downtown scene percolating and skewing its politics decidedly leftward.

 p213

The Drive >> Take VT 9 west along the Molly Stark scenic byway for 40 miles to Bennington. After an ear-popping climb, 5 miles past the turnoff for the town of Marlboro, you'll come to the Hogback Mountain overlook; make sure to stop and admire the three-state views over Massachusetts, New Hampshire and Vermont.

❷ Bennington

Bennington is divided into three sections: workaday town (Ben-

LINK YOUR TRIP

8 **Mohawk Trail**
Explore New England's oldest scenic highway in Massachusetts. From Bennington, drive 13 miles south on US 7 to Williamstown.

21 **Connecticut River Byway**
Follow the river and visit college towns in New Hampshire. From Brattleboro drive 23 miles north on I-91 to Walpole.

nington proper), college town (North Bennington) and **Old Bennington**, which is where you'll find the main sights. The charming hilltop Colonial site is studded with 80 Georgian and Federal houses and the **Old First Church** (802-447-1223; www.oldfirstchurchbenn. org; cnr Monument Ave & VT 9; 10am-4pm Mon-Sat, from 1pm Sun Jul–mid-Oct, weekends only late May-Jun), built in 1806 in Palladian style. Its churchyard holds the remains of five Vermont governors, numerous soldiers of the American Revolution and poet Robert Frost (1874–1963), one of the best-known and best-loved American poets of the 20th century.

Up the hill to the north, the **Bennington Battle Monument** (802-447-0550; www.bennington battlemonument.com; 15 Monument Circle, Old Bennington; adult/child $5/1; 9am-5pm late Apr-Oct) commemorates the crucial Battle of Bennington, fought during the American Revolution. Had Colonel Seth Warner and the local 'Green Mountain Boys' not helped weaken British defenses during this battle, the colonies might well have been split. The obelisk, built between 1887 and 1891, offers impressive views – an elevator whisks you two-thirds of the way up the 306ft tower.

 p213

The Drive >> Head out of town along scenic VT 7A and drive 4 miles north to the Robert Frost Stone House Museum. As the road winds along the valley the southernmost section of the Green Mountains emerges on your left.

❸ Shaftsbury

When he moved his family to Shaftsbury, Robert Frost was 46 years old and at the height of his career. The **Robert Frost Stone House Museum** (802-447-6200; www.frostfriends.org; 121 VT 7A; adult/child $10/5; 11am-5pm Wed-Sun May-Oct) opens a window into the life of the poet, with one entire room dedicated to his most famous work, 'Stopping by Woods on a Snowy Evening,' which he penned here in the 1920s.

The Drive >> Drive 5 miles north along scenic VT 7A to Shaftsbury itself, then continue 6 miles further through bucolic farmland and wooded hollows to Arlington.

❹ Arlington

Arlington's tiny maple-syrup shop (the sweet stuff is made on-site) houses the **Norman Rockwell Exhibition** (802-375-6747; www.sugarshackvt. com/norman-rockwell-exhibit; Sugar Shack Lane; 10am-4:30pm Mon-Fri, 9am-4pm Sat & Sun Mar-late Dec), a homage to the artist, who lived in Arlington from 1939 to 1953. A section of the shop displays 500 of Rockwell's *Saturday Evening Post* covers and shows a short film about his life. (Exhibition hours vary; call to confirm.)

The Drive » Continue for 8 miles north along scenic VT 7A, passing the base of imposing Mt Equinox as you approach Hildene, on the southern outskirts of Manchester. The area is an excellent place for an overnight stay – oodles of B&Bs and hotels congregate in Manchester proper and along VT 7A as you approach town.

❺ Hildene

Abraham Lincoln's wife, Mary Todd Lincoln (1818–82), and their son, Robert Todd Lincoln (1843–1926), came here during the Civil War; as an adult Robert built **Hildene** (☎general info 800-578-1788, tour reservations 802-367-7968; www.hildene.org; 1005 Hildene Rd/VT 7A; adult/child $23/6, guided tour $7.50 extra; ⏰9:30am-4:30pm), a 24-room Georgian Revival mansion. Robert enjoyed the house until his death in 1926, and his great-granddaughter lived here until her death in 1975. Soon after, it was converted into a museum filled with Lincoln family personal effects and furnishings, including the hat Abraham Lincoln probably wore when he delivered the Gettysburg Address, and a brass cast of his hands, the right one swollen from shaking hands while campaigning for the presidency.

The surrounding grounds feature 8 miles of **walking trails**, an exquisite flower garden designed to resemble a stained-glass Roman-esque cathedral window and a solar-powered barn where you can watch Hildene goat's cheese being produced.

The Drive » Continue north on VT 7A for 2 miles to central Manchester.

TRIP HIGHLIGHT

❻ Manchester

Manchester has been a fashionable resort town for almost two centuries. These days, the draws are the nearby skiing and hiking, the relaxed New England town vibe and the upscale outlet shopping (Manchester contains more than 100 shops, from Armani to Marimekko).

Two families put the place on the map –

DETOUR: MERCK FOREST

Start: ❻ Manchester

Encompassing more than 2700 acres of high-country farmland, meadow and forest, **Merck Forest & Farmland Center** (☎802-394-7836; www.merckforest.org; 3270 VT 315, Rupert; ⏰visitor center 9am-4pm; 👫) is a blissful place to experience Vermont's natural beauty and agricultural heritage. The park's centerpiece is a working organic farm with animals, vegetable gardens, renewable energy installations and a sugar house where you can watch maple syrup being produced during sugaring season (generally mid-March to early April). It's hidden away on a gorgeous hilltop only 25 minutes from Manchester – but a world apart from the village hustle and bustle.

The center offers a wide range of hikes, environmental education programs and events such as sheepdog trials. It also rents out cabins and tent sites, which are spread around the property. Sales of produce and syrup, coupled with voluntary contributions, help sustain the nonprofit foundation at its heart.

To get here from Manchester, take VT 30 northwest 8 miles to East Rupert, then head 2 miles south on VT 315, looking for signs on your left at the top of the hill.

Hildene Gardens

the Lincolns and the Orvises. Franklin Orvis (1824–1900) established the Equinox House Hotel; his brother, Charles, founded the Orvis Company, makers of fly-fishing equipment with a worldwide following. Orvis Company products are showcased in the **American Museum of Fly Fishing** (📞802-362-3300; www.amff.org; 4070 Main St/VT 7A; adult/child $5/3; 🕙10am-4pm Tue-Sun Jun-Oct, Tue-Sat Nov-May), with fly collections and rods used by Ernest Hemingway, Bing Crosby and several US presidents.

Hikers can hit the trail for the dramatic climb to the summit of Mt Equinox (3848ft), which looms large just south of town. The five-hour hike (2918ft elevation gain) will reward you with exhilarating views; look for the trailhead behind the Equinox Hotel.

🍴 🛏 p49, p213

The Drive ⟫ Follow VT 11 northeast for 15 miles toward Londonderry, then take VT 100 another 5 miles north into Weston.

- - - - - - - - - - - - - - - - - -

⑦ Weston

Crowds flock to Weston for three main reasons:

to browse the shelves at the Vermont Country Store (p174), to attend the renowned summer theater festival at Vermont's oldest professional theater, the **Weston Playhouse** (📞802-824-5288; www.westonplayhouse.org; 703 Main St; 🕙performances late Jun-early Sep), or simply to bask in the glow of one of Vermont's most picturesque villages. From the gazebo at the center of Weston's circular town green, the views upstream to the town's waterfall and 19th-century mill are the stuff of tourist legend.

The Drive ⟫ Head 12 miles east on Weston–Andover Rd and VT 11 through the gorgeous stone village of Chester, then turn south on VT 35 and continue 7 miles south to Grafton.

- - - - - - - - - - - - - - - - - -

TRIP HIGHLIGHT

⑧ Grafton

One of Vermont's prettiest villages, Grafton exudes a peaceful grace reminiscent of a bygone century. It's not that way by accident. In the 1960s the private Windham Foundation established a preservation program for the entire village, burying all electrical and telephone lines and re-

storing historic buildings and covered bridges. The town's most picturesque building is the **Grafton Inn** at the center of town. Stop for a bite at the formal New England dining room or the casual tavern in the carriage house out back.

South of town, the **Grafton Trails & Outdoor Center** (📞802-843-2350; www.graftoninnvermont.com/grafton-trails; 783 Townshend Rd) offers year-round recreation on its network of mountain-biking, hiking and cross-country ski trails, along with canoeing, swimming, snow-tubing and adventure camps for kids. Along the same road you'll also find the **Grafton Village Cheese Company** (📞800-472-3866; www.graftonvillagecheese.com; 533 Townshend Rd; 🕙hours vary), whose mouthwatering and nose-tingling cheddars regularly win awards at international cheese festivals.

🍴 🛏 p213

The Drive ⟫ Continue 27 miles south along Grafton–Townshend Rd, VT 35 and VT 30 into Brattleboro, taking time to stop and admire the Georgian and Greek Revival architecture in postcard-worthy Newfane.

Eating & Sleeping

Brattleboro

✗ TJ Buckley's — American $$$

(☎802-257-4922; www.tjbuckleysuptowndining.com; 132 Elliot St; mains incl salad $45; ☺5:30-9pm Thu-Sun year-round, plus Wed mid-Jun–early Oct) Chef-owner Michael Fuller founded this exceptional, upscale little eatery in an authentic 1925 Worcester dining car over 30 years ago. Ever since, he's been offering a verbal menu of four seasonally changing items, sourced largely from local farms. Locals rave that the food here is Brattleboro's best. The diner seats just 18 souls, so reserve ahead. No credit cards.

🛏 Latchis Hotel — Hotel $$

(☎802-254-6300; www.latchishotel.com; 50 Main St; r $100-210, ste $190-240; 🛜) You can't beat the location of these 30 reasonably priced rooms and suites, in the center of downtown and adjacent to the historic theater (p208) of the same name. The hotel's art-deco overtones are refreshing, and wonderfully surprising for New England.

Bennington ❷

✗ Pangaea — International $$

(☎802-442-7171; www.vermontfinedining.com; 1 Prospect St, North Bennington; mains $9-31; ☺lounge 5-10pm daily, restaurant to 9pm Tue-Sat) Whether you opt for the casual lounge, the riverside terrace or the more upscale dining room, you can expect exceptional food at this cozy North Bennington favorite. The varied menu ranges from burgers, salads, crab cakes, eggplant parmigiana and Thai stir-fries on the lounge side to herb-crusted halibut, roast duck and rack of lamb in the tastefully decorated restaurant.

Manchester ❻

✗ Moonwink — Burmese $$

(☎802-768-8671; www.facebook.com/moonwinkvt; 4479 Main St; mains $12-13; ☺11:30am-7pm Tue-Sat) Nothing fancy here, but Moonwink – opened in 2018 by Burmese-born chef May Stannard and her Vermonter husband Wes – makes some of the best authentic Asian food you'll find in rural New England. Order a Burma bowl (rice and sprouted peas with curry), a delicious vegetarian or vegan salad, or daily specials such as fish stew or coconut chicken noodle soup.

🛏 Aspen at Manchester — Motel $$

(☎802-362-2450; www.aspenvt.com; 5669 Main St/VT 7A; r $89-199, 6-person cottage $289-369; ❄🛜🐾) An affordable standout, this family-run motel set back serenely from the road has 27 comfortable rooms, a swimming pool and a convenient location within walking distance of Manchester Center. Two adjacent cottages sleeping up to six make an attractive option for families.

Grafton ❽

✗ Phelps Barn — Pub Food $$

(☎802-234-8718; www.graftoninnvermont.com/dining/phelps-barn; mains $13-28; ☺4-8:30pm Sun-Thu, to 9:30pm Fri & Sat) Tucked into a historic carriage house, the casual on-site tavern at the Grafton Inn serves light pub fare – burgers, fish and chips, *steak frites* – and a wide range of Vermont microbrews. Pop in on Thursday evenings, when a burger and a pint go for $13, or on Friday and Saturday evenings, when there's live music from 7pm to 9:30pm.

🛏 Grafton Inn — Inn $$

(☎802-843-2248; www.graftoninnvermont.com; 92 Main St; r $159-279; 🛜) With a double porch that serves as Grafton's most picturesque landmark, this venerable inn has played host to such notable guests as Rudyard Kipling, Theodore Roosevelt and Ralph Waldo Emerson. While the original brick inn is quite formal, many of the 45 guest rooms and suites – scattered around houses within the village – are less so.

STRETCH YOUR LEGS
STOWE

Start/Finish: Quiet Path

Distance: 2.5 miles

Duration: Two to three hours

This walk takes you along the Quiet Path, a circular walk through pastoral countryside, then into the center of Stowe village. You'll cross a pedestrian covered bridge, visit local galleries and shops, and learn about Stowe's skiing and snowboarding history.

Take this walk on Trips

Quiet Path

Start your exploration of Stowe along the Quiet Path, a delightful, easy 1.8-mile walk that features mountain views and leads you through bucolic farmland along the west branch of the Little River. Along the way, you'll see dogs out for a walk with their owners, painters capturing Stowe's beautiful landscape on canvas and special plaques explaining the ecosystem of the area. The loop is blissfully devoid of cyclists or anything else that moves quickly.

The Walk >> Access the walk from the parking lot beneath Stowe Community Church. Follow signs to the recreation path, veering right after the second bridge. After looping back to the start, walk uphill, turn right at the church, then right onto Mountain Rd.

Stowe Walkway

A pedestrian covered bridge (built 1972), the Stowe Walkway runs parallel to the main road across the Waterbury River. One of Stowe's most photographed spots, it's a mini, skinny version of the covered bridges you see all over Vermont and features a sweet Stowe sign at the entrance.

The Walk >> Cross the pedestrian bridge. At the other end, cross the street and turn left; your next stop is on your right.

Stowe Craft

Stowe has no shortage of galleries and craft shops displaying work by artists of local and international renown. One of the best, in the heart of Stowe village, is **Stowe Craft** (☑802-253-4693; www.stowecraft.com; 55 Mountain Rd; ☺10am-6pm), with adventurous, eclectic and surreal works of art and craft.

The Walk >> Follow Mountain Rd 300ft south to its junction with Main St, then cross Main St to reach your next stop.

Vermont Ski & Snowboard Museum

Located in an 1818 meeting house that was rolled to its present spot by oxen in

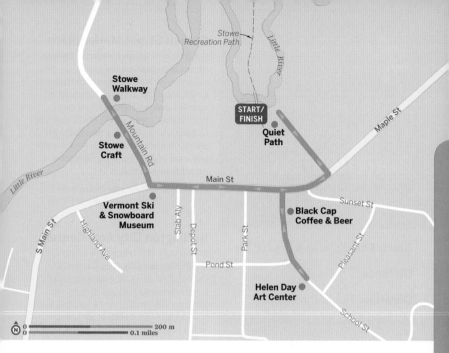

the 1860s, the **Vermont Ski & Snowboard Museum** (📞802-253-9911; www.vtssm.com; 1 S Main St; suggested admission $5; ⊙ noon-5pm Wed-Sun) is a tribute to skiing and boarding, with over 7500 cataloged items. It tells the tale of the famous 10th Mountain Division of skiing troops from WWII history, traces the evolution of equipment (85 years of Vermont ski lifts) and gives you a chance to chuckle at 1970s slope-side fashion.

The Walk ≫ Turn right out of the museum and walk down Main St — you'll pass oodles of shops and restaurants. Turn right onto School St and walk three blocks until you see your next stop on the right.

Helen Day Art Center

This gently provocative **community art center** (📞802-253-8358; www.helenday.com; 90 Pond St; ⊙10am-5pm Tue-Sat) hosts rotating traditional and avant-garde exhibits. It also sponsors 'Exposed,' an annual, town-wide outdoor sculpture

show running from mid-July to mid-October.

The Walk ≫ Walk back down School St the way you came. At Main St, the next stop is on your right at the corner.

Black Cap Coffee & Beer

What's art without coffee? After your visit to the art center, grab a cuppa and unwind over baked goods or sandwiches at this homey, refurbished **cafe** (📞802-253-2123; www.facebook.com/blackcapcoffeeandbeer; 144 Main St; sandwiches $7-9; ⊙7am-6pm Sun-Thu, to 7pm Fri & Sat; 🛜) in the heart of the village, set in an inviting old house with armchairs, couches and a small but delightful front porch. The attached shop stocks an impressive collection of microbrews and hosts regular beer-tasting events.

The Walk ≫ To return to the beginning of the Quiet Path, cross Main St and walk down the hill (the church will be on your right) to the parking lot.

STRETCH YOUR LEGS
BURLINGTON

Start/Finish: Pearl & Church Sts

Distance: 3 miles

Duration: Two to three hours

Stroll down Burlington's main drag and pedestrian hang-out strip, and then along the city's finest asset, Lake Champlain. Learn about the city's history and the lake's ecosystem, and see where Burlington's residents sail, cycle and run a few steps from the town center.

Take this walk on Trips

Church Street Marketplace

Get a dose of urban culture at **Church Street Marketplace** (www.churchstmarket place.com; 🚶), the city's commercial and social hub. This attractive pedestrian zone is lined with shops, food carts, restaurants, cafes, street musicians and climbing rocks that are popular with young children. It's packed with locals any time of day and is the epicenter of nightlife on weekends.

The Walk ≫ Walk along the pedestrian mall. After College St, you will see your next stop on the right.

Burlington City Arts Center

A mainstay of Burlington's cultural life, the **Burlington City Arts Center** (BCA Center; ☎802-865-7166; www.burlingtoncity arts.org/bca-center; 135 Church St; ☻noon-5pm Tue-Thu & Sun, to 8pm Fri & Sat, closed Sun Nov-Apr) features Vermont artists, as well as those from further afield, with a focus on contemporary art.

The Walk ≫ From Church St, turn right onto Main St. You'll immediately see the lake looming in front of you. Walk downhill; the road dead-ends at your next stop.

Union Station

The brick beaux-arts-style structure (built in 1915) is **Union Station** (1 Main St), the former station for the Central Vermont railway; look for the quirky steel-winged monkeys looming on top of the building. Inside, admire the revolving local art; head downstairs to see murals detailing the history and development of Burlington, along with *Train Ball,* a sculpture by Lars Fisk (former artistic director for Vermont's legendary band Phish).

The Walk ≫ Exit on the bottom floor and turn right. You'll pass the old platform, which looks like it could receive passengers anytime. Walk on the path following the tracks.

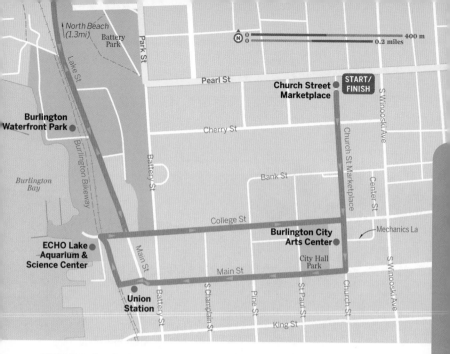

ECHO Lake Aquarium & Science Center

Nature-lovers, or those interested in green architecture, will definitely want to explore the ECHO Leahy Center for Lake Champlain (p202), a waterfront science museum that is LEED-certified for its state-of-the-art environmentally friendly design. Focusing on Lake Champlain's ecosystem, it features a moderate-sized aquarium with local fish and hands-on touch tanks. Don't miss the stand devoted to the lake's mythical sea creature, 'Champ.'

The Walk » Cross the roundabout and you'll see the boathouse off to the left and the boardwalk up ahead, both part of your next stop.

Burlington Waterfront Park

Refreshingly unencumbered by the souvenir stands that crowd the more developed waterfronts, the park has a low-key promenade with four-person swinging benches and swaths of grassy spots. Its marina contains **Splash at the Boathouse** (☎802-658-2244; www. splashattheboathouse.com; College St, at Lake Champlain; ☺11am-9pm mid-May–mid-Oct), an outdoor restaurant and bar on a floating dock that's perfect for watching the sun set over the lake and the Adirondack Mountains beyond with a cocktail (it's best for the drinks and views, not the food).

The Walk » Walk down the boardwalk and continue past the sailing club to Burlington Recreation Path, a paved path that takes you along the lake. Follow the shoreline 1.3 miles to North Beach – the elevation increases slightly, giving excellent views from above.

North Beach

This wide stretch makes you feel like you've landed on a small ocean. Wriggle your feet in the sand, breathe in the crisp air and, if it's summer, dive in.

The Walk » Return to the Burlington Recreation Path and walk back to the waterfront park. Then walk east along College St and north up Church St until you return to the Church St Marketplace.

217

New Hampshire

THE BEST THING ABOUT A TRIP THROUGH THE GRANITE STATE? The whole place is one big scenic attraction. You don't have to drive through miles of suburbia to get to the good stuff because most of it *is* the good stuff: lofty peaks, shimmering lakes, crashing waterfalls and powerful rivers. After crossing the state line, everything's within a half-day's trip. In the north, the word 'presidential' best describes the scenery. Mt Washington (New England's highest peak) anchors the magnificent Presidential Range, replete with trails and high granite summits. It's all about lake views and water fun at Lake Winnipesaukee, where wildlife roams in nearby hills. Vistas are gentler along the Connecticut River and in towns near Mt Monadnock, regions that draw artists and families with their museums and covered bridges.

Keene Mt Monadnock
DENISTANGNEYJR/GETTY IMAGES ©

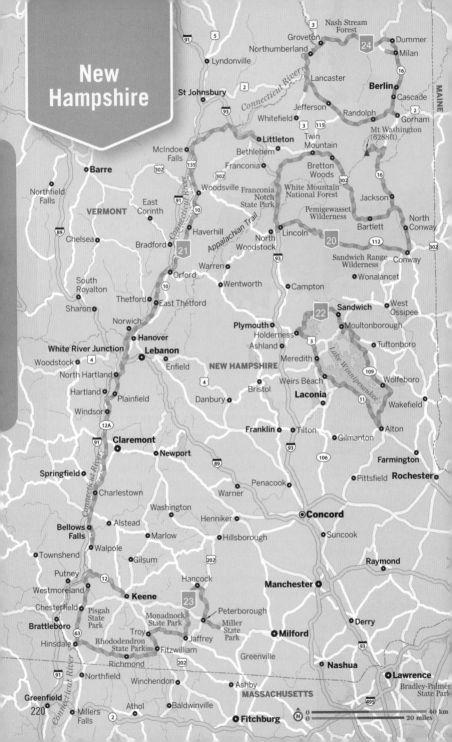

Moultonborough Loon Center

 DON'T
MISS

Kancamagus Highway

Drive past majestic vistas of granite peaks and watch out for moose on Trip 20

Moat Mountain Smokehouse & Brewing Co

After hiking up Mt Washington, swap lies about the trail at this North Conway pub on Trip 20

Burdick Chocolate

A decadent dessert here is a must, but the quiche might be the best you've ever tasted. Try it on Trip 21

Hiking Mt Monadnock

If Thoreau liked it twice, the view must be good. Conquer America's most popular summit for yourself on Trip 23

Wildlife Watching

Learn about local wildlife from folks who are helping it thrive at Squam Lakes Natural Science Center and Loon Center on Trip 22

White Mountains Loop

20

Adventure calls from every trailhead on this notch-linking loop that swoops along the Kancamagus Highway, climbs the slopes of Mt Washington and passes the mighty flume at Franconia Notch.

TRIP HIGHLIGHTS

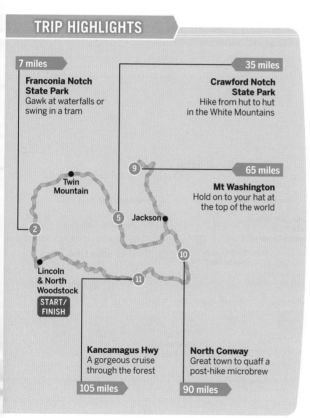

7 miles

Franconia Notch State Park
Gawk at waterfalls or swing in a tram

35 miles

Crawford Notch State Park
Hike from hut to hut in the White Mountains

65 miles

Mt Washington
Hold on to your hat at the top of the world

Twin Mountain

Jackson

Lincoln & North Woodstock

START/ FINISH

Kancamagus Hwy
A gorgeous cruise through the forest

105 miles

North Conway
Great town to quaff a post-hike microbrew

90 miles

**3 DAYS
135 MILES / 217KM**

GREAT FOR...

BEST TIME TO GO
Visit from May to October for warm days and full foliage.

ESSENTIAL PHOTO
Capture presidential peaks from the CL Graham Wangan Grounds Overlook.

BEST FOR HISTORY
Bretton Woods, where the World Bank was created.

20 White Mountains Loop

Hikers, lace up your boots and grab your walking sticks. The White Mountain National Forest, with help from the Appalachian Mountain Club, is home to one of the most impressive trail networks in the nation. You'll experience waterfalls crashing through gorges, streams rippling past an abandoned settlement and mountain huts serving up meals and beds. Not a hiker? Train rides through leafy terrain and a fairy-tale theme park bring the adventure to you.

1 Lincoln & North Woodstock

Outdoor shops, an adventure outfitter and a gob-smacking array of pizza joints line the Kancamagus Hwy on its run through Lincoln and nearby North Woodstock. Start at the **White Mountains Visitor Center** (📞National Forest info 603-745-3816, visitor info 603-745-8720; www.visitwhitemoun tains.com; 200 Kancamagus Hwy, off I-93, exit 32, North Woodstock; ⏰visitor center 8:30am-5pm year-round, National Forest desk 9am-

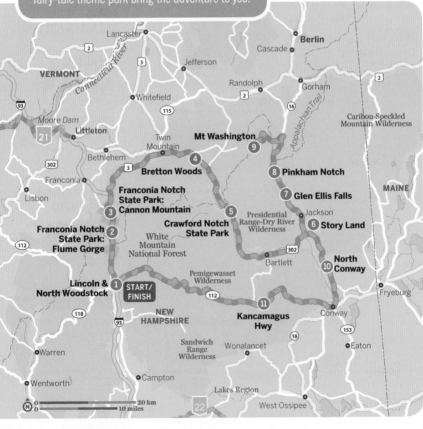

3:30pm mid-May–mid-Oct, Fri-Sun rest of year), where a stuffed moose sets a mood for adventure. This is also the place to grab brochures and trail maps and purchase a White Mountain National Forest Recreation Pass ($5 day pass), which is required for extended stops at some national forest trailheads.

Want to leave the planning to others? Try **Alpine Adventures** (603-745-9911; www.alpinezipline.com; 41 Main St, Lincoln; zipline tours from $39; ⏱9am-5pm;) a few doors down. These knowledgeable folks lead backwoods safaris and zipline tours.

LINK YOUR TRIP

21 Connecticut River Byway

Drive toward Littleton on I-93 north from Franconia Notch to start a pastoral drive along the Connecticut River.

22 Lake Winnipesaukee

Leave the mountains behind and discover New Hampshire's beautiful lakes region; from Lincoln, it's a 45-minute drive to Weirs Beach via I-93 and NH 104.

🛏 p229

The Drive » Drive 4 miles north on I-93 to exit 34A and follow the signs 0.5 miles further to Flume Gorge.

- -

TRIP HIGHLIGHT

② Franconia Notch State Park: Flume Gorge

Expect crowds at **Flume Gorge** (🎫603-745-8391; www.flumegorge.com; I-93, exit 34A; adult/6-12yr $16/14; ⏱8:30am-5pm early May-Jun & Sep–mid-Oct, to 5:30pm Jul & Aug), a natural granite sluice with 90ft walls in Franconia Notch State Park. But don't let elbow jostling keep you away – the verdant, moss-covered cliffs and rushing stream are worth it. The trail has a sturdy walkway, making it accessible for everyone. If you plan to ride the Cannon Mountain Aerial Tramway, buy the Discovery Pass (adult/child $30/24), which covers the flume and the tram at a reduced rate.

Take a walk or a bike ride on the 8-mile **Recreation Trail** beside the Pemigewasset River or stroll 500ft to the **Basin**, the first of several waterfalls accessed from the Basin parking lot north of the Flume Gorge Visitor Center.

The Drive » Follow US 3 for 1 mile north to join I-93, then continue 4.5 miles north to

---

exit 34B. Here in the heart of Franconia Notch State Park, I-93 and US 3 merge into a single highway, flanked closely on either side by the Kinsman and Franconia mountain ranges.

- -

③ Franconia Notch State Park: Cannon Mountain

A short drive north, the **Cannon Mountain Aerial Tramway** (🎫603-823-8800; www.cannonmt.com; 260 Tramway Dr; round trip adult/6-12yr $18/16; ⏱8:30am-5pm Jun–mid-Oct; 🅿🚡) whisks you to a lookout point so lofty that you'll feel you've sprouted wings.

Every New Hampshirite mourns the **Old Man of the Mountain**, a rock formation that remains the state symbol despite its collapse in May 2003. Near the Tramway Valley Station, the departure point for the tram, you'll find the **Old Man of the Mountain Museum** (I-93, exit 34B; ⏱10am-5pm late May–mid-Oct; 🅿), where there are forensically accurate diagrams of 'the Profile's' collapse, and tributes to this beloved bit of state history.

The Drive » Follow I-93 north to exit 35, taking US 3 north to Twin Mountain, where you'll pass a prison-striped moose at the police station. Fill up the tank at Foster's Crossroads, then follow US 302 east. The drive is 17 miles.

4 Bretton Woods

From July 1 to July 22, 1944, the Mount Washington Hotel (p229) hosted the Bretton Woods International Monetary Conference. This history-making summit established the World Bank and helped stabilize the global economy as WWII ended. World leaders were determined to avoid the disastrous economic fallout that occurred after WWI. Today, spend a sumptuous night in one of the resort's 200 rooms or simply stop by to wander past the historic photographs beside the lobby. A drink on the veranda with its view of Mt Washington is also a pleasant diversion.

🛏 p229

The Drive » Follow US 302 south 4 miles to the park.

TRIP HIGHLIGHT

5 Crawford Notch State Park

The **Pond Loop** and **Sam Tilley** trails are two easy riverside hikes in this **state park** (☎603-374-2272; www.nhstateparks.org; 1464 US 302, Hart's Location; ⏱ visitor center 9:30am-5pm late May–mid-Oct, park year-round unless posted otherwise; ℗) at the base of the White Mountains. For details about local trails, stop by the **AMC Highland Center** (☎603-466-2727; www.outdoors.org;

NH 302; ⏱ 24hr), one of the country's best launch-pads for outdoor exploration. There's an information desk, a dining room and a small outdoor retail shop. Overnight lodging is also available, and hikers can link to the AMC's popular hut-to-hut trail system from here. The huts are lodge-like dorms offering meals, bunks and stellar views. The Highland Center is just north of the park.

The Conway Scenic Railroad's Notch Train stops at the nearby 1891 **Crawford Depot & Visitor Center** (www.outdoors.org; NH 302; ⏱ 9am-2pm Mon-Fri, to 4pm Sat & Sun Jun-Sep), which contains a small but good collection of train-related history.

🛏 p229

The Drive » Continue east on US 302 for 16 miles, passing Dry River Campground and the Crawford Notch General Store. Turn left at NH 16, and continue 0.25 miles to Story Land.

6 Story Land

With its bright, off-kilter facade, **Story Land** (☎603-383-4186; www.storylandnh.com; 850 NH 16, Glen; $39; ⏱ 9:30am-6pm Jul & Aug, to 5pm mid-late Jun, to 5pm Sat & Sun late May–mid-Jun & Sep–mid-Oct; ℗ 👶) is like a Venus flytrap, luring families in for a closer look, then preventing escape with scenes of kiddie-minded fun just beyond its protective

wall. What's inside this roadside theme park? Shows, games, costumed characters and 20 rides based on fairy tales and make-believe. This popular place gets a thumbs-up from kids and parents alike.

The Drive » Drive north on NH 16. In 2 miles, take a photo break at the covered bridge in tiny Jackson. Continue 8 miles to the trailhead for Glen Ellis Falls.

7 Glen Ellis Falls

Only a stone's throw off NH 16, stop at Glen Ellis Falls for a few snapshots. This easy walk brings you 0.3 miles to a 60ft waterfall, one of the prettiest in the region. Most can make the hike without breaking a sweat.

The Drive » Continue north almost 1 mile to the visitor center.

8 Pinkham Notch Visitor Center

Hikers tackling Mt Washington should stop by the **Pinkham Notch Visitor Center** (☎603-466-2721; www.facebook.com/pg/JoeDodgeLodge; 361 NH 16; ⏱ 6:30am-10pm Jun-Oct, to 9pm Nov-May) for information, maps and a diorama that spotlights area trails. The 4.2-mile **Tuckerman Ravine Trail** to the summit starts behind the visitor center. Appropriate preparation for this brutal climb – which can

Franconia Notch State Park Flume Gorge

be deadly in bad weather – is imperative.

🛏 p229

The Drive » Drive 3 miles north to the entrance to the Auto Rd. From here it's 7.6 miles to the summit.

TRIP HIGHLIGHT

⑨ Mt Washington

Welcome to Mt Washington, New England's highest peak and the site of the world's second-highest recorded wind gust: 231mph (and the highest ever observed by humans). To reach the summit, pay the toll for the **Mt Washington Auto Road** (☎603-466-3988; www.mountwashingtonauto road.com; NH 16; car & driver $31, extra adult/5-12yr $9/7, guided tours adult/child $36/16; ☺8am-6pm mid-Jun–Aug, shorter hours May–mid-Jun & Sep-late Oct) then hold tight to the

wheel as you twist 7.6 miles to the summit on a narrow road with steep drop-offs and no guard rails. But the views of the Presidential Range are superb. Guided tours are also available if you want to leave the driving to someone else.

Up top, stop in for souvenirs, refreshments, views from the observation deck and a visit to the **Extreme Mt Washington** (☎800-706-0432; www. mountwashington.org/visit-us; Mt Washington summit; $2, free with Auto Road ticket; ☺hours vary depending on weather; 🅿) museum, where you can contemplate Mt Washington's claim as 'home of the world's worst weather' and learn how scientists track climate conditions year-round despite hurricane-force winds and Arctic temperatures.

Aspiring athletes take note: a handful of runners have reached the top in less than one hour (!) during the annual Mt Washington Road Race.

The Drive » Backtrack to the junction of NH 16 and US 302. Follow US 302/NH 16 southeast for 5 miles to North Conway, stopping at the Intervale Scenic Vista for views, brochures and restrooms.

TRIP HIGHLIGHT

⑩ North Conway

North Conway is the perfect mountain town: lively pubs, top-notch breakfast joints and numerous quaint inns. Shopaholics can pop into one of the 80 outlet stores (including LL Bean) at **Settlers Green** (www.settlersgreen.com; 1699 White Mountain Hwy; ☺hours vary by store). North Conway is also home to the **Conway Scenic**

TOP TIP:
HIKER SHUTTLE

Need transportation before or after a strenuous one-way hike in the White Mountain region? Use the **AMC hiker shuttle** (☑reservations 603-466-2727; www.outdoors.org/lodging/lodging-shuttle.cfm; one-way trip AMC members/nonmembers $20/24; ⊙daily Jun–mid-Sep, Sat & Sun mid-Sep–mid-Oct) system for your pick-up or drop-off. These shuttles run daily from June to mid-September, then on weekends to mid-October. One-way rides cost $24 ($20 for AMC members) and are best reserved in advance.

Railroad (☑603-356-5251; www.conwayscenic.com; 38 Norcross Circle; Notch Train coach/1st class/dome car $59/73/85; ⊙Notch Train mid-Jun–Oct; 🚺🐕), which runs half-day train trips up into Crawford Notch. On sunny days they may attach the open-air coach car, a restored Pullman with no glass in the windows that's perfect for shutterbugs.

✕ 🏠 p49, p229

The Drive » US 302 splits from NH 16 south of downtown. Follow NH 16 heading south for 2.5 miles, taking it through Conway, then hop onto NH 112, which is better known as the Kancamagus Highway.

TRIP HIGHLIGHT

⑪ Kancamagus Highway

Roll down the windows and slip on your shades. It's time to drive. This 34.5-mile byway, named for a peace-seeking Native American chief, rolls through the **White Mountain National Forest** unhampered by commercial distractions or pesky stoplights – although you do need to gauge your speed and watch for wildlife. Stop by the **Saco Ranger District Office** (☑603-447-5448; www.fs.usda.gov/detail/whitemountain/about-forest/

offices; 33 Kancamagus Hwy, Conway; ⊙9am-4:30pm Mon, 8am-4:30pm Tue-Sun) for maps, information and a recreation pass ($5 per day) if you plan to park and explore. National park passes work too.

Fifteen miles west, pull over at **Sabbaday Falls** for an easy climb to flumes cascading through granite channels and small pools. After the falls, the road starts rising and leafy maples are replaced by dark conifers. The serene view at **Kancamagus Pass** (elevation 2855ft) can be beat only by Mt Washington. For camera-ready panoramas, stop at the **CL Graham Wangan Grounds Overlook** just east of the pass, or the **Pemi Overlook** just west.

The **Lincoln Woods Trail** (☑603-630-5190; www.fs.usda.gov; NH 112/Kancamagus Hwy; day-use fee $5; ⊙visitor center 9am-3:30pm) at the parking area further west follows the Pemigewasset River for 2.9 miles. Kids enjoy the suspension bridge beside the visitor center.

The Drive » From here, drive west on NH 112 to return to Lincoln and North Woodstock.

Eating & Sleeping

Lincoln & North Woodstock ❶

🛏 Notch Hostel   Hostel $

(📞603-348-1483; www.notchhostel.com; 324 Lost River Rd, North Woodstock; dm $30, d $75-90; 🅿 @ 🛜 🐾) Tibetan prayer flags mark your arrival at this gorgeous hostel, the brainchild of outdoor enthusiasts (and husband-and-wife team) Serena and Justin. A class act all round, it welcomes guests with outdoor decks, a spacious kitchen, a mountain-themed library, a sauna for chilly winter nights and a cozy vibe. Lots of info and support for Appalachian Trail through-hikers.

Bretton Woods ❹

🛏 Omni Mt Washington Hotel & Resort   Hotel $$$

(📞603-278-1000; www.omnihotels.com; 310 Mt Washington Hotel Rd; r/ste from $449/619; 🅿 ❄ @ 🛜 🐾) Even if you're not staying here, don't miss the view of Mt Washington from a wicker chair on the veranda of this historic hotel, preferably with a cocktail in hand. Open since 1902, this grand place maintains a sense of fun – note the moose's head overlooking the lobby and the framed local wildflowers in many of the guest rooms.

Crawford Notch ❺

🛏 AMC Highland Center Lodge   Lodge $$

(📞front desk 603-278-4453, reservations 603-466-2727; www.outdoors.org; NH 302, Bretton Woods; r incl breakfast & dinner per adult/child/teen $176/54/103, without bath $121/54/103; 🅿 🛜) This cozy Appalachian Mountain Club lodge is set amid the splendor of Crawford Notch, an ideal base for hiking the trails crisscrossing the Presidential Range. The grounds are beautiful, rooms are basic but comfortable, meals are hearty and guests are outdoor enthusiasts. Discounts for AMC members. The information center, open to the public, has loads of information about regional hiking.

Pinkham Notch ❽

🛏 Joe Dodge Lodge   Lodge $

(📞603-466-2727; www.outdoors.org/lodging/lodges/pinkham; 361 NH 16; r per person adult/3-12yr/13-17yr incl breakfast & dinner from $86/39/74; 🅿 ❄ 🛜) The AMC complex at Pinkham Notch incorporates this lodge, with dorms holding 100-plus beds. Rooms come in a variety of configurations and the price is per person. With the Tuckerman Ravine trailhead a few steps away, this cozy facility is a great place to overnight before hiking to the summit of Mt Washington. Reservations recommended.

North Conway ❿

🍴 May Kelly's Cottage   Irish, American $$

(📞603-356-7005; www.maykellys.com; 3002 White Mountain Hwy; mains $11-27; ⏱4-9pm Wed, noon-9pm Thu, noon-10pm Fri & Sat, noon-8pm Sun) Irish conviviality and friendliness? May Kelly's is the real deal. Local-attic decor, helpful servers, mountain views, sandwiches and hearty mains like the Ploughman's Dinner (top sirloin steak, Irish potato cake, brown bread and baked beans) make it a local favorite.

🍴 Stairway Cafe   Breakfast $

(📞603-356-5200; www.stairwaycafe.com; 2649 White Mountain Hwy; mains $4-15; ⏱7am-3pm) The all-day breakfast treats are scrumptious at this brightly decorated, six-table upstairs cafe, from specials like homemade cinnamon muffins to lobster Benedict. Omelets come with grilled red Maine potatoes, veg baked beans or homemade apple sauce, and there's a range of wild-game sausages (try the venison-merlot-blueberry or wild-boar-cranberry-shiraz varieties). Lunches include burgers, wraps and salads.

🛏 Golden Gables   Motel $$

(📞603-356-2878; www.goldengablesinn.com; 1814 White Mountain Hwy; r $155-209, ste $209-429; 🅿 ❄ 🛜 🐾) The balconies with mountain views close the deal at this stylish motel. Mini-refrigerator and microwave in each room. There's a back lawn perfect for letting the kids run free.

Connecticut River Byway

21

Crossing back and forth between New Hampshire and Vermont, this drive follows the roaring, rippling southbound flow of the mighty Connecticut River, linking mill towns, white-clapboard villages, farms and historical museums.

TRIP HIGHLIGHTS

0 miles

Littleton
The world's longest candy counter sells gummy eggs!

1 START

Orford

3 — **59 miles**

Montshire Museum of Science
Touch the tooth of a mastodon

Claremont

132 miles — **8 FINISH**

Walpole
Dawdle over a double-shot mocha at Burdick Chocolates

**2 DAYS
132 MILES / 212KM**

GREAT FOR...

BEST TIME TO GO

April to November for spring flowers, summer greenery and fall foliage.

 ESSENTIAL PHOTO

The Cornish-Windsor Covered Bridge linking Vermont and New Hampshire.

 BEST FOR FOODIES

Dig into fancy chocolates and savory fare at Burdick Chocolates in Walpole.

---

21 Connecticut River Byway

Taking this leisurely, winding road trip through the Connecticut River's Upper Valley is like earning a liberal arts degree in one weekend. There's the Colonial history of the Fort at No 4, natural sciences at the Montshire Museum and a mini-session in the arts among the sculpture-dotted grounds of Saint-Gaudens. Along the way, you'll be greeted by lush farms and maple-covered hillsides rolling down to meet New England's longest river.

TRIP HIGHLIGHT

❶ Littleton, New Hampshire

Littleton may be off the beaten path, but it's an inspirational place to start this trip. The White Mountains hover to the southeast, the Ammonoosuc River churns through town, a towering steeple overlooks Main St and the world's longest candy counter beckons with a rainbow's array of sweets at **Chutters** (📞603-444-5787; www.chutters.com; 43 Main St; ⏰9am-5pm Mon-Thu, to 7pm Fri & Sat, 10am-5pm Sun); for more Littleton shops see p234.

On Main St, the **Littleton Chamber of Commerce Welcome Center** (📞603-444-6561; www.littletonareachamber.com; 107 Main St, Thayer's Inn; ⏰hours vary) provides a walking-tour brochure with a stop at the **Littleton Grist Mill**. Built in 1797, it's back in service as a mill after renovations initiated in the 1990s. The adjacent Ammonoosuc drops 144ft as it crashes through town. The **covered bridge** here, built in 2004, looks like it's barely hanging onto the riverbank – but it's perfectly safe for walking.

🍴 🛏 p237

The Drive ≫ Take I-93 north to exit 44 and NH 135 south. This bucolic road passes fields, red barns and cattle-crossing signs as it hugs the river. Snap a photo of the covered bridge in Woodsville, then continue south on NH 10. In Orford, look left for the impressive Seven Ridge Houses, built in the Bullfinch style by local craftspeople between 1773 and 1839. Cross the bridge to Fairlee (VT) and continue south along US 5, following the Connecticut River down to East Thetford. The drive is 58 miles.

❷ Cedar Circle Farm, East Thetford, Vermont

With its vast fields stretching out toward the banks of the Connecticut River and bins overflowing with homegrown organic produce, **Cedar Circle Farm** (📞802-785-4737; www.cedarcirclefarm.org; 225 Pavilion Rd; ⏰10am-6pm Mon-Sat, to 5pm Sun late Apr-Oct; 🚼) is like a roadside farm stand on steroids. Wander through the lush fields of produce, pick your own berries, flowers and pumpkins, lounge in an Adirondack chair by the river, or simply stop in at the cafe to pick up a snack for the road ahead. Summer and fall events include dinners in the field, workshops on canning and freezing, and strawberry (June) and pumpkin (October) festivals.

The Drive ≫ Follow US 5 south for 11 miles to Norwich, VT, then take Montshire Rd to the Montshire Museum.

TRIP HIGHLIGHT

③ Montshire Museum of Science, Norwich, Vermont

Rub the tooth of a mastodon. View current images from the Hubble telescope. Watch leafcutter ants at work. But whatever you do at the **Montshire** (☎802-649-2200; www.montshire. org; 1 Montshire Rd; adult/child $18/15 late Jun-early Sep, $16/13 rest of year; ☺10am-5pm; 🚻), don't park your car near the planet Neptune – it's part of a model solar system that stretches the length of the parking lot and beyond (and Neptune is way, way out there).

Located on a 110-acre site beside the Connecticut River, this kid-friendly museum offers exhibits covering ecology, technology, and the natural and physical sciences. It's also the regional visitor center for

LINK YOUR TRIP

Ivy League Tour

Cross the river near the Montshire museum to tour Dartmouth College.

23 Monadnock Villages

From Walpole, take NH 12 to Keene for a stroll through downtown.

233

the **Silvio Conte National Fish & Wildlife Refuge** – look for the life-size moose and the displays that highlight local flora and fauna. In summer, water-focused and sensory exhibits in the Montshire's outdoor **Science Park** will fascinate younger kids.

🛏 p237

The Drive ≫ Cross the river back to Hanover, NH, taking NH 10 past the strip-mall wasteland of West Lebanon, where you pick up NH 12A south to Saint-Gaudens; the drive is 18 miles. (For variety, the river can be tracked along US 5 in Vermont between a village or two, with regular bridges connecting New Hampshire and Vermont until you reach Walpole.)

LOCAL KNOWLEDGE: SHOPPING & STROLLING DOWNTOWN LITTLETON

Lined with 19th- and early-20th-century buildings, Littleton's Main St is a delightful place to stroll, with some attractive, independently owned stores. For outdoor gear and clothing, step into **Lahout's** (☑603-444-5838; www.lahouts.com; 245 Union St; ☻10am-5:30pm Mon-Sat, to 4:30pm Sun), America's oldest ski shop. A few doors down, the **League of New Hampshire Craftsmen** (☑603-444-1099; www.littleton.nhcrafts.org; 81 Main St, lower level; ☻10am-6pm Mon-Sat, 10:30am-5pm Sun) runs a gallery that sells jewelry, pottery and other New Hampshire–made arts and crafts. For lunch and a slice of local life, grab a seat at the **Coffee Pot** (☑603-444-5722; www.thecoffeepotrestaurant.com; 30 Main St; mains $5-11; ☻6:30am-4pm Mon-Fri, to 2pm Sat, to noon Sun) on Main St, or head round the corner to the 18th-century grist mill by the Ammonoosuc River, where you can soak up river views over craft brews and pizza at Schilling Beer Co (p237).

---

④ Saint-Gaudens National Historic Site, New Hampshire

In the summer of 1885, the sculptor Augustus Saint-Gaudens rented an old inn near the town of Cornish and came to this beautiful spot to work. He returned summer after summer and eventually bought the place in 1892. The **estate** (☑603-675-2175; www.nps.gov/saga; 139 St Gaudens Rd, Cornish; adult/under 16yr $10/free; ☻bldgs 9am-4:30pm Jun-Oct, visitor center only 9am-4pm Mon-Fri Nov-May, grounds dawn-dusk year-round; ℗)), where he lived until his death in 1907, is now open to the public.

Saint-Gaudens is best known for his public monuments, including the Robert Gold Shaw Memorial across from the state house in Boston. Recasts of his greatest sculptures dot the beautiful grounds. Visitors can also tour his home and wander the studios, where artists-in-residence sculpt. Exhibit buildings are closed in winter, but the visitor center is usually open 9am to 4pm weekdays.

The Drive ≫ Head 1.5 miles south on NH 12A to reach the Cornish-Windsor Covered Bridge.

---

⑤ Cornish-Windsor Covered Bridge

Built in 1866, this 449ft-long beauty is the longest wooden covered bridge in the United States and you can still drive across it! One bit of trivia, in case you were wondering: the whole thing belongs to the state of New Hampshire, so you won't actually cross into Vermont until you touch the riverbank on the far side.

The Drive ≫ Cross the covered bridge into Windsor, VT, then take US 5 north to the Old Constitution House at 16 N Main St.

---

⑥ Windsor, Vermont

Affectionately known as the 'Birthplace of Vermont,' Windsor is home

Littleton Ammonoosuc River

to the **Old Constitution House State Historic Site** (http://historicsites. vermont.gov/directory/ old_constitution). This small museum occupies the former tavern where a devoted band of Vermonters – rejecting the competing claims of New York and New Hampshire to their territory – officially declared Vermont's independence in July 1777. The groundbreaking constitution signed here was the first in the New World to outlaw slavery, create a free public education system for both men and women, and give every man (regardless of property ownership) the right to vote.

Vermont held its ground as an independent republic for 14 years (eat your heart out, Texas!) before finally joining the union as the 14th state in 1791. Visitors can tour the museum here and learn about Vermont's early history on weekends from Memorial Day to Columbus Day.

The Drive » Bop back into New Hampshire via the Cornish-

Windsor Bridge and turn right to follow the Connecticut River downstream. Not quite 1 mile south, bear left onto Town House Rd at the fork for two more covered bridges, then continue south for another 17 miles on NH 12A, which soon rejoins NH 12, to Charlestown.

- - - - - - - - - - - - - - - - -

❼ Fort at No 4, Charlestown, New Hampshire

Named for a 1700s land grant, the original fort was built in the 1740s to protect pioneer farmers from Native Americans and the French. The original fort, which was no longer needed by the late 1770s and no longer exists, was reconstructed in the 1960s as a **living history museum** (☎603-826-5700; www.fortat4.org; 267 Springfield Rd/NH 11; adult/6-12yr/13-17yr $10/6/8; ◷10am-4:30pm Wed-Sat, to 3:30pm Sun May-Oct; P), with a layout based on a detailed drawing sketched in 1746.

Visitors can explore the different rooms of the fort, wander the riverside grounds and watch historical re-enactors, whose activities vary from

weekend to weekend. Check the Facebook page for current activities.

The Drive » Rolling mountains, as well as fields, train tracks, river views and a sugar house, decorate the 14-mile drive on NH 12 south to Walpole.

- - - - - - - - - - - - - - - - -

TRIP HIGHLIGHT

❽ Walpole, New Hampshire

The carefully crafted desserts at **Burdick Chocolates** look like they attended finishing school – no slovenly lava cakes or naughty whoopee pies here. But you'll find more than just rich chocolate indulgences. The adjoining bistro serves creative new American dishes, plus artisanal cheeses and top-notch wines; the creamy quiche is fantastic.

Purchase local art and crafts across the street at the **Walpole Artists Cooperative** (☎603-756-3020; www.walpoleartisans. org; 52 Main St; ◷10am-5pm Wed-Sat, 11:30am-3pm Sun).

✖ p237

Eating & Sleeping

Littleton ❶

✖ Cold Mountain Cafe & Gallery International $$

(☎603-869-2500; www.coldmountaincafe.com; 2015 Main St, Bethlehem; sandwiches & salads $8.50-10, dinner mains $12-21; ☺11am-3pm & 5-9pm Mon-Sat, closed Nov) Among the region's finest restaurants, this casual cafe and gallery has an eclectic, changing menu, featuring gourmet sandwiches, salads and quiches at lunchtime, and luscious dinner options, such as bouillabaisse, Indian-spiced lamb stew or its signature black bean cakes. There's occasional live music, from jazz to folk. Be prepared to wait for your table (outside, since the place is cozy).

✖ Schilling Beer Co Pizza, Pub Food $

(☎603-444-4800; www.schillingbeer.com; 18 Mill St; pizzas $11-16; ☺noon-10pm Mon-Thu, noon-11pm Fri, 11am-11pm Sat, 11am-10pm Sun) In a historic mill by the Ammonoosuc River, this bustling microbrewery serves delicious crunchy-crusted, wood-fired pizzas along with bratwurst and a nice selection of home brews, from Konundrum sour pale ale to Erastus Belgian abbey-style tripel. The post-and-beam-style main room, looking out at a covered bridge, makes for a convivial setting, as does the riverside deck.

🛏 Littleton Motel Motel $

(☎603-444-5780; www.littletonmotel.com; 166 Main St; r $78-108, ste $128-158; ☺May-Oct; P ❄ 🛜 🏊) Why, yes, I would like to stay in New Hampshire's oldest motel. But don't worry – the 20 rooms at this old-school motor inn, which opened in 1948, have refrigerators, microwaves, air-con and wi-fi.

Norwich ❸

🛏 Norwich Inn Inn $$

(☎802-649-1143; www.norwichinn.com; 325 Main St; r $189-269, ste $299; P ❄ 🛜) Just across the Connecticut River in Norwich, this is both a historic inn and a microbrewery. Rooms in the main house are decorated with Victorian antiques and traditional country furniture, and the two adjacent buildings include modern furnishings and gas fireplaces in each room.

Walpole ❽

✖ Burdick Chocolates Cafe $

(☎603-756-2882; www.burdickchocolate.com/chocolateshop-cafe-walpole.aspx; 47 Main St; pastries from $3; ☺7am-5pm Mon, to 9pm Tue-Sat, 9am-5pm Sun) Locals descend from surrounding villages to dine at this fabulous eatery. Originally a New York City chocolatier, Burdick relocated to this tiny gem of a New Hampshire village and opened a sophisticated cafe to showcase its desserts. Complementing these rich chocolaty indulgences is the adjacent Restaurant at Burdick's.

✖ Restaurant at Burdick's Bistro $$

(☎603-756-9058; www.47mainwalpole.com/the-restaurant.html; 47 Main St; mains lunch $17-27, dinner $17-33; ☺11:30am-2:30pm Mon, 11:30am-3pm & 5:30-9pm Tue-Sat, 10am-2pm Sun) This spectacular restaurant in tiny Walpole serves French-themed dishes, such as onion soup, *steak frites* and *mussels mariniere*, plus a few regional dishes like New England oysters, accompanied by artisanal cheeses and top-notch wines. It's a lovely spot for dressing up just a bit.

Lake Winnipesaukee

This trip loops around the state's largest lake, swinging past a wildlife preserve, trails, museums and a drive-in – there's something for toddlers, teens, the kids in between and good ol' mom and dad.

TRIP HIGHLIGHTS

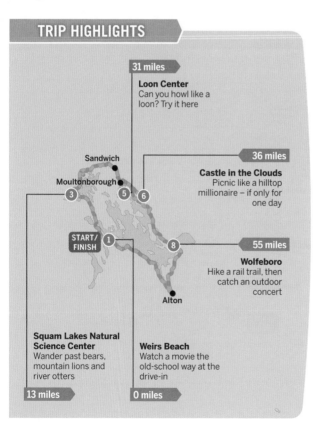

31 miles
Loon Center
Can you howl like a loon? Try it here

Sandwich
Moultonborough
3 **5** **6**

36 miles
Castle in the Clouds
Picnic like a hilltop millionaire – if only for one day

START/ FINISH **1** **8**

55 miles
Wolfeboro
Hike a rail trail, then catch an outdoor concert

Alton

Squam Lakes Natural Science Center
Wander past bears, mountain lions and river otters
13 miles

Weirs Beach
Watch a movie the old-school way at the drive-in
0 miles

2 DAYS
85 MILES / 137KM

GREAT FOR...

BEST TIME TO GO
June to September: school's out and the weather is warm.

ESSENTIAL PHOTO
The Weirs Beach Boardwalk – it's a classic!

BEST FOR WILDLIFE
Visit Squam Lakes Natural Science Center for critter-watching and live animal demos.

Weirs Beach Boardwalk

22 Lake Winnipesaukee

Weirs Beach drive-in has shown movies on the big screen since 1949. Across the lake, Bailey's Bubble has scooped ice cream for generations of appreciative families. Summer camps in the area have thrived for decades too. There's something special about this mountain-ringed lake, a place that summons people back year after year. But it's not just the beauty. It's the little moments of family fun and summer camaraderie that make it truly magical.

TRIP HIGHLIGHT

❶ Weirs Beach

A word of warning: if you're traveling with kids, they're going to want to stay here all day. With its colorful distractions – video arcades, slippery waterslides, souvenir stands and a bustling boardwalk – Weirs Beach is the lake region's center of tacky fun. Escape the hoopla on the **Winnipesaukee Scenic Railroad** (✆603-745-2135; www.hoborr.com; 211 Lakeside Ave; adult/

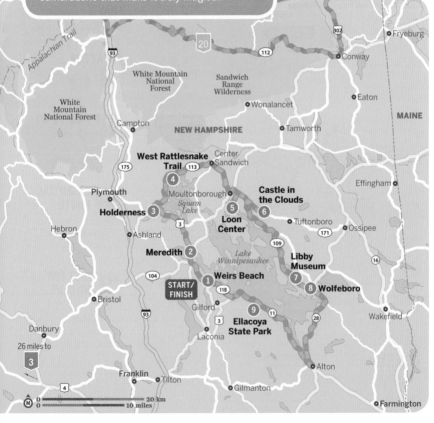

child 3-11yr 1hr $18/14;), whose '20s and '30s train cars travel to the lake's southern tip at Alton Bay and back – kids love the ice-cream-parlor car. The train depot is also the departure point for MS *Mt Washington*.

After a day on the beach, unwind with a movie at the **Weirs Drive-In** (☑603-366-4723; www.weirsdrivein.com; 76 Endicott St/US 3; per car $28; ⏰7-11pm mid-May–early Sep;). Opened in 1949 and in continuous operation since then, the WDI is a revered institution. Note that every car will be charged, at a minimum, $28, which covers up to four people.

✘ 🛏 p245

The Drive ›› Go north on US 3/Endicott St, which runs parallel to the lake. Soon after passing the high-flying ropes course at Monkey Trunks (www. monkeytrunks.com), US 3's local name changes to Daniel

LINK YOUR TRIP

3 **Ivy League Tour**
Follow I-93 to the Ivies for guided tours about history and traditions.

20 **White Mountains Loop**
From Holderness, drive north to the Notches for trains, hiking and cascades.

Webster Hwy. Meredith is 5 miles north of Weirs Beach.

- - - - - - - - - - - - - - - - - - -

② Meredith

Upscale Meredith is a lively lakeside town with attractive Colonial and Victorian homes flanking a commercial center. In Meredith village, boutiques, art and craft stores, galleries and restaurants line US 3 and Main St.

Just south of the village roundabout, stop in at **Mill Falls Marketplace** (www.millfalls.com/shop; 312 Daniel Webster Hwy/US 3; ⏰10am-5:30pm Mon-Thu, to 9pm Fri & Sat), a restored linen mill that houses a dozen shops and restaurants. Climb to the top floor and settle in at **Waterfall Cafe** (☑603-677-8631; www.millfalls.com/dine; mains $6-10; ⏰6:30am-1pm Mon-Fri, 7am-1:30pm Sat, 7am-1pm Sun), a cozy spot where you can enjoy omelets, buttermilk pancakes, eggs Benedict, salads and sandwiches against the backdrop of a spectacular wall mural depicting Lake Winnipesaukee and the surrounding rolling hills.

The Winnipesaukee Scenic Railroad and the MS *Mt Washington* boat (Monday only July and August) both stop in Meredith.

✘ p245

The Drive ›› From Meredith, continue 5 miles north on

woodsy, easy-driving US 3. Don't be surprised if you see lots of motorcyclists. Squam Lake soon nudges into view to the northeast.

- - - - - - - - - - - - - - - - - - -

TRIP HIGHLIGHT

③ Holderness

The site of the movie *On Golden Pond,* Squam Lake and Holderness remain placid and peaceful, perfect for a pair of waders and fly-fishing, or for plopping your butt in a beach chair and soaking up the sun. If you hike in the shady forests you'll frequently surprise deer, moose and even a black bear or two.

It's all about the wildlife at **Squam Lakes Natural Science Center** (☑603-968-7194; www.nhnature.org; 23 Science Center Rd, off NH 113; adult/child 3-15yr $20/15, boat tours $27/23; ⏰9:30am-5pm May-Oct; 🅿), where four nature paths weave through the woods and around the marsh. The 0.75-mile **Gephardt Trail** is a highlight, leading past large trailside enclosures that hold bobcats, mountain lions, river otters and raptors. (Most of the animals were orphaned or injured and are unable to live on their own in the wild.) The center also offers informative 90-minute tours of the lake and educational live animal demonstrations.

✘ 🛏 p245

The Drive ≫ From the nature center, follow NH 113 northeast for 5 miles. About 0.25 miles after the 'Rockywold Deephaven Camps' sign, look for the 'West Rattlesnake Trail' sign. Park in the parking lot or in a permissible space on either side of the road, wherever you don't see a 'No Parking' sign. The trail is on the lakeside.

④ West Rattlesnake Trail

The West Rattlesnake Trail climbs to a rocky outcrop atop Rattlesnake Mountain that yields stunning views of Squam Lake. It's less than a mile to the top, making this a good hike for families. (Just watch younger kids on the rocks.)

The Drive ≫ NH 113 twists past cottages, pine trees and rock walls, offering glimpses of Squam Lake to the southeast before entering Center Sandwich. From this white clapboard village, pick up NH 109 south for 4.5 miles to NH 25/Whittier Hwy. Turn right onto NH 25 and follow it about 0.5 miles to Blake Rd and turn left. Follow Blake Rd to Lees Mill Rd and turn right.

TRIP HIGHLIGHT

⑤ Loon Center

Loons may be water birds, but their closest relatives are actually penguins, not ducks or geese. Known for their unique and varied calls (the wail sounds like a howling wolf), loons experienced a sharp decline in the 1970s.

The Loon Preservation Committee monitors the birds and works to restore a strong, healthy population. At its secluded **Loon Center** (☎603-476-5666; www.loon.org; 183 Lees Mill Rd, Moultonborough; ⊙9am-5pm daily Jul-early Oct, Mon-Sat May, Jun & mid-Oct, Thu-Sat late Oct-Apr; 👪), wildlife enthusiasts can learn about the birds' plumage, habitat and distinctive calls and watch an award-winning video. There are also details about protecting the birds. Kid-friendly activities include interactive games, a scavenger hunt and a junior biologist's guide.

The center sits within the 200-acre **Markus Wildlife Sanctuary** (www.loon.org/loon-center-markus-sanctuary.php; ⊙dawn-dusk; 🅿). The sanctuary's **Loon Nest Trail** is a haven for birds: the 1.7-mile path winds through the forest and past a marsh to the shores of Lake Winnipesaukee. The best time for loon spotting is nesting season, in June and July.

The Drive ≫ Follow Lees Mill Rd to Lee Rd. Turn right and continue to NH 109. Turn right. Continue 1.2 miles to the junction of NH 109 and the start of NH 171/Old Mountain Rd. Drive about 2 miles on NH 171. The entrance to Castle in the Clouds will be on the left.

TRIP HIGHLIGHT

⑥ Castle in the Clouds

Perched on high like a king surveying his territory, the Arts and Crafts–style **Castle in the Clouds** (☎603-476-5900;

CRUISING ON MS MOUNT WASHINGTON

Boasting 183 miles of coastline, Lake Winnipesaukee is prime cruising territory. The classic **MS Mount Washington** (☎603-366-5531; www.cruisenh.com; 211 Lakeside Ave; adult/5-12yr regular cruises $32/16, Sun brunch cruises $52/26; ⊙mid-May–late Oct) steams out of Weirs Beach on a relaxing 2½-hour scenic lake cruise, departing twice daily in July, August and late September to mid-October (reduced schedule May, June and early September).

Special trips include the Sunday champagne brunch cruise and the evening sunset, plus fall foliage and theme cruises (tribute to Elvis, Lobsterfest etc) running throughout summer and fall ($32 to $52). From late June through August, the boat stops in Meredith on Monday and in Wolfeboro daily from Tuesday to Saturday (Monday through Saturday in Wolfeboro in September and October).

Moultonborough Castle in the Clouds

www.castleintheclouds.org; 455 Old Mountain Rd/NH 171, Moultonborough; adult/5-17yr $17/10; ⊙10am-5:30pm daily late May–late Oct, Sat & Sun mid-May–late May; 🅿) wows with its stone walls and exposed-timber beams, but it's the views of lakes and valleys that draw the crowds – in fall the kaleidoscope of rust, red and yellow beats any postcard. The 5500-acre estate features gardens, ponds and a path leading to a small waterfall. Admission includes the 2-mile scenic road to the mansion and stories about the eccentric millionaire, Thomas Plant, who built it.

From late June to late August, make reservations for sunset music performances with dinner on Monday and Thursday nights. Check the online calendar for other events, ranging from yoga on the lawn to stargazing.

The Drive » Return to NH 109 south, following a woodsy route that tracks Lake Winnipesaukee (although you won't always be able to see the water). After Melvin Village, cross Mirror Lake on a pinch of land before hitting the outskirts of Wolfeboro. The drive is 10 miles.

---

❼ Libby Museum

At the age of 40, Henry Forrest Libby, a local doctor, began collecting things. In 1912 he built a home for his collections, which later became the eccentric little **Libby Museum** (☎603-569-1035; www.thelibbymuseum.org; 755 N Main St/NH 109, Winter Harbor; adult/under 16yr $5/ free; ⊙10am-4pm Tue-Sat, noon-4pm Sun Jun–mid-Sep). Starting with butterflies and moths, the amateur naturalist built up a private natural-history collection that now includes numerous stuffed mammals and birds.

Other collections followed, including Abenaki relics and early American farm and home implements. The museum sits in a lovely spot across from Winter Harbor on Lake Winnipesaukee.

The Drive >> Drive 3.2 miles southeast on NH 109 to downtown Wolfeboro.

TRIP HIGHLIGHT

8 Wolfeboro

The self-proclaimed 'Oldest Resort in America' is a nice place to wander for a few hours. The waterfront is picturesque, with a grassy lakeside park, and in summer there are lots of free concerts and art events. (It's also garnered fame as the site of Republican presidential candidate Mitt Romney's summer home.)

Stretch your legs on the **Cotton Valley Rail Trail** (www.cottonvalleyrail trail.org; Central Ave), which runs for 12 miles along a former train track. It passes two lakes, climbs through Cotton Valley and winds through forests and fields. The trail starts behind the **Wolfeboro Chamber of Commerce** (☑603-569-2200; www.wolfeborochamber.com; 32 Central Ave; ◷10am-3pm Mon-Sat, to noon Sun late May–mid-Oct, shorter hours rest of year), inside the former train depot, which carries a fantastic map detailing the walk. Before leaving, buy a scoop of ice cream downtown from **Bailey's Bubble** (☑603-569-3612; www.facebook.com/BaileysBubble; 5 Railroad Ave; ice cream from $3.50; ◷11am-10pm early May-early Oct), where

they've served generations of families.

🍴 🛏 p245

The Drive >> Leave NH 109 in Wolfeboro, picking up NH 28 east just south of downtown. Summer camps dot the 10-mile drive toward Alton. Turn right on Old Bay Rd to pick up NH 11 north and drive for another 10 miles, passing the trailhead for the Mt Major Trail, a 1.5-mile one-way path leading to big views of the lake.

9 Ellacoya State Park

This has been a busy trip, so if you're ready to relax in a lovely setting, unpack your beach towel for a sunny day at lakeside **Ellacoya State Park** (☑603-293-7821; www.nhstateparks.org; 266 Scenic Rd, Gilford; adult/6-11yr $5/2; ◷9am-5pm daily mid-Jun–early Sep, Sat & Sun late May-early Jun), which has a 600ft-wide beach with gorgeous views across the lake to the Sandwich and Ossipee Mountains. This is an excellent place for swimming, fishing and canoeing. If your timing is right you might even see the MS *Mt Washington* cruising across the still waters – it's a pretty scene!

The Drive >> To complete the loop, return to Weirs Beach by taking NH 11 and NH 11B north for 7 miles.

THE GREAT PUMPKIN WAS HERE

One of the state's quirkiest annual gatherings, the **New Hampshire Pumpkin Festival** (www.facebook.com/NHPumpkinFestival; Main St, Laconia; ◷Oct), held on the third or fourth Saturday in October, draws in thousands of visitors to admire the world's largest tower of jack-o'-lanterns. Started in 1991 by merchants in Keene, the event exploded over the years, with the town's 2003 tally of nearly 29,000 pumpkins setting a Guinness world record. In 2015 the festival moved to Laconia, about 7 miles south of Weirs Beach.

In addition to gazing into the eyes of the plump, artfully carved orange fruit, visitors can enjoy a craft fair, a costume parade, seed-spitting contests and fireworks. Live bands play on the surrounding streets as local merchants dish up clam chowder, fried sausages, mulled cider and plenty of pumpkin pie.

Eating & Sleeping

Weirs Beach ❶

✖ Union Diner   Diner $

(📞603-524-6744; www.theuniondiner.com; 1331
Union Ave, Laconia; mains $5-14; ⏱6am-3pm
Mon-Wed, to 8pm Thu-Sat, to 1pm Sun) Escape
the waterfront hubbub at this classic American
diner 3 miles south of Weirs Beach, housed
in a converted 1950s railway dining car with
oak-mahogany woodwork and decorative floors.
Grab a booth or a counterside stool and treat
yourself to early-bird breakfast specials or a
lunch of homemade meatloaf, lobster stew, or
roast turkey with stuffing and cranberry sauce.

🛏 Proctor's
Lakehouse Cottages   Apartment $$$

(📞603-366-5517; www.lakehousecottages.com;
1144 Weirs Blvd/US 3, Weirs Beach; cottages
$250-340, ste $315; ⏱mid-May-early Oct;
P❄🐾🛜🏊) This welcoming family-owned
collection of cottages and suites, all with
kitchens, is blissful. The more modern suites
clustered in the main structure feature porches,
while cottages exude old-school New England
with original wood walls and rustic (but well-
kept) furnishings. All have views of the lake
(there's a tiny beach and deck), and every unit
comes with its own lakeside grill.

Meredith ❷

✖ Lakeside Deli & Grille   Sandwiches $

(📞603-677-7132; www.facebook.com/
LakesideDeliGrille; 2 Pleasant St; most
sandwiches $6-11; ⏱11am-4pm Sun, Mon, Wed
& Thu, to 8pm Fri & Sat) For a delicious lunch
with prime Lake Winnipesaukee views, hit the
front porch of this deli just east of downtown,
beloved for its reasonably priced sandwiches,
homemade soups, and fish tacos with fresh
haddock and chipotle mayo.

Holderness ❸

✖ Walter's Basin   American $$

(📞603-968-4412; www.waltersbasin.com; 859
US 3; mains $10-26; ⏱11:30am-9pm Sun-Thu, to

9:30pm Fri & Sat) Lake trippers are encouraged
to dock their boats and come in for a meal at
this casual waterfront spot. Located on Little
Squam Lake near the bridge, the friendly
restaurant features pan-fried haddock, elk
meatloaf, grilled steak tip sandwiches, lobster
macaroni and cheese, and other comfort fare.
Sip a craft beer at the easygoing Basshole
Lounge.

🛏 Manor on Golden Pond   B&B $$$

(📞603-968-3348, 800-545-2141; www.
manorongoldenpond.com; 31 Manor Dr; r $285-
415, ste $485; ⏱closed 1 week Christmas & 1
week early spring; P@🛜🏊) This inviting B&B
is perched on Shepard Hill, overlooking serene
Squam Lake. Quaintly elegant rooms (some with
fireplaces and hot tubs), gourmet breakfasts
(included in rates) and a lovely private beach
make this a fine lake region retreat. Extra perks
include clay tennis courts, a full-service spa and
an excellent dining room. Children under 12 are
not welcome.

Wolfeboro ❽

✖ Wolfetrap Grill & Rawbar   Seafood $$

(📞603-569-1047; www.wolfetrapgrillandrawbar.
com; 19 Bay St; mains $9-26; ⏱11am-9pm
Tue-Sat May-late Nov) Nantucket meets new
Hampshire at this airy eatery tucked away
on Back Bay, an inlet of Lake Winnipesaukee.
Inside tables are covered with parchment
paper – ready for you to attack and get
messy with shellfish (oysters, clams, shrimp,
lobster) – while the deck has loungey chairs
overlooking the water. The bar keeps going, as
the bartenders say, 'till the wolf howls.'

🛏 Wolfeboro Inn   Inn $$$

(📞603-569-3016; www.wolfeboroinn.com; 90 N
Main St; r $219-279, ste $319-359; P@🛜🏊)
The town's best-known lodging is right on the
lake with a private beach. One of the region's
most prestigious resorts since 1812, it has 44
rooms across a main inn and a modern annex.
Rooms have modern touches like new beds
and contemporary furnishings: it feels less
historic but oh-so luxurious. Facilities include a
restaurant and pub, Wolfe's Tavern.

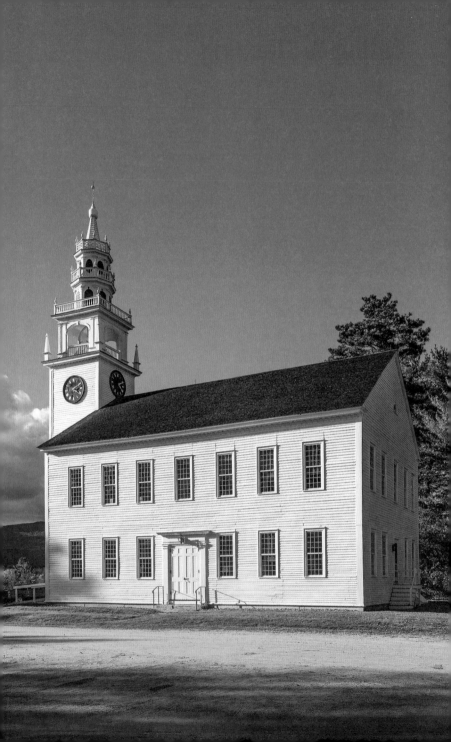

Monadnock Villages

Driving between the villages encircling Mt Monadnock is like gliding through a 19th-century landscape painting – one brought vividly to life with hikers, blooming rhododendrons and abundant wildlife.

23

TRIP HIGHLIGHTS

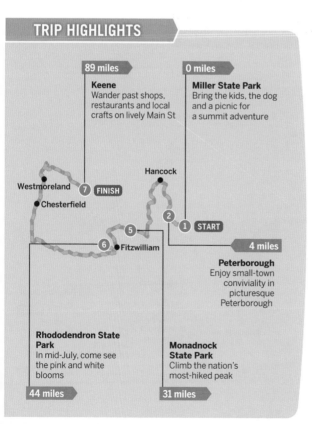

89 miles
Keene
Wander past shops, restaurants and local crafts on lively Main St

0 miles
Miller State Park
Bring the kids, the dog and a picnic for a summit adventure

Hancock

Westmoreland **7** **FINISH**

● Chesterfield

2

1 **START**

5

6 ● Fitzwilliam

4 miles

Peterborough
Enjoy small-town conviviality in picturesque Peterborough

Rhododendron State Park
In mid-July, come see the pink and white blooms

Monadnock State Park
Climb the nation's most-hiked peak

44 miles

31 miles

2 DAYS
89 MILES / 143KM

GREAT FOR...

BEST TIME TO GO
April through October for festivals, foliage and hiking.

ESSENTIAL PHOTO
From Kimball Farm, photograph Mt Monadnock, then order your ice cream.

BEST FOR OUTDOORS
A hike to the summit of Mt Monadnock – views are superb!

Monadnock Villages

Striking peaks, birch-lined streams, white-painted villages – it's no wonder artists and writers such as Henry David Thoreau, Willa Cather and Thornton Wilder found inspiration here. But the camaraderie in the towns, with their attractive communal spaces, surely added oomph to their oohs and aahs. This convivial spirit continues today, from the shared sense of adventure on the White Dot Trail to the ice-cream fans toughing out the winds on a chilly day at Kimball Farm.

TRIP HIGHLIGHT

① Miller State Park

If Mt Monadnock is the main course, then **Pack Monadnock** is the appetizer. Just 4 miles east of Peterborough, this 2290ft mountain is the heart of **Miller State Park** (📞603-924-3672; www.nhstateparks.org; 13 Miller Park Rd; adult/child 6-11yr $4/2; ⊙8am-6pm Sun-Fri, to 8pm Sat late May–early Sep, hours vary rest of year; **P**). Established in 1891, the park is New Hampshire's oldest, and a good one to visit if you're

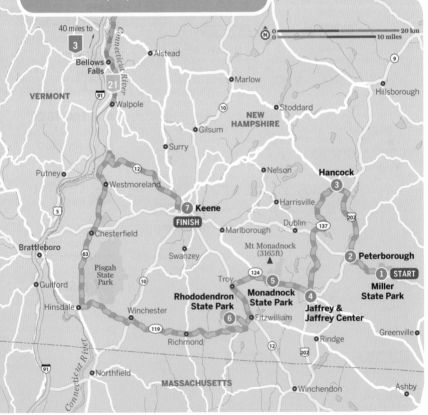

traveling with young children and pets. Two separate trails, the **Womack Trail** and the **Marion Davis Trail**, lead 1.4 miles from the parking lot to the summit, where you can climb a **fire tower** (built in 1939) for sweeping views. Short on time? Drive the 1.3-mile paved road to the top.

The Drive » Take NH 101 west for 4 miles into Peterborough.

TRIP HIGHLIGHT

2 Peterborough

This charming village of redbrick houses and tree-lined streets, with the idyllic Nabasuit River coursing through its historic center, is a particularly nice place for an extended stop. Its atmosphere is enhanced by the artistic influence of the nearby MacDowell Colony.

LINK YOUR TRIP

3 Ivy League Tour
Head north from Keene to Hanover via NH 12 and I-91 for a tour of New England's most legendary colleges.

21 Connecticut River Byway
Swoop west from Keene on NH 12 to join the beautiful valley of the Connecticut River.

ATTENTION: ARTISTS AT WORK!

The MacDowell Colony, Peterborough's century-old art colony, draws more than 250 poets, composers, writers, architects and playwrights to the Monadnock region each year. Playwright Thornton Wilder wrote *Our Town*, a play openly inspired by Peterborough, while at the colony. On the first Friday of every month between March and November, MacDowell fellows share their work through the MacDowell Downtown program, a series of free performances and panel discussions open to the general public.

Pop into the **Mariposa Museum** (☏603-924-4555; www.mariposamuseum.org; 26 Main St; adult/child $6/4; ☺11am-5pm Tue-Sun; 🚸) for folk art and folklore from around the world. It's a 'please touch' kind of place, and kids are encouraged to try on costumes and play the musical instruments. Visit during one of the periodic interactive performances featuring musicians and storytellers. The indie bookstore **Toadstool Bookshop** (☏603-924-3543; www. toadbooks.com; 12 Depot Sq; ☺10am-6pm Mon-Fri, to 5pm Sat, to 4pm Sun; 🖥) has a welcoming vibe and a good selection of books. Its small cafe, **Aesop's Tables** (☏603-924-1612; www.facebook.com/aesops tablescafe; mains breakfast $4-7, lunch $7-9; ☺7:30am-4pm Mon-Fri, 9am-1pm Sat), has a few patio tables and sells coffee, quiches, salads and sandwiches.

🍴 🛏 p253

The Drive » From Peterborough, drive 9 miles northwest on US 202/NH 123, along a woodsy route also popular with motorcyclists.

---

3 Hancock

In the first half of the 1800s, wandering artists would paint colorful landscape murals on bedroom walls in homes and inns throughout New England. Rufus Porter, an inventor who started *Scientific American* magazine, was one of the most famous of these traveling artists; unfortunately, many of his stencils and paintings were subsequently covered, and ruined, by wallpaper. Two murals are still visible inside the Hancock Inn (p253), a three-story B&B in the heart of town. The inn is the oldest in New Hampshire and has been in continuous operation since 1789 – when George Washington was president! Although the murals are in guest rooms, you can enjoy a Porter-style mural – with a cocktail – in the inn's sitting room before a meal at the restaurant.

🛏 p253

The Drive » NH 137 winds past marshes, stone walls and lichen-covered rocks on its way to NH 101, which is 6.5 miles south. Continue south on NH 137 for 7 miles to Jaffrey or, if you need to break for a meal, turn left and continue to Peterborough, then head south to Jaffrey on US 202.

④ Jaffrey & Jaffrey Center

Jaffrey Center, 2 miles west of Jaffrey, is another tiny, picture-perfect village of serene lanes, 18th-century homes and a dramatic white-steepled meetinghouse. All of its historic sites are clustered around the wee historic district, located on both sides of Gilmore Pond Rd off NH 124. The most intriguing sights include the towering 1775 **meetinghouse** (www.townofjaffrey.com; Blackberry Lane; **P**), the frozen-in-time **Little Red School House** and the **Melville Academy** (www.townofjaffrey.com; 39 Thorndike Pond Rd; ⏱2-4pm Sat & Sun Jul & Aug), which houses a one-room museum of rural artifacts. Willa Cather, a frequent visitor to Jaffrey, is buried in the **Old Burying Ground** behind the meetinghouse, with a

quote from *My Antonia* gracing the headstone.

Jaffrey is perhaps best known as the home of Kimball Farm (p252), an ice-cream shop that is favored by Mt Monadnock hikers.

🍴 p253

The Drive » From Jaffrey Center, drive under a half-mile on NH 124 and turn right on Dublin Rd. Pass a church camp and follow the signs to the park.

TRIP HIGHLIGHT

⑤ Monadnock State Park

Roughly 125,000 people climb this commanding 3165ft **peak** (☎603-532-8862; www.nhstateparks.org; 169 Poole Rd, Jaffrey; day use adult/6-11yr $5/2; **P**) every year, helping it earn the honor of the most-climbed peak in the USA. Writer and philosopher Henry David Thoreau climbed it several times in the mid-1800s. Displays inside the visitor center explain that *monadnock* comes from the Abenaki word meaning 'special' or 'unique.' The word is now used geologically to describe a residual hill that rises alone from a plain.

Twelve miles of un-groomed **ski trails** lure

Monadnock State Park Peak climb

cross-country skiers in winter, while more than 40 miles of **hiking paths** draw the trail-hungry hordes in summer. Numerous combinations of trails lead to the summit. The 1.9-mile one-way **White Dot Trail** (www. nhstateparks.org; 169 Poole Rd) is the most direct route, running from the visitor center to the bare-topped peak; it's a 3.9-mile round-trip hike if you return on the **White Cross Trail**, and the whole trip takes about 3½ hours. Most people ascend on the slightly shorter White Dot Trail. On clear days, you can gaze 100 miles across all six New England states.

The park's seasonal Gilson Pond Campground (p253) is well placed for a sunrise ascent.

🛏 p253

The Drive ›› Return to NH 124 and follow it 4.5 miles west, then bear left onto Troy Rd/ Monadnock St and continue 2.5 miles west to join NH 12 near Troy. Turn left onto southbound NH 12 and drive 4 miles to Fitzwilliam, whose town green is surrounded by lovely old houses and a towering steeple. Follow NH 119 about 1 mile west, then turn right on Rhododendron Rd and drive for 2 miles.

TRIP HIGHLIGHT

⑥ Rhododendron State Park

The 16-acre rhododendron grove in this serene **park** (☎603-532-8862; www.nhstateparks.org; 424 Rockwood Pond Rd, US 119W, Fitzwilliam; adult/6-11yr $4/2; ☉year-round unless otherwise posted; 👶) is the largest in New England. It makes for a nice stroll in mid-July, when thick stands of the giant plant (*Rhododendron maximum*) bloom white and pink along the 0.6-mile **Rhododendron Trail**

LOCAL KNOWLEDGE: KIMBALL FARM

After a hike to the summit of Mt Monadnock, everyone knows that the best reward is ice cream from **Kimball Farm** (📞603-532-5765; www.kimballfarm. com/jaffrey; 158 Turnpike Rd/NH 124, Jaffrey; mains $7-32, small ice cream $5; ⏰10am-10pm mid-Apr–early Oct). Consider the 40 flavors, order at the window, then find a seat at a picnic table out front. Perennial favorites include maple walnut, vanilla peanut butter, raspberry chocolate chip and coffee Oreo. Take note: the scoops are huge.

circling the grove. The blooms can last for weeks and the final blossoms may occur as the leaves are turning. Listen for songbirds in the foliage while on the trail. The trail is also accessible to people with disabilities.

Hikers can hook onto the adjacent **Wildflower Trail**, where they may see mountain laurel blooms in June and berries in the fall. More ambitious ramblers can link from the Rhododendron Trail to the **Little Monadnock Mountain Trail**, which climbs to the 1883ft summit of Little Monadnock Mountain. On the way it joins the 117-mile **Meta-Comet–Monadnock Trail** (nicknamed the M&M Trail), which continues to the summit of Mt Monadnock.

The Drive ⟫ Drive west on NH 119, crossing NH 32 before heading into Winchester. Continue west on NH 119, passing one entrance to Pisgah State Park. Turn right on NH 63 for a bucolic spin past cows and red barns. Cross NH 9 to begin a particularly scenic drive past Spofford Lake, pine trees and the startlingly impressive Park Hill Meeting House. Turn right on NH 12 at Stuart & John's Sugar House and drive toward Keene. The drive is 47 miles.

TRIP HIGHLIGHT

7 Keene

Keene is like the hub of a giant wheel, with a half-dozen spokes linking to dozens of outlying villages that encircle the city, providing an endless supply of scenic loops. You really can't go wrong with any of them.

Keene itself is a great place to explore, particularly along its pleasant and lively Main St, which is lined with indie shops

and cozy eateries. For local crafts, foodstuffs and gifts, stop by **Hannah Grimes Marketplace** (📞603-352-6862; www. hannahgrimesmarketplace. com; 42 Main St; ⏰10am-6pm Mon-Thu, to 7pm Fri & Sat, to 4pm Sun).

Main St is crowned by a small tree-filled plaza (Central Sq) with a fountain at one end. The elegant, redbrick **Keene State College** (📞603-358-2276; www.keene. edu; 229 Main St) anchors the western end of Main St and the students inject downtown with an energetic vibe, as well as a youthful, artistic sensibility. The spacious, skylit halls at the **Thorne-Sagendorph Art Gallery** (📞603-358-2720; www.keene.edu/tsag; Wyman Way; ⏰noon-7pm Wed & Thu, to 5pm Fri-Sun) showcase rotating exhibits of regional and national artists. The small permanent collection includes pieces by national artists who have been drawn to the Monadnock region since the 1800s.

In the evening, see what's doing at the 90-year-old **Colonial Theater** (📞603-352-2033; www.thecolonial.org; 95 Main St), which offers a diverse lineup of entertainment.

🍴 🛏 p253

Eating & Sleeping

Peterborough ②

✗ Waterhouse Modern American $$
(☎603-924-4001; www.waterhousenh.com; 18 Depot St; mains lunch $12-18, dinner $24-30; ⏱11:30am-9pm Mon-Sat, to 2:30pm Sun; ✐) Feeling a tad fancy? Step into the bright wood-floored dining room and grab a table beside the floor-to-ceiling windows directly overlooking the rushing Nubanusit. The lunch menu abounds in revisited American classics like BLTs, fish and chips, burgers and tuna melts, while dinner expands to include steak and seafood.

🛏 Little River Bed & Breakfast B&B $
(☎603-924-3280; www.littleriverbedand breakfast.com; 184 Union St; r $145-155; 🛜) One mile west of the village center on the gorgeous Nubanusit River, this 19th-century farmhouse once served as housing for artists at the nearby MacDowell Colony. Innkeepers Paula and Rob Fox have converted it into a cozy B&B with four immaculate guest rooms and tasty breakfasts featuring homemade granola and muffins.

Hancock ③

🛏 Hancock Inn Inn $$$
(☎603-525-3318; www.hancockinn.com; 33 Main St; r $178-395; ❄🛜🐾) New Hampshire's oldest inn (1789) has 14 rooms, each with its own charms. Room prices vary according to size and features: some include dome ceilings (ones that used to be part of a ballroom), fireplaces and private patios. The cozy Fox Tavern dining room is open to the public for dinner (Tuesday to Saturday) and features locally grown fare.

Jaffrey & Jaffrey Center ④

✗ Sunflowers Cafe $$
(☎603-593-3303; www.sunflowerscatering. com; 21 Main St, Jaffrey; mains lunch $10-14, dinner $11-26; ⏱11am-2pm Mon-Fri, to 3pm Sat, 5-7:30pm Mon, Wed & Thu, to 8:30pm Fri & Sat, 9am-2pm Sun) In the heart of Jaffrey (2 miles east of Jaffrey Center), this cozy cafe with its cheerful blue and yellow facade is the perfect place to relax and enjoy the good life with creative salads and sandwiches at lunch and baked haddock dinners and steaks for dinner. Burgers are always on the menu.

Monadnock State Park ⑤

🛏 Gilson Pond Campground Campground $
(☎info 603-532-2416, reservations 877-647-2757; www.nhstateparks.org; 585 Dublin Rd/ NH 124, Jaffrey; tent sites $25; ⏱early May-Oct; 🅿) Well placed for a sunrise ascent up the mountain, this state park campground has 35 peaceful, well-shaded sites. From November through April, when Gilson Pond is closed, camping is available at the park's Headquarters Campground, near the main entrance, on a first-come, first-served basis. The latter is usually open only to youth groups in summer.

Keene ⑦

✗ Luca's Mediterranean Café Italian $$
(☎603-358-3335; www.lucascafe.com; 10 Central Sq; mains lunch $8-16, dinner $16-30; ⏱11am-2pm Mon-Sat, 5-9pm Sun-Thu, to 10pm Fri & Sat) Luca's serves tasty salads and gourmet sandwiches and burgers at lunch, while dinner sees a tempting array of pastas, fish dishes and steaks. Alfresco dining is a good choice on pleasant nights.

🛏 Fairfield Inn & Suites Keene Downtown Hotel $$$
(☎603-357-7070; www.marriott.com; 30 Main St; r $249-279; 🅿❄🛜) In a picture-perfect Main St location, this venerable century-old hotel (formerly known as the Lane Hotel) has 40 attractive rooms, each individually furnished in a classic style, ensuring you won't get the cookie-cutter experience. There are plenty of creature comforts (individual climate control, high-speed internet connections, on-site breakfast) and a good restaurant on the 1st floor.

Woodland Heritage Trail

24

Embrace the solitude on this loop through the North Woods, where the stories of entrepreneurs, immigrants, lumberjacks and one very effective conservationist are as fascinating as the scenery.

TRIP HIGHLIGHTS

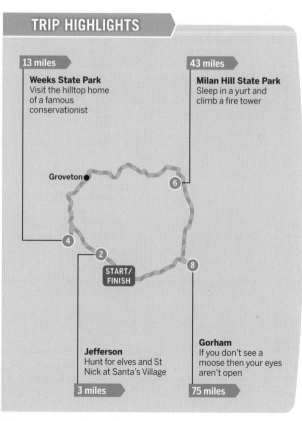

13 miles

Weeks State Park
Visit the hilltop home of a famous conservationist

43 miles

Milan Hill State Park
Sleep in a yurt and climb a fire tower

Groveton

6

4

2

START/ FINISH

8

Jefferson
Hunt for elves and St Nick at Santa's Village

3 miles

Gorham
If you don't see a moose then your eyes aren't open

75 miles

**2 DAYS
90 MILES / 145KM**

GREAT FOR...

BEST TIME TO GO

June to October for warm weather, fall foliage and open-for-business attractions.

ESSENTIAL PHOTO

Stark Covered Bridge, which anchors a picturesque village.

BEST FOR FAMILIES

Hop aboard the Jingle Bell Express train then climb a fire tower.

Stark Stark Covered Bridge

24 Woodland Heritage Trail

Why is northern New Hampshire so wild? Because a forward-thinking US senator from the Granite State, John W Weeks, introduced a bill in 1909 that birthed the modern national forest system. This trip makes the most of his vision by circling the White Mountain National Forest's rugged Kilkenny District, plunked dramatically between the Connecticut and Androscoggin Rivers and the Presidential Range. But it's not all lumberjacks and moose – Santa himself has somehow muscled onto the landscape.

① Water Wheel

This trip starts with blueberry buttermilk pancakes and pure maple syrup at the appropriately named Water Wheel (p261) – look for the big red wheel, or at least half of one. You can also stock up on New Hampshire gifts at this cozy place.

✗ p261

The Drive » From the Water Wheel, look both ways for logging trucks, then turn right on US 2 and head to Jefferson, 3 miles away.

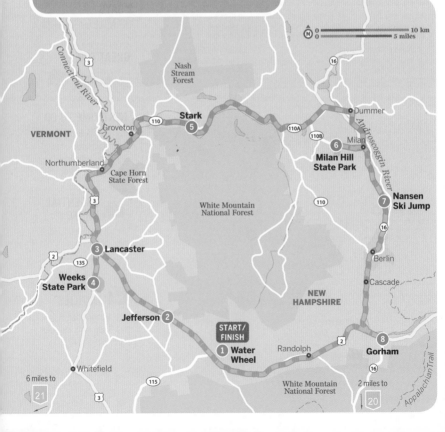

② Jefferson

Just west of mountain-ringed Jefferson is every child's dream: **Santa's Village** (☏603-586-4445; www.santasvillage.com; 528 Presidential Hwy/US 2, Jefferson; $33; ☺9:30am-6pm daily Jul & Aug, to 5pm late Jun, 9:30am-5pm Sat & Sun late May, early Jun & Sep–early Oct; P 🐾). Inside this cheery theme park, look for Santa's 26 elves as you enjoy the kiddie-focused rides, a Ferris wheel and the *Jingle Bell Express* train. Kids can even visit Santa himself, usually found relaxing at home. The attached water park, **Ho Ho H2O**, is open from late May into early October. The park also opens weekends in December for holiday visits.

LINK YOUR TRIP

20 White Mountains Loop

From Gorham drive south to Mt Washington, New England's highest peak.

21 Connecticut River Byway

Vistas are bucolic on the Connecticut River Byway, which rolls south from Lancaster.

LIVE FREE OR DIE

New Hampshire is the most politically conservative state in New England, with a libertarian streak that runs deep. It's tough and rugged, and its citizens still cling with pride to the famous words uttered by General John Stark, victor at the crucial Battle of Bennington: 'Live Free or Die!' The famous saying graces local license plates and appears all over the state.

🛏 p261

The Drive » Continue west 7 miles from Santa's Village to Lancaster, passing clapboard homes, logging trucks and commanding views of the Presidential Range.

---

③ Lancaster

Photo op! Substitute your face for Paul Bunyan's at the **Great North Woods Welcome Center** (☏603-788-3212; www.northerngatewaychamber.org; 25 Park St; ☺10am-4pm Mon-Sat) in downtown Lancaster. Here you can pick up maps and brochures before wandering past the boutiques and antique stores lining nearby Main St.

The Drive » Follow US 3 for 3 miles south out of downtown Lancaster. The Weeks State Park entrance is on the left, across the street from a scenic pull-off.

---

④ Weeks State Park

Named for US senator John Weeks, **Weeks State Park** (☏603-788-4004; www.nhstateparks.org; 200

Weeks State Park Rd, off US 3, Lancaster; adult/6-17yr $5/3; ☺10am-5pm late May-early Oct; P 🐾) sits atop Mt Prospect. Weeks was a Lancaster native who introduced legislation in 1909 that helped to stem the degradation of local lands caused by un-regulated logging, with legislation that became known as the Weeks Act. By authorizing the federal government to purchase land at the head of navigable streams, the Act kick-started the national forest system, adding more than 19 million acres of land to the nation's holdings.

The park encompasses the 420-acre **Weeks estate**, where you can drive the 1.5-mile scenic road, explore the Weeks home and enjoy 360-degree mountain views from the property's stone **fire tower**.

The Drive » From Lancaster, drive north on US 3, also known as the Daniel Webster Hwy, through Coos Junction, passing bogs and paralleling the train tracks. In Groveton,

10 miles north, snap a photo of the covered bridge before continuing east on NH 110 for 21 miles to Stark.

---

5 Stark

Fans of George RR Martin's novel *A Game of Thrones* can't be blamed if they ask directions to Winterfell, the northern holdfast of the Stark family that sits on the fringes of the lonely Wolfswood. But there aren't any wildling or wargs in this roadside village (that we saw, anyway), just the impossibly picturesque **Stark Covered Bridge**. This white, 134ft Paddleford truss bridge – constructed in 1862 and subsequently rebuilt and strengthened – spans the Upper Ammonoosuc River. It's flanked by the white **Union Church** (1850) and a white schoolhouse, making for an eye-catching photo. General John Stark was a famous commander during the American Revolution.

Two miles east, pull over for the **Camp Stark Roadside Marker**, which describes the WWII prisoner-of-war camp located nearby, where

Milan Hill State Park Yurt accommodations

prisoners were put to work cutting pulpwood. It was the only war camp in New Hampshire.

The Drive ≫ Continue east for 2.7 miles. Make a sharp left onto NH 110A at the junction of NH 110 and NH 110A. Drive just over 3.5 miles (you'll pass 110B) to NH 16 and a view of the mighty Androscoggin River. Turn right and follow NH 16 south toward Berlin for 4 miles. Turn right at 110B for a short drive to Milan Hill State Park.

TRIP HIGHLIGHT

⑥ Milan Hill State Park

How often do you get to spend the night in a purple yurt? Yep, that's an option at **Milan Hill State Park** (☎603-449-2429; www. nhstateparks.org; 72 Fire Tower Rd, Milan; day-use adult/6-11yr $4/2; ☺year-round; P🐾), also known for its cross-country skiing and snowshoe trails. The 45ft **fire tower** provides expansive views of New Hampshire's mountains, as well as of mountain ranges in Vermont, Maine and Canada. The park is pet-friendly, so bring Fido for a walk or picnic. It's

BOOM PIERS

Driving south on NH 16 from Milan to Gorham, it's hard to miss the compact clusters of wood that rise from the middle of the river. Are they beaver dams? Small islands? Nope, those eye-catching clusters are boom piers, human-made islands that were used by lumbermen to separate logs by owner during the annual log drives. (Stamps that identified the owners were hammered into the end of the logs.) The log drives ended in 1963.

open year-round but only staffed seasonally; no day-use fee is collected in the low season.

The park is just south of New Hampshire's **13 Mile Woods Scenic Area**, which stretches along NH 16 and the Androscoggin River a few miles north and is known to be a popular strip for free-ranging moose.

🛏 p261

The Drive ➤ Continue south on NH 16 from Milan for 4 miles, keeping your eyes open for moose, particularly in the morning and early evening. The road hugs the western side of the birch-lined Androscoggin River, a log-carrying highway in the first half of the 20th century.

7 Nansen Ski Jump

South of Milan, on the way to Gorham, pull over at the historic marker describing the **Nansen Ski Jump**, which is visible on the adjacent hill as you look north. This 171ft ski jump, first used in 1936, was the site of Olympic ski-jump trials in 1938. It was last used in 1982.

The Drive ➤ Continue another 11 miles south on NH 16 to reach Gorham.

TRIP HIGHLIGHT

8 Gorham

Gorham is a regional crossroads, linking roads flowing in from the North Woods, from Mt Washington and North Conway, and from the Rangeley Lakes region of northwestern Maine. Stop here for one of the area's best restaurants, Libby's Bistro. Housed in an old bank building, it has a relaxed, speakeasy feel and uses local produce, in-season vegetables and New Hampshire seafood. Original wall safes speak of the building's banking past.

By this point, you've probably seen several moose-crossing signs dotting the route. If you still haven't seen an actual moose, join a moose safari with **Gorham Moose Tours** (📞877-986-6673, 603-466-3103; www.gorhammoosetours.org; 69 Main St; adult/5-12yr $30/20; ☺late May-Sep). These determined folks know where the moose are and have a 93% to 97% moose-spotting success rate (and, yes, they've done the math!).

🍴 🛏 p261

The Drive ➤ Complete the loop by returning to Jefferson, just west of the junction of US 2 and NH 115.

Eating & Sleeping

Water Wheel ❶

✕ Water Wheel   American $

(☎603-586-4313; www.waterwheelnh.com;
1955 Presidential Hwy/US 2; mains $3-9;
🕐6am-2pm Jun-Aug, Thu-Mon Sep-May) A red
water wheel marks the spot at this down-home
eatery where decorative bears hang from the
wooden rafters. Portions are hearty, service can
be a tad slow and breakfast is served all day.

Jefferson ❷

🛏 Evergreen Motel   Motel $

(☎603-586-4449; www.evergreenmotelnh.com;
537 Presidential Hwy/US 2; r $105; P ❄ 🛜 🏊)
This 18-room mom-and-pop establishment is
across the street from Santa's Village (p257).
There's also a complimentary 18-hole miniature
golf course on-site. Snowmobilers can ride to
their doors from the Corridor 5 route. Breakfast
included in rates.

🛏 Jefferson Inn   B&B $

(☎603-586-7998; www.jeffersoninn.com; 6
Renaissance Lane/US 2; r $125-145, ste $175;
P ❄ 🛜 🏊) Eleven homespun rooms – with
quilts, old brooms and washboards on the wall
– fill this attractive Victorian house perched on
a hill above the Presidential Hwy. Four rooms
have air-con and two rooms are pet friendly.
Breakfast included in rates.

Milan Hill State Park ❻

🛏 Milan Hill State
Park Campground   Campground $

(☎603-449-2429; www.nhstateparks.org; 72
Fire Tower Rd, Milan; tent & RV sites $23-29,
yurts $50; 🕐mid-May–Oct; P) Four furnished
yurts, each sleeping four people, are on offer
at this state park campground. There are
also six campsites, four of them available by
reservation. Campsite 6 has a covered shelter.

Gorham ❽

✕ Libby's Bistro
& Saalt Pub   International $$

(☎603-466-5330; www.libbysbistro.org; 111 Main
St/NH 16; mains $12-23; 🕐 bistro 5-9pm Fri & Sat,
pub 5-9pm Wed-Sun) A labor of love for acclaimed
chef Liz Jackson, this 20-year-old spot serves a
seasonally changing, globally inspired menu that
draws on locally sourced ingredients; offerings
run from Latin American to Middle Eastern,
Vietnamese to Mediterranean. You'll also find
creative burgers, a Thai fried chicken salad and
four-cheese baked penne.

✕ White Mountain
Cafe & Bookstore   Cafe $

(☎603-466-2511; www.whitemountaincafe.com;
212 Main St; sandwiches $5-9; 🕐7am-4pm) This
cozy cafe is darn near perfect: pleasant staff, fine
coffee and very tasty sandwiches for breakfast
and lunch. Plus there are books! Located on
US 2, White Mountain makes a convenient and
worthwhile stop if you're traveling between the
Great North Woods and North Conway.

🛏 Mt Madison
Inn & Suites   Motel $

(☎800-516-1778, 603-466-3622; www.
mtmadisoninnandsuites.com; 365 Main St; r
$134-144, ste $189; P ❄ @ 🛜 🏊 🏊) The
upgraded king and queen rooms at this 32-room
motel have all been re-carpeted and come with
microwaves, coffee makers and refrigerators. A
few rooms are pet friendly; pets are $10 per pet
per night. Other amenities include a heated pool
and hot tub.

🛏 Top Notch Inn   Motel $

(☎603-466-5496, 800-228-5496; www.
topnotchinn.com; 265 Main St; r $119-127, house
$199; P ❄ @ 🛜 🏊 🏊) A brown moose
stands guard outside the welcoming Top
Notch. In addition to standard but stylish motel
rooms, the inn offers the three-room Pinkham
House, a restored farmhouse, that sleeps up
to eight people. A heated pool and laundry
facilities are available. The pet fee is $10 per
pet per night.

STRETCH YOUR LEGS
PORTSMOUTH

Start/Finish: Colby's

Distance: 1.5 miles

Duration: Four hours

This easy stroll reveals the abundant charms of Portsmouth's vibrant historic district. Fuel up at the city's favorite breakfast joint, then set off to discover Colonial churches and mansions, a pretty waterfront park and one of New England's premier history museums.

Take this walk on Trip

Colby's

If you get to **Colby's** (☎603-436-3033; 105 Daniel St; mains $4-11; ⏰7am-2pm) after 8am on the weekend, there's going to be a wait, so give 'em your name and enjoy a cup of free coffee on the patio. Once in, egg lovers can choose from a multitude of Benedicts, and there's always the huevos rancheros and the chalkboard specials. Colby's owners are serious about preserving their eatery's intimate appeal. In 2012, management posted a 'No Politicians, No Exceptions' sign on the door in the days before New Hampshire's presidential primary – campaign staff and candidates were disrupting business in the 28-seat restaurant.

The Walk » Turn left out of Colby's and walk a block and a half to Market Sq.

Market Square

A public gathering place since the mid-1700s, this lively square, anchored by the 1854 **North Church**, is still the heart of Portsmouth. Nearby are open-air cafes, colorful storefronts and tiny galleries with banjo-playing buskers for entertainment on warm summer nights. There's public wi-fi here, and an information kiosk is open in summer.

The Walk » Stroll down Pleasant St, passing the US Custom House, built in 1860. Next, on the left, is Governor John Langdon's House, where the three-term governor hosted George Washington in 1789. Bear left on Gates St and follow it to Marcy St, where you'll turn right and continue one block to find the meetinghouse on your right.

South Ward Meetinghouse

The towering **meetinghouse** (280 Marcy St), completed in 1866, replaced a parish meetinghouse that had been on the site since 1731. The 1st floor of the new building held a school, and the 2nd floor was used for meetings. Black citizens celebrated Emancipation Day here in January 1882. The meetinghouse is also a stop on the **Portsmouth Black Heritage Trail** (☎603-436-8433; www.portsmouthhistory.org/portsmouth-black-heritage-trail/self-guided-tour; guided tour $20; ⏰tours 2pm most Sat mid-Apr–early Nov).

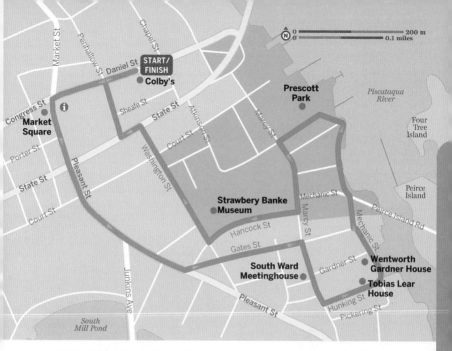

The Walk >> From the front of the meetinghouse, cross Marcy St and walk down Hunking St.

Tobias Lear & Wentworth Gardner Houses

Tobias Lear House, built in 1740, was in the Lear family for 120 years. The fifth Tobias Lear served as private secretary to President George Washington, who visited Lear's mother here in 1789. Around the corner is the 1760 **Wentworth Gardner House** (☎603-436-4406; www.wentworthlear.org; 50 Mechanic St; adult/under 18yr $6/3; ⏰11am-4pm Thu-Mon Jun-Oct), one of the finest Georgian houses in the USA. Elizabeth and Mark Hunking Wentworth were among Portsmouth's wealthiest citizens, so no expense was spared in building the home, which was a wedding gift for their son.

The Walk >> Turn left on Mechanic St and follow it past the windswept headstones at Point of Graves to Prescott Park.

Prescott Park

Overlooking the Piscataqua River, this leafy **park** (www.cityofportsmouth.com/ prescottpark; 105 Marcy St) is the backdrop for a summer **arts festival** (www.prescott park.org; ⏰Jun-early Sep; 🚹), with free music, dance and theater. The design of the shoreside **Sheafe Warehouse** (c 1705) made it easy for flat-bottomed boats to load and unload cargo.

The Walk >> Turn left into Marcy St and continue to the parking lot of the Strawbery Banke Museum on the corner of Marcy and Hancock Sts.

Strawbery Banke Museum

Spread across 10 acres, the **museum** (☎603-433-1100; www.strawberybanke.org; 14 Hancock St; adult/5-17yr $19.50/9; ⏰10am-5pm May-Oct, special events only Nov-Apr; ℗ 🚹) is a blend of period homes dating from the 1690s. Costumed guides recount tales that took place among the 38 historic buildings. The museum includes **Pitt Tavern** (1766), a hotbed of Revolutionary sentiment, and **Goodwin Mansion**, a grand 19th-century house from Portsmouth's most prosperous time.

The Walk >> Follow Washington St northwest to State St, turn left, walk a few steps then turn right onto Penhallow St and return to Daniel St.

Maine

YOU KNOW THERE'S SOMETHING SPECIAL ABOUT A STATE when its most prominent citizens donate their land for the enjoyment of all. Governor Percival Baxter provided the wilderness for Baxter State Park, while John D Rockefeller and his neighbors donated land for Acadia National Park. Today, private timber companies allow recreational access to vast swaths of woodland. For travelers, a coastal drive north from Portland swooshes past the legendary LL Bean flagship store, shipbuilding villages, Acadia National Park and first-in-the-nation sunrises. And we haven't even mentioned the lighthouses and lobster shacks. Inland, scenic byways hug rivers, lakes, forests and mountains. If you're lucky, you'll spy a moose; even if you don't, we're pretty certain you'll relish the quirky towns, charming inns, locavore dishes and excellent local brews you'll encounter.

Baxter State Park Moose
PAUL TESSIER/SHUTTERSTOCK ©

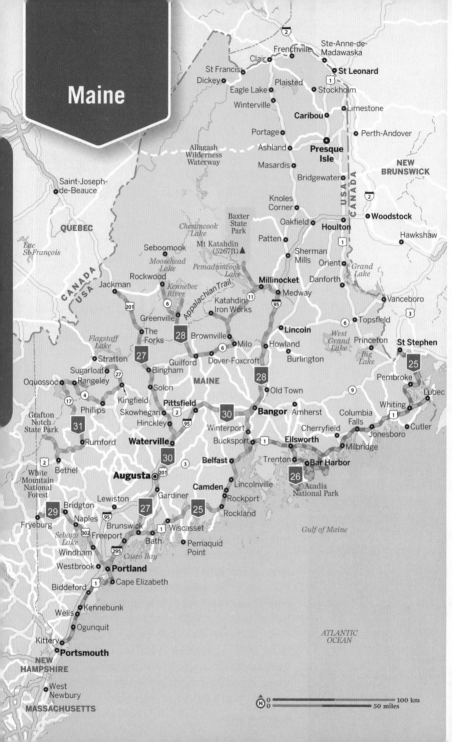

Rockland Harbor Rockland Breakwater Lighthouse

Maritime Maine 5 Days
25 Lighthouses, lobster shacks, maritime museums and early sunrises link Kittery to Calais. (p269)

Acadia National Park 3 Days
26 Swoop up Cadillac Mountain, and roll past cliffs on Mount Desert Island. (p279)

Old Canada Road 2 Days
27 White-water rafting, cabinets of curiosity and logging history make this a well-rounded adventure. (p289)

Great North Woods 3 Days
28 Escape into lonely backwoods to discover Maine's largest lake and highest peak. (p297)

Lakes Tour 2 Days
29 B&Bs, campgrounds and water sports abound on this scenic lake country jaunt. (p305)

Mainely Art 3 Days
30 This pretty loop ribbons through art museums, galleries and lovely landscapes. (p313)

Moose & Mountains: Western Maine 2 Days
31 Canoe, bike, ski or hike – and watch for moose – in Maine's western mountains. (p321)

Lighthouse Hike
You'll earn your view of the coast after a hike across granite blocks to the Rockland Breakwater Lighthouse. View it on Trip **25**

Heavenly Views
Lie on the sand and ponder the universe during the Stars over Sand Beach program at Acadia National Park. Enjoy it on Trip **26**

Gifford's Ice Cream Stand
Fuel up for the North Woods with a scoop of Maine Blackberry or Caramel Caribou from Gifford's. Try it on Trip **27**

Moose Safari
Haven't spotted a moose? Increase your odds on a Northwoods Outfitters safari. Try your luck on Trip **28**

Museums & Murals

View works by American masters at the Portland Museum of Art, and snap photos of Maine-inspired murals down the street. Take them all in on Trip **30**

Classic Trip

Maritime Maine

25

US 1 between Kittery and Calais is a route meant for lingering: fog-wrapped lighthouses, oceanfront picnic tables, seafaring artifacts in dusty museums, and one sprawling outdoors store.

TRIP HIGHLIGHTS

78 miles

Bath
Seafaring artifacts are a link to Maine's maritime past

265 miles

Lubec & Quoddy Head
Crashing waves, an eerie foghorn and a lonely lighthouse

FINISH
Calais

11

Camden
9

127 miles

Rockland Breakwater Lighthouse
A granite walkway leads to the distant beacon

7

3

Ogunquit

Kittery
START

Cape Elizabeth
Snap photos of the lighthouse and wander past WWII bunkers

42 miles

---

5 DAYS
285 MILES / 459KM

GREAT FOR...

BEST TIME TO GO

Summer is great, but you'll shake the crowds in September and October.

ESSENTIAL PHOTO

Stand on the rocks for a photo of Pemaquid lighthouse.

BEST FOR HISTORY

Exhibits on seafaring are captivating at the Maine Maritime Museum.

Pemaquid Lighthouse Park Pemaquid Point Light

25 Maritime Maine

The rugged complexity of the Maine coast hits home at Rockland's visitor center, where a giant state map — complete with lighthouses — sprawls across the floor. Islands, peninsulas, harbors — it's no wonder this state has such a strong maritime heritage. And it's this heritage that makes the trip memorable. The sunrises and rocky coasts are lovely, but it's the stories about lighthouse-keepers, brave captains and shipyard Rosie the Riveters that make this coastal drive unique.

① Kittery

The drive to **Fort Foster Park** (http://fortfoster.weebly.com; Pocahontas Rd; car/walk-in $10/5; ⏰10am-8pm daily Jun-Aug, Sat & Sun May & Sep; 👣) twists past flowers, Victorian homes and tantalizing ocean glimpses. The seaside park is a nice place to walk some trails, have a picnic, and play in rocky tide pools. Look out to sea for **Whaleback Ledge** (1831), the first lighthouse on this trip.

To get here from US 1, take ME 103 for 5 miles, then cross a small channel to Gerrish Island. Follow Pocahontas Dr through the woods.

From Kittery, you can pop across to Portsmouth (p262) for a walking tour.

The Drive » Continue north on US 1. There's a nice but potentially crowded sand beach at Ogunquit. Seven miles north of Ogunquit, turn right onto Laudholm Farm Rd.

② Wells

Wildlife-lovers, bird-watchers and families enjoy wandering the 7 miles of trails at the 2250-acre **Wells National Estuarine Research Reserve** (📞207-646-1555; www.wellsreserve.org; 342 Laudholm Farm Rd; adult/child $5/1; ⏰trails 7am-sunset, nature center 10am-4pm; 🅿), a protected coastal ecosystem (no pets permitted). Down the road, the **Rachel Carson National Wildlife Reserve** (📞207-646-9226; www.fws.gov/refuge/rachel_carson; 321 Port Rd; ⏰dawn-dusk; 🅿) holds more than 14,000 acres of protected coastal areas, with four trails scattered along

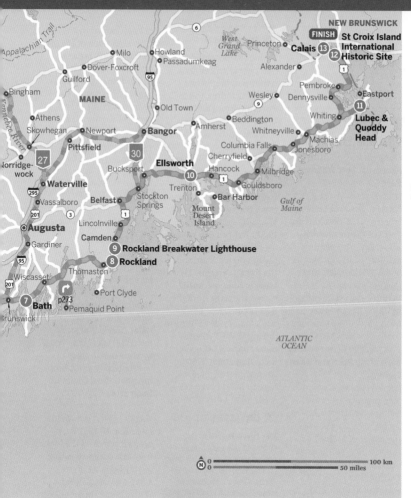

50 miles of shoreline. The 1-mile, pet-friendly **Carson Trail** meanders along tidal creeks and salt marshes.

The Drive » Follow US 1 north, passing through Saco. In Scarborough, turn right onto ME 207. Follow it almost 3 miles to ME 77 and turn left. Drive just over 7 miles, passing Two Lights Rd, to Shore Rd. Turn right.

LINK YOUR TRIP

27 **Old Canada Road**
From Bath, drive to Brunswick to wander a museum about arctic explorers, then continue the route north along the stunning Kennebec River.

30 **Mainely Art**
In Rockland, join a cultural loop of Maine's artistic heritage and contemporary culture.

Classic Trip

③ Cape Elizabeth

Good photo opportunities abound at **Fort Williams Park** (☎207-767-3707; https://fortwilliams.org; 1000 Shore Rd; ☼ sunrise-sunset), where you can explore the ruins of the fort, which was a late-19th-century artillery base, and check out WWII bunkers and gun emplacements (a German U-boat was spotted in Casco Bay in 1942). The fort guarded the entrance to the bay until 1964.

A favorite feature of the park is the **Portland Head Light** (☎207-799-2661; https://portlandheadlight. com; museum adult/child $2/1; ☼ museum 10am-4pm Jun-Oct, Sat & Sun only Apr, May & Nov), the oldest of Maine's 52 functioning lighthouses. Commissioned by George Washington in 1791, it was staffed until 1989, when machines took over. The keeper's house is now a museum, which traces the maritime and military history of the region.

✗ p277

The Drive >> Drive north 1 mile on Shore Rd, then turn right onto Preble St. Drive another mile, then turn right on Broadway then left onto Breakwater Dr. Just ahead, turn right onto Madison St.

④ Portland

Maine's largest city and port is graced by a handful of handsome lights, including the 1875 **Portland Breakwater Light** (Madison St, South Portland), with Corinthian columns. Dubbed the 'Bug Light' because of its tiny size, it sits in a small park in South Portland with a panoramic view of downtown across the harbor. You can't enter the Bug Light, but you can traipse over the stone breakwater and walk around the light's exterior. The **Liberty Ship memorial**, across the park from the Bug Light, describes the site's history as a shipyard during WWII, when more than 30,000 people, including about 3750 women, were employed here to build cargo vessels, called Liberty Ships.

✗ ⮕ p277, p311, p319

The Drive >> Follow I-295 north and take exit 17. DeLorme cartographic company will be on your right off the ramp (signed 'Global Village'). You can also follow US 1 north from Portland.

⑤ Yarmouth

On the way to the stores of Freeport, geography buffs shouldn't miss a visit to the DeLorme cartographic company – its lofty office atrium is home to a giant rotating globe named **Eartha** (2 DeLorme Dr; ☼ 8:30am-5pm Mon-Fri). Eartha has a diameter of 41.5ft and has been acknowledged by the Guinness Book of Records as the world's largest revolving and rotating globe. The detail on it is impressive (it took two years to build), as is the opportunity for visitors to stop by for a look.

The Drive >> Follow US 1 north 4.5 miles past outlet stores and motels to LL Bean. There's a large parking lot on the left between Howard Pl and Nathan Nye St.

⑥ Freeport

A century ago Leon Leonwood Bean opened a shop here to sell equipment and provisions to hunters and fishers. His success lured other retailers and today nearly 200 stores line US 1, leading to traffic jams in summer.

Fronted by a 16ft hunting boot, the flagship **LL Bean store** (☎877-755-2326; www.llbean.com; 95 Main St; ☼ 24hr) is a Maine must-see. In 1951 Bean himself removed the locks from the doors, deciding to stay open 24 hours a day, 365 days a year. With almost three million visitors annually, the store is one of the state's most popular attractions. There's a 3500-gallon aquarium and trout pond, a stuffed moose, and eating outlets – not to mention outdoor clothing and gear, spread over a small campus of stores (one dedicated to hunting and fishing, another to bike, boat and ski, and another to home furnishings).

Two 'Bootmobiles' travel the country on a mission to inspire people to get outside. The **LL Bean Outdoor Discovery School** (📞888-615-9979; www.llbean.com/ods) offers an array of courses, from instore bike-maintenance clinics to first aid, plus fantastic excursions, tours and classes locally and across the state – from archery to snowshoeing by way of fly-fishing and bird-watching.

🛏 p277

The Drive » Follow US 1 north 18 miles through Brunswick to Bath. Pass Middle St, turn right on Washington St and drive 1.2 miles to the maritime museum.

TRIP HIGHLIGHT

7 Bath

This quaint Kennebec River town was once home to more than 20 shipyards producing more than a quarter of early America's wooden ships. Bath Iron Works, founded in 1884, is still one of the largest and most productive shipyards in the nation.

On the western bank of the Kennebec, the **Maine Maritime Museum** (📞207-443-1316; www.mainemaritime museum.org; 243 Washington St; adult/child $17.50/10.50; ⊙9:30am-5pm) preserves the town's traditions with paintings, models and exhibits that tell the tale of the last 400 years of seafaring. Landlubbers and old salts alike will find something of interest,

whether it's an 1849 ship's log describing the power of a hurricane or a hands-on tugboat pilot's house. On the grounds, look for the remains of the *Snow Squall,* a three-mast 1851 clipper ship that foundered near the Falkland Islands, and a life-size sculpture of the *Wyoming,* the largest wooden sailing vessel ever built.

In summer, the museum offers a variety of **boat cruises**, taking in assorted lighthouses and bird-rich bays ($34 to $50 per person, including museum admission). It also has a trolley tour that gives an insider's perspective of the Bath Iron Works.

The Drive » Return to US 1 and continue north 40 miles, taking a moment to ogle the long line at Red's, a popular lobster shack in Wiscasset known for its lobster rolls. Continue north to Rockland.

8 Rockland

This thriving commercial port boasts a large fishing fleet and a proud year-round population. Settled in 1769, it was once an important shipbuilding center and a transportation hub for river cargo. Today, tall-masted ships still fill the harbor because Rockland (along with nearby Camden) is a center for Maine's **windjammer cruises** (📞800-807-9463; www.sailmainecoast. com; ⊙cruises late May–mid-Oct), which are multiday sailings on wind-powered schooners.

A map of Maine's coast, with all of its lighthouses, spreads across the floor of the **Penobscot Bay Regional Chamber of Commerce** (📞207-596-0376; www. camdenrockland.com; 1 Park Dr; ⊙9am-5pm Jun-Oct, to

DETOUR: PEMAQUID POINT

Start: 7 Bath

Maine's most famous lighthouse these days is the 1827 **Pemaquid Point Light**, which was featured on the special-edition Maine quarter. It's perched dramatically above rock-crashing surf in **Pemaquid Lighthouse Park** (📞207-677-2492; www.facebook.com/pemaquidlighthouse; 3115 Bristol Rd, Bristol; adult/child $2/free; ⊙9am-5pm May-Oct). The keeper's house now serves as the **Fisherman's Museum** (📞207-677-2494; www.thefishermensmuseum.org; 3007 Bristol Rd; ⊙9am-5pm May-Oct). Staffed by volunteers (so with occasionally irregular hours), it displays fishing paraphernalia and photos. From Damariscotta, between Wiscasset and Waldoboro, follow ME 130 south.

Classic Trip

WHY THIS IS A CLASSIC TRIP
AMY C BALFOUR, WRITER

There's a certain thrill in joining the crowds at the iconic spots along the coast. In Freeport, I was directed down to the marina to feast on lobster at the iconic red-painted seafood shack of the Harraseeket Lunch & Lobster Co (www. harraseeketlunchandlobster.com). If it's nice out, you can grab a picnic table – or just do like the locals and sit on the roof of your car. Make sure you finish with a slice of blueberry pie. And be there early to beat the crowds. It's BYOB and cash only, so come prepared.

Above: Lobster roll
Left: Fort Williams Park, Cape Elizabeth
Right: Rockland Breakwater Lighthouse

4pm Mon-Fri Nov-May) beside Rockland Harbor. Ask for the list that identifies the lighthouses on the map. The chamber of commerce shares a roof with the **Maine Lighthouse Museum** (☎207-594-3301; www.mainelighthousemuseum. org; 1 Park Dr; adult/child $8/ free; ⏱10am-5pm Mon-Fri, to 4pm Sat & Sun Jun-Oct, 10am-4pm Thu-Sat Nov-May; 🚹), which exhibits vintage Fresnel lenses, foghorns, marine instruments and ship models.

✕ 🛏 p277, p319

**The Drive ›› ** Follow Main St/ US 1 north just over 1 mile from downtown to Waldo Ave. Turn right and drive half a mile. Turn right onto Samoset Rd, following it to a small parking lot.

- - - - - - - - - - - - - - - - - -

TRIP HIGHLIGHT

❾ Rockland Breakwater Lighthouse

Feeling adventurous? Tackle the rugged stone breakwater that stretches almost 1 mile into Rockland Harbor from Jameson Point at the harbor's northern shore. Made of granite blocks, this 'walkway' – which took 18 years to build – ends at the **Rockland Breakwater Lighthouse** (☎207-542-7574; www.rock landharborlights.org; Samoset Rd; ⏱10am-5pm Sat & Sun late May–mid-Oct). Older kids should be fine; just watch for slippery rocks and ankle-twisting gaps between stones. Bring a

sweater, and don't hike if a storm is on the horizon.

The Drive » US 1 hugs the coast as it swoops north past the artsy enclaves of Rockport, Camden and Belfast, curving east through Bucksport before landing in Ellsworth, about 60 miles from Rockland.

⑩ Ellsworth

Cooks and coffee-lovers, this stop's for you. In old-school Ellsworth, pull over for **Rooster Brother** (📞207-667-8675; www. roosterbrother.com; 29 Main St; ⏰store 9:30am-5:30pm Mon-Sat, coffee from 7:30am Mon-Fri), a kitchenware boutique that also sells amazing roasted coffee. Step downstairs from the retail store for a coffee sample – but be careful, you'll likely end up buying a full cup or a pound to go. Check out the excellent fresh cookies, especially the super-tasty ginger and molasses. Wine, chocolate, cheese and fresh bread are also for sale.

 p277

The Drive » From Ellsworth, drive east on US 1. Consider taking ME 182, the most direct route north, but it's a more scenic option to follow US 1 south onto the Schoodic Peninsula. ME 182 hooks back onto US 1 at Cherryfield. From

here, enter 'Down East' Maine, an unspoiled region dotted with traditional fishing villages. For a good meal and convenient lodging, stop in Machias.

TRIP HIGHLIGHT

⑪ Lubec & Quoddy Head

Lubec is a small fishing village that makes its living off transborder traffic with Canada and a bit of tourism. South of town, a walking trail winds along towering, jagged cliffs at the 541-acre **Quoddy Head State Park** (📞207-733-0911; www.maine.gov/ quoddyhead; 973 S Lubec Rd; adult/child $4/1; ⏰sunrise-sunset), a moody place when the mist is thick and the foghorn blasts its lonely wail. The tides here are dramatic, fluctuating 16ft in six hours. Look for whales migrating along the coast in summer. The park is also the site of the 1858 **West Quoddy Light**, which looks like a barber's pole.

The Drive » Return to US 1 north, passing Pembroke and Perry. About 3 miles north of Perry look for a pull-off on the left marking the 45th parallel, the halfway point between the North Pole and the equator. Continue 8.5 miles north.

⑫ St Croix Island International Historic Site

The site of one of the first European settlements in the New World is visible from this **historic park** (www.nps.gov/sacr; 84 St Croix Dr, Calais; ⏰park dawn-dusk year-round, visitor center 9am-5pm Thu-Mon Jun & Sep, 9am-5pm daily Jul & Aug), 8 miles southeast of Calais. In 1604 a company of settlers sailed from France to establish a French claim in North America. They built a settlement on a small island in Passamaquoddy Bay, between Maine and New Brunswick, Canada. The settlers were ill-prepared for winter, and icy waters essentially trapped them on the island with limited food until spring. Many perished. The settlement was abandoned in 1605 and a new home was established in Port Royal, Nova Scotia. A short trail at the park winds past bronze statues and historic displays; a visitor center is staffed from mid-May to mid-October.

The Drive » Return to US 1 and drive 5 miles north to a rest area on your right. If you end up in Canada – or pass the local high school – you've gone too far.

⑬ Calais

Maine's northernmost lighthouse is **Whitlocks Mill Light** (www.stcroix historical.com; US 1), visible from a rest area 3.5 miles south of Calais. To spot the lighthouse, look for the sign, walk down to the fence and look north.

Eating & Sleeping

Cape Elizabeth ❸

✕ Lobster Shack at Two Lights
Seafood $$

(☎207-799-1677; www.lobstershacktwolights.com; 225 Two Lights Rd; mains $5-25; ⏱11am-8pm Apr-Oct) Crack into a lobster dinner, lobster roll or chowder bowl at this well-loved seafood shack, with killer views of the Atlantic from indoor and outdoor seating areas. It's about 7.5 miles south of downtown Portland.

Portland ❹

🛏 Pomegranate Inn
B&B $$$

(☎207-772-1006; www.pomegranateinn.com; 49 Neal St; r $189-409; ❄🛜) Whimsy prevails at this eight-room inn, a historic home and showcase for antiques and contemporary art: life-size statues, leopard rugs and Corinthian columns. Common spaces are a riot of colors and patterns; guest rooms come with hand-painted, oversized flower patterns and a wild mix of antique and contemporary furniture.

Freeport ❻

🛏 Harraseeket Inn
Inn $$

(☎800-342-6423, 207-865-9377; www.harraseeketinn.com; 162 Main St; r $155-310; ❄🛜🏊🐾) This big, white clapboard inn is a Freeport tradition, with a lodge-style lobby complete with crackling fireplace and afternoon tea. While most rooms have a classic but fresh look, the Thomas Moser Room is decked out in sleek slate and wood. A short walk from the LL Bean outlet.

🛏 Recompence Shore Campground
Campground $

(☎207-865-9307; www.freeportcamping.com; 134 Burnett Rd; campsites $30-65, cabins $225-250; ⏱May-Oct; 🅿🛜) Adjacent to the Wolfe's Neck Woods State Park, this fabulous, family-oriented, 626-acre campground has waterfront and wooded sites spread over a working saltwater farm. It's part of a nonprofit organization dedicated to promoting sustainable agriculture and outdoor recreation; it's open for the public to check out the animals and walk the trails.

Rockland ❽

✕ Primo
Italian $$$

(☎207-596-0770; www.primorestaurant.com; 2 Main St/ME 73; mains $32-48; ⏱5-10pm Wed-Sun mid-May–Oct) In a sprawling Victorian house a mile from downtown sits Primo, considered one of Maine's best restaurants. Chef Melissa Kelly has reached celebrity status for her creative ways with New England ingredients. Try scallops atop local wild leek and fiddlehead ferns, or farm-raised chicken with ricotta *gnudi* (dumplings). The menu, a farm-to-table ode, changes daily.

🛏 Captain Lindsey Hotel
Boutique Hotel $$

(☎207-596-7950; www.lindseyhotel.com; 5 Lindsey St; r $215; ❄🛜) There's a sophisticated seafaring theme at this nine-room boutique hotel on a side street just steps from Main St. The building started as a sea-captain's home; check out the 'snack vault' and the handsome oak-paneled breakfast room, or get cozy by the fire in your guest room or in the hotel library.

Ellsworth (Machias) ❿

✕ Helen's Restaurant
American $

(☎207-255-8423; www.helensrestaurantmachias.com; 111 Main St/US 1, Machias; mains $8-30; ⏱6am-8pm Mon-Sat, 7am-2pm Sun; 🅿) Helen's is the kind of friendly locals' joint where waitresses call you 'hon,' but their food makes your standard American diner fare look like mud in comparison. Fresh haddock is moist and flakey, salads are made with local goat's cheese, the hot roast-beef sandwich comes on homemade bread, and the blueberry pie is the envy of restaurants across the state.

🛏 Machias River Inn
Motel $$

(☎207-255-4861; www.machiasriverinn.com; 103 Main St/US 1, Machias; r $84-144, ste $110-160, apt $120-175; ❄🛜🏊) Next to Helen's, this roadside lodge exceeds expectations with its clean, comfortable rooms and more spacious suites and apartments. All have mini-fridges, microwaves and Keurig coffeemakers; pricier rooms have great views of the Machias River out back. Bikes are available for hire.

Classic Trip

Acadia National Park

26

For adventurers, Mount Desert Island is hard to beat. Mountain hiking. Coastal kayaking. Woodland biking. Bird-watching. When you're done exploring, unwind by stargazing on the beach.

TRIP HIGHLIGHTS

3 DAYS
112 MILES / 180KM

GREAT FOR...

BEST TIME TO GO

May through October for good weather and open facilities.

 ESSENTIAL PHOTO

Capture that sea-and-sunrise panorama from atop Cadillac Mountain.

☑ **BEST FOR OUTDOORS**

Hike a 'ladder trail' up a challenging cliff.

---

68 miles

Bar Harbor
Shop, dine and slurp ice cream in this preppy town

30 miles

Carriage Roads
Cyclists and walkers love these car-free paths

Hulls Cove
START

⑦ ⑨

⑥

Schoodic Peninsula
FINISH

⑤

Northeast Harbor

Seal Cove

Southwest Harbor

Bass Harbor

18 miles

Jordan Pond House
Popovers and tea make the perfect après-hike

Cadillac Mountain
Climb high for sunrise and sunset views

24 miles

Cadillac Mountain Sunrise over Acadia National Park

279

Classic Trip

26 Acadia National Park

Drivers and hikers can thank John D Rockefeller Jr and other wealthy landowners for the aesthetically pleasing bridges, overlooks and stone steps that give Acadia National Park its artistic oomph. Rockefeller in particular worked diligently with architects and masons to ensure that the infrastructure complemented the surrounding landscape. Today, park explorers can put Rockefeller's planning to good use — tour the wonderful Park Loop Rd by car, but be sure to explore on foot and by bike wherever you can.

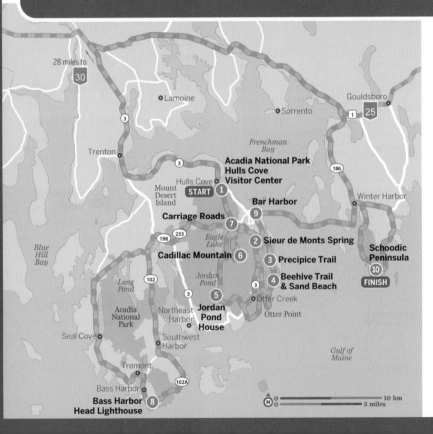

① Acadia National Park Hulls Cove Visitor Center

Whoa, whoa, whoa. Before zooming into Bar Harbor on ME 3, stop at the **park visitor center** (☎207-288-3338; www.nps. gov/acad; ME 3; ☉8:30am-4:30pm mid-Apr–Jun, Sep & Oct, 8am-6pm Jul & Aug) to get the lay of the land and pay the admission fee. Inside, head directly to the large diorama, which provides a helpful overview of Mount Desert Island (MDI). As you'll see, Acadia National Park shares the island with several non-park communities, which are tucked here and there beside Acadia's borders.

From the visitor center, the best initiation to the park is to drive the 27-mile **Park Loop Rd**, which links the park's highlights in the eastern section of MDI. It's one

LINK YOUR TRIP

25 **Maritime Maine**
Enjoy Bass lighthouse? Hop on US 1 for more photogenic beacons.

30 **Mainely Art**
Take US 1 south to Rockland for galleries, museums and local artists.

TOP TIP: PARK SHUTTLES

With millions of visitors coming to the park each summer, traffic and parking can be a hassle. On arrival, drive the Park Loop Rd straight through for the views and the driving experience. Then leave the driving to others by using the Island Explorer (www.exploreacadia.com), which is free with park admission. Shuttles run along nine routes that connect visitors to trails, carriage roads, beaches, campgrounds and in-town destinations. They can even carry mountain bikes.

way (traveling clockwise) for most of its length.

The Drive » From the visitor center, turn right onto the Park Loop Rd, not ME 3 (which leads into Bar Harbor). Take in a nice view of Frenchman Bay on your left before passing the spur to ME 233. A short distance ahead, turn left to begin the one-way loop on the Park Loop Rd.

② Sieur de Monts Spring

Nature-lovers and history buffs will enjoy a stop at the Sieur de Monts Spring area at the intersection of ME 3 and the Park Loop Rd. Here you'll find a nature center and the summer-only branch of the **Abbe Museum** (☎207-288-3519; www.abbemuseum.org; 49 Sweetwater Circle; adult/child $3/1; ☉10am-5pm late May-Oct), which sits in a lush, nature-like setting. Twelve of Acadia's biospheres are displayed in miniature at the **Wild Gardens of Acadia** (Park

Loop Rd & ME 3), from bog to coniferous woods to meadow. Botany enthusiasts will appreciate the plant labels. There are also some amazing stone-step trails here, appearing out of the talus as if by magic.

The Drive » If you wish to avoid driving the full park loop, you can follow ME 3 from here into Bar Harbor. Push on for the full experience – you won't regret it.

③ Precipice Trail

What's the most exciting way to get a bird's-eye view of the park? By climbing up to where the birds are. Two 'ladder trails' cling to the sides of exposed cliffs on the northeastern section of the Park Loop Rd, dubbed Ocean Dr. If you're fit and the season's right, tackle the first of the ladder trails, the steep, challenging 1.6-mile **Precipice Trail**, which climbs the east

Classic Trip

face of Champlain Mountain on iron rungs and ladders. (Note that the trail is typically closed late spring to mid-August because it's a nesting area for peregrine falcons. If it is closed, you might catch volunteers and staff monitoring the birds through scopes from the trailhead parking lot.) Skip the trail on rainy days.

The Drive » Continue south on the Park Loop Rd. The Beehive Trail starts 100ft north of the Sand Beach parking area.

----

❹ Beehive Trail & Sand Beach

Another good ladder trail is the **Beehive Trail**. The 0.8-mile climb includes ladders, rungs, narrow wooden bridges and scrambling – with steep drop-offs. As with the Precipice Trail, it's recommended that you descend via a nearby walking route, rather than climbing down.

Don't let the crowds keep you away from **Sand Beach**. It's home to one of the few sandy shorelines in the park, and it's a don't-miss spot. But you don't have to visit in the middle of the day to appreciate its charms. Beat the crowds early in

the morning, or visit at night, especially for the **Stars over Sand Beach** program. During these free one-hour talks, lie on the beach, look up at the sky and listen to rangers share stories and science about the stars. Even if you miss the talk, the eastern coastline along Ocean Dr is worth checking out at night, when you can watch the Milky Way seemingly slip right into the ocean.

The Drive » Swoop south past the crashing waves of Thunder Hole. If you want to exit the loop road, turn right onto Otter Cliff Rd, which hooks up to ME 3 north into Bar Harbor. Otherwise, pass Otter Point then follow the road inland past Wildwood Stables.

ISLAND VISIT PLANNER

Acadia National Park

Orientation & Fees

Park admission is $30 per vehicle (including passengers), $20 per motorcycle and $12 for walk-ins and cyclists. Admission is valid for seven days.

Camping

There are two great rustic campgrounds on Mount Desert Island, with nearly 500 sites between them. Both are densely wooded and near the coast; reservations are essential (except in winter at Blackwoods). **Seawall** (☏877-444-6777; www.recreation. gov; 668 Seawall Rd, Southwest Harbor; tent sites $22-30, RV sites $30; ⊙late May–mid-Oct) is 4 miles south of Southwest Harbor on the 'Quietside' of Mount Desert Island, while **Blackwoods** (☏877-444-6777; www.recreation.gov; ME 3; tent & RV sites $30; ⊙year-round) is closer to Bar Harbor (5 miles south, on ME 3).

Bar Harbor & Mount Desert Island

Before your trip, check lodging availability at the **Bar Harbor Chamber of Commerce** (www.visitbarharbor.com). Staff can mail you a copy of the visitor guide. Otherwise, stop by the welcome center for lodging brochures, maps and local information. It's located north of the bridge onto Mount Desert Island. There is a second **visitor center** (Acadia Welcome Center; ☏207-288-5103; www.visitbarharbor.com; 2 Cottage St; ⊙8am-4pm) in Bar Harbor itself.

Jordan Pond House

TRIP HIGHLIGHT

❺ Jordan Pond House

Share hiking stories with other nature-lovers at the lodge-like **Jordan Pond House** (☏207-276-3316; https://jordanpondhouse.com; Park Loop Rd; tea & popovers $11, mains $13-29; ⏲11am-7pm mid-May–mid-Oct), where afternoon tea has been a tradition since the late 1800s. Steaming pots of Earl Grey come with hot popovers (hollow rolls made with egg batter) and strawberry jam. Eat on the broad lawn overlooking the lake. On clear days the glassy waters of 176-acre Jordan Pond reflect the image of Mt Penobscot like a mirror. Take the 3.2-mile nature trail around the pond after finishing your tea.

The Drive ❯❯ Look up for the rock precariously perched atop South Bubble from the pull-off almost 2 miles north. Continue north to access Cadillac Mountain Rd.

TRIP HIGHLIGHT

❻ Cadillac Mountain

Don't leave the park without driving – or hiking – to the 1530ft summit of Cadillac Mountain. For panoramic views of Frenchman Bay, walk the paved 0.5-mile **Cadillac Mountain Summit loop**. The summit is a popular place in the early morning because it's long been touted as the first spot in the USA to see the sunrise. The truth? It is, but only between October 7 and March 6. The crown is passed to northern coastal towns the rest of the year because of the tilt of the earth. But, hey, the sunset is always a good bet.

The Drive ❯❯ Drunk on the views, you can complete the loop road and exit the park, heading for your accommodations or next destination. But consider finding a parking lot and tackling walking trails, or heading to Bar Harbor to hire bikes.

TRIP HIGHLIGHT

❼ Carriage Roads

John D Rockefeller Jr, a lover of old-fashioned horse carriages, gifted Acadia some 45 miles of crisscrossing carriage roads. Made from crushed stone, the roads are free of cars and are popular with cyclists, hikers and equestrians. Several of them fan out from Jordan Pond House, but if the lot is too crowded continue north to the parking area at **Eagle Lake** on US 233 to

Classic Trip

WHY THIS IS A CLASSIC TRIP
BENEDICT WALKER, WRITER

New England's one-and-only national park turned 100 in 2016 and continues to live up to its celebrity status — around 2 million visitors each year make it one of the most popular parks in the USA. The best way to get oriented is to drive Park Loop Road, but don't be afraid to venture off the beaten track, or take the 'other' loop to explore the scenic Schoodic Peninsula. You'll find pristine inlets and sleepy coves on the 'Quietside,' the occasional working lobster shack, and nature, the star performer, thriving at every turn.

Above: Beehive Trail, Acadia National Park
Left: Carriage road, Acadia National Park
Right: Bass Harbor Head Lighthouse

ZACK FRANK/SHUTTERSTOCK ©

link to the carriage-road network. If you're planning to explore by bike, the Bicycle Express Shuttle runs to Eagle Lake from the Bar Harbor Village Green from late June through September. Pick up a *Carriage Road User's Map* at the visitor center.

The Drive » Still in the mood for cruising? Before you head for the bright lights of Bar Harbor, take a detour: drive ME 233 toward the western part of MDI, connecting to ME 198 west, then drop south on ME 102 toward Southwest Harbor. Pass Echo Lake Beach and Southwest Harbor, then bear left onto ME 102A for a dramatic rise up and back into the park near the seawall.

---

⑧ Bass Harbor Head Lighthouse

There is only one lighthouse on Mount Desert Island, and it sits in the somnolent village of Bass Harbor in the far southwest corner of the park. Built in 1858, the 36ft lighthouse still has a Fresnel lens from 1902. It's in a beautiful location that's a photographers' favorite. The lighthouse is a coast guard residence, so you can't go inside, but you can take photos. You can also stroll to the coast on two easy trails near the property: the **Ship Harbor Trail**, a 1.2-mile loop, and the **Wonderland Trail**, a 1.4-mile round trip. These trails are

Classic Trip

spectacular ways to get through the forest and to the coast, which looks different to the coast on Ocean Dr.

The Drive » For a lollipop loop, return on ME 102A to ME 102 through the village of Bass Harbor. Follow ME 102 then ME 233 all the way to Bar Harbor.

TRIP HIGHLIGHT

9 Bar Harbor

Tucked on the rugged coast in the shadows of Acadia's mountains, Bar Harbor is a busy gateway town with a J Crew joie de vivre. Restaurants, taverns and boutiques are scattered along Main St, Mt Desert St and Cottage St. Shops sell everything from books and camping gear to handicrafts and art. For a fascinating collection of natural artifacts related to Maine's Native American heritage, visit the **Abbe Museum** (☑207-288-3519; www.abbemuseum. org; 26 Mount Desert St; adult/child $8/4; ☉10am-5pm May-Oct, to 4pm Thu-Sat Nov-Apr, closed Jan). The collection holds more than 50,000 objects, such as pottery, tools, combs and fishing instruments spanning

the last 2000 years, including contemporary pieces. (There's a smaller summer-only branch in Sieur de Monts Spring; p281.)

Done browsing? Spend the rest of the afternoon, or early evening, exploring the area by water. Sign up in Bar Harbor for a half-day or sunset sea-kayaking trip. Both **National Park Sea Kayak Tours** (☑800-347-0940; www.acadiakayak.com; 39 Cottage St; half-day tour $55; ☉late May-early Oct) and **Coastal Kayaking Tours** (☑207-288-9605; www. acadiafun.com; 48 Cottage St; 2½hr/half-day tours $46/56; ☉mid-May–mid-Oct) offer guided trips along the jagged coast.

 p287

The Drive » There's another part of the park you haven't yet explored. Reaching it involves a 44-mile drive (north on Rte 3 to US 1, following it about 17 miles to ME 186 S). ME 186 passes through Winter Harbor and then links to Schoodic Point Loop Rd. It's about an hour's drive one way. Alternatively, hop on a Downeast Windjammer ferry from the pier beside the Bar Harbor Inn.

----

10 Schoodic Peninsula

The Schoodic Peninsula is the only section of Acadia National Park that's part of the

mainland. It's also home to the Park Loop Rd, a rugged, woodsy drive with splendid views of Mount Desert Island and Cadillac Mountain. You're more likely to see a moose here than on MDI – what moose wants to cross a bridge?

Much of the drive is one way. There's an excellent **campground** (☑877-444-6777; www.recreation.gov; 54 Farview Dr, Winter Harbor; campsites $22-30; ☉late May–mid-Oct) near the entrance, then a picnic area at **Frazer Point**. Further along the loop, turn right for a short ride to **Schoodic Point**, a 440ft-high promontory with ocean views.

The full loop from Winter Harbor is 11.5 miles. If you're planning to come by ferry, you could rent a bike beforehand at **Bar Harbor Bicycle Shop** (☑207-288-3886; www.barharborbike. com; 141 Cottage St; rental per day $25-50, half-day from $19; ☉8am-6pm) – the Park Loop Rd's smooth surface and easy hills make it ideal for cycling.

In July and August, the Island Explorer Schoodic shuttle bus runs from Winter Harbor to the peninsula ferry terminal and around the Park Loop Rd. It does not link to Bar Harbor.

Old Canada Road

The Kennebec River offers a stunning backdrop for photographers, a link to the past for history students, a white-water mecca for rafters and a source of inspiration for, well, everyone.

27

TRIP HIGHLIGHTS

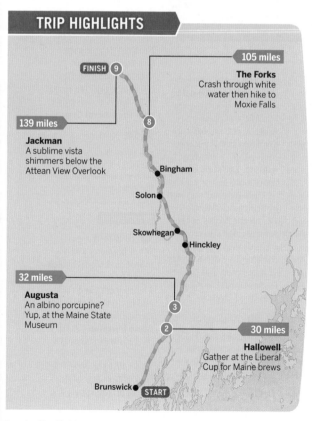

105 miles

The Forks
Crash through white water then hike to Moxie Falls

FINISH 9

139 miles

Jackman
A sublime vista shimmers below the Attean View Overlook

8

Bingham

Solon

Skowhegan

Hinckley

32 miles

Augusta
An albino porcupine? Yup, at the Maine State Museum

3

2

30 miles

Hallowell
Gather at the Liberal Cup for Maine brews

Brunswick **START**

2 DAYS
139 MILES / 224KM

GREAT FOR...

BEST TIME TO GO

July to October for top rafting and hiking.

ESSENTIAL PHOTO

From the Attean View Overlook, take a sunset shot of Attean Lake and distant mountains.

☑ **BEST FOR OUTDOORS**

White-water-rafting trips launch onto the Kennebec and Dead Rivers near The Forks.

Kennebec River Fly fishing

289

Old Canada Road

The Old Canada Rd is a 'hands-on' museum for history buffs. Stretching north from Hallowell to the Canadian border along US 201, it tracks the Kennebec River for most of the drive, passing farms, old ports, private timberlands and rafting companies – all of the industries that have sustained the region over the last few centuries. You're also following the trail of Benedict Arnold, who marched this way for George Washington during the Revolutionary War.

① Brunswick

What better place to start a road trip than a museum dedicated to an intrepid explorer? On the campus of Bowdoin College, the **Peary-MacMillan Arctic Museum** (☏207-725-3416; www.bowdoin.edu/arctic-museum; 9500 College Station, Bowdoin College campus, Hubbard Hall; ⏰10am-5pm Tue-Sat, 2-5pm Sun) displays memorabilia from the expeditions of Robert Peary and Donald MacMillan, who were among the first explorers to reach the North Pole – or a spot pretty darn close to it. Exhibits include an oak-and-rawhide sledge used to carry the expedition to the pole and Peary's journal entry reading 'The pole at last!' Also notable are MacMillan's black-and-white Arctic photos and displays examining the Inuit people and Arctic wildlife. The stuffed polar bears look...not so cuddly.

The surrounding town of Brunswick, which sits on the banks of the Androscoggin River, is a handsome, well-kept community with a pretty village green and historic homes tucked along its tree-lined streets.

✕ ⏸ p295, p319

The Drive » Follow US 201 north past meadows, fruit stands, old Chevy pickup trucks and Dunkin' Donuts (they're everywhere!) on this 30-mile stretch.

TRIP HIGHLIGHT

② Hallowell

Hallowell, a major river port for many years, thrived on the transportation of granite, ice and timber. There's a nice view of the town and the Kennebec River from the **Kennebec-Chaudière International Corridor Information Panel**, located at a small pull-off south of town and describing the 233-mile international heritage trail between Québec City and coastal Maine. Hallowell dates from 1726, and it's a sociable place, dubbed 'the New Orleans of the North.' The compact downtown is home to numerous historic buildings, antique stores, cafes, and an easygoing pub, the **Liberal Cup**.

✕ ⏸ p295

The Drive » From Hallowell, follow US 201 just 1.5 miles north to downtown Augusta and the State Capitol complex.

TRIP HIGHLIGHT

③ Augusta

What happens when a moose and his rival lock horns in mortal combat? Their interlocked racks end up in the Cabinet of Curiosities at the **Maine State Museum** (☏207-287-2301; www.mainestatemuseum.org; 230 State St; adult/child $3/2; ⏰9am-5pm Tue-Fri, 10am-4pm Sat) in Augusta, the state

capital. The museum, a four-story ode to all things Maine, is situated around a multistory mill that churns by water power. The newest permanent exhibit, 'At Home in Maine,' looks at homes throughout the years; in the mod 1970s house you can watch a family filmstrip and dial a rotary phone.

Across the parking lot, take a tour (guided or self-guided) of the **State House** (☎207-287-2301; www.legislature.maine.gov/lio; cnr State & Capitol Sts; ⏱8am-5pm Mon-Fri), built in 1832 and enlarged in 1909. It was designed by Boston architect Charles Bulfinch, the same architect behind the nation's Capitol building in Washington, DC.

The Drive » On the 19-mile drive to Winslow you'll cross the river and pass a barn or two, a taxidermy shop, pine trees, creeks and small churches.

LINK YOUR TRIP

28 Great North Woods
From Jackman, take ME 6 east to Rockwood to tour Maine's largest lake.

30 Mainely Art
Visit the Bowdoin College Museum of Art in Brunswick, then stroll through galleries along the coast.

④ Waterville & Winslow

The oldest blockhouse fortification in the USA is located at the **Fort Halifax State Historic Site**, in a small park on the banks of the Kennebec River in Winslow. The log blockhouse is all that remains of a larger palisaded garrison built by British Americans in 1754, designed to guard against attacks by the French and their allied Native American tribes. In 1987 the blockhouse's logs came apart during a flood and floated downstream. They were recovered, and the fortification was rebuilt. It sits in pretty Fort Halifax Park on US 201, a mile south of the Winslow-Waterville Bridge (well hidden among gas stations).

 p295

The Drive » Cross the Winslow-Waterville Bridge and continue on US 201 north through downtown Waterville. From here it's a 9-mile drive. Look out for logging trucks as the road approaches Hinckley.

⑤ LC Bates Museum

Any road trip worth its stripes includes at least one eccentricity. This one earns its stripes – and its spots and feathers – with the nicely nonconformist **LC Bates Museum** (☏207-238-4250; www.gwh.org; 14 Easler Rd, Hinckley; adult/child $3/1; ☉10am-4:30pm Wed-Sat, 1-4:30pm Sun Apr-Sep, other times by appointment). Housed in a 1903 brick school building on the Good Will-Hinckley educational complex south of Hinckley, the museum embraces the concept of

SEAN PAVONE/GETTY IMAGES ©

NORTH WOODS RIVER-RAFTING TRIPS

Some of the best white water in America rushes through Maine's North Woods. From early May to mid-October, dozens of companies run organized rafting trips on the Kennebec, Dead and Penobscot Rivers. Bingham and The Forks serve as bases for rafting companies, and trips range in difficulty from Class II to Class V. For a one-day trip on the Kennebec, expect to pay between $69 and $129, with prices at their highest in July and August.

The following recommended rafting companies, all with lodges for accommodations and meals, plus other outdoor activities on offer (including river tubing, fishing, wildlife-spotting and winter snowmobiling), are all based in The Forks.

Crab Apple Whitewater (☏800-553-7238; www.crabapplewhitewater.com; Lake Moxie Rd; rafting $81-121)

Northern Outdoors (☏207-663-4466; www.northernoutdoors.com; 1771 US 201; rafting $69-149)

Three Rivers Whitewater (☏207-663-2104; www.threeriverswhitewater.com; 2265 US 201; ☉rafting $94-124)

Augusta Maine State House

the 20th-century Cabinet of Curiosities, with a huge assortment of natural, geologic and artistic artifacts. On the 1st floor, look for an amazing array of taxidermied birds. The basement holds stuffed mammals (including one of the last caribou shot in Maine), rocks, minerals and fossils. There are treasures here, and staff members are glad to point out the more interesting finds and answer questions. **Nature trails** meander through the forest out back.

The Drive ≫ The Kennebec stays in the picture on the 10-mile drive to Skowhegan, former home of Margaret Chase Smith, the first woman elected to both the US House of Representatives and Senate.

----

6 Skowhegan

At Skowhegan's hard-to-resist ice-cream stand **Gifford's** (☎207-474-2257; www.giffordsicecream.com; 307 Madison Ave/US 201; cones from $3.75; ⏰ hours vary Apr–mid-Oct), **every flavor sounds delicious**, from Maine Wild Blueberry to Caramel Caribou to Moose Tracks, made

with peanut-butter cups and fudge. If you don't pull over for a scoop, you'll never hear the end of it if you've got kids or a co-pilot on board. But don't worry, these creamy concoctions are delicious. Plus: if you need a real leg-stretch, there's a mini-golf course here too.

The Drive ≫ From Skowhegan, drive 10 miles north to the junction of US 201 and ME 43, which marks the start of the Old Canada Road National Scenic Byway – a particularly lovely stretch of the longer Old Canada Rd.

BENEDICT ARNOLD SLEPT HERE

About 12 miles north of Bingham, on the left side of the road, a small stone memorial marks the spot where Benedict Arnold and his soldiers left the Kennebec River in October 1775 during the Revolutionary War. Arnold, at the time still loyal to America, had been placed in command of 1100 men by George Washington. His mission? To follow the Kennebec and Dead Rivers north to defeat the British forces at Québec. The soldiers used bateaux (shallow-draft river boats) to travel up the Kennebec and encountered numerous difficulties along the way. Many men were lost through desertion and illness. A weakened force of about 500 reached Québec, where they were ultimately defeated.

7 Robbins Hill Scenic Area

Take a picnic and your camera to the overlook at Robbins Hill near the start of the national byway. Look west for views of Saddleback Mountain, Mt Abraham and other mountains in Maine's Rangeley Lakes region. Signboards detail the history of the communities along the Old Canada Rd, from the region's agricultural beginnings in the late 1700s to the effects of the railroad and the arrival of the timber industry.

The Drive » Pass white clapboard houses in Solon and another roadside pull-off, this one overlooking the Kennebec River. Here you'll find informational plaques about the railroad and the logging industries, including a picture of the last American log drive here

in 1976. Continue past anglers' cabins, rafting businesses and brewpubs.

TRIP HIGHLIGHT

8 The Forks

After passing through Bingham and Moscow, US 201 follows a gorgeous stretch of river into The Forks. At this dot on the map, the Dead River joins the Kennebec River, setting the stage for excellent white-water rafting. At the junction of US 201 and Lake Moxie Rd, there's a small rest area with picnic tables, an information kiosk and a footbridge over the Kennebec River. From here, drive 2 miles east on Lake Moxie Rd to the trailhead for the easy walk (0.6 miles one way) to the dramatic **Moxie Falls**. At 90ft, this is one

of the highest waterfalls in the state.

 p295

The Drive » On this 20-mile push, you'll ascend Johnson Mountain before reaching the Lake Parlin overlook, where there are details about the American moose – which can reach speeds of 35mph.

TRIP HIGHLIGHT

9 Jackman

Jackman knows how to throw out the welcome mat. Just south of town, the **Attean View Overlook** greets road-trippers with a dramatic view of Attean Lake and distant mountains – a landscape that sweeps into Canada.

The lake and overlook are named for Joseph Attean, a Penobscot Indian leader who guided Henry David Thoreau on trips through the Maine woods in 1853 and 1857. Attean died during a log drive on July 4, 1870. Legend says that his boots were hung from a pine knot near where his body was found, a tradition for river drivers killed while working the waterway. Today, Jackman is a good base for outdoor fun, including fishing, canoeing, hiking, biking, snowmobiling and cross-country skiing. Its ATV trails are considered some of the state's best.

🛏 p295

Eating & Sleeping

Brunswick ❶

✕ Tao Yuan   Asian $$
(☎207-725-9002; www.tao-yuan.me; 22 Pleasant St; small plates $6-22; ⊗5-9pm Tue-Thu, to 10pm Fri & Sat) At this high-quality pan-Asian eatery, the accomplished dishes dazzle palates with fresh flavor. Small plates range from lobster ravioli served in a rich, coconut-laced *massaman* broth with basil to Peking duck with caramelized hoisin sauce to cold Thai beef salad. Order family style and share, and make reservations.

⊨ Black Lantern   B&B $
(☎207-725-4165; www.blacklanternbandb.com; 57 Elm St, Topsham; r $95-140; ☎) Looking like something from a postcard, this mid-19th-century home houses three pretty, affordable guest rooms, plus a lovely garden that stretches down to the river's edge. It's in Topsham, just a mile from downtown Brunswick, across the Androscoggin River.

Hallowell ❷

✕ Slates
Restaurant & Bakery   American $$
(☎207-622-4104; www.slatesrestaurant.com; 165 Water St; mains lunch $11-23, dinner $17-30; ⊗3-8pm Mon, 11:30am-8:30pm Tue, 8am-8:30pm Wed-Sat, 10am-2pm Sun) Inside this big yellow house on the main street, the crowd-pleasing menu includes crabmeat crepes, grilled pesto pizzas and beef tenderloin *au poivre*. At lunchtime, chicken pie and crab cakes are a hit. The bakery next door serves breakfast goodies, breads, sandwiches and coffee from 7am daily.

⊨ Maple Hill Farm B&B   B&B $$
(☎207-622-2708; www.maplebb.com; 11 Inn Rd; r $115-219; ❄☎) Hosted by former Maine state senator Scott Cowger, this laid-back B&B sits 3 miles west of Hallowell amid acres of rolling hayfields and forests crisscrossed by hiking trails. The eight rooms are bright and comfortable, with loads of homey furnishings (brass lamps, oil paintings and big armchairs). The best rooms have fireplaces, private terraces and two-person hot tubs.

Waterville & Winslow ❹

✕ Big G's Deli   American $
(☎207-873-7808; www.big-g-s-deli.com; 581 Benton Ave, Winslow; mains $7-12; ⊗6am-7pm) The sandwiches here are *huge* and inexpensive (trust us, you only need a half-portion), making Big G's a good stop for travelers on a budget. Grab your sandwich to go and take it down to the river for a picnic. Breakfast is available until noon.

The Forks ❽

✕ Kennebec
River Brewery   Pub Food $$
(☎207-663-4466; www.northernoutdoors.com; 1771 US 201, The Forks; mains $10-19; ⊗7am-9pm Jan-Mar & May-Oct, 4-9pm Nov) After a day of rafting, enjoy a burger or steak and a 'Let 'er Drift' summer ale. The brewpub is inside the main lodge at the Northern Outdoors Adventure Resort and serves up a full day's worth of hearty eats to snowmobilers (from January to mid-March), white-water rafters (from May to mid-October) and hunters (in November, evenings only).

Jackman ❾

⊨ Bishops Country Inn Motel   Motel $
(☎207-668-3231; www.bishopsmotel.com; 461 Main St; d $95-110, tr $105-120, q $115-130; ❄☎) The plain but spacious rooms here work well for gear-laden adventurers and come with microwave, refrigerator and flat-screen TV. Peak season here is winter (January to March), when snowmobilers hit town to revel in Jackman's surrounding forest trails.

Great North Woods

Welcome to the highlands, a land of superlatives where you can hike Maine's highest mountain, canoe its largest lake and ogle the stomping grounds of America's spookiest author – if you dare.

28

TRIP HIGHLIGHTS

210 miles
Lily Bay State Park
Lie on the beach in the backwoods of Maine

88 miles
Baxter State Park
This is where the wild things are

Rockwood
FINISH

3

Millinocket

7

6

● Brownville

START **1**

Greenville & Moosehead Lake
Enjoy a lake cruise on a 1914 steamboat

Bangor
Check out an ax-wielding lumberman and spooky gates

200 miles

0 miles

---

3 DAYS
250 MILES / 402KM

GREAT FOR...

BEST TIME TO GO
July and August brings warm weather and no blackflies.

ESSENTIAL PHOTO
Capture Mt Katahdin rising behind Baxter State Park's southern entrance.

BEST FOR OUTDOORS
Hike through the vast virgin wilds of Baxter State Park.

28 Great North Woods

Texts. Tweets. Twenty-four hours of breaking news. If you need a respite from the modern world, grab your map – a paper one! – and drive directly to the Maine highlands, part of the sprawling North Woods. What will you find? Silence and solitude. Water and pines. The unfettered wildness of Baxter State Park. And access to 175,000 acres of private forest thrown open for public recreation.

TRIP HIGHLIGHT

❶ Bangor

Bangor is the last city on the map before the North Woods. So it seems appropriate that a towering **statue of Paul Bunyan** (Main St btwn Buck & Dutton Sts) stands near the center of downtown. The 31ft statue has watched over Bangor since the 1950s, but the ax-wielding lumberman isn't getting much love these days. His view of the Penobscot River is now blocked by a casino,

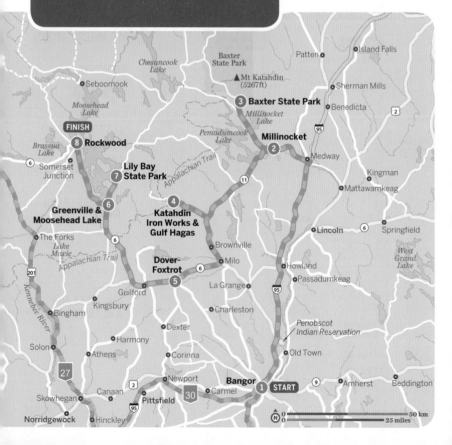

and a new multipurpose arena has risen behind him.

But Paul's not the only star in town. Stephen King, the mega-best-selling author of horror novels such as *Carrie* and *The Shining,* resides in an appropriately Gothic red Victorian **house** (West Broadway) off Hammond St. You can't go inside, but you can snap a photo of his splendidly creepy wrought-iron front fence, adorned with spiderwebs and bats. The house is in a residential neighborhood, so please keep your shrieking to a minimum.

 p303, p319

The Drive ›› The 60-mile drive on I-95 north to exit 244 for Millinocket isn't that interesting. But it's efficient, and the rest of the drive will blow this ho-hum stretch from your memory. From

LINK YOUR TRIP

27 Old Canada Road

Head west to US 201 from Rockwood for rafting and riverside history.

30 Mainely Art

In Bangor, kick-start a loop of Maine's finest art and culture with a visit to the University of Maine Museum of Art.

exit 244, drive northwest on ME 11/157.

② Millinocket

Baxter State Park is far, far off the beaten path, and many of its rules and policies differ from those at other Maine state parks – so do a bit of planning before driving out here. The town of Millinocket, with its motels, inns and eating outlets, works well as a base camp. Eighteen miles from the park, it's also the closest town to the southern entrance. For park information and a copy of *Windnotes,* the helpful park visitor guide, stop by the **Baxter State Park Authority Headquarters** (207-723-5140; www.baxterstatepark

authority.com; 64 Balsam Dr/ME 157; 8am-4pm daily mid-May–mid-Oct, 8am-4pm Mon-Fri mid-Oct–mid-May); it's just beside the McDonald's.

 p303

The Drive ›› The drive from Millinocket to Baxter State Park takes in bogs, birches and pine trees and then some very narrow roads. Gape at Katahdin from the Keep Maine Beautiful sign, then continue to Togue Pond gate.

TRIP HIGHLIGHT

③ Baxter State Park

In the 1930s, Governor Percival Baxter began buying land for **Baxter State Park** (207-723-5140; www.baxterstatepark.org; Baxter Park Rd; entry per day $15, season pass $40; main gates usually

6am-10pm mid-May–mid-Oct), using his own money. By the time of his death in 1969, he had given, in trust, more than 200,000 acres to the park as a gift to the people of Maine. **Mt Katahdin** is the park's crowning glory. At 5267ft it is Maine's tallest mountain and the northern endpoint of the 2190-mile Appalachian Trail.

Baxter also left an endowment fund for the support and maintenance of the park. His greatest desire was for the land to remain wild and to serve as a 'sanctuary for beasts and birds.' To ensure that his vision is followed, the park is kept in a primitive state and there is very little infrastructure inside its boundaries. And what a difference this makes. Baxter is Maine at its most primeval: the wind whips around dozens of peaks, black bears root through the underbrush, and hikers go for miles without seeing another soul.

🛏 p303

The Drive ❯❯ From Millinocket, follow ME 11 south for about 25 miles. Turn right onto Katahdin Iron Works Rd, and drive 6.3 miles on a dirt road. If you get to Brownsville Junction on ME 11, you missed Katahdin Iron Works Rd.

----

❹ Katahdin Iron Works & Gulf Hagas

A reminder of a time when blast furnaces and charcoal kilns smelted iron all day, the **iron works** (www.maine.gov/katahdinironworks; Katahdin Iron Works Rd; adult/child $14/free, Maine residents $9/free; ☺9am-sunset) were built in 1843. Eventually the costs of operating in such isolation meant the facility was unable to compete with foundries in Pennsylvania and

---

BAXTER STATE PARK PLANNER

Admission
In order to protect the park from overuse, day-use is limited by the capacity of trailhead parking lots. Parking lots for the most popular Katahdin-access trailheads fill very early (by 6:30am) on sunny summer weekends.

Parking space at the most popular day-use parking lots is reservable ($5) under the park's Day Use Parking Reservation (DUPR) system – see the website www.baxterstateparkauthority.com. Reservations can be made up to two weeks before your visit.

Baxter's two main gates are **Togue Pond gate** in the south and **Matagamon gate** in the north. Both are generally open 6am to 10pm from mid-May to mid-October.

Togue Pond is 18 miles from Millinocket; there's a visitor center (offering canoe rental) just south of the gate. The less-popular access point at Matagamon is 26 miles from the town of Patten.

There is a $15 admission fee per vehicle per day (free for Maine residents).

Hiking
Read the park's website thoroughly. To hike, you need a car-parking reservation. A few spots may be available on a first-come, first-served basis, but don't count on that on a summer weekend. Make a DUPR booking online.

For an easy day in the southern part of the park, try the mile-long walk to **Katahdin Stream** falls or the pleasant 2-mile nature path around **Daicey Pond**. See the park's website for maps and details about hiking **Mt Katahdin**.

Katahdin Iron Works Charcoal kiln

other states, and it closed in 1890.

From here, Katahdin Iron Works Rd leads another 6.5 miles to the trailhead for **Gulf Hagas** (📞207-435-6213; www.northmainewoods.org; day use adult/child $14/free; ⏰6am-9pm May-early Oct), dubbed the Grand Canyon of Maine. The gorge features a stunning 500ft drop studded with waterfalls over the course of its 3 miles. Carved over five million years by water eroding the slate bedrock, the gulf is a national natural landmark and is surrounded by

some of Maine's oldest white pines. An 8-mile rim-trail hiking loop is remote and challenging, so come very prepared. Gulf Hagas is within the KI-Jo Mary Multiple-Use Forest, which is owned and managed by private timber interests but allows public use. Pay the entrance fee at the checkpoint across from Katahdin Iron Works. Visit the website for maps as well as details about access and trails at Gulf Hagas.

The Drive » From Brownville, south of Brownsville Junction,

continue south on ME 11. Take ME 6 west to Dover-Foxcroft.

----

⑤ Dover-Foxcroft

It's a bit of a haul between the iron works and Greenville. This route swings below the private logging roads of the North Woods. Take a break for **Butterfield's Ice Cream** (📞207-564-2513; www.butterfields icecream.com; 946 W Main St; cones from $3.50; ⏰11:30am-8pm Mon-Sat, noon-8pm Sun mid-Apr–late Sep, to 9pm daily Memorial Day-Labor Day) in Dover-Foxcroft. Walk up to the window, choose your scoop, grab a seat and enjoy your licks beside the smiling cow.

The Drive >> Follow ME 6 west through Guilford and Abbot Village. North of Monson, look for a pull-off on your right beside the Appalachian Trail. From this trailhead it's 112 miles north to Katahdin. This trailhead marks the southern start of a very remote section of the trail. The pull-off is about 11 miles south of Greenville.

TRIP HIGHLIGHT

6 Greenville & Moosehead Lake

Silver-blue and dotted with islands, Moosehead Lake sprawls over 120 sq miles of North Woods wilderness. Named, some say, after its shape from the air, it's one of the state's most glorious places. Greenville is the main settlement of the region.

Owned and maintained by the Moosehead Marine Museum, the steamboat **SS Katahdin** (207-695-2716; www.katahdincruises.com; Lily Bay Rd, Greenville; 3hr cruise adult/child $35/5; Jun–mid-Oct) was built in 1914. It still makes the rounds on Moosehead Lake from Greenville's center, just

like it did in Greenville's heyday. The lake's colorful history is preserved in the **Moosehead Marine Museum** (207-695-2716; www.katahdincruises.com/museum; 12 Lily Bay Rd, Greenville; entry by donation; 9am-5pm Tue-Sat, 10am-4pm Sun & Mon mid-Jun–mid-Oct), next to the dock. For moose-spotting safaris, white-water rafting, ATV tours, guided fishing trips and canoe adventures, stop by **Northwoods Outfitters** (207-695-3288; www.maineoutfitter.com; 5 Lily Bay Rd, Greenville; 8am-7pm) in the center of town. It also rents and sells outdoor gear.

The **Moosehead Lake Region Chamber of Commerce** (207-695-2702; www.destinationmoosehead lake.com; 480 Moosehead Lake Rd/ME 15; 10am-4pm) runs a useful visitor center located south of downtown.

✕ 🛏 p303

The Drive >> Tantalizing glimpses of Moosehead Lake peek through the trees on the 8-mile drive from Greenville on Lily Bay Rd, culminating in grand views from Blair Hill.

TRIP HIGHLIGHT

7 Lily Bay State Park

To camp on the shores of Moosehead Lake, pitch your tent at one of the 90 campsites at this lovely, 925-acre **park** (207-695-2700; www.maine.gov/lilybay; 13 Myrle's Way, Greenville; adult/child $6/1). Relax on the sandy beach, bird-watch and stroll the 2-mile shoreline trail.

The Drive >> Return to Greenville, then drive 20 miles north on ME 6, passing the Lavigne Memorial Bridge and marker, memorializing a local son who died in WWII.

8 Rockwood

The distinctive **Mt Kineo** is a 1769ft rhyolite mountain rising from the bottom of Moosehead Lake. For a good silhouette of its steep, towering face, which juts more than 700ft above the lake, pull over in the village of Rockwood north of Greenville. From Rockwood, return to Greenville or continue 26 miles through the woods on a lovely ribbon of road with lake views to US 201 near Jackman.

Eating & Sleeping

Bangor ❶

✕ Fiddlehead　　　　American $$

(📞207-942-3336; www.thefiddleheadrestaurant.
com; 84 Hammond St; mains $18-29; ⏱4-9pm
Tue-Fri, 5-10pm Sat, 5-9pm Sun) The young chef
at this downtown place has been earning raves
(and a packed dining room) for her international
spin on local, seasonal ingredients. Think
okonomiyaki (Japanese pancake) with Maine
shrimp, seared halibut with *char siu* pork, and
rose-petal crème brûlée. Exposed brick walls,
cool cocktails and a bar crowded with hipsters
make this a definite hot spot.

Millinocket ❷

✕ River Drivers
Restaurant & Pub　　　Pub Food $$

(📞207-723-8475; www.neoc.com/river-drivers-
restaurant-maine; 30 Twin Pines Rd, Millinocket
Lake; mains $14-28; ⏱7am-9pm; 🛜🚗🎔) At
this handsomely designed restaurant at the
NEOC Twin Pines Camp , enjoy upscale comfort
fare (blackened haddock tacos, vegetarian
lasagna, pork with pineapple-mango salsa)
in a laid-back setting with a great view of Mt
Katahdin. It's open year-round, but it's worth
checking the latest opening hours online (or on
the restaurant's Facebook page). It's signed off
the road to Baxter State Park.

🛏 NEOC Twin Pines Camp　　Cabin $$$

(📞207-723-5438, 800-634-7238; www.neoc.
com; 30 Twin Pines Rd, Millinocket Lake; cabin
$296-750; 🛜🐾) En route to Baxter State Park,
the New England Outdoor Center (NEOC) offers
a delectable slice of rural Maine, with creature
comforts in abundance in a glorious lakeside
setting. Spread over the property are 22 comfy
cabins and stylish lodges with all mod cons
(including full kitchen); some can sleep up to 14.

Baxter State Park ❸

🛏 Baxter State
Park Campgrounds　　Campground $

(📞207-723-5140; www.baxterstatepark.org;
tent sites $32, dm $12, cabins $57-135) Baxter
State Park has 11 campgrounds, a handful of
bunkhouses and basic cabins sleeping from
two to six, and numerous backcountry sites
($21), including some sites with lean-tos and
bunkhouses. Locations, facilities and opening
dates are outlined on the park website. Summer
season is generally mid-May to mid-October;
winter season is from December to March. Make
reservations well in advance.

Greenville & Moosehead Lake ❻

✕ Auntie M's　　　　American $

(📞207-695-2238; 13 Lily Bay Rd, Greenville;
mains $5-10; ⏱5am-3pm; 🚗) Eat breakfast
all day at this cozy eating spot near the center
of town. Burgers, wraps and Mexican pizza are
served at lunch. It also sells bag lunches ($6.50)
with a sandwich and snacks, perfect for those
heading out into the woods. Cash only.

🛏 Blair Hill Inn　　　　B&B $$$

(📞207-695-0224; www.blairhill.com; 351
Lily Bay Rd, Greenville; r $329-499; ⏱late
May–mid-Oct; 🛜) The Chicago socialite who
commissioned this dreamy hilltop cottage in
the late 1800s had it cleverly built atop a 20ft-
high stone foundation, thus providing views of
Moosehead Lake from almost every window.
Today it's a 10-room B&B, whose smallest
detail whispers good taste: plush, white down
comforters, fluffy robes, in-room fireplaces and
a sleek wooden bar. There's also a spa.

🛏 Moose Mountain Inn　　　Motel $

(📞207-695-3321; www.moosemountaininn.
com; 314 Rockwood Rd/ME 15; r $90-150;
❄🛜🚗🐾) Owned by Northwoods Outfitters,
this no-frills two-story motel offers 15 simple
rooms that come with refrigerator, microwave
and flat-screen TV. It's 3 miles northwest of
Greenville, en route to Rockwood.

Lakes Tour

Bright blue lakes dapple the landscape like drops from Mother Nature's paintbrush, luring travelers with sandy beaches, excellent kayaking, small-town strolling and New England's favorite state fair.

29

TRIP HIGHLIGHTS

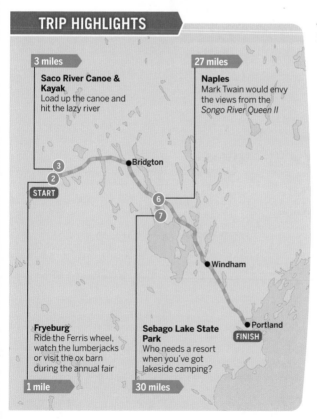

3 miles

Saco River Canoe & Kayak
Load up the canoe and hit the lazy river

27 miles

Naples
Mark Twain would envy the views from the *Songo River Queen II*

● Bridgton

3
2
START

6
7

● Windham

Fryeburg
Ride the Ferris wheel, watch the lumberjacks or visit the ox barn during the annual fair

Sebago Lake State Park
Who needs a resort when you've got lakeside camping?

● Portland
FINISH

1 mile

30 miles

2 DAYS
60 MILES / 97KM

GREAT FOR...

BEST TIME TO GO

To enjoy swimming and boating, visit from May to October.

 ESSENTIAL PHOTO

Stake your position on the Naples causeway for sweet pics of Long Lake.

 BEST FOR FAMILIES

Spend a lazy afternoon canoeing the Saco River near Fryeburg.

29 Lakes Tour

US 302 in southeast Maine is the quickest link between North Conway's outlet stores and the LL Bean store just north of Portland, but the road is also the lifeline for the stunning Lakes region. Filled with glacier-made lakes and ponds, this summer hot spot is home to the state's most popular campground as well as a beloved paddle wheeler and the family-friendly Saco River. Lovely B&Bs encourage lingering with water views and scrumptious breakfasts.

1 Fryeburg Visitor Information Center

Just east of the Maine state line, this state-run **visitor center** (☎207-935-3639; www.mainetourism.com; 97 Main St/US 302, Fryeburg; ☺9am-5:30pm Nov-Apr, 8am-6pm May-Oct) can prepare you for an adventure anywhere in the Pine Tree State. It's well stocked with brochures, and the staff are very helpful. Want to stretch your legs? A 4.2-mile section of the new **Mountain Division Trail** begins just behind the visitor center.

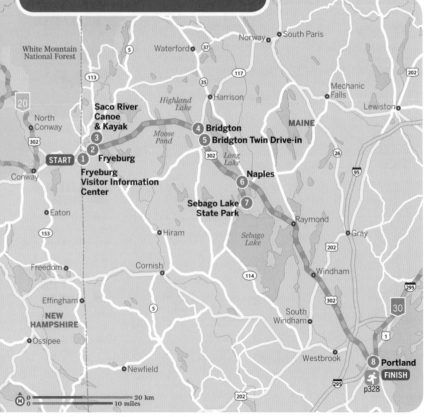

If all goes to plan, the hiking and biking trail will eventually extend 52 miles from Fryeburg to Portland.

The Drive » From the visitor center, follow US 302 east into downtown.

- - - - - - - - - - - - - - - - -

TRIP HIGHLIGHT

❷ Fryeburg

Sitting prettily on the banks of the Saco River, Fryeburg is best known for hosting the annual **Fryeburg Fair** (☎207-935-3268; www.fryeburgfair.org; 1154 Main St; adult/child $12/ free, parking $5; ☀early Oct), an eight-day state agricultural fair that started in 1851. Today it attracts more than 300,000 people. Events and attractions include everything from livestock and flower shows to a whoopie-pie

LINK YOUR TRIP

20 **White Mountains Loop**

Take US 302 west to North Conway, NH, to hop a train ride to the Presidential Range.

30 **Mainely Art**

For cultural inspiration, join this gallery-filled route, starting with the American landscapes at the Portland Museum of Art.

contest, a pig scramble (local pigs only, please), a horse-pulling contest and Woodsmen's Day, when male and female lumberjacks chisel poles of timber with their chainsaws and hurl their mighty axes.

The rest of the year, the big draw is the Saco River. If you want to feel the sand under your feet after hiking through the White Mountains in next-door New Hampshire, relax on **Weston's Beach**. To get there, take a left onto ME 113/River Rd just before entering Fryeburg from the visitor center. Parking is ahead on the right after crossing the river.

🛏 p311

The Drive » Follow ME 5 north for half a mile till the junction of US 302 and ME 5, where signs advertising chowder suppers and community dinners tempt weary travelers.

- - - - - - - - - - - - - - - - -

TRIP HIGHLIGHT

❸ Saco River Canoe & Kayak

Ready to get out on the water? The friendly folks at **Saco River Canoe & Kayak** (☎207-935-2369; www.sacorivercanoe.com; 1009 Main St, Fryeburg), who've run self-guided trips for more than 40 years, will set you up on the family-friendly Saco River. The river flows about 120 miles from Saco Lake in New Hampshire's upper White

Mountains through Crawford Notch and into Maine. In Maine, the Saco runs parallel to US 302 as it makes its way to the Gulf of Maine southwest of Portland. The river is particularly pleasant around Fryeburg, with leafy banks and sandy shores, mountain views and gentle conditions. Trips can range from one hour to several days. Canoe and kayak rentals run from $33 to $45 per day, depending on watercraft and season. Delivery and pick-up services are charged separately, and cost $7 to $16 per trip (minimum charge from $15). Service to the nearby Swans Fall access point is free.

The Drive » US 302 passes Christmas-tree farms and diamond-blue lakes on its 15-mile run east to Bridgton.

- - - - - - - - - - - - - - - - -

❹ Bridgton

Bridgton is prime digs for a weekend getaway. Main St runs for 1.5 miles past a museum, a movie house, an inviting park and an eclectic array of indie shops (p310). The well-regarded **Rufus Porter Museum** (☎207-647-2828; www.rufusportermuseum.org; 121 Main St; adult/child $8/free; ☀11am-4pm Wed-Sat early Jun-early Oct; ♿) looks at the work of 19th-century Renaissance man Rufus Porter. Porter is recognized

throughout New England for the landscape murals he painted in hundreds of houses in the region between 1825 and 1845. Also an inventor, he sold the concept of the revolving rifle to Samuel Colt in 1844, and created *Scientific American* magazine.

Take a moment to walk through the photogenic Bob Dunning Memorial Bridge – built by district craftseople in 2007 to honor a local conservationist. It marks the northern entrance to **Pondicherry Park** (www. loonecholandtrust.org; access from Depot St; ⏱dawn-10pm),

a 66-acre woodland park filled with trails and wildlife. The park sits behind the **Magic Lantern** (☎207-647-5065; www.magiclanternmovies. com; 9 Depot St; adult/child $7.50/6; ⏱Wed-Sun), a beloved community movie house – and the site of a tannery in the 1800s – that anchors downtown. Congenial staff, a pub with a 23ft screen and three themed theaters make this a pleasant spot to catch a blockbuster, an indie flick or the big game.

✗ ⊨ p311

The Drive » From downtown Bridgton drive 1 mile east on US 302.

⑤ Bridgton Twin Drive-in

One of just six drive-ins remaining in the state, **Bridgton Twin Drive-in** (☎207-647-8666; 383 Portland Rd/US 302; adult/child $7.50/5; ⏱mid-Apr–early Oct) has been going strong for some 60 years. It shows movies on two screens, and is a popular choice with families. Visit its Facebook page to see what's playing.

The Drive » US 302 rolls east out of Bridgton, turning in

Sebago Lake State Park Songo Beach

a more southerly direction as it approaches Naples, 8 miles to the south.

TRIP HIGHLIGHT

6 Naples

Restaurants and shops cluster around the Causeway in downtown Naples, which sits on a spit of land between Long Lake and Brandy Pond. A walk along the Causeway affords grand views of bright blue Long Lake. The big draw here, beyond the eating outlets and bars with lake views, is the red-and-white **Songo River Queen II** (207-693-6861; www.

songoriverqueen.net; US 302; tours adult/child 1hr $15/8, 2hr $25/13; noon, 2:30pm, & 4pm daily late Jun-early Sep, Sat & Sun only late May-late Jun & Sep-mid-Oct), a 93ft paddle wheeler with a covered upper deck. The boat churns up the east coast of the lake, then comes back down the west side (or vice versa). You'll get a look at Mt Washington and the Presidential Range during the cruise. The *Songo* holds 350 people, so reservations are not typically needed.

✗ p311

The Drive › From the Causeway, turn left onto ME 114 and drive 2 miles south. Turn left onto State Park Dr and take a woodsy cruise to the park entrance.

TRIP HIGHLIGHT

7 Sebago Lake State Park

With 250 campsites scattered throughout the woods beside the sandy shores of Sebago Lake, this 1500-acre **state park** (207-693-6231; www.maine. gov/sebagolake; 11 Park Access Rd, Casco; adult/child $8/1; park year-round, camping late May-early Sep) is a popular and scenic place

SHOPS OF BRIDGTON

Welcoming proprietors and an eclectic mix of shops in close proximity make downtown Bridgton (p307) a great spot for an hour or two of shopping.

Bridgton Books (☎207-647-2122; 140 Main St; ⏱9:30am-5:30pm Mon-Sat, 11am-4:30pm Sun) There's a large inventory of new and used books in this independent bookstore, and helpful staff.

Gallery 302 (☎207-647-2787; www.gallery302.com; 112 Main St; ⏱11am-4pm Mon-Fri, 10am-5pm Sat & Sun) This co-op with 60 member artists displays and sells art in all its forms.

Renys (☎207-647-3711; www.renys.com; 151 Main St; ⏱8am-8pm Mon-Sat, 9am-5pm Sun) A discount mini department store found throughout Maine, with 17 locations. They sell clothing, housewares and lots of outdoor essentials for Maine adventures.

to swim, picnic and camp on the way to Portland. Sebago Lake is Maine's second-largest lake, at 45 sq miles. Visitors can enjoy the beaches (Songo Beach is a pearl), grills and picnic tables, and if the beach gets too crowded, just step into the woods, where you can wander several miles of easy to moderate trails or bike the roadways. There's also a nature center. In summer,

rangers lead talks, hikes and canoe trips; look for details on the bulletin board at the park entrance. Pets are not allowed on the beaches or in the campground.

🛏 p311

The Drive » Continue southeast on US 302, passing through Windham. Suburbia and development creep in as Portland approaches.

❽ Portland

Well, hello there. Is that a brew house at the eastern end of US 302, on the fringes of downtown Portland? Yes? Cheers, we say! And welcome to the **Great Lost Bear** (☎207-772-0300; www.greatlostbear.com; 540 Forest Ave; ⏱11:30am-11:30pm Mon-Sat, noon-11pm Sun; 🛜), a fun and quirky place in a fun and quirky city. Decked out in Christmas lights and flea-market kitsch, this rambling bar and restaurant is a Portland institution. Seventy-eight taps serve primarily Northeastern brews, including 40 from Maine, making the GLB one of America's best regional beer bars. The atmosphere is family friendly (at least early in the evening), with a massive menu of burgers, quesadillas and other bar nibbles. It's the perfect fuel-stop before further explorations of Portland's museums, mansions and working wharves (p328).

🍴 🛏 p277, p311, p319

Eating & Sleeping

Fryeburg

🛏 Oxford House Inn   B&B $$

(☎207-935-3442; www.oxfordhouseinn.com;
548 Main St; r $150-190) Enjoy Saco River
views from this century-old house with four
stylish rooms. The owners are chefs and the
highly regarded on-site restaurant serves
contemporary American dishes (dinner mains
$26 to $34) from a seasonal menu; much of the
produce is sourced from Weston Farms, behind
the property. A cozy, inviting pub, Jonathan's, is
on the lower level.

Bridgton ④

✗ Campfire Grille   American $$

(☎207-803-2255; www.thecampfiregrille.com;
518 Portland Rd/US 302; mains $10-24; ⏱11am-
10pm Mon-Thu, to 11pm Fri & Sat, to 9pm Sun)
Around 3 miles southeast of Bridgton (along US
302), this easygoing spot serves pub-grub dishes
with gourmet flair: burgers, steaks, flatbread
pizzas, and appetizers like 'caribou curds'
(cheese curds with sriracha aioli) and 'bobcat
bites' (battered and fried brussels sprouts). The
weekday lunch special ($8 to $10) is great value.

🛏 Noble House Inn   B&B $$

(☎207-647-3733; www.noblehousebb.com; 81
Highland Rd; r $165-275; ❄🐾🛜) The bottomless
cookie jar is just one of the details that make
the eight-room Noble House Inn so inviting.
Breakfasts are typically sourced from locally
grown, organic ingredients. Wildlife carouses
on the lawn or in the adjacent pine grove, while
Highland Lake beckons across the street.

🛏 Highland Lake Resort   Motel $

(☎207-647-5301; www.highlandlakeresort.com;
115 N High St/US 302; r $110-160; ⏱May-Oct; ❄
🛜) Overlooking Highland Lake, this 1950s-style
motel has been given a modern makeover, and
it's a great base for outdoor activities. There's
a two-story row of well-equipped rooms, all set
with comfy furnishings, quality mattresses, mini-
fridges, microwaves and coffeemakers. All rooms
have lake views, and the grassy lawn leads down
to a private sandy beach.

Naples ⑥

✗ Rick's Cafe   American $$

(☎207-693-3759; www.rickscafenaples.com;
US 302; mains $10-24; ⏱11:30am-9pm late
May-early Sep) In the thick of Naples' Causeway
action, Rick's is good for camaraderie, drinks
and lake views (with a side order of live music
Thursday to Saturday nights). It serves burgers,
seafood and Tex-Mex dishes, with the bar
staying open until late.

Sebago Lake State Park ⑦

🛏 Sebago Lake
State Park Campground   Campground $

(☎park 207-693-6231, reservations 207-624-
9950; www.campwithme.com; 3 Campground
Rd, Naples; sites $35, with hookup $45)
Campgrounds are in hot demand due to their
proximity to Sebago Lake State Park. This 250-
site campground starts accepting reservations
each February 1 at 9am. All sites become
first-come, first-served after mid-September.
Prices don't include the reservation fee ($5 per
site per night) or the 9% state lodging tax. Maine
residents get a $10-per-site discount.

Portland ⑧

✗ Susan's Fish & Chips   Seafood $

(☎207-878-3240; http://susansfishnchips.com;
1135 Forest Ave; mains $10-20; ⏱11am-8pm;
🐾) Pop in for fish and chips and plenty of deep-
fried seafood at this no-fuss, family-friendly
eatery on US 302. It's low on pretension, high on
good cheer and set up in a former garage with
under-the-sea decor.

🛏 Press Hotel   Hotel $$$

(☎207-573-2425; www.thepresshotel.com; 119
Exchange St; r $220-413; 🅿❄🛜) This is a
creative conversion of the building that once
housed the offices and printing plant of Maine's
largest newspaper. The press theme shines in
unique details – a wall of vintage typewriters,
old headlines on hallway wallpapers. The smart,
navy-toned rooms are sexy.

Mainely Art

30

Up the river, into the woods and down the coast. On this drive you'll view the work of Maine's finest painters inside art museums and lovely galleries, then cruise past the landscapes that inspired them.

TRIP HIGHLIGHTS

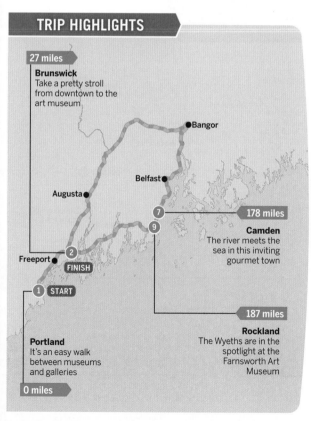

27 miles

Brunswick
Take a pretty stroll from downtown to the art museum

Bangor

Belfast

Augusta

7

9

178 miles

Camden
The river meets the sea in this inviting gourmet town

Freeport

2

FINISH

1 **START**

187 miles

Rockland
The Wyeths are in the spotlight at the Farnsworth Art Museum

Portland
It's an easy walk between museums and galleries

0 miles

3 DAYS
200 MILES / 322KM

GREAT FOR...

BEST TIME TO GO

May through October is high season for art walks.

 ESSENTIAL PHOTO

Capture all of island-dotted Penobscot Bay from the top of Mt Battie in Camden Hills State Park.

 BEST FOR CULTURE

Galleries, museums and a mural keep Portland cutting-edge.

Camden Hills State Park Penobscot Bay

30 Mainely Art

Art museums in Maine spotlight native sons and daughters and other American artists who found inspiration here. It's a talented bunch that includes Winslow Homer, George Bellows, Edward Hopper, Louise Nevelson and the Wyeths. But really injecting energy into the contemporary art scene are the fantastic special exhibits that explore the issues of our day, from conservation and urban planning to social networking, in unexpected but thought-provoking works.

TRIP HIGHLIGHT

① Portland

A great introduction to Maine's artistic treasure trove is found in the **Portland Museum of Art** (207-775-6148; www.portlandmuseum.org; 7 Congress Sq; adult/child $15/free, 4-8pm Fri free; ◷10am-6pm Sat-Wed, to 8pm Thu & Fri, shorter hours Oct-May), founded in 1882. This well-respected museum houses an outstanding collection of American works. Maine artists

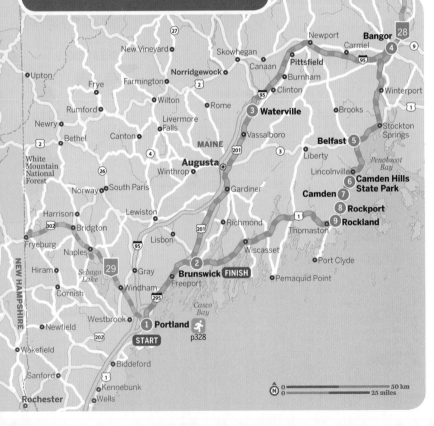

are particularly well represented. You'll also find a few paintings by European masters. From here, some of the city's coolest highlights (p328) are within easy walking distance.

 p277, p311, p319

The Drive » If you want to make good time, hop on I-295 and drive 25 miles north to Brunswick. For LL Bean and the outlet stores, make a detour onto US 1 at Freeport.

TRIP HIGHLIGHT

② Brunswick

Tidy Brunswick, with its well-kept central green and dramatic perch over the Androscoggin River, is a landscape painting come to life. The view stays inspiring on the Bowdoin College campus, where stately buildings surround a

LINK YOUR TRIP

28 Great North Woods

From Bangor, a short drive on I-95 leads to the North Woods and Mt Katahdin.

29 Lakes Tour

Hop on US 302 in Portland and head northwest for a bright-blue lake-dappled landscape.

LOCAL KNOWLEDGE: CULINARY GEMS

Seafood is big in Portland, naturally – look for New England specialties like periwinkles, quahog clams and, of course, lobster. Cafe and bakery culture is strong, too. The buzziest restaurants cluster in and around the Old Port District, but Munjoy Hill and the West End also have some culinary gems. Most eateries of all stripes offer great local beers to accompany food.

---

tree-dotted quad. The dramatic glass entrance pavilion at the **Bowdoin College Museum of Art** (☎207-725-3275; www.bowdoin.edu/art-museum; 9400 College St; ⊙10am-5pm Tue-Sat, to 8:30pm Thu, noon-5pm Sun) injects this pastoral scene with a bit of modernity, and sets a compelling tone for further exploration. The 20,000-piece collection is particularly strong in the works of 19th- and 20th-century European and American painters, with some surprising antiquities, too.

 p295, p319

The Drive » For inspiring views of the Kennebec River and time on the historic Old Canada Rd, follow US 201 north. The quickest route for the 50-mile drive is I-295 north to I-95 north.

----

③ Waterville

Another bucolic college campus, another outstanding art collection

---

– this time, it's the **Colby College Museum of Art** (☎207-859-5600; www.colby.edu/museum; 5600 Mayflower Hill Dr; ⊙10am-5pm Tue-Sat, noon-5pm Sun), fresh from a marvelous expansion and the addition of a 26,000-sq-ft glass pavilion. The space displays works from a nearly 500-piece collection gifted to Colby by longtime benefactors Peter and Paula Lunder. It is one of the largest gifts of art to a liberal-arts college; highlights of the collection are numerous, with works by James McNeill Whistler, Winslow Homer and Georgia O'Keeffe, among others, and a focus on American and contemporary art.

p295

The Drive » From Waterville, I-95 swoops along the edges of the Maine highlands as it angles north and then east on its 55-mile swing to Bangor.

④ Bangor

The small **University of Maine Museum of Art** (☎207-581-3300; www.umma.umaine.edu; 40 Harlow St; ⏰10am-5pm Tue-Sat) in Bangor is the northernmost art museum on the **Maine Art Museum Trail** (www.maineartmuseums.org). It's not the largest or most impressive collection in the state, but Bangor is a pleasant gateway for exploring the moody Maine highlands to the north and the Midcoast art towns just south. The university's collection spotlights mid-century modern American artists as well as contemporary pieces by David Hockney, Roy Lichtenstein, Andy Warhol and others. The special exhibits can really shine, so check the online calendar to see what's on display.

✕ p303, p319

The Drive » This 45-mile jaunt south on US 1A west to US 1 south passes the Paul Bunyan statue in downtown Bangor then tracks the Penobscot River, passing the informative Penobscot Marine Museum in Searsport.

⑤ Belfast

There aren't any art museums in Belfast, but this working-class community with Scots-Irish roots does have an inviting downtown with 12 or so galleries and studios. The oceanfront town is also the site of the nation's oldest shoe store, **Colburn Shoe** (79 Main St), which opened in 1832! Stop by **High Street Studio & Gallery** (☎207-338-8990; www.facebook.com/HighStreetStudioGallery; 149 High St; ⏰10am-5pm Mon-Thu, to 8pm Fri, to 4pm Sat) for bright paintings by a trio of local women, plus painting classes. The art-deco **Colonial Theatre** (☎207-338-1930; www.colonialtheatre.com; 163 High St; adult/child $8.50/5.50) has shown movies since 1912, luring moviegoers with a neon sign and a rooftop elephant. See what's happening at **Waterfall Arts** (☎207-338-2222; www.waterfallarts.org; 256 High St; ⏰10am-5pm Tue-Fri, hours vary for events), a nonprofit

contemporary arts center that hosts exhibitions, lectures, art classes, musical performances, film screenings and more.

The Drive » Follow US 1 south for 16 miles, mostly along the coast, passing Ducktrap and Lincolnville.

⑥ Camden Hills State Park

A favorite hike in **Camden Hills State Park** (☎207-236-3109; www.maine.gov/camdenhills; 280 Belfast Rd/US 1; adult/child $6/1; ⏰9am-sunset) is the half-mile climb up **Mt Battie**, offering outstanding views of

TOP TIP:
GALLERY GUIDE & ART NEWS

For a list of galleries and studios throughout the state, pick up the free *Maine Gallery & Studio Guide* at art museums and galleries. It's also available online at cafedesartistes.mainegalleryguide.com.

Portland Museum of Art

Penobscot Bay. Feeling sluggish? You can drive up the mountain, too.

🛏 p319

The Drive 》 Drive 2 miles south on US 1 to downtown Camden.

TRIP HIGHLIGHT

➐ Camden

Camden and its picture-perfect harbor, framed against the mountains of Camden Hills State Park, is one of the prettiest sites in the state. The Megunticook River crashes dramatically into the sea beside the public landing behind US 1 in the center of town. At the landing you'll also find the helpful **Penobscot Bay Regional Chamber of Commerce** (☎207-236-4404; www.camdenrockland.com; 2 Public Landing; ⏰9am-5pm Mon-Fri, 10am-4pm Sat & Sun late May–mid-Oct, 9am-4pm Mon-Fri rest of year). Camden offers **windjammer cruises** (www.sailmainecoast.com) – anything from two-hour rides to multiday journeys up the coast. There are also galleries, fine seafood restaurants and back alleys for exploring. Enjoy a good meal at **Fresh & Co** (☎207-236-7005; www.freshcamden.com; 1 Bayview Landing; mains $21-35; ⏰11:30am-2:30pm & 5-9pm Thu-Tue Jul & Aug, shorter hours rest of year).

🛏 p319

The Drive 》 By the time you get your seatbelt buckled you're almost in Rockport, just a 2-mile drive south on US 1.

➑ Rockport

Photographers flock to Rockport, a sleepy harborside town, for more than just the picturesque coast. Rockport is the home of the world-renowned **Maine Media Workshops** (☎207-236-8581; www.mainemedia.edu; 70 Camden St), one

MIDCOAST ART WALKS

If it's a Friday night in July or August, and you're driving along Maine's Midcoast, you're going to drive past an art walk. For a list of art walks throughout the state, visit www.artwalkmaine.org.

Bath 4pm to 7pm, third Friday of the month, June to September; www.visitbath.com/events/artwalk

Belfast 5:30pm to 8pm, fourth Friday of the month, May to September; www.belfastcreativecoalition.org/art-walk

Brunswick 5pm to 8pm, second Friday of the month, May to October; www.artwalkmaine.org/brunswick

Portland 5pm to 8pm, first Friday of the month, year-round; www.liveworkportland.org/arts/walk

Rockland 5pm to 8pm, first Friday of the month, May to November; www.artsinrockland.org

of the world's leading instructional centers in photography, film and digital media. The institute offers hundreds of workshops and master classes throughout the year. Student and faculty works are displayed in a gallery at 18 Central St.

But let's not forget the most important attraction in town: the granite statue of **Andre the Seal** (Pascal Ave, Rockport Marine Park), about half a mile off US 1 via Main St. Andre was a crowd-pleasing showboat who swam to the harbor from Boston every summer from the 1970s until his death in the mid-'80s. He was the subject of a children's book, *Andre the Seal,* and a 1994 movie.

The Drive >> Leave Andre behind as you turn left onto Pascal Ave, following it to US 1. Rockland is 6 miles to the south.

TRIP HIGHLIGHT

❾ Rockland

Rockland is a cool little town. Its commercial port adds vibrancy, and its bustling Main St is a window into the city's sociocultural diversity, with working-class diners, bohemian cafes and high-end bistros beside galleries and old-fashioned storefronts.

Just off Main St, the **Farnsworth Art Museum** (☎207-596-6457; www.farnsworthmuseum.org; 16 Museum St; adult/child $15/free; ⊗10am-5pm Jun-Oct, to 8pm Wed Jul-Sep, closed Mon Nov, Dec, Apr & May, 10am-4pm Wed-Sun Jan-Mar) is one of the country's best small regional museums, with works spanning 200 years of American art. The 'Maine in America' collections spotlight artists who have lived

or worked in the state. Exhibits about the Wyeths – Andrew, NC and Jamie – are housed in galleries throughout the museum and in the Wyeth Center, a former Methodist church across the garden.

The wonderful **Archipelago Fine Arts** (☎207-596-0701; www.thearchipelago.net; 386 Main St; ⊗9:30am-5:30pm Mon-Fri, to 5pm Sat, 11am-4pm Sun) sells jewelry, paintings and arts and crafts by artists living on Maine's islands and coast. It works in partnership with the **Island Institute** (www.islandinstitute.org), an organization whose goal is to support Maine's remote coastal and island communities.

✕ ⎸ 277, p319

The Drive >> From Rockland, continue south along the coast on US 1 to loop back to Brunswick.

Eating & Sleeping

Portland ❶

✖ Fore Street
Modern American $$$

(📞207-775-2717; www.forestreet.biz; 288 Fore St; small plates $12-16, mains $26-42; ⏰5:30-10pm Sun-Thu, to 10:30pm Fri & Sat) Fore Street is the lauded, long-running restaurant many consider to be the originator of today's food obsession in Portland. Chef-owner Sam Hayward has turned roasting into a high art: chickens turn on spits in the open kitchen as chefs slide iron kettles of mussels into the wood-burning oven. Local, seasonal eating is taken very seriously and the menu changes daily.

🛏 Danforth Inn
Boutique Hotel $$$

(📞207-879-8755; www.danforthinn.com; 163 Danforth St; r $199-359, ste $699; 🅿 ❄ 📶) Staying at this ivy-shrouded West End boutique hotel feels like being a guest at an eccentric millionaire's mansion. Shoot pool in the wood-paneled games room (a former speakeasy) or climb into the rooftop cupola for views across Portland Harbor. The nine rooms are decorated in a sophisticated mix of antique and modern.

Brunswick ❷

🛏 Brunswick Inn
B&B $$

(📞207-729-4914; www.thebrunswickinn. com; 165 Park Row; r $169-189, cottage $299; ❄ 📶) Overlooking Brunswick's town green, this elegant guesthouse has rooms ranging from small to spacious. Each is individually designed in an airy, farmhouse-chic style, a mix of worn woods and modern prints. There's a self-contained garden cottage that's ideal for families. Enjoy drinks by the fire in the bar, or on the porch overlooking the Town Mall.

Bangor ❹

✖ Bagel Central
Cafe $

(📞207-947-1654; www.bagelcentralbangor.com; 33 Central St; mains $6-8; ⏰6am-6pm Mon-Fri, to 2pm Sat & Sun; 📶 ✏) Vast and cafeteria-like, Bagel Central bakes up over two dozen varieties of bagels (including vegan and gluten-free

options), which can be transformed into sandwiches spilling over with smoked salmon, melted cheese, eggs and other tasty fillings. Omelets and other breakfast fare are served all day. Sweet treats, too – including strudel, danishes and baklava.

Camden Hills State Park ❻

🛏 Camden Hills State Park
Campground $

(📞Feb-Apr 207-236-0849, May-Oct 207-236-3109; www.campwithme.com; 280 Belfast Rd/US 1; tent sites $35, RV sites with/without hookups $45/35; ⏰mid-May–mid-Oct; 📶) The park's appealing campground has hot showers and wooded sites, some with electric hookups. There's also wi-fi. Reserve online through Maine's government reservations portal.

Camden ❼

🛏 Norumbega
B&B $$$

(📞207-236-4646; www.norumbegainn.com; 63 High St; r $289-389, ste $449-539; 📶) Looking like something out of a slightly creepy fairy tale, this 1886 turreted stone mansion is now Camden's poshest and most dramatically situated B&B, on a hill above the bay, with 11 distinctive rooms and suites. The coolest choices are the two-story Library Suite, with a book-lined upper balcony, and the Penthouse, with a private deck and panoramic water views. Guests can take up the option of the $75 seven-course tasting menu, prepared by the owner-chef.

Rockland ❾

✖ Suzuki Sushi Bar
Japanese $$

(📞207-596-7447; www.suzukisushi.com; 419 Main St; sushi $4-9, mains $14-22; ⏰5-9pm Tue-Sat) The super-fresh seafood of midcoast Maine is put to exquisite use at Suzuki's, where the sushi chefs are women (in a field dominated by men). Sashimi and sushi govern the menu, though noodles and *donburi* (rice-bowl dishes) made with local crab and dashi are also available. Closing times flexible.

Moose & Mountains: Western Maine

31

This trek feels akin to flying. Leafy byways soar up the sides of mountains. Pristine forests float beneath lofty overlooks. And bumpy frost heaves add turbulence on the back roads.

TRIP HIGHLIGHTS

68 miles

Height of Land
Enjoy sweeping views of Mooselookmeguntic Lake

93 miles

Rangeley Lakes Trails Center
Nordic skiing and hiking on wooded lakeside trails

FINISH — Sugarloaf

Oquossoc

⑥

④ Small Falls

Houghton

② Mexico

START ①

Grafton Notch State Park
Inspire your inner artist at beautiful Screw Auger Falls

Bethel
A stylish base camp for multi-season adventure

18 miles

0 miles

**2 DAYS
160 MILES / 257KM**

GREAT FOR...

BEST TIME TO GO

June through March is good for hiking, leaf-peeping and skiing.

ESSENTIAL PHOTO

Frame a shot of Mooselookmeguntic Lake from the Height of Land overlook.

BEST FOR WILDLIFE

ME 16 between Rangeley and Stratton is a local moose alley.

Height of Land Mooselookmeguntic Lake

321

31

Moose & Mountains: Western Maine

The first time you see a moose standing on the side of the road, it doesn't seem unusual. You've been prepped by all of the moose-crossing signs. But then it registers. 'Hey, that's a moose!' And you simultaneously swerve, slam on the brakes and speed up. Control these impulses. Simply slow your speed and enjoy the gift of wildlife.

TRIP HIGHLIGHT

① Bethel

If you glance at the map, tiny Bethel doesn't seem much different from the other towns scattered across this alpine region. But look more closely. The town is cocooned between two powerful rivers, and several ski resorts and ski centers call the community home. Four state and national scenic byways begin within an 85-mile drive.

Of the ski resorts, **Sunday River** (☎800-543-

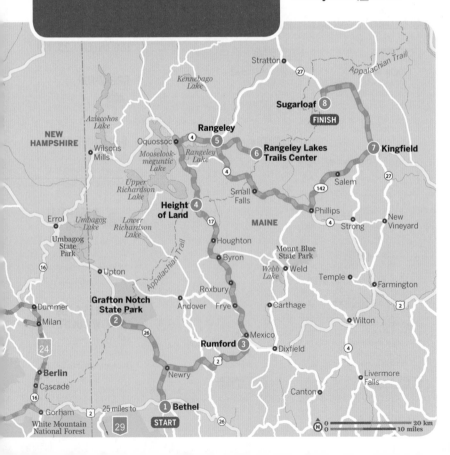

2754; www.sundayriver.com; 15 S Ridge Rd, Newry; lift ticket adult/teen/child $105/79/69;) is the biggest draw, luring skiers with eight interconnected peaks, 135 trails and a host of winter activities. From July until early October, the resort opens 25 mountain-bike trails and runs trips up to North Peak on its fast-moving **Chondola** (round trip adult/child $15/10; ☺10am-4pm Thu-Sun late Jun-early Sep, 10am-4pm Fri-Sun Sep-early Oct). There's also a six-line **zipline tour** (adult/child $69/59; ☺9am, 10am, 11:30am & 2pm Thu-Sun late Jun-early Sep, Fri-Sun early Sep-early Oct). Several outdoor centers, including **Carter's X-C Ski Center** (☎207-824-3880; www.cartersxcski.com; 786 Intervale Rd; day pass adult/child $15/10; ☺9am-4pm mid-Dec–Mar), are base camps for cross-country skiing

LINK YOUR TRIP

24 Woodland Heritage Trail
Take US 2 west to learn the history of logging on the Androscoggin River.

29 Lakes Tour
Follow the Pequawket Trail Scenic Byway along ME 113 to a riverside beach in Fryeburg and more lakes beyond.

SCENIC BYWAYS IN THE LAKES & MOUNTAINS REGION

Read more at www.exploremaine.org/byways.

Grafton Notch Scenic Byway From Bethel, follow US 2 north, then turn left at Newry and take ME 26 through Grafton Notch State Park.

Pequawket Trail Scenic Byway Follow the Androscoggin River west from Bethel on US 2. Turn south onto ME 113 at Gilead and follow it to Fryeburg.

State Route 27 Scenic Byway From stop 7, in Kingfield, follow ME 16/27 to Sugarloaf, then continue north on ME 27 to Canada.

Rangeley Lakes National Scenic Byway Drive east on US 2 from Rumford to Mexico, then turn north on US 17. The byway begins about 15 miles north, just beyond the town of Byron.

and snowshoeing, with 'fat biking' (on mountain bikes with wide tires) growing in popularity.

 p327

The Drive » Follow ME 5/ME 26/US 2 north from Bethel, tracking the Sunday River about 6 miles north. Keep left on NH 26 as it leaves ME 5/US 2 and becomes Bear River Rd, which leads to the park 11 miles west.

- - - - - - - - - - - - - - - - -

 TRIP HIGHLIGHT

2 Grafton Notch State Park

Sitting astride the Grafton Notch Scenic Byway within the Mahoosuc Range, this rugged **park** (☎207-824-2912; www.maine.gov/graftonnotch; 1941 Bear River Rd/ME 26; adult/child $4/1; ☺9am-sunset) is a stunner. Carved by a glacier that retreated 12,000 years ago, the notch is a four-season playground,

chock-full of waterfalls, gorges, lofty viewpoints and hiking trails, including over 20 miles of the Appalachian Trail. Peregrine falcons build nests in the cliffs, helping the park earn its spot on the Maine Birding Trail (www.mainebirdingtrail.com); the best viewing is May to October. Cross-country skiers and snowshoers enjoy the park in winter. If you're short on time, simply wander the path beside **Screw Auger Falls**, off the main parking lot. This 23ft waterfall crashes dramatically through a narrow gorge. If you have more time, try the 2.4-mile round-trip hike up to **Table Rock overlook** or the 2.2-mile **Eyebrow Loop Trail**. There are excellent picnicking opportunities within the park – the Spruce

Meadow picnic area is signed off ME 26.

The Drive » Return to US 2 north. On the 16-mile drive, you'll pass stone walls and antique stores, and enjoy the Androscoggin River tagging along on your right.

3 Rumford

How do you know you've arrived? When the giant, ax-wielding **Paul Bunyan** says 'Hey there.' According to legend, the red-shirted lumberman was born in Maine but was later sent west by his parents. Today, he stands tall beside the **River Valley Chamber of Commerce Visitor Center** (☑207-364-3241; www.rivervalleychamber.com; 10 Bridge St; ☺9am-5pm Jun-Oct, 10am-2pm Nov-May). Walk a few steps beyond the building for a fantastic view of the wild and woolly **Rumford Falls**. The highest falls east of Niagara, they drop 176ft over a granite ledge. The small park here holds a black marble memorial honoring local son and former US senator Edmund Muskie, who authored the Clean Water Act.

The Drive » Leave Rumford and US 2, picking up ME 17 north in Mexico. From here ME 17 runs parallel to pines, farms, meadows and the rocky Swift River. Snap a photo of the river barreling through metamorphic rock at the Coos Canyon Rest Area in Byron, then head north, picking up the Rangeley Lakes

National Scenic Byway north of Houghton.

TRIP HIGHLIGHT

4 Height of Land

The entrance to this photogenic **overlook** sneaks up on you – it's on the left as you round a bend on Brimstone Mountain, just after a hiker warning sign. But don't slam on your brakes and swerve across the grass divider if you miss the turn (we saw this happen), because there's another entrance just north. But you *should* pull over. The expansive view of island-dotted **Mooselookmeguntic Lake**, the largest of the Rangeley Lakes, as it sweeps north toward distant mountains is astounding. Views of undeveloped forest stretch for up to 100 miles; you can even see the White Mountains in New Hampshire. The dogged Appalachian Trail runs alongside the viewpoint, and an interpretive sign shares a few details about the 2190-mile footpath.

The Drive » Drive north to the village of Oquossoc, then turn right onto ME 4/16. Take a photo at the Rangeley Scenic Overlook, where there is a panoramic view of Rangeley Lake. This overlook is about 5.5 miles from Height of Land. From here, continue east.

5 Rangeley

An adventure hub, with tidy inns and down-home

restaurants, Rangeley makes a useful base for skiing, hiking, whitewater rafting and mountain biking in the nearby mountains. Snowmobilers can zoom across 150 miles of trails. For information, stop by the **Rangeley Lakes Chamber of Commerce** (☑207-864-5571; www.rangeleymaine.com; 6 Park Rd; ☺10am-4pm Mon-Fri, to 2pm Sat), which has handouts about restaurants, lodging options, local trails and moose-watching. Just behind the visitor center, **Rangeley Town Cove Park** (Park Rd; ☺5am-10pm) is a nice spot to enjoy a

Sunday River Downhill skiing

picnic by the lake. On rainy days, ask at the Chamber about the local museums.

✕ ⊨ p327

The Drive » ME 4 breaks from ME 16 in downtown Rangeley. From the chamber of commerce, follow ME 4 east. Turn left onto Dallas Hill Rd, then in 2.5 miles bear right on Saddleback Mountain Rd and continue another 2.5 miles.

❻ Rangeley Lakes Trails Center

A green yurt marks your arrival at the **Rangeley Lakes Trails Center** (📞207-864-4309; www.range leylakestrailscenter.com; 524 Saddleback Mountain Rd; day pass $10-20), a four-season trail system covering gorgeous woodland terrain beside Saddleback Lake. Here there are more than 40 miles of trails for cross-country skiing and snowshoeing during snow season (rental equipment is available inside the yurt, along with hot soup!). In summer, the cross-country trails double as hiking trails, and the snowshoe trails allow single-track biking. The yurt is closed in summer, but trail maps are available from an information board (or from the chamber of commerce in Rangeley).

The Drive » Follow ME 4 southeast, passing another Rangeley Lake overlook. Continue southeast. You'll pass another Appalachian Trail crossing before entering prime moose country. Follow ME 12 east to NE 16/27 north.

❼ Kingfield

If you enjoy hiking and cross-country skiing, but not backpacking, consider a hut-to-hut trip through **Maine Huts & Trails** (📞207-265-2400; www.mainehuts.org; 496 Main St; per person incl meals $96-138), a wonderful

HERE A MOOSE, THERE A MOOSE

Moose-crossing signs are as ubiquitous as logging trucks in these parts. But spotting one of these chunky beasts, which can reach a height of 7ft at the shoulder and weigh anywhere from 1000lb to 1400lb, is trickier. You'll most likely see them eating on the side of the road in the morning, in the evening and between noon and 2pm. According to a handout from the Rangeley Lakes Chamber of Commerce, these are some of the top moose-spotting sites in the area:

Route 4 Phillips to Rangeley

Route 16 Rangeley to Stratton; Wilsons Mills to the New Hampshire border

Route 17 Between the Height of Land overlook and the Rangeley Lake overlook

Route 16/27 Stratton to Carrabassett Valley

When driving these routes stay extra vigilant and slow down, particularly at night. Moose don't always leap out of the way like deer, and in the dark your vehicle's headlights won't always reflect off the animals' eyes, due to their height. If you come upon a moose standing in the road, do not get out of the car (they can charge the vehicle) or drive around it. Wait for the moose to mosey off the road.

nonprofit organization based in Kingfield that operates four ecolodges along an 80-mile trail system near Sugarloaf (with more huts planned). Choose a dorm bed or a private bunkroom and enjoy three meals (including a packed lunch) and pretty plush off-the-grid relaxation. Pillows and blankets are provided, but not bedding. Winter and summer are peak popularity for the huts; in the off-season you can still stay overnight, but without meal service (and with reduced prices). There is no vehicle access to the lodges (two are less than 2 miles from a trailhead).

The Drive » From Kingfield, NH 16 joins ME 27, unfurling beneath the pines, with the Carrabassett River tumbling merrily alongside.

- - - - - - - - - - - - - - - - - - -

❽ Sugarloaf

The Rangeley area's most popular **ski resort** (☎800-843-5623, 207-237-2000; www.sugarloaf.com; 5092 Access Rd, Carrabassett Valley; full-day lift ticket adult $99, child $69-79), Sugarloaf has a vertical drop of 2820ft, with 162 trails and glades, and 13 lifts. This is Maine's second-highest peak (4237ft).

Summer activities include lift rides, ziplines and golf. The resort village complex has an enormous mountain lodge, an inn and rental condos. Nearby towns of Kingfield and Stratton are also good bases.

Near Sugarloaf's slopes, the **Sugarloaf Outdoor Center** (☎207-237-2000; ME 27/ME 16, Carrabassett Valley; day pass adult/child $23/15, half-day pass $18/11; ☺9am-5pm Sun-Fri, to 8pm Sat Dec-Mar) has 56 miles of groomed cross-country trails, plus guided snowshoeing safaris and public ice-skating on an NHL-size rink.

Eating & Sleeping

Bethel ❶

✖ Cho Sun
Asian $$

(📞207-824-7370; www.chosunrestaurant.com;
141 Main St; mains $18-27; ⏰5-9pm Wed-Sun)
Korea meets rural Maine at this unassuming
Victorian house, whose interior has been
transformed into an Asian oasis of bamboo and
paper lanterns. Try flavor-filled dishes from the
owner's native South Korea, like *bibimbap* (rice
pot with steamed veggies and chicken, shrimp,
calamari or tofu) or *bulkalbi* (barbecue beef
short ribs). There's also a high-quality sushi bar
and a (booze) bar.

✖ DiCocoa's Market & Bakery
Cafe $

(📞207-824-6386; www.cafedicocoa.com; 125
Main St; sandwiches $6-8; ⏰7am-4pm; 🛜📶)
This funky orange bungalow is a morning must
for espresso-based drinks, and draws a loyal
local crowd. It also serves wholegrain baked
goods, croissants, bagel sandwiches, deli
salads, and granola and yogurt. The fresh-baked
fruit-filled pies are worth the indulgence.

✖ Good Food Store
Sandwiches $

(📞207-824-3754; www.goodfoodbethel.com;
212 Mayville Rd/ME 26; salads & sandwiches
$7-8; ⏰store 9am-8pm, takeout 11am-6pm)
Buy super sandwiches, salads and heat-and-eat
meals at this gourmet organic market and wine
shop. The homemade cookies and dried fruit
are fantastic.

🛏 Chapman Inn
B&B $

(📞207-824-2657; www.chapmaninn.com; 2
Church St; dm $40, r $90-140; ❄🛜) Run by
a friendly, globe-trotting retiree, this roomy
downtown guesthouse has character in spades.
Set in an 1865 building (one of Bethel's oldest),

the 10 private rooms are done up in florals and
antiques, with slightly sloping floors attesting
to the house's age. The cozy common space
is stocked with Monopoly and other rainy-day
games, and there are free bikes for guest use.

Rangeley ❺

✖ Red Onion
American $

(📞207-864-5022; www.therangeleyredonion.
com; 2511 Main St; mains $10-20; ⏰11am-9pm
Mon-Sat, noon-9pm Sun; 📶) A big plate of
eggplant Parmesan with a side of pasta after a
day on the slopes has been a Rangeley tradition
for some four decades. This boisterous Italian-
American joint is also known for its pizzas and
its 1970s wood-paneled bar.

🛏 Loon Lodge
Inn $$

(📞207-864-5666; www.loonlodgeme.com; 16
Pickford Rd; r $110-165; ❄🛜) Hidden in the
woods by the lake, this century-old log-cabin
lodge has eight rooms, most with a backwoods-
chic look, with wood-plank walls and handmade
quilts (no TVs). There's a formal dining room
on-site, plus the intimate, friendly Pickford Pub,
serving classics such as steak, burgers and fish
and chips.

🛏 Rangeley Inn & Tavern
Inn $$

(📞207-864-3341; www.therangeleyinn.com;
2443 Main St; r $135-295; ❄🛜) Behind the
inn's pretty powder-blue facade, you can relax
by the fire and admire the mounted bear and
moose head in the lobby. Rooms are simple and
old-fashioned in this creaky, turn-of-the-20th-
century lodge, and come with floral wallpaper
and brass beds. There's also a motel-style lodge
on the property.

STRETCH YOUR LEGS
PORTLAND

Start/Finish: Portland Museum of Art

Distance: 2 miles

Duration: Four hours

This walk takes in museums and a magically transformed landmark before dropping to the bars and boutiques of the hard-charging Old Port District. Re-energize along the working wharves, then head to the West End for a sun-dappled finale among the mansions.

Take this walk on Trips

Portland Museum of Art

Paintings by Winslow Homer and other Maine artists are highlights at this **museum** (☎207-775-6148; www.portland museum.org; 7 Congress Sq; adult/child $15/ free, 4-8pm Fri free; ☺10am-6pm Sat-Wed, to 8pm Thu & Fri, shorter hours Oct-May), which anchors the city's Arts District. The collection sprawls across three separate buildings. Most pieces are in the postmodern Charles Shipman Payson Building, designed by the firm of IM Pei. Don't miss the flying staircase in the 1801 Federal-style McClellan House in the back.

The Walk ❯❯ Leave the museum and turn right onto Free St. You'll pass the Children's Museum. Turn left on Oak St and return to Congress St. Turn right and follow Congress two blocks. The Wadsworth-Longfellow House is on the left.

Wadsworth-Longfellow House

The revered American poet Henry Wadsworth-Longfellow (1807–82) grew up in this Federal-style **house** (☎207-774-1822; www.mainehistory.org; 489 Congress St; guided tour adult/child $15/4; ☺noon-5pm May, 10am-5pm Mon-Sat, noon-5pm Sun Jun-Oct), built in 1785 by his Revolutionary War–hero grandfather. The house has been impeccably restored to look as it did in the 1800s, complete with original furniture and artifacts. The ticket price includes admission to the **Maine Historical Society Museum** next door, which has rotating exhibits about life in Maine over the past few centuries.

The Walk ❯❯ Continue along Congress St, walking past Monument Sq and the bronze statue dedicated to Portland's Civil War experience. Turn right onto Exchange St.

Press Hotel

From old Portland to new: the **Press Hotel** (☎207-573-2425; www.thepresshotel. com; 119 Exchange St) is a clever, creative conversion of the building that once housed the offices and printing plant of

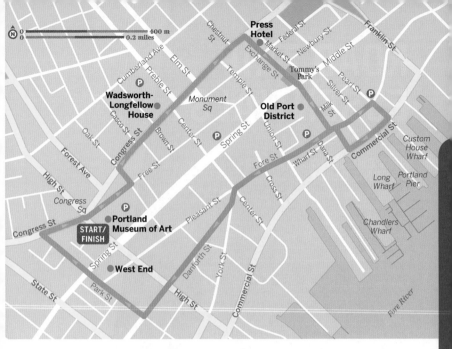

Maine's largest newspaper. The press theme shines in whimsical details – a wall of vintage typewriters, old headlines revived on hallway wallpaper, and letterpress artwork behind the reception desk. Drop by for a coffee or microbrew in **Inkwell**, the lobby bar, and pop downstairs to check out the mini art gallery that features works by local artists.

The Walk » A walk down Exchange St toward the waterfront takes you through a pretty little green pocket known as Tommy's Park – look out for the hot-dog vendor here, a fixture for the past decade.

Old Port District

Handsome 19th-century brick buildings line the streets of Old Port, with the city's most enticing stores, pubs and restaurants. By night, flickering gas lanterns add to the atmosphere. Wander down Exchange St and its offshoots for fresh seafood, local microbrews and tiny galleries. To sign up for a sightseeing boat tour or order lobster to ship

home (if home's in the USA), walk down to the wharves.

The Walk » Follow Fore St west to its junction with Danforth St, where there's a statue of movie director and native son John Ford. Continue west on Danforth St.

West End

Get lost in this hillside enclave of brick town houses, elegant gardens and stately mansions; some date from the neighborhood's founding in 1836. Be sure to walk past the **Victoria Mansion** (☏207-772-4841; www.victoriamansion.org; 109 Danforth St; adult/child $15/5; ☉10am-3:45pm Mon-Sat, 1:15-4:45pm Sun May-Oct). This Italianate palace, whose exterior would work well in a Tim Burton movie, dates from 1860. If you have time, delving further west into the neighborhood brings rewards, including the scenic **Western Promenade**, a grassy pathway with fine views over the harbor, especially around sunset.

The Walk » Return to the art museum by taking Park St northwest to Congress St.

ROAD TRIP ESSENTIALS

New England Driving Guide

Scenic, generally well-maintained roads make New England a delightful road-trip destination. Let us answer all your driving-related questions, including where to pahk your cah.

DRIVING LICENSE & DOCUMENTS

All drivers must carry a driving license, the car registration and proof of insurance. If your license is not in English, you will need an official translation or an International Driving Permit (IDP). You will also need a credit card to rent a car.

INSURANCE

Liability All drivers are required to obtain a minimum amount of liability insurance, which would cover the damage that you might cause to other people and property in case of an accident. Liability insurance can be purchased from rental-car companies for about $12 per day.

Collision For damage to the rental vehicle, a collision damage waiver (CDW) is available from the rental company for about $18 a day.

Alternative sources Your personal auto insurance may extend to rental cars, so it's worth investigating before purchasing liability or collision from the rental company. Additionally, some credit cards offer reimbursement coverage for collision damages if you rent the car with that credit card; again, check before departing. Most credit-card coverage isn't valid for rentals of more than 15 days or for exotic models, SUVs, vans and 4WD vehicles.

HIRING A CAR

Rental cars are readily available. With advance reservations for a small car, the daily rate with unlimited mileage starts around $50, while typical weekly rates run $200 and up. Rates for midsize cars are often only a tad higher. Dropping off the car at a different location from where you picked it up usually incurs an additional fee. It always pays to shop around between rental companies on sites such as www.kayak.com and www.expedia.com.

Having a major credit card greatly simplifies the rental process. Without one, some agencies simply will not rent vehicles, while others require prepayment, a deposit higher than the cost of your rental, plus pay stubs, proof of round-trip airfare and more.

Alamo (www.alamo.com)

Avis (www.avis.com)

Budget (www.budget.com)

Dollar (www.dollar.com)

Enterprise (www.enterprise.com)

Hertz (www.hertz.com)

National (www.nationalcar.com)

Rent-A-Wreck (www.rentawreck.com) Rents out cars that may have more wear and tear than your typical rental vehicle, but are actually far from wrecks.

Thrifty (www.thrifty.com)

Driving Fast Facts

Right or left? Drive on the right

Legal driving age 16

Manual or automatic? Most rental cars will come with automatic transmission

Top speed limit 75mph (on interstate in rural Maine)

BRINGING YOUR OWN VEHICLE

Generally, crossing the US–Canada border is straightforward. The biggest hassle is usually the length of the lines. All travelers entering the USA are required to carry passports, including citizens of Canada and the USA. Citizens of other nationalities must have the appropriate visa/visa waiver, issued electronically or otherwise, before departing their home country.

MAPS

Detailed state highway maps are distributed free by state governments. You can call or write to state tourism offices in advance to request maps, or you can pick them up at highway tourism information offices (welcome centers) when you enter a state on a major highway. Another excellent resource is DeLorme (www.delorme.com), which publishes individual state road atlases. These contain large-format maps with topographic detail and exhaustive coverage of backcountry roads. The scale ranges from 1:65,000 to 1:135,000. The New England box set includes all six states for $61.95, or you can buy individual state atlases for $19.95 to $22.95 each.

ROAD CONDITIONS

New England roads are very good – even the warren of hard-packed dirt roads that crisscross Vermont. A few hazards to be aware of:

➡ Some of the region's big, old cities can be difficult to navigate. Boston in particular is notorious for its scofflaw drivers and maddening maze of one-way streets. Park your car and use alternative means to get around.

➡ Traffic is heavy around urban areas during rush hour (7am to 9am and 4pm to 7pm Monday through Friday).

➡ Some roads across northern mountain passes in Vermont, New Hampshire and Maine are closed during the winter, but good signage gives you plenty of warning.

Toll Roads

You are likely to encounter tolls for some roads, bridges and tunnels while driving in New England, including the following:

➡ Blue Star (New Hampshire) Turnpike (I-95)

➡ Claiborne Pell Newport Bridge (Rhode Island)

➡ Frederick E Everett Turnpike (Central New Hampshire Turnpike)

➡ Maine Turnpike (I-95)

➡ Massachusetts Turnpike (I-90)

➡ Mt Equinox Skyline Dr (Vermont)

➡ Mt Mansfield Auto Toll Rd (Vermont)

➡ Mt Washington Auto Rd (New Hampshire)

➡ Spaulding Turnpike (New Hampshire)

➡ Sumner Tunnel (Massachusetts)

➡ Ted Williams Tunnel (Massachusetts)

➡ Tobin Bridge (Mystic River Bridge; Massachusetts)

Driving Problem-Buster

What should I do if my car breaks down? Call the service number provided by the rental-car company and it will make arrangements with a local garage. If you're driving your own car, it's advisable to join the American Automobile Association (AAA), which provides emergency assistance.

What if I have an accident? If any damage is incurred, you'll have to call the local police (☏ 911) to come to the scene of the accident and file an accident report for insurance purposes.

What should I do if I get stopped by the police? Always pull over to the right at the first available opportunity. Stay in your car and roll down the window. Show the police officer your driver's license and automobile registration. For any violations, you cannot pay the officer issuing the ticket; rather, payment must be made by mail or by internet.

How do the tolls work? Most tolls are payable in cash only. Tollbooths are usually staffed, so exact change is not required. Alternatively, consider purchasing an E-Z Pass for the state you will be traveling in (this is not transferable to other states).

ROAD RULES

The maximum speed limit on most New England interstates is 65mph, but some have a limit of 55mph, and one stretch of I-95 in rural Maine has a limit of 75mph. On undivided highways, the speed limit will vary from 30mph to 55mph. Police enforce speed limits by patrolling in police cruisers and in unmarked cars. Fines vary by state but can run into hundreds of dollars.

➡ Driving laws are different in each of the New England states; all except New Hampshire require the use of seat belts.

➡ In every state, children under four years of age must be placed in a child safety seat secured by a seat belt.

➡ Most states require motorcycle riders to wear helmets whenever they ride. In any case, use of a helmet is highly recommended.

➡ All six New England states prohibit texting while driving, while Vermont, New Hampshire and Connecticut have banned handheld cellphone use by drivers.

Road Trip Websites

American Automobile Association (www.aaa.com) Provides maps and info, travel discounts and emergency assistance for members. Members get discounts on car rentals, air tickets, hotels and attractions, as well as emergency road service and towing. AAA has reciprocal agreements with automobile associations in other countries. Bring your membership card from your country of origin.

Gas Buddy (www.gasbuddy.com) Find the cheapest gas in town.

New England Travel Planner (www.newenglandtravelplanner.com) Routes, reviews and other travel resources.

Traffic.com (www.traffic.com) Real-time traffic reports, with details about accidents and traffic jams.

PARKING

Public parking is readily available in most New England destinations, whether on the street or in parking lots. In rural areas and small towns, it is often free. Bigger towns and cities typically have coin- or credit card-fed parking meters, which will limit the amount of time you can leave your car (usually two hours or more). Parking can be a challenge in urban areas, especially Boston and cities with a high volume of tourist traffic, such as Newport. In both cities, street parking is limited, so you will probably have to pay for parking in a private lot or garage.

FUEL

Gas stations are ubiquitous and many are open 24 hours. Small-town stations may be open only from 7am to 8pm or 9pm. Prices vary, tending to be more expensive in remote areas, or in states with high fuel taxes (Connecticut's taxes are the highest; New Hampshire's are the lowest). Some stations offer specially discounted prices one day per week; watch for signs. Gas prices in New England ranged between $2.25 and $2.55 per US gallon at the time of research.

At some stations, you must pay before you pump; at others, you may pump first. More modern pumps have credit-/debit-card terminals built into them, so you can pay with plastic right at the pump. At 'full service' stations, an attendant will pump your gas for you; no tip is expected.

SAFETY

New England does not present any particular safety concerns for drivers. That said, travelers are advised to always remove valuables and lock all car doors, especially in urban areas.

Driving can be tricky in big cities, where narrow streets, clogged traffic and illogical street layouts can make unfamiliar drivers miserable. New England drivers are notoriously impatient. Beware the 'Boston left,' where the first left-turning vehicle jumps out in front of oncoming traffic.

Be extra cautious driving at night on rural roads, which are often not well lit and may be populated by deer, moose and other creatures that can total your car if you hit them the wrong way. In winter, snow tires or all-season tires are a must, especially for mountain driving.

RADIO

Maine WCYY (94.3FM), based in Portland, specializes in alternative rock, with a good mix of oldies and newbies.

Massachusetts Boston is blessed with two public radio stations – WGBH (89.7FM) and WBUR (90.9FM) – broadcasting news, classical music and radio shows.

New Hampshire The Freewaves (91.3FM), run by the students of the University of New Hampshire, offers indie, classical, jazz and folk.

Vermont WRUV (90.1 FM) – also known as Burlington's Better Alternative – is a nonprofit student- and volunteer-run radio station, playing a mix of music at the DJs' discretion, but absolutely no songs that were ever in the Billboard Hot 100.

FERRY CROSSINGS

Several ferry companies serve New England's offshore islands. Park your car in port ($10 to $20 per day) – or, if you want to bring your vehicle along, book well in advance and expect to pay high prices.

Bay Ferries (www.ferries.ca/thecat) Operates the summertime CAT service, sailing daily between Portland, ME, and Yarmouth, Nova Scotia, Canada (5½ hours).

Block Island Ferry (www.blockislandferry. com) Operates car ferries and high-speed passenger ferries between Point Judith, RI, and Block Island, RI.

Bridgeport & Port Jefferson Steamboat Company (www.88844ferry.com) Year-round ferries from Port Jefferson (Long Island), NY to Bridgeport, CT (1¼ hours).

Cross Sound Ferry (www.longislandferry. com) Year-round car ferries (80 minutes) and seasonal high-speed passenger ferries (40 minutes) from Orient Point (Long Island), NY to New London, CT.

Fishers Island Ferry (www.fiferry.com) Year-round ferries between Fishers Island, NY and New London, CT (45 minutes).

Fort Ti Ferry (www.forttiferry.com) Makes regular crossings from Shoreham, VT to Ticonderoga Landing, NY (seven minutes) between May and October.

Seastreak (www.seastreak.com) High-speed weekend ferry service from New York City to Martha's Vineyard, MA (5¼ hours) and Nantucket, MA (6½ hours) between late May and early September.

Road Distances (miles)

	Boston, MA	Provincetown, MA	Portsmouth, NH	Portland, ME	Bar Harbor, ME	Burlington, VT	Brattleboro, VT	Norwich, VT/ Hanover, NH	Hartford, CT
Provincetown, MA	114								
Portsmouth, NH	58	171							
Portland, ME	108	221	51						
Bar Harbor, ME	267	380	210	159					
Burlington, VT	217	330	207	209	334				
Brattleboro, VT	120	220	124	175	354	151			
Norwich, VT/Hanover, NH	127	240	116	167	346	96	69		
Hartford, CT	101	206	150	201	380	236	85	152	
Providence, RI	50	120	106	157	336	265	137	175	86

New England Travel Guide

GETTING THERE & AWAY

While the two most common ways to reach New England are by air and car, you can also get here easily by train and bus. Boston is the region's hub for air travel, but some international travelers fly into New York City to do some sightseeing before heading up to New England.

AIR

Because of New England's location on the densely populated US Atlantic seaboard between New York and eastern Canada, air travelers have a number of ways to approach the region.

The major gateway to the region is Boston's **Logan International Airport** (BOS; ☑800-235-6426; www.massport.com/logan-airport/), which offers many direct, nonstop flights from major airports in the USA and abroad.

Depending on where you will be doing the bulk of your exploring, several other airports in the region receive national and international flights. It's also feasible to fly into one of New York City's major airports.

Bangor International Airport (BGR; ☑866-359-2264; www.flybangor.com; 287 Godfrey Blvd) Bangor, ME is served by regional carriers associated with American Airlines, Delta and United.

Bradley International Airport (BDL; ☑860-292-2000; www.bradleyairport.com; Schoephoester Rd, Windsor Locks) New England's second largest airport, 12 miles north of Hartford, CT in Windsor Locks (I-91 exit 40), is served by American Airlines, Delta, JetBlue, Southwest Airlines and United.

Burlington International Airport (BTV; ☑802-863-2874; www.btv.aero; 1200 Airport Dr, South Burlington) Vermont's major airport.

Green Airport (PVD; ☑888-268-7222; www.pvdairport.com; 2000 Post Rd, Warwick) Located 20 minutes south of Providence, RI.

Manchester-Boston Regional Airport (MHT; ☑603-624-6556; www.flymanchester.com; 1 Airport Rd; ☎) A quiet alternative to Logan, Manchester Airport is just 55 miles north of Boston in New Hampshire.

Portland International Jetport (PWM; ☑207-874-8877; www.portlandjetport.org; 1001 Westbrook St) Serves coastal Maine.

Worcester Regional Airport (ORH; www.massport.com; 375 Airport Dr) Serves central Massachusetts.

BUS

You can get to New England by bus from all parts of the USA and Canada, but the trip will be long and may not be much less expensive than a discounted flight. Bus companies usually offer special promotional fares.

Greyhound (www.greyhound.com) The national bus line, serving all major cities in the USA.

Peter Pan Bus (www.peterpanbus.com) Regional bus company serving over 50 destinations in Massachusetts, Connecticut and Rhode Island, with connections as far south as Washington, DC.

Several other bus companies offer service from New York City to New England, including Go Bus (www.gobuses.com), Lucky Star Bus (www.luckystarbus.com), Megabus (www.megabus.com) and Dartmouth Coach (www.dartmouthcoach.com).

CAR & MOTORCYCLE

Interstate highways crisscross New England and offer forest, farm and mountain scenery, once you're clear of urban areas and the I-95 corridor between Boston and New York. These interstate highways connect the region to New York; Washington, DC; Montréal, Canada; and points west. Major interstate highways include:

I-95 Along the Atlantic seaboard from New York City through Providence, Boston and Portland to the Canadian border.

I-91 Up the Connecticut River valley from New Haven through Hartford and central Massachusetts, then along the Vermont–New Hampshire line to Canada.

I-90 (Mass Pike) Spanning Massachusetts east-west from Albany, NY to Boston.

I-89 Northwest from Concord, NH through New Hampshire and Vermont to the Canadian border (near Montréal).

I-93 North from Boston through New Hampshire into Vermont.

TRAIN

Amtrak (www.amtrak.com) is the main rail passenger service in the USA. Services along the Northeast Corridor (connecting Boston, Providence, RI and New Haven, CT with New York and Washington, DC) are some of the most frequent in Amtrak's system, running several times daily in each direction. Amtrak's high-speed *Acela Express* makes the trip from New York City to Boston in 3¾ hours. Amtrak also offers the following once-daily services to New England:

➜ The *Ethan Allen Express* travels from New York City north to Rutland, VT (5½ hours) via Albany, NY.

➜ The *Vermonter* runs north to St Albans, VT from Washington, DC (12¾ hours) and New York City (9¼ hours), passing en route through New Haven and Hartford, CT, Springfield and Amherst, MA, and several towns in Vermont.

➜ The *Lake Shore Limited* runs from Chicago to Boston (22 hours), passing through Cleveland, OH, Buffalo, NY and Albany, NY, then continuing east through Massachusetts, with stops in Pittsfield, Springfield and Worcester.

Connecticut is also served by commuter trains from New York City, operated by Metro-North (www.mta.info) and Shore Line East (www.shorelineeast.com).

DIRECTORY A–Z

ACCESSIBLE TRAVEL

Travel within New England is gradually becoming less difficult for people with disabilities. Public buildings are now required by law to be wheelchair accessible and also to have appropriate restroom facilities. Public transportation services must be made accessible to all, and telephone companies are required to provide relay operators for the hearing impaired. Many banks provide ATM instructions in braille, curb ramps are common, many busy intersections have audible crossing signals, and most chain hotels have suites for guests with disabilities.

Mobility International USA (www.miusa.org) advises travelers with disabilities on mobility issues and runs educational international exchange programs.

Download Lonely Planet's free Accessible Travel guides from shop.lonelyplanet.com/categories/accessible-travel.com.

ACCOMMODATIONS

New England provides an array of accommodations, but truly inexpensive options are rare. Reservations are recommended, especially in high season.

B&Bs, Inns & Guesthouses

Accommodations in New England range from small B&Bs to rambling old inns that have sheltered travelers for several centuries. Accommodations and amenities can vary widely, from the very simple to the luxurious (and prices vary accordingly). Many inns require a minimum stay of two or three nights on weekends, and some

Efficiencies

An 'efficiency,' in New England parlance, is a room in a hotel, motel or inn with cooking and dining facilities: a stove, a sink, a refrigerator, a dining table and chairs, cooking utensils and tableware. Efficiency units are located throughout New England. They cost slightly more than standard rooms.

Practicalities

Discount Cards Many museums and other attractions offer discounts to college students with a valid university ID. Travelers aged 50 years and older can also receive rate cuts and benefits, especially members of the American Association of Retired Persons (www.aarp.org). AAA members (www.aaa.com) are also eligible for many discounts at sights and hotels.There are several programs that offer discounts to Boston-area attractions, including City Pass (www.citypass.com) and Smart Destinations (www.smartdestinations.com).

Radio & TV National Public Radio (NPR) can be found at the lower end of the FM dial. The main TV broadcasting channels are ABC, CBS, NBC, FOX and PBS (public broadcasting); the major cable channels are CNN (news), ESPN (sports), HBO (movies) and Weather Channel.

Smoking Five out of six New England states have banned smoking in bars, restaurants and non-hospitality workplaces – so, essentially, anywhere that anyone works. Only New Hampshire is less restrictive, but smoking is nonetheless prohibited in bars and restaurants.

Video Systems NTSC standard (incompatible with PAL or SECAM); DVDs are coded for Region 1 (USA and Canada only).

Weights & Measures Weights are measured in ounces (oz), pounds (lb) and tons; liquids in fluid ounces (fl oz), pints, quarts and gallons (gal); and distances in feet (ft), yards (yd) and miles (mi).

only accept payment in cash or by check (not by credit card). Some inns do not welcome children under a certain age.

Reserve rooms directly with the inn or through agencies such as New England Inns & Resorts (www.newenglandinnsand resorts.com), which books B&Bs and inns in all six New England states.

Camping

With few exceptions, you'll have to camp in established campgrounds (there's no bivouacking on the side of the road). Make reservations well in advance (especially in July and August) for the best chance of getting a site. Most campgrounds are open from mid-May to mid-October.

Rough camping is occasionally permitted in the Green Mountain National Forest or the White Mountain National Forest, but it must be at established sites. State park sites usually offer services like flush toilets, hot showers and dump stations for RVs. Campsites at these places cost between $15 and $30. Private campgrounds are usually more expensive ($25 to $40) and less spacious than state parks, but they often boast recreational facilities such as playgrounds, swimming pools, game rooms and miniature golf.

The following resources provide camping information:

Connecticut Department of Environmental Protection (www.ct.gov/dep) Has a large section on outdoor recreation in Connecticut.

Maine Bureau of Parks and Land (www.parksandlands.com) Offers camping in 12 state parks.

Massachusetts Department of Conservation and Recreation (www.mass.gov/eea) Offers camping in 29 state parks.

National Park Service (www.nps.gov/subjects/camping) Camping info for Acadia National Park, ME and Cape Cod National Seashore, MA.

Plan Your Stay Online

For more accommodation reviews by Lonely Planet authors, check out www.lonelyplanet.com. You'll find independent reviews, as well as recommendations on the best places to stay.

New Hampshire State Parks (www.nhstateparks.org) Details on the Granite State's 20 state park campgrounds.

Northeast Campground Association (www.campnca.com) Features private campgrounds throughout the Northeast.

Rhode Island Division of Parks & Recreation (www.riparks.com) Info on Rhode Island's five state park campgrounds.

Vermont State Parks (www.vtstateparks.com) Complete camping and parks information.

Cottages & Cabins

Cottages and cabins are generally found on Cape Cod, Nantucket and Martha's Vineyard, as well as in New England's woods. They are typically one- to three-room vacation bungalows with basic furnishings, a bathroom and a kitchen. Rates vary greatly, from $50 to several hundred dollars per night, depending upon the location, season and size. Rental condos are popular at New England's larger ski resorts and can often be booked directly through the resort.

Hotels & Resorts

New England hotels, mostly found in cities, are generally large and lavish, except for a few 'boutique' hotels (which are small and understatedly lavish). Resorts often offer a wide variety of guest activities, such as golf, horseback riding, skiing and water sports. Prices range from $100 upwards per night.

Hostels

Hosteling isn't as well developed in New England as it is in other parts of the world. But some prime destinations – including Boston, Cape Cod, Martha's Vineyard and Nantucket, MA; Portland and Bar Harbor, ME, Burlington, VT; and the mountains of New Hampshire and Vermont – have hostels that allow you to stay in $150-per-night destinations for as little as $30 per night.

Some hostels are private, while others are affiliated with Hostelling International USA (www.hiusa.org). The latter organization officially requires a membership card, available on-site or through the hosteling association in your home country – though nonmembers can generally still stay in US hostels for a slightly higher rate.

Motels

Motels, located along main roads, at interstate highway exits or on the outskirts of towns and cities, range from 10-room places in need of a fresh coat of paint to having resort-style facilities. Prices run from around $75 to $150. Motels offer standard accommodations: a room with a private entrance, a private bathroom, a cable TV, heat and air-con. Some have small refrigerators, and many provide a simple breakfast, often at no extra charge.

ELECTRICITY

Type B
120V/60Hz

FOOD

Eating in New England is a treat, whether feasting on fresh seafood, munching berries from the bush or dining at one of the region's top, chef-driven restaurants.

The finest dining and most innovative cooking takes place in New England's cities, especially Boston, MA, Portland, ME, Providence, RI and Burlington, VT. At high-end restaurants, reservations for dinner are usually recommended, especially during peak tourist seasons and on weekends. Reservations are not usually needed for lunch.

Except in the most rural areas or the smallest towns, vegetarians will have no problem finding animal-free eats. Other dietary restrictions are also usually accommodated.

INTERNET ACCESS

Many hotels, restaurants and cafes offer wireless access for free or for a small fee. Most public libraries also offer free online computer access, and some cities and towns have free public wi-fi hot spots. If you bring a laptop with you from outside the USA, it's worth investing in a universal AC and plug adapter.

LGBTIQ+ TRAVELERS

Out and active gay communities are visible across New England, especially in cities such as Boston, MA and New Haven, CT, which have substantial LGBTIQ+ populations. Several smaller cities also have well-established queer communities, including Portland, ME, Northampton, MA and Burlington, VT.

Cities throughout the region also stage well-attended pride festivals, with Boston Pride (www.bostonpride.org), Rhode Island PrideFest (www.prideri.org), Pride Portland! (www.prideportland.org) and Northampton's NoHo Pride (www.noho pride.org) being among the biggest.

The Rainbow Times (www.therainbow timesmass.com) is a great New England–wide resource for news and entertainment listings with an LGBTIQ+ focus.

Eating Price Ranges

The following price ranges refer to a standard main course at dinner. Unless otherwise stated, a service charge and taxes are not included.

$ less than $15

$$ $15–25

$$$ more than $25

MONEY

ATMs & Cash

ATMs are ubiquitous in towns throughout New England. Most banks in New England charge at least $2 per withdrawal. The Cirrus and Plus systems both have extensive ATM networks that will give cash advances on major credit cards and allow cash withdrawals with affiliated ATM cards.

If you're carrying foreign currency, it can be exchanged for US dollars at Logan International Airport in Boston. Many banks do not change currency, so stock up on dollars when there's an opportunity to do so.

Credit Cards

Major credit cards are widely accepted throughout New England, including at car-rental agencies and at most hotels, restaurants, gas stations, grocery stores and tour operators. However, some restaurants and B&Bs do not accept credit cards. We have noted in our reviews when this is the case.

Visa and MasterCard are the most common credit cards. American Express and Discover are less widely accepted.

Tipping

Many service providers depend on tips for their livelihoods, so tip generously for good service.

Baggage carriers $1 per bag

Housekeeping $2 to $5 per day, $5 to $10 per week

Servers and bartenders 15% to 20%

Taxi drivers 15%

Tour guides $5 to $10 for a one-hour tour

OPENING HOURS

The following is a general guideline for opening hours. Shorter hours may apply during low seasons, when some venues close completely. Seasonal variations are noted in the listings.

Banks and offices 9am to 5pm or 6pm Monday to Friday; sometimes 9am to noon Saturday

Bars and pubs 5pm to midnight, some til 2am

Restaurants Breakfast 6am to 10am, lunch 11:30am to 2:30pm, dinner 5pm to 10pm daily

Shops 9am to 7pm Monday to Saturday; some open noon to 5pm Sunday, or until evening in tourist areas

PUBLIC HOLIDAYS

New Year's Day January 1

Martin Luther King Jr Day Third Monday of January

Presidents' Day Third Monday of February

Easter March or April

Patriots' Day Third Monday of April (Maine and Massachusetts only)

Memorial Day Last Monday of May

Independence Day July 4

Labor Day First Monday of September

Columbus Day Second Monday of October

Veterans Day November 11

Thanksgiving Fourth Thursday of November

Christmas Day December 25

SAFE TRAVEL

You're unlikely to come across any major problems while traveling in New England. Most of the region enjoys high standards of living, and tourists are usually well taken care of.

Outdoor Hazards

Outdoor activities, from beach-going to mountain-hiking, can be dangerous anywhere in the world. Pay attention to weather and water conditions before setting out on any sort of adventure.

➡ The White Mountains are notorious for strong winds and wild weather, but conditions can be dangerous on any of the New England mountain trails. Hypothermia is a key concern in chilly, windy or damp weather; carry adequate clothing for changing conditions.

➡ Always stay on marked trails and do not disturb wildlife while hiking.

➡ In recent years, shark sightings have not been uncommon off Cape Cod, and beaches may close for that reason. In 2018, the region saw its first fatal shark attack in nearly a century. Not all public beaches are guarded, so inquire about riptides and other dangers before swimming at area beaches.

Weather

It snows a lot in New England. If you're visiting between December and March, there's a good chance you'll experience a major snowstorm, possibly impeding your progress until roads are plowed.

TELEPHONE

All phone numbers in the USA consist of a three-digit area code followed by a seven-digit local number. You must dial 1 plus all 10 digits for local and long-distance calls in most areas, particularly in Eastern Massachusetts.

Always dial '1' before toll-free (800, 888 etc) and domestic long-distance numbers. Remember that some toll-free numbers may only work within the region or from the US mainland.

To make direct international calls, dial 011 plus the country code plus the area code plus the number. (An exception is calls made to Canada, where you dial 1 plus the area code, plus the number. International rates apply to Canada.) For international operator assistance, dial 0.

If you're calling New England from abroad, the international country code for the USA is 1. All calls to New England are then followed by the area code and the seven-digit local number.

Cell Phones

The US uses a variety of cell-phone frequencies, most of which are incompatible with the GSM 900/1800 standard traditionally used throughout Europe, Asia and Australasia. However, most modern quad-band smartphones work on multiple frequencies, making them suitable for international use. Check with your cellular service provider before departure about using your phone in New England, and inquire about international roaming charges, which can be quite high. If your phone is unlocked, you'll often save money by purchasing a pre-paid SIM card in the United States.

Network Coverage

Verizon has the most extensive cellular network in New England; AT&T, T-Mobile and Sprint also offer coverage in the region, though service can be spotty depending on where you're traveling. Once you get up into the mountains and off the main interstates in Vermont, New Hampshire and Maine, cell-phone reception is often downright nonexistent. Don't count on being able to use your phone on hiking trails or in other remote rural locations.

Phonecards

These private prepaid cards are available from convenience stores, supermarkets and pharmacies. Cards sold by major telecommunications companies such as AT&T may offer better deals than upstart companies.

TOURIST INFORMATION

Connecticut Office of Tourism (www. ctvisit.com)

Greater Boston Convention & Visitors Bureau (www.bostonusa.com)

Maine Office of Tourism (www.visit maine.com)

Massachusetts Office of Travel & Tourism (www.massvacation.com)

New Hampshire Division of Travel & Tourism (www.visitnh.gov)

Rhode Island Tourism Division (www. visitrhodeisland.com)

Vermont Division of Tourism (www. vermontvacation.com)

Chambers of Commerce

Often associated with convention and visitors' bureaus (CVBs), these are membership organizations for local businesses including hotels, restaurants and shops. Although they often provide maps, lodging recommendations and other useful information, they focus on establishments that are members of the chamber.

A local chamber of commerce often maintains an information booth at the entrance to town or in the town center, frequently open only during tourist seasons.

VISAS

Citizens of many countries are eligible for the Visa Waiver Program, which requires prior approval via Electronic System for Travel Authorization.

Electronic System for Travel Authorization

Since January 2009 the USA has had the Electronic System for Travel Authorization (ESTA), a system that was implemented to mitigate security risks concerning those who travel to the USA by air or sea (travelers entering by land, such as via Canada, do not need to file an ESTA application). This pre-authorization system applies to citizens of approximately three dozen countries that fall under the Visa Waiver Program. This process requires that you register specific information online, prior to entering the USA. Information required includes details such as your name, current address and passport information, including the number and expiration date, and details about any communicable diseases you may carry (including HIV). It is recommended that you fill out the online form as early as possible, and at least 72 hours prior to departure. You will receive one of three responses:

➡ 'Authorization Approved' usually comes within minutes; most applicants can expect to receive this response.

➡ 'Authorization Pending' means you should go back online to check the status within roughly 72 hours.

➡ 'Travel not Authorized' indicates that your application is not approved and you will need to apply for a visa.

Once approved, registration is valid for two years, but note that if you renew your passport or change your name, you will need to re-register. The cost is $14. The entire process is stored electronically and linked to your passport, but it is recommended that you bring a printout of the ESTA approval just to be safe. If you don't have access to the internet, a travel agent can apply on your behalf.

Visa Applications

Citizens of non-Visa Waiver Program countries must generally apply for a nonimmigrant visa using Form DS-160 (ceac.state.gov/genniv), pay a nonrefundable application fee ($160) and schedule an interview at a US embassy or consulate.

Documentation required for visa applications:

➡ Information about your family, your US point of contact, your education, employment and travel history, and your proposed itinerary, along with answers to Security and Background questions.

➡ A recent photo (240KB or less if uploading digitally, or 50.8mm by 50.8mm in print form).

➡ Documents of financial stability and/or guarantees from a US resident are sometimes required, particularly for those from developing countries.

➡ Visa applicants may be required to 'demonstrate binding obligations' that will ensure their return home. Because of this requirement, those planning to travel through other countries before arriving in the US are generally better off applying for their US visa while they are still in their home country rather than while on the road.

The validity period for a US visitor visa depends on your home country. The actual length of time you'll be allowed to stay in the US is determined by the Bureau of Citizenship and Immigration Services at the port of entry.

As with the Visa Waiver Program, your passport should be valid for at least six months longer than your intended stay.

Visa Waiver Program

The USA has a Visa Waiver Program in which citizens of certain countries may enter the USA for stays of 90 days or less without first obtaining a US visa. This list is subject to continual re-examination and bureaucratic rejigging. For an up-to-date list of countries included in the program, see the US Department of State website (www.travel.state.gov). Under the program you must have a round-trip ticket (or onward ticket to any foreign destination) that is nonrefundable in the USA and you will not be allowed to extend your stay beyond 90 days.

To participate in the Visa Waiver Program, travelers are required to have a passport that is machine readable. Also, your passport should be valid for at least six months longer than your intended stay.

BEHIND THE SCENES

SEND US YOUR FEEDBACK

We love to hear from travelers – your comments help make our books better. We read every word, and we guarantee that your feedback goes straight to the authors. Visit **lonelyplanet. com/contact** to submit your updates and suggestions.

Note: We may edit, reproduce and incorporate your comments in Lonely Planet products such as guidebooks, websites and digital products, so let us know if you don't want your comments reproduced or your name acknowledged. For a copy of our privacy policy visit lonelyplanet.com/legal.

WRITER THANKS

BENEDICT WALKER

A special thanks to Cheryl Cowie and Keri Berthelot for their guidance, support and Reiki II's on the road. As always, to Trish Walker for countless hours in the prayer chair, and a big shout-out to family; Andy, Sally and P for making sure I didn't overdo the lobster! In memory of Kevin Hennessy, Ainsley Crabbe and Ben Carey, my fellow adventurers who passed away in other lands while I was researching this title. A little part of you remains in Rhode Island for me, always. You'll like it there!

ISABEL ALBISTON

Thanks to everyone in Massachusetts who answered my questions so patiently and treated me so kindly, especially to all the museum guides who showed me around along the way. Thanks also to Leah, Julie and Andrea for your warm hospitality and to Trisha for commissioning me for such a great project. Lastly, huge thanks to Ellie, Alan and Liz for traveling out to join me at the end of my trip.

AMY C BALFOUR

Thank you Amy Scannell and Michael Billings for your hospitality and NH expertise. Eleanor Barnes and Whit Andrews, endless gratitude for climbing Mt Washington with me. Peaches and Genienne Hockensmith, thanks for sharing the best of Keene! Cheers to the crew atop New England at Mt Washington Observatory: Adam, Ian, Brian, Zach, Tessa, Bruce and Priscilla. Your passion for weather and your regional recs are much appreciated. Thanks for key assistance Lynn Neumann and Randy Propster. Duby Thompson, thanks for lunch in Littleton!

ROBERT BALKOVICH

Thank you to my family – my mother, father and sister – and friends for their love and support. Special thanks to Michael, Raghnild, Elizabeth and Ming for their hospitality and wealth of tips, and to Matthew for your friendship on the road. And thank you to Trisha Ping for this opportunity, and many others.

GREGOR CLARK

Thanks to the many fellow Vermonters who shared their favorite spots in the Green Mountain State with me this

THIS BOOK

This 5th edition of *New England's Best Trips* was researched and written by Benedict Walker, Isabel Albiston, Amy C Balfour, Robert Balkovich, Gregor Clark, Adam Karlin, Brian Kluepfel, Regis St Louis and Mara Vorhees. This guidebook was produced by the following:

Destination Editor Trisha Ping

Senior Product Editors Martine Power, Kirsten Rawlings, Vicky Smith

Product Editors Hannah Cartmel, Kate James

Senior Cartographer Alison Lyall

Cartographers Anita Banh, Rachel Imeson

Book Designers Ania Bartoszek, Gwen Cotter

Assisting Editors Imogen Bannister, Michelle Bennett, Nigel Chin, Katie Connolly, Samantha Cook, Lucy Cowie, Peter Cruttenden, Carly Hall, Kellie Langdon, Kristin Odijk, Mani Ramaswamy, Monica Woods

Cover Researcher Gwen Cotter

Thanks to Evan Godt, Sonia Kapoor, Claire Naylor, Karyn Noble, Amanda Williamson

edition – especially Shawn O'Neil, Margo Whitcomb, Victoria St John, Jim Lockridge and Joy Cohen – and to Gaen, Meigan and Chloe for a lifetime of companionship on our family adventures in this gorgeous place we call home.

ADAM KARLIN

Thanks to: Trisha Ping for letting me poke around the Pine Tree state, the Barclays for hosting us, friends and family and kind strangers met along the way, and Rachel and Sanda, my two favorite partners for climbing up rocks and swimming in the cold ocean.

BRIAN KLUEPFEL

First and always, to my wife Paula, my co-pilot in life. Secondly, to all my kinfolk who helped on this journey: June and Alan Kluepfel (formerly of Noank), Neil Kluepfel and his wife Irene Koenig of Stonington, and Jim and Eileen Flynn of Mystic. Thirdly (and crucially), to Trisha Ping who gave me such a delightful assignment.

REGIS ST LOUIS

I am grateful to countless innkeepers, park rangers, baristas and shop owners and folks 'from away' who provided shared Maine insight. Special thanks to Brother Arnold for a fabulous meal at Sabbathday Shaker Village, Scott Cowger for the tips and barn tour in Hallowell, Jack Burke and Julie Van De Graaf for their kindness in Castine, and Gregor Clark and Diane Plauche for general Maine suggestions. Special thanks to my family, who make coming home the best part of travel.

MARA VORHEES

To the server at a Gloucester restaurant, who recommended that I spend my afternoon at a certain delightful beach (which is not in this book). Thanks for sharing your secret spot. I won't tell.

ACKNOWLEDGEMENTS

Climate map data adapted from Peel MC, Finlayson BL & McMahon TA (2007) 'Updated World Map of the Köppen-Geiger Climate Classification', *Hydrology and Earth System Sciences*, 11, 1633–44.

Front cover photographs (clockwise from top): Autumn trees in New England, Leena Robinson/Shutterstock ©; Lobster traps and buoys, James Kirkikis/Shutterstock ©; Washington, Maine, 1949 Chevrolet 3100 pickup, Ken Morris/Shutterstock ©

Back cover photograph: Bass Harbor Head Lighthouse in Acadia National Park, Maine, Sara Winter/Shutterstock ©

INDEX

BRIAN KLUEPFEL

Brian lived in three states and seven different residences by the time he was nine, and just kept moving, making stops in Berkeley, Bolivia, the Bronx and the 'burbs further down the line. His journalistic work across the Americas has ranged from the Copa America soccer tournament in Paraguay to an accordion festival in Quebec. His titles for Lonely Planet include *Venezuela, Costa Rica, Belize & Guatemala, Bolivia* and *Ecuador*. He's an avid birder and musician and dabbles in both on the road.

REGIS ST LOUIS

Regis grew up in a small town in the American Midwest — the kind of place that fuels big dreams of travel — and he developed an early fascination with foreign dialects and world cultures. He spent his formative years learning Russian and a handful of Romance languages, which served him well on journeys across much of the globe. Regis has contributed to more than 50 Lonely Planet titles, covering destinations across six continents. His travels have taken him from the mountains of Kamchatka to remote island villages in Melanesia, and to many grand urban landscapes. When not on the road, he lives in New Orleans.

MARA VORHEES

Mara Vorhees writes about food, travel and family fun around the world. Her work has been published by *BBC Travel, Boston Globe, Delta Sky,* the *Vancouver Sun* and more. For Lonely Planet, she regularly writes about destinations in Central America and Eastern Europe, as well as New England, where she lives. She often travels with her twin boys in tow, earning her expertise in family travel. Follow their adventures and misadventures at www.havetwinswilltravel.com.

AMY C BALFOUR

Amy practiced law in Virginia before moving to Los Angeles to try to break in as a screenwriter. After a stint as a writer's assistant on *Law & Order*, she jumped into freelance writing, focusing on travel, food and the outdoors. She has hiked, biked and paddled across Southern California and the Southwest. Books authored or co-authored include Lonely Planet's *Los Angeles Encounter, Los Angeles & Southern California, Caribbean Islands, California, California Trips, USA, USA's Best Trips* and *Arizona*.

ROBERT BALKOVICH

Robert was born and raised in Oregon, but has called New York City home for almost a decade. When he was a child and other families were going to theme parks and grandma's house he went to Mexico City and toured Eastern Europe by train. He's now a writer and travel enthusiast seeking experiences that are ever so slightly out of the ordinary to report back on. Follow him on Instagram @oh_balky.

GREGOR CLARK

Gregor is a US-based writer whose love of foreign languages and curiosity about what's around the next bend have taken him to dozens of countries on five continents. Chronic wanderlust has also led him to visit all 50 states and most Canadian provinces on countless road trips through his native North America. Since 2000, Gregor has regularly contributed to Lonely Planet guides, with a focus on Europe and the Americas. Gregor earned his degree in Romance Languages at Stanford University and has remained an avid linguist throughout careers in publishing, teaching, translation and tour leadership.

ADAM KARLIN

Adam has contributed to dozens of Lonely Planet guidebooks, covering an alphabetical spread that ranges from the Andaman Islands to the Zimbabwe border. As a journalist, he has written on travel, crime, politics, archaeology and the Sri Lankan Civil War, among other topics. He has sent dispatches from every continent barring Antarctica (one day!) and his essays and articles have featured in the BBC, NPR, and multiple nonfiction anthologies.

Adam is based out of New Orleans, which helps explain his love of wetlands, food and good music. Learn more at http://walkonfine.com/, or follow him on Instagram @adamwalkonfine.

OUR WRITERS

OUR STORY

A beat-up old car, a few dollars in the pocket and a sense of adventure. In 1972 that's all Tony and Maureen Wheeler needed for the trip of a lifetime – across Europe and Asia overland to Australia. It took several months, and at the end – broke but inspired – they sat at their kitchen table writing and stapling together their first travel guide, *Across Asia on the Cheap*. Within a week they'd sold 1500 copies. Lonely Planet was born.

Today, Lonely Planet has offices in the US, Ireland and China, with a network of over 2000 contributors in every corner of the globe. We share Tony's belief that 'a great guidebook should do three things: inform, educate and amuse'.

BENEDICT WALKER

Born in Newcastle, Australia, Ben holds notions of the beach core to his idea of self, though he's traveled hundreds of thousands of kilometres from the sandy shores of home to live in Leipzig, Germany. Ben was given his first Lonely Planet guide *(Japan)* when he was 12. Two decades later, he'd write chapters for the same publication: a dream come true. A communications graduate and travel agent by trade, Ben whittled away his twenties gallivanting around the globe. He thinks the best thing about travel isn't as much where you go as who you meet: living vicariously through the stories of kind strangers enriches one's own experience. Come along for the ride on Instagram @wordsandjourneys.

ISABEL ALBISTON

After six years working for the *Daily Telegraph* in London, Isabel left to spend more time on the road. A job as a writer for a magazine in Sydney, Australia, was followed by a four-month overland trip across Asia and five years living and working in Buenos Aires, Argentina. Isabel started writing for Lonely Planet in 2014 and has contributed to 12 guidebooks. She's currently based in Ireland.

 MORE WRITERS

Published by Lonely Planet Global Limited
CRN 554153
5th edition – Aug 2022
ISBN 978 1 7886 836 16
© Lonely Planet 2022 Photographs © as indicated 2022
10 9 8 7 6 5 4 3 2 1
Printed in China